Competition and the World Economy

Competition and the World Economy

Comparing Industrial Development Policies in the Developing and Transition Economies

Francisco Sercovich

with

Authors

Choong-Yong Ahn
Claudio Frischtak
Mojmir Mrak
Herman Muegge
Wilson Peres
Samuel Wangwe

Edward Elgar
Cheltenham, UK • Northampton, MA, USA

United Nations Industrial Development Organization

Published by
Edward Elgar Publishing Limited
Glensanda House
Montpellier Parade
Cheltenham
Glos GL50 1UA
UK

Edward Elgar Publishing, Inc.
136 West Street
Suite 202
Northampton
Massachusetts 01060
USA

A catalogue record for this book
is available from the British Library

Library of Congress Cataloguing in Publication Data
Competition and the world economy : comparing industrial development policies in the developing and transition economies / Francisco C. Sercovich ... [et al.].
"Prepared for the United Nations Industrial Development Organization."
Includes indexes.
1. Industrial policy—Developing countries. 2. Industrial capacity—Government policy—Developing countries. 3. Industrial policy—Europe, Eastern. 4. Industrial capacity—Government policy–-Europe, Eastern. 5. Post-communism. 6. Competition, International. I. Sercovich, Francisco Colman.
HD3616.D452C65 2000
338.9'009172'4—dc21 99–33957
CIP

ISBN 1 84064 192 4

Printed and bound in Great Britain by Bookcraft (Bath) Ltd.

Contents

Tables

Figures

Boxes

Abbreviations

AFTA	American Free Trade Association
AIA	ASEAN Investment Area
AIC	Advanced industrial country
AICO	ASEAN Industrial Complementation
AIP	ASEAN Industrial Programme
AIJV	ASEAN Industrial Joint Venture
ALADI	Latin American Integration Association
APEC	Asia–Pacific Economic Cooperation
ASEAN	Association of South-East Asian Nations
ATC	Air Tanzania Corporation
BBC	Brand-to-brand complementation
BIS	Basic industrial strategy
BNDES	National Development Bank (Brazil)
b.p.	Basis point
CACM	Central American Common Market
CAD	Computer-aided design
CARMATEC	Center for Agricultural Mechanization and Rural Technology (United Republic of Tanzania)
CBES	Sino-Brazilian Programme of spatial Cooperation
CCI	Chamber of Commerce and Industry
CEECs	Central and East European Countries
CET	Common external tariff
CMEA	Council for Mutual Economic Assistance
CNC	Computer numerically controlled
CNI	National Confederation of Industry (Brazil)
COIME	Committee on Industry, Minerals and Energy (ASEAN)
COSTECH	Commission for Science and Technology (United Republic of Tanzania
CPI	Consumer price index
CTA	Centro Tecnológico da Aeronáutica (Brazil)
EAC	East African Community

EAEC East-Asian Economic Caucus
EC European Commission
ECA Economic Commission for Africa
EPZs Export processing zones
ERC Engineering Research Center (Republic of Korea)
ERP Economic Recovery Programme (United Republic of Tanzania)
ESAP Economic and Social Action Programme (United Republic of Tanzania)
ESRF Economic and Social Research Foundation (United Republic of Tanzania)
EU European Union
FDI Foreign direct investment
FINAMEX Programa da Financiamento à Produção e Exportaçao de Màquinas e Equipamento (Brazil)
FINEP Financiadore d'Etudos e Projetos
FUNCEX Fundação Centro de Comércio Exterior (Brazil)
GATS General Agreement on Trade in Services
GATT General Agreement on Tariffs and Trade
GDP Gross Domestic Product
GRI Government-supported research institution
HCIs Heavy and chemical industries
HPTC High Precision Technology Center (United Republic of Tanzania)
HRD Human resource development
ICOR Incremental capital–output ratio
ICT Information and communications technologies
IFC International Finance Corporation
IMF International Monetary Fund
IMPI Institute for Small and Medium-sized Enterprises (Spain)
IMS GT Indonesia–Malaysia–Singapore growth triangle
INPE Instituto Nacional de Pesquisas Espaciais (Brazil)
IPC Investment Promotion Centre (United Republic of Tanzania)
IPI Institute of Product Innovation (United Republic of Tanzania)
IPRs Intellectual property rights
IRP Integrated Roads Programme (United Republic of Tanzania)
ISO International Standards Organization
JIT Just in time
LACCs Latin American and Caribbean countries

LART	Loans and Advances Realization Trust (United Republic of Tanzania)
LCRs	Local content rules
LDCs	Less developed countries
LIBOR	London Inter-Bank Offered Rate
MAI	Multilateral agreement on investment
MERCOSUR	Southern Common Market
MICT	Ministry of Industry, Commerce and Trade (Brazil)
MIE	Multi-industrial enterprise
MITI	Ministry of International Trade and Industry (Malaysia)
MNC	Multinational corporation
MOST	Ministry of Science and Technology (Republic of Korea)
MOTIE	Ministry of Trade, Industry and Energy (Republic of Korea)
MVA	Manufacturing value-added
NAFTA	North American Free Trade Agreement
NASACO	National Shipping Agencies Corporation (United Republic of Tanzania)
NBC	National Bank of Commerce (United Republic of Tanzania)
NC	Numerically controlled
NESP	National Economic Survival Programme (United Republic of Tanzania)
NGO	Non-governmental organization
NIE	Newly industrializing economies
NOE	Newly opened economy
NTBs	Non-tariff barriers
NTRs	Non-tariff restrictions
NUWA	National Urban Water Authority (United Republic of Tanzania)
NVTC	National Vocational Training Centre (United Republic of Tanzania)
OAU	Organization of African Unity
OECD	Organization of Economic Cooperation and Development
OGL	Open general licence
PBQP	Brazilian Programme of Quality and Productivity
PHARE	EU Programme for the East European Countries
PICAB	Programme of Integration and Cooperation
PPP	Purchasing power parity
PROEX	Programa de Financiamento às Exportações (Brazil)
PSRC	Parastatal Sector Reform Commission (United Republic of Tanzania)

Q&P	Quality and productivity
QRs	Quantitative restrictions
R&D	Research and development
RD&E	Research, development and engineering
RPED	Regional Private Enterprise Development Programme (United Republic of Tanzania)
RTA	Regional trade arrangement
RTC	Regional trading corporation (United Republic of Tanzania)
RULCs	Relative unit labour costs
S&T	Science and Technology
SADC	Southern Africa Development Community
SAP	Structural Adjustment Programme
SBIC	Small business investment company (USA)
SEBRAE	Brazilian SME Support Service
SENAI	Serviço Nacional de Aprendizgem Industrial (Brazil)
SIDO	Small Industries Development Organization (United Republic of Tanzania)
SMEs	Small and medium-sized enterprises
SMIs	Small and medium-scale industries
SOE	State-owned enterprises
SRC	Scientific Research Centre (Republic of Korea)
SSRTA	South–South regional trade agreements
ST&E	Science, technology and engineering
STC	State Trading Organization (United Republic of Tanzania)
TANESCO	Tanzania Electrical Supply Company
TE	Transition economy
TEMDO	Tanzania Engineering and Manufacturing Design Organization
TFP	Total factor productivity
THA	Tanzania Harbours Authority
TIRDO	Tanzania Industrial Research Development Organization
TISCO	Tanzania Industrial Studies and Consulting Organization
TNC	Transnational corporation
TPC	Tanzania Postal Corporation
TQC	Total quality control
TQM	Total quality management
TRC	Tanzania Railways Corporation
TRIMs	Trade-related industrial measures
TRIP	Trade-related industrial property
ULC	Unit labour cost
UNCTAD	United Nations Conference on Trade and Development
WTO	World Trade Organization

Notes on Authors

The following are the co-authors' respective contributions, academic degrees and positions occupied at the time of preparation of the manuscript:

C.-Y. Ahn: Chapter 8 (Ph.D., Ohio State University; Director, Economic Research Institute, Chung-Ang University, Seoul, Republic of Korea)

C. Frischtak: Chapters 4 and 9 (Ph.D., Stanford University; Vice-President, World Invest Ltd, Rio de Janeiro, Brazil)

M. Mrak: Chapter 5 (Ph.D., University of Belgrade; Professor, University of Ljubljana, Slovenia)

H. Muegge: Chapter 10 (Ph. D., University of Bonn; former Director, Strategic Planning Office, UNIDO, Vienna, Austria)

W. Peres: Annex 9.C (Ph.D., University of Oviedo; Chief, Joint ECLAC/UNIDO Industrial and Technological Unit, ECLAC, Santiago, Chile)

F. Sercovich: Chapters 1, 2, 3, 6, 7 (Chapter 7 is partly based on contributions by the co-authors) and 12; methodological design, overall coordination and substantive revision (Ph.D., University of Sussex; Team Leader, Policy Research, Studies and Research Branch, UNIDO, Vienna, Austria)

S. Wangwe: Chapter 11 (Ph.D., University of Dar es Salaam; Executive Director of the Economic and Social Research Foundation, Dar es Salaam, Tanzania)

Foreword

The role of industrial development policy in an open, market-driven economy led by private investment is, for the most part, still undefined in most developing countries and economies in transition. It constitutes a dilemma from which they are slowly and laboriously emerging, with high social costs and risks.

Competition and the World Economy: Comparing Industrial Development Policies in Developing and Transition Economies shows that much of the controversy over industrial policy during the last decade or so has diverted attention from matters critical to the development prospects of developing countries and transition economies. While industrial development is about productivity growth, sustainable resource mobilization, capacity building and technological progress, much of the policy controversy has focused on short-term measures geared to redistribution of resources through subsidies, import controls, credit allocations and the like. Industrial policy has today become synonymous with the kind of redistribution associated with rent-seeking. By contrast, this book provides a developmental perspective on the matter.

Import-substitution industrialization policies have been largely responsible for blurring the distinction between industrial development policy, on the one hand, and industrial policy, on the other. But, in taking stock of the redistributive aspects of import-substitution policies, their historical role should not be underestimated. For all their shortcomings and distortive effects, these and related policies have contributed in considerable measure to raising living standards as well as building crucial industrial infrastructure and capabilities required for successful export-oriented manufacturing in today's more open and market-driven developing and transition economies. In any event, industrial policies based on import substitution, closed economies and strong state intervention have certainly exhausted their life cycle.

The book also highlights the crucial role of industrial development policies in addressing multiple market failures due to market imperfections and ill-developed or missing markets. For this challenging task to succeed, it cannot be tackled merely by trying to fill the gaps in other policies in such spheres as macroeconomics, investment, education, institutions, environment and regional and social matters. On the contrary, these need to be finely integrated with industrial development policies. They do not substitute but complement one another.

The impact of globalization on industrial development policies is a major focus of the book. The analysis presented reveals that the performance of firms, sectors and national economies in the world market, as well as respective policies and strategies, are increasingly being measured against world standards. No single economy in the world, no matter how large, can ignore this. Yet, as the book shows, different countries take different approaches to the issue of policy convergence and are likely to continue to do so.

Failure to heed these policy-related maxims has led to serious problems in implementing macroeconomic stabilization and reform programmes in the developing countries and economies in transition. By assuming swift market responses to changes in the incentive system, the expected success of such programmes has often been grossly overestimated, leading to costly distortions in policy implementation.

Industrial development is fundamentally about the slow, long-term, incremental acquisition of skills and technological capabilities required to attain world standards in the production of goods and services. This involves complex microeconomic and institutional transformations that markets alone cannot accomplish, even with the right macroeconomic fundamentals.

To help unravel these intricate relationships, *Competition and the World Economy: Comparing Industrial Development Policies in Developing and Transition Economies* offers policy makers, entrepreneurs and researchers unique perspectives on industrial development policy in today's world. It serves as a comprehensive guide to the multitude of considerations necessary to understanding and formulating the kind of policies crucial to national industrial development and integration into the global economy. In its role as a world forum for industry, UNIDO has produced the book to enable those concerned with policy in developing countries and economies in transition to take informed decisions and cope better with the challenges and opportunities of the global economy.

Carlos A. Magariños
Director-General

Preface

This book is a remarkable contribution to the debate on the worldwide crisis of structural adjustment. It was in the late 1970s that economists began to speak of structural adjustment and to recognize that the world economy could no longer continue on the high growth trajectory of the 1950s and 1960s. Whereas it was fashionable at the time to blame the OPEC crisis of the 1970s for many of these problems, it is now more generally recognized that there were many other contributory factors which led to the slowdown of economic growth and structural unemployment experienced in many countries. Among these, the nature and direction of technical change and the impact of globalization on world trade and investment flows are clearly of great importance.

So far from leading to a more harmonious development of the world economy and to a convergence of growth rates across the globe, the impact of these forces has up to now been to accentuate the uneven development of the various regions and countries of the world. This uneven development was already apparent in the 1980s, when the countries of Eastern Asia mostly continued to grow at a very fast rate while many countries in Latin America and Africa actually experienced negative growth in per capita incomes. In the 1990s these divergent trends became even more evident with the collapse of the high growth in East Asia, the even more serious collapse of the Russian economy and the very serious downturn in Brazil and several other Latin American countries.

These divergent trends call for very specific analysis of each group of countries as well as generalizations about the worldwide trends in technology, trade and development. The great merit of this book is that it has succeeded in this analysis of divergence in response to global structural change. The classification by four groups of countries in Part III of the book permits a far more focused analysis of the major trends in all parts of the world economy. This part also contains four country studies (of the Republic of Korea, Brazil, Hungary and the United Republic of Tanzania), each of which illustrates a number of the problems of each of the four groups.

These features make the UNIDO study a particularly valuable source for understanding contemporary changes. The editor and authors are to be congratulated on their success in analysing and interpreting the extremely complex and uneven process of global structural change.

Chris Freeman, Emeritus Professor
Science Policy Research Unit
University of Sussex, UK

Acknowledgements

This book is an output of UNIDO's policy research programme. Messrs J.W. Suh, Director of the Research and Studies Branch, his successor B. Svensson, and F. Richard, Director of the Industrial Policy and Research Branch, created an environment conducive to its completion. K.-Y. Nam provided overall assistance and R. Cox editorial assistance. B. Dissmann gave technical assistance. A. Teter was responsible for the preparation of the camera-ready copy. To all of them, the authors wish to express their utmost appreciation.

If we can learn about government policy options that have even small effects on the long-term growth rate, then we can contribute much more to improvements in standards of living than has been provided by the entire history of macroeconomic analysis of counter cyclical policy and fine-tuning.[1]

One of the major roles of development strategy is to serve as a catalyst, for example, by identifying the areas of a country's (dynamic) comparative advantage. Identifying these areas and publicizing such information is a *public good*, and as such is a responsibility of government.[2]

[1]R.J. Barro and X. Sala-I-Martin, *Economic Growth*, McGraw-Hill, New York, 1995, pp. 4–5.

[2]J. Stiglitz, 'Towards a new paradigm for development; strategies, policies, and processes', 1998 Prebisch Lecture at UNCTAD (http://www.worldbank.org/html/extdr/extme/jssp101998.htm), p. 9.

PART I

INTRODUCTION

1. Overview

OBJECTIVES AND TARGET AUDIENCE

The aim of this book is threefold: first, to provide an updated review of new trends and challenges in manufacturing competitiveness and industrial development policies in developing countries and economies in transition; second, to make information on policy developments in the manufacturing competitiveness and industrial development fields more accessible, transparent and comparable; and third, to promote awareness of policy matters affecting industrial development.

The book is addressed to policy makers in the broadest sense, including policy formulators and practitioners and policy consultants, specialists and analysts in the private and public sectors and academia. It is part of a broader UNIDO initiative to develop a policy dialogue aimed at comparing practices, developing common indicators and criteria for assessment, agreeing on common rules and calibration systems and setting up an interactive information network and management system for data.

POLICY EFFECTIVENESS AND TRANSPARENCY

Developing countries and economies in transition are expected to account for nearly 30 per cent of world manufacturing value-added by 2005, affirming their role as the engine of world manufacturing growth. Faced with slowly growing markets in the advanced industrial countries, developing countries and economies in transition face mounting pressures to enhance productivity and adjust their trade patterns while fighting poverty and unemployment. This calls for effective policies aimed at structural change, resource mobilization and capability building.

Increasing economic interdependence worldwide, coupled with ever more stringent international codes and covenants in the fields of trade, investment and technology, compels policy makers in developing countries and economies in transition continuously to enhance their knowledge and understanding of policy trends abroad. For this they need to strengthen their analytical skills and their ability to gain access to relevant information in a usable and timely fashion. As recent turmoil in world markets has made painfully clear, developing countries and countries with economies in transition need to substantially shorten lead-times in experience sharing.

Interdependence calls for predictability which, in turn, calls for transparency. The latter is of vital importance for the policy-making process. Greater transparency of information on policy developments has become an essential international public good.

Advanced industrial countries and the most successful performers among the developing countries and economies in transition attach high priority to monitoring policy developments abroad. The gap in policy-monitoring capability between them and the bulk of the developing countries and economies in transition is considerable. Appropriate and updated systems for methodical learning in the policy field are still in their infancy or in need of a major overhaul in most developing countries and economies in transition.

Many attempts at explaining why some countries do better than others are inconclusive or, when the results are forthcoming, they often rely on highly restrictive assumptions, which limit their usefulness for policy makers eager to learn from international experience.

This book is intended to make international policy experience more accessible to government and private sector decision makers in developing countries and economies in transition. A pragmatic approach to the matter is, therefore, mandatory – while avoiding, as Keynes put it, 'falling prey to the dogmas of defunct economists'.

POLICY TRADE-OFFS AND CONSTRAINTS ON REPLICABILITY

Rather than judge policies *in and of themselves*, the book assesses how far they have succeeded in reaching widely shared developmental goals and ultimately, to account for the factors that underlie success or failure.

Manufacturing competitiveness and industrial development policy success means achieving *sustainable* gains in welfare – growth, equity, jobs, earnings and quality of life – over time. Although there are short-term trade-offs between these different goals, they reinforce one another in the medium and long term. For example, recent research shows that social equity in terms of access to jobs, education, health and the like is instrumental to, rather than in conflict with, macroeconomic stability and growth.

Grading countries according to normative achievement criteria is far easier, although less germane to the book, than *explaining* performance. Moreover, along with policy, structural, institutional and behavioural factors are also key parts of the explanation. The book focuses, therefore, on policy within the specific environment where it evolves and performs. Such a specification, on which the comparative value of the findings depends, plays a critical role in assessing policy effectiveness and defining the scope for cross-country replicability (see Chapter 2).

The great diversity among developing countries and economies in transition is a key constraint. To facilitate comparability, the book considers four country groupings according to the key policy challenges they face, rather than along solely regional lines. From a comparative perspective, differences *among* and *within* these groupings are as relevant as commonalities (see Part III).

Policy comparisons face two major challenges. One is to decipher domestic policies so as to highlight the elements that are most useful for purposes of experience-sharing among countries. The other consists of the analytical problems involved in assessing policy. This concerns, especially, the complex array of interfaces between macroeconomic stabilization and structural reform programmes, short-term manufacturing competitiveness policies and medium- to long-term industrial development policies. The key dilemmas and trade-offs faced by most policy makers today are about macroeconomic versus microeconomic reform and short-term versus longer-term goals rather than protectionist versus open policies (see Part II).

The links between macroeconomic and short-run competitiveness policies, on the one hand and policies for structural change and capability building in the medium and long term, on the other, are particularly hard to define. Yet, an increasing number of decision makers, as much in the advanced industrial countries as among developing countries and economies in transition, are of the view that differences in competitive performance are explained by skills, entrepreneurship and framework conditions conducive to innovation, technology diffusion and resource mobility. These factors are the focus of industrial development policies.

POLICY PARADIGMS

Policy and institutions, together with natural resources, the labour force, skills and entrepreneurship, are among the country-specific factors that underlie the ability to compete in the medium and long term. Since national economies need to adjust to changing technology, skill requirements and demand patterns, externalities, market failures and the need for coordination make manufacturing competitiveness and industrial development policies a key factor in the development process.

The analytical skills and resources required for manufacturing competitiveness and industrial development policy management based on market-based incentives and the role of the government as inducer and catalyser rather than driving force are more demanding than those needed for traditional industrial policy.

The traditional approach to industrial policy has been to influence the behaviour of economic agents through subsidies and privileges. By contrast, benchmarking- and market-based policies consist of constant monitoring of strengths and weaknesses in manufacturing competitiveness and industrial development performance as a guide to structuring the incentive system with the aim of countering market failures. This entails a rigorous assessment of relevant firm-centred, sector-specific and industry-wide factors that underlie such performance – including skills, technological capabilities and framework conditions – and requires a thorough mastery of all the variables and processes involved (see Chapter 3).

Developing countries and economies in transition share a pressing need to develop capabilities to conduct objective and accurate manufacturing competitiveness and industrial development policy benchmarking while helping respective best practices to be widely spread. At a time of increasing pressure towards policy harmonization and policy competition to attract capital and technology and to open export outlets, the risk is *understating* developing countries' and economies in transitions' scope for manoeuvre in the policy arena rather than *overstating* it. Some advanced industrial countries are among the most aggressive in offering incentives to attract foreign direct investment (FDI) or to foster foreign market penetration at a time when these practices are being decried as a regrettable legacy of the past.

LEVELLING THE PLAYING FIELD

Levelling the playing field is a key priority for policy-making. Assessing which policies meet this objective is at least as important as evaluating which policies best promote manufacturing competitiveness, industrial development, employment creation and poverty eradication.

The emerging globalized system of production, investment, technology and trade is predicated on relentless competitive rivalry. Countries and firms are taking steps to position themselves as advantageously as possible (see Part III). Firms do this by improving their competitive abilities, adopting best practices and forging business alliances to become viable competitors. But they do not operate in a regulatory and institutional vacuum. While they may compete internationally, the quality of their home base is vital to success. A great deal of their performance relies on the business environment at home and this, in turn, is strongly affected by government policies.

Governments address the challenge of global competition mainly through domestic policy reform programmes aimed at facilitating the adjustment of the domestic economic, as well as the social and institutional, structure to an increasingly market- and technology-driven world economy. The convergence towards international policy and best business practices does not mean the demise of national policy.[1]

A basic effect of this process is the simultaneous growth of interdependence and unevenness in the distribution of costs and benefits. Such unevenness is apparent *within* as well as *between* countries. For instance, the incidence of financial costs in manufacturing competitiveness may differs among firms *within* countries more than it does *between* countries (see Chapter 5). Another example is the removal of cross-border price distortions at the expense of their absorption into the domestic economy (see Chapter 8).

Adequate access to information, especially about policies, is vital for all countries and requires a level playing field. Yet even equal opportunity of access to quality assessments of international policy design and implementation may prove insufficient for many countries if they lack effective support for institutional development and skill formation through technical assistance programmes.

LOOKING AHEAD

Developing countries and economies in transition, where most future industrial development is to take place, will soon account for nearly a third of total world manufacturing value-added (MVA) and manufacturing exports. The impact of industrial development on trade, employment and allocation of resources and vice versa will be strongly influenced by policy. The increasing need of countries to draw on international experience makes comparative manufacturing competitiveness and industrial development policy assessment more necessary than ever before.

The emerging industrial culture of developing countries and economies in transition is steering away from such rent-seeking enticements as subsidies and non-tariff barriers (NTBs) to become more upstream-, factor- and framework-oriented (see Annex to Chapter 3). This permeates such diverse policies as deregulation, privatization, taxation, competition, investment, labour legislation and technological and regional development. One of the essential considerations of this new view is that, for open economies to succeed, active policies in relation to manufacturing competitiveness and industrial development are required. Services may generate jobs, but so far they are not a substitute for industry's role as an engine of growth. Services support producers and consumers but are largely non-tradable and comprise important non-competitive segments. Nevertheless, manufacturing competitiveness depends vitally on the competitiveness of the service sector (see Chapter 4).

Widespread adoption of manufacturing competitiveness policies is steering countries towards better focused policies for raising productivity, upgrading skills and technology, promoting innovation, attaining dynamic efficiency gains from learning, specialization and stimulating competition rather than towards protectionist policies, competitive devaluations and the like. The former policies, which address the core of industrial development, hold the only sustainable long-term answer to enhancing manufacturing competitiveness.

COLLABORATIVE EFFORT

In addition to the Bretton Woods institutions, the regional development banks and economic commissions make an important contribution to monitoring manufacturing competitiveness and industrial development policy from a regional perspective. Moreover, the Organisation for Economic

Cooperation and Development (OECD) has extended the scope of its policy work to cover a number of recently graduated developing countries and economies in transition. This book complements this vital work, especially from an interregional perspective.

This kind of effort has its own learning curve. Over time, improvements are expected in manufacturing competitiveness and industrial development policy monitoring and benchmarking methodology as well as in the identification of strengths and weaknesses in the approach adopted so far. For instance, specification of strategic groups of countries that share similar policy paradigms and growth dynamics may enhance the effectiveness of policy benchmarking.

SHORT SUMMARY

The book presents three main messages that stem from the international comparisons of policy-making experience and country case studies it contains.

First, a distinction needs to be made between *industrial policy*, which is aimed at changing the sectoral allocation of resources through short-run redistributive measures such as subsidies, import restrictions and credit allocation, on the one hand, and *industrial development policy*, which is aimed at increasing the productivity of resources in the medium- and long-run through capability building, on the other. Capability building refers to skill enhancement, scientific and technological progress, capital accumulation, quality upgrading, resource mobilization, environmental sustainability and market, institutional and regional development.

Second, because of the multiplicity of tasks and market failures it addresses, industrial development policy needs to be finely tuned to the working of the economic and social incentive system and to take full note of the reciprocal influence between macro- and microeconomics, monetary and real variables, short- and longer-term elements and economic and social factors.

Third, as globalization of the world economy proceeds, competitive performance at the firm, sectoral and national levels is increasingly measured by world standards. So are respective policies and strategies.

ORGANIZATION OF THE BOOK

The book is divided into three Parts.

Part I introduces some key issues that underlie current concerns of policy makers, not just in developing countries and transitional economies (TEs), but also in advanced industrial countries, such as international best practices, policy convergence and policy benchmarking.

Part II discusses three issues of prior concern for policy makers: the concept and measurement of manufacturing competitiveness and respective policies, the incidence of financial factors and the implications of the macro/micro policy dichotomy for cross-country replicability.

Finally, Part III addresses the specific experience of countries and regions and lessons therefrom. It covers four types of country: newly industrializing economies, newly open economies, economies in transition and less developed countries (LDCs), and provides respective country and region case studies. Since the original manuscript was completed, the state of the world economy, and particularly that of developing and transition economies, has undergone important changes. The significance of these changes and their implications from the point of view of the subject-matter of this book are discussed in Chapter 2.

Two important issues do not receive the special treatment they deserve within the scope of this book. They are environmental sustainability and local and regional policies at the national level.

NOTE

1. The latest *World Development Report* (World Bank, 1997) raises an intriguing paradox, perhaps inadvertently, when it suggests that countries with scarce institutional resources are relatively more prone to policy failures and should, therefore, limit themselves to minimal interventions (health, law and order, property rights, defence). And yet these are the same countries where market failures, because of missing markets, are more pervasive. See Chapter 8.

REFERENCE

World Bank (1997), *World Development Report,* Washington D.C.

2. Best Practices and Policy Convergence

THE IMPACT OF GLOBALIZATION

Globalization has put the issue of the international convergence of policies and institutions on the world's agenda.[1] The spread of universal best practices, such as those agreed by a large number of World Trade Organization (WTO) Member countries, appears to have become inexorable and is intended to smooth the way towards a level playing field in the international economy.[2] The deadlines involved impart an added sense of urgency and priority for compliance with uniform and universal standards underscored by the impact they will have on economic and social development in developing countries and economies in transition.

The commitment to policy convergence is undeniable. Of the 109 developing countries and economies in transition that have launched major market-oriented reform programmes since the 1980s, 75 have done so since 1989 (see Annex 2A). At the same time, 107 of the 134 members of the WTO are developing countries and economies in transition, while another 28, including China, the Russian Federation and Taiwan Province, are actively negotiating their entry under special conditions (see Chapter 12). According to the agreement on trade-related industrial measures (TRIMs), by 2000, developing countries (and by 2002, LDCs) must abolish all restrictions on FDI that affect imports, exports or foreign exchange balances, including local content rules (LCRs).

The Asian, Russian and Brazilian crises of the late 1990s have shattered the smooth running of the process of convergence. Requests for waivers and exemptions in enforcing TRIMs deadlines by a number of WTO members, as well as by countries that are still negotiating their entry, should not be ruled out. Both will try to comply with the required policy changes only when activities deemed critical for their future development become competitively sustainable. Thus debates on the legitimacy of various forms and timing of application of the infant-industry argument can be expected.

Convergence towards WTO 2000 is taking place in an uneven way, particularly from the interregional perspective; to the extent that, as a result, the 'particular difficulties' allowed for by WTO are extensively invoked, and the universal application of the TRIMs, together with the levelling of the playing field, may be jeopardized (see Chapter 12).[3]

This raises the question whether universal, peremptory compliance with a uniform set of rules is necessarily the best or only route to a level playing field. Can universal best-practice rules be applied in a uniform, costless and almost immediate way by all countries, regardless of their stage of development and national conditions?

VERIFYING HYPOTHESES ON CONVERGENCE

Hypotheses and predictions on productivity and income convergence among countries rely on the theory of economic growth, whose key building blocks were laid by the classical economists and their direct successors. Such blocks include the role of decreasing returns in physical and human capital accumulation, the relation between per capita income and population growth, the effect of technological progress on the specialization of labour and the influence of monopoly power on technological change.[4]

Neoclassical models of growth predict a *conditional* convergence whereby the lower a country's initial real per capita gross domestic product (GDP) compared to its long-term, steady-state level, the higher its rate of growth as a result of higher relative returns to investment, *provided that* such things as saving rates, initial levels of human capital, population growth, government policy and technological change are not factored in.

The neoclassical theory of growth declined as a field of research by the early 1970s because of lack of empirical relevance. Since then, macroeconomic research has focused on short-term fluctuations. The theory of growth reappeared towards the mid-1980s, when a period of great intellectual effervescence ensued.[5]

What conclusions has available empirical research arrived at regarding the hypotheses on productivity and income convergence? A comparison of the evolution of real per capita GDP among 129 countries during 1960–90 shows that the level of dispersion has *increased* and that the most advanced country in the sample, the United States, went from a real per capita GDP 39 times higher than the most backward country, Ethiopia, in 1960, to one 65 times higher in 1990. At Japan's historical rate of growth between 1890 and 1990, of 2.75 per cent, Ethiopia would reach the United States' 1990 level towards 2149. At the more moderate historical rate of growth of the

United States, of 1.75 per cent, that would occur towards 2236 (Barro and Sala-I-Martin, 1995, p. 3).[6]

The average rate of growth of real per capita GDP during 1960–90 for a sample of 114 countries was 1.8 per cent, with the Republic of Korea, at 6.7 per cent, at one extreme and the Islamic Republic of Iraq, at –2.11 per cent, at the other. The other 16 countries included in the sample – most of them from the sub-Saharan region – also suffered negative rates of growth. The representative country of this region required 30 years to grow 1.3 times, against 7.4 times for the Republic of Korea (Barro and Sala-I-Martin, 1995, pp. 3–4).

Thus the hypothesis that the more backward a country's initial position is in terms of real per capita GDP the higher its rate of growth has not been verified, except in the conditional sense defined above. But even in a homogeneous world in every respect except in rate of growth, the rate of convergence would be so low that to bridge the gap between actual and potential GDP would take a minimum of 70 years.

In the case of Latin America and the Caribbean, available estimates indicate that the gap in total factor productivity (TFP) with the advanced industrial and newly industrializing countries has widened considerably since the Second World War, particularly since the mid-1960s (Ramos, 1996). Convergence in manufacturing labour productivity levels with respect to the United States is not verified either for 1970–94, except during 1973–82 (Benavente et al., 1996).

The economic convergence hypothesis is being confirmed only among similar advanced industrial countries and a few newcomers such as the Republic of Korea, which have still to pass some critical maturity tests.

Beyond the hypotheses of the theory of growth a distinction can be drawn between economic convergence, on the one hand, and institutional convergence, on the other. Imperfect competition, asymmetry in power and information, increasing returns to scale and externalities may prevent convergence in productivity, not just across nations, but also across firms, sectors and regions. Institutional convergence, which consists of a growing similarity of institutional forms and of responses to political, economic and social disequilibria, originating either abroad or at home, is deterred by multiple configurations of the balance between the market and the mix of public regulations, private and public hierarchies and institutional arrangements and legacies at the national level. These relationships vary widely in factor and product markets.

Comparable long-term economic performance records can be compatible with very different institutional configurations, so that the scope for institutional heterogeneity is considerably wider than in the strict sense of the stylized variables of economic growth theory (see below).

If, as observed, the hypothesis of *economic* convergence is hard to verify, the hypothesis of *institutional* convergence is even harder to verify, given the persistence of national specificities (Boyer, 1996; see also Przeworski, 1991).

The debate on convergence refers, in the last resort, to the rivalry among various civilizations and their influence on the configuration of the world order in terms of degree of admissible diversity. The relationships between universality and specificity are the object of a secular controversy today, revived by the transformation of the post-cold war era (see Huntington, 1997, esp. ch. 12).

REPLICATION OF BEST PRACTICES AND DISPARITIES IN INITIAL CONDITIONS AND STRATEGIC CHALLENGES

In contrast to the converging trend towards international production and policy best practices, the developing world and the economies in transition have faced growing differentiation in recent decades. This has led to, on the one hand, a gradation of economic and social winners and losers and, on the other, sharply differing policy challenges that lessen the scope for emulating development success across borders.

Table 2.1 presents some key dimensions of the problem reflected in the diversity of strategic challenges faced by four categories of countries: newly opened economies (NOEs), which have moved from inward-looking to substantially open economies; newly industrializing economies (NIEs), which are those of East and South-East Asia; economies in transition, that is, the former command economies; and less developed countries (LDCs), which are the world's poorest economies. Beyond sharp intra-group contrasts of a historical, geographical, economic, social and institutional nature, the differences in policy challenges facing these four groups of countries have acquired historical proportions, associated with epochs almost as distinct as those that exist between them, on the one hand, and the advanced industrial countries, on the other. These differences cover the whole spectrum that goes from persistent laggardness to successful catching up.[7]

At one extreme, for instance, newly industrializing economies overcame a good many of the obstacles to convergence in income and productivity with advanced industrial countries within a few decades. At the other extreme, less

Table 2.1. Specificity of strategic challenges to industrial development by country category

Country category	Key policy challenges
Newly opened economies (NOEs)	To couple increasing integration into the global economy with the consolidation of manufacturing sector's competitiveness
Newly industrializing economies (NIEs)	To renew manufacturing competitiveness and offset declining rates of return on investment by emphasizing endogenous innovation and technical change
Transition economies (TEs)	To redefine the role of the state, establish a market system, restructure industry, modernize management systems and close important structural adjustment gaps
Less developed countries (LDCs)	To promote reform by enhancing domestic supply responses through structural change, resource accumulation and development of institutional capacities and appropriate incentive systems

developed countries have yet to emerge from economic and social backwardness. The former are now aiming to generate domestic sources of innovation and technical change while consolidating their progress towards higher unit value-added activities. The latter are struggling in their search for viable forms of achieving economic and social progress and for sustainable approaches to accumulate resources, create markets and develop skills and capabilities required for structural change. In contrast to the two former country groupings, newly opened economies and economies in transition are pursuing routes that demand profound changes in economic regime, strategic orientation and linkages with the world market. Such a wide range of challenges highlights the difficulty in devising universal, ubiquitous policy packages. To expect countries so diverse to converge in their policies within a few years would be unrealistic.

Analogous policies and similar strategic guidelines hardly apply to developing countries and economies in transition. Even among the so-called

Table 2.2. Lean production, skill development and corporate governance: limits to cross-border replicability of best practices among members of the 'convergence club'

Best practice (origin)	Key attributes in the country of origin	Restrictions to the scope for replicability
1. Lean production* (Japan)	Decentralization of responsibility, elimination of 'dead' times and induction of constant work effort Teamwork, polyvalent skills Motivation through stress and reciprocal obligation	*Germany and Japan:* Skills are occupational, standardized, portable rather than general, and focused on firm-specific organizational and labour environments as in Japan. Portability of skills facilitates labour mobility among independent enterprises; non-portability favours labour markets *internal* to the firm or conglomerate. In Germany priority is given to workers' dedication to their own performance and labour ethos rather than to their loyalty and devotion to the employer. Performance prevails over seniority. Teamwork rests on individual skills, rather than on team capabilities as such.

2.	Technical training (Germany)	Efficient mechanism of collective bargaining between employers and employees; low pressures on unit labour cost rises; trade union's aversion to inflation and protectionism Training as an explicit component of collective bargaining Trade unions respond to technical change by demanding the upgrading of skills and increases in the share of skilled workers in the labour force	*France:* The tradition of owners' control and the propensity towards adversarial labour relations have blocked the assimilation of the German government/enterprise/trade unions tripartite dialogue practices, which is vital to consensus on effective and sustainable technical training programmes.
3.	Corporate governance (United States and Japan)	Minimization of transaction costs (Japan) versus Minimization of agency costs (USA)	*United States and Japan:* Both countries have advanced along separate tracks in regard to transaction costs versus agency costs, so that their corporate governance systems are not reciprocally replicable. Similar contrasts between the United Kingdom and Germany have blocked progress towards common European legislation in this field.

*Applies to manual work in assembly operations.

Source: Based on Berger and Dore (1996).

'convergence club' of the advanced industrial countries, replication of best practices is hindered by substantive disparities. Table 2.2 presents some examples of this while Boxes 2.1 and 2.2 give some examples of best-practice benchmarking, which is discussed in Chapter 3.

The principles of lean production have produced a quantum leap as compared with traditional Fordism, so that the former can be considered as exemplifying an international best practice worth emulating. This constituted the direction followed by enterprises around the world, particularly in advanced industrial countries, including Germany. Different institutions, practices and forms of social conduct have, however, narrowed significantly the scope for universal application of the principles of lean production. The case of Germany provides a good illustration (see Table 2.2; see also Box 2.1).

Box 2.1 OECD: benchmarking business environments in the global economy

OECD's project on Framework Conditions for Industry was developed in response to the interest of OECD Governments in comparing the characteristics, strengths and weaknesses of their domestic business environments in a dynamic perspective. Country-specific snapshots in matrix form and benchmarks are provided in eight areas: R&D infrastructure; educational profile of the labour force; corporate governance environments; employment regulations; labour costs; corporate taxation; energy costs; and telecommunication costs and infrastructure. The aim is *not* to rank countries on a unidimensional scale of competitiveness. The next step in the inquiry would be to assess the general (macro-level) attractiveness and supportiveness of national business environments for private investment, taking into account the uneven growth of different industries and the specific framework needs of the most dynamic ones. The project approaches industrial competitiveness policy as a new way for governments to respond to globalization of industry and technological change by predominantly indirect means of shaping the framework conditions, or the business environment, for industry.

Major quantitative and qualitative differences were identified across OECD countries. For instance, the proportion of researchers in private enterprises in the total research population ranges from some 20 per cent in New Zealand and Iceland to some 70 per cent in Switzerland and Japan, with an OECD average of around 40 per cent. There are also major differences in sectoral orientation. New Zealand and Iceland focus 25 per cent of their R&D efforts on agro-technologies, while Japan and Germany devote more than 60 per cent of R&D to industrial machinery. Resources dedicated to education and training also vary widely. In some OECD countries most of the working population has below secondary-level education; in others, the bulk of the workforce has received advanced secondary education. Significant differences also exist in terms of professional specialization of the highly skilled segments of the labour force. Graduates in the physical sciences and engineering account for between 30 and 40 per cent of degrees awarded in Switzerland and Germany, while most university degrees in other OECD countries are obtained in law, liberal arts and social sciences.

Even within OECD countries, there are wide differences in the absolute levels of hourly compensation costs for manufacturing workers. In 1993, they varied from US$42.56 in Mexico to US$25.70 in Germany, with an OECD average of US$16.07. Unit labour costs ranged from 0.27 in Mexico to 0.52 in Australia and 0.75 in Sweden, with an OECD average of 0.61.

In 1994, electricity end-use prices for industry were high in Japan (US$0.173/kWh) and Portugal (US$0.116/kWh) and low in Sweden (US$0.037/kWh) and New Zealand (US$0.036/kWh). The telecommunications infrastructure also differs markedly among OECD countries, owing to uneven capital investment and a variety of institutional and regulatory arrangements. The number of main telephone lines per 100 inhabitants is highest in Sweden, with nearly 70 main lines per 100 inhabitants in 1994 and lowest in Mexico, with less than 10. The OECD average is about 48. In 1994, Sweden had more than nine cellular mobile subscribers per 100 inhabitants, with the OECD average above three. Business telephone charges, both local and international, were found to be highest in Turkey and lowest in the Scandinavian countries.

Source: OECD (1997)

France and the United Kingdom have faced difficulties in trying to emulate efficient German practices in the field of training and skill formation. France has failed not just in replicating German practices in education and training but also in R&D, labour relations and industrial restructuring. A number of Latin American countries also have experienced serious problems in trying to benefit from the German dual system owing, among other things, to poor standards of basic education.

Box 2.2 Best-practice policies for small and medium-scale industries (SMIs)

SMIs' dynamism in creating jobs, spreading technological progress, stimulating entrepreneurship and contributing to economic and social well-being is widely recognized. But, because of market asymmetries, SMIs require government support. In search of best support practices, an OECD Industry Committee's Working Party identified four broad areas where governments can have a significant impact by facilitating (i) efficient and unbiased financial markets, (ii) a suitable business environment, education, training and competitiveness and (iii) access to information, networking and the global marketplace.

Financing Venture capital is not a source of finance for most SMIs, but it is used for funding high-risk/high-return businesses. Technology-based firms are often the focus for such types of initiatives. Government support through provision of venture capital varies widely between the more hand-on approaches of the Republic of Korea and Finland and the hands-off approach of Switzerland and the United States, both with considerable success. SMIs establish partnerships through joint ventures, strategic alliances, licensing agreements, franchises and other forms of networking. Governments can help to maximize synergies of this kind, for instance, by sponsoring international trading opportunities through initiatives such as *Europartenariat*.

Business environment Steps toward reducing administrative and regulatory burdens on SMIs is another important policy area. The Dutch and Portuguese experiences show the need for political commitment at the highest level if these actions are to be effective. Yet progress may be slow if support does not consist of highly practical initiatives.

Management capability To effectively assist in improving the quality of management, it is vital that the assistance provided be focused, as shown by the French and Dutch experiences. A major question is whether governments should stimulate and subsidize the purchases of external consultancy and advisory services as opposed to improving internal capability. Italy introduced a scheme of 'mentors' to young people establishing a business for the first time. Although expensive in terms of monitoring costs, this scheme shows impressive results: 80 per cent of businesses survived for at least four years.

Access to markets Governments facilitate market development through electronic commerce and information technology. Several questions were raised by the US experience. SMIs require simple and user-friendly databases for electronic commerce. More sophisticated procedures are needed, however, if the service is to serve not just SMIs but also their advisers and consultants. There is also a question about whether national databases and commercial information should be accessible to non-nationals who do not share in the cost of setting up the databases. Another topic is access to new markets by SMIs from Central and Eastern Europe, which face major hurdles in accessing OECD markets due to lack of familiarity with customer needs, limited packaging experience and linguistic problems. Development of mentoring capability in ethnic groups located in OECD countries and fostering the participation of SMIs in international fairs and exhibitions is a way of overcoming the problem. The Greek scheme to encourage micro enterprises to sell abroad met great success.

(continued)

Box 2.2 continued

SMI policy areas	Topics	Country	Best practice
Financing	Venture capital: alternative sources of financing	Finland	Regional network of venture capital funds, focused on seven Finnish science parks.
		Republic of Korea	Venture capital policy of Ministry of Trade, Industry and Energy (MOTIE) for SMI start-ups.
		Switzerland	Venture capital for new enterprises. Federal guarantee against innovation risks for SMEs.
		United States	US Government's innovative financing programme to facilitate establishment of small business investment companies (SBICs) without intervening in their management and investment decision taking.
		Canada	Leveraging government resources to support joint ventures and other forms of business partnering. Government to encourage SMIs to develop partnerships without influencing their nature. Focus on creating infrastructure to exchange information.
	SMEs and joint ventures	Spain	Promotion by the Spanish Institute for Small and Medium-sized Enterprises (IMPI) of joint ventures between Spanish SMIs and SMIs in developing countries. Government-sponsored business cooperation programme to encourage partnerships between domestic and Latin American SMIs.

Business environment	Reduction of administrative and regulatory burdens on SMIs	Netherlands	New commission on deregulation chaired by the Prime Minister. Areas investigated to reduce burden: taxation, social insurance, environment, labour conditions, statistics and information technology.
		Portugal	Task force under a state secretary to modernize administration and a business administration committee to discuss and implement 90 measures with the consent of business groups.
Management capability	Quality: tools to improve SMI competitiveness	Netherlands	'Enterprise house': mechanism to deliver management development programmes at the local level to minimize confusion amongst SMEs caused by various agencies offering assistance. Assistance by consultants to stimulate information flows to SMEs.
	Mentoring: improving the internal capability of SMIs	Italy	Mentoring scheme underpinned by statutory law to stimulate new SMIs in South Italy.
Access to markets	Business networks: government facilitation of market development through electronic commerce and information technology	United States	United States Small Business Administration provides information services to SMEs on the Internet through customized database.
		Spain	Business networks in framework of action programme for SMEs: set of interconnected information systems for integrated provision of value-added products and services specially designed for SMEs, along with communications facilities.

Box 2.2 continued

SMI policy areas	Topics	Country	Best practice
	Access to new markets for SMIs of Central and Eastern European and OECD countries	Finland	To promote SMIs' access to external markets between Finland and four economies in transition (Czech Republic, Estonia, Hungary and Poland), Ministry of Trade and Industry together with Finnish Foreign Trade Association developed information system and networking of Finnish SMIs, providing market information services, services related to the domestic regional network and export centres and services to promote networking and making Finnish products better known (credit guarantees).
	Programme to foster SMIs' participation in international fairs and exhibitions	Greece	Development of scheme, funded primarily by the EU, to encourage micro-enterprises to sell overseas. Subsidy of 50 per cent of costs of marketing studies, printing of sales brochures and costs of travel to international fairs and exhibitions.

Source: OECD (1997).

Another example of divergence for best practice among the advanced industrial countries lies in the field of corporate governance. Management practices based on large industrial conglomerates in countries such as Germany, Italy, Japan and Switzerland are relatively efficient in terms of lower transaction costs due to the use of implicit contracts and permanent, stable and foreseeable relationships among enterprises. On the other hand, the Anglo-American system facilitates lower agency costs associated with the separation between ownership and control. What represents an advantage in one system translates into a disadvantage in the other and vice versa. An analogous contrast exists within the EU, with Germany and the United Kingdom in the antipodes, and France and Italy somewhere in between, which has led to a paralysis in the timetable towards common legislation for best practice. This suggests that there is a multiplicity of best practices in any given field associated with country-specific historical, institutional and social legacies.

If the workability of convergence is plagued with difficulties even among the countries of the convergence club, the uniform impact of globalization on domestic microeconomic scenarios raises even stronger doubts with the considerable differences in national institutions, policies and practices.[8] Divergences in the microeconomic domain are greater and more resilient than those in the macroeconomic since they involve more deeply rooted national institutions, practices and traditions. This challenges the notion that globalization reduces national states to passivity and impotence.[9]

Evidence that microeconomic policies and institutions can be successfully replicated across borders is not very convincing. It is even likely that the number of cases of failure exceeds that of successes. Best practices espoused in the management literature mostly refer to issues of operational efficiency. Yet the essence of entrepreneurial strategies and related public policy guidelines concerns choices among alternatives specific to the economic and social milieu. Techniques geared to improve operational efficiency, such as total quality management or 'time-based' competition, can be replicated with some ease. But the opposite is true when it comes to deciding how best to draw on such techniques within a specific entrepreneurial environment (Porter, 1996).

Technological learning, production of public goods, skill and capability formation and similar endogenous processes are spheres of national policy that the governments of even the most advanced countries are reluctant to leave to other hands, visible or invisible. Rather than universally superior practices, best practices are normally hybrids that result from adoption and then adaptation to specific national conditions.

EMERGING GLOBAL STANDARDS: SCOPE AND IMPLICATIONS FOR DOMESTIC POLICY MAKING

Notwithstanding the hurdles pointed out above, the spread of global standards adds pressure towards convergence across countries in policies, practices and institutions, both directly through interactions with global markets and institutions and indirectly through the broadening and deepening of regional integration processes.

Exposure to international competition renders national policies vulnerable to the increasing influence of the external environment. It also raises the stakes of effective policy making and adherence to global standards. The quality of political, social and business institutions around which industrial activity is organized is increasingly being judged in international fora in terms of the extent of their adherence to such norms. The need for developing and transition economies to gain credibility and access to the global capital market has become a key incentive to comply with them. As the pace of internationalization of policies accelerates, particularly through regional integration processes, lead-times to respond are becoming shorter.

National systems are being required to adjust to international protocols and conventions and voluntary agreements in a growing range of areas encompassing governance, environment, trade, finance, investment, labour and technical standards (see Box 2.3). Voluntary standards tend to become binding over time.[10]

Box 2.3. Examples of established and emerging binding and voluntary global standards and covenants in the trade, investment, technical, environmental and financial fields

A. Trade, technical standards and investment

- WTO agreements on trade-related industrial measures (TRIMs), trade-related industrial property (TRIPs), General Agreement on Trade in Services (GATS), anti-dumping, technical barriers to trade, rules of origin, government procurement
- OECD Multilateral Agreement on Investment*
- ISO 9000*

B. Environment

- Montreal Protocol (chlorofluorocarbons)
- Kyoto Protocol (greenhouse effects)
- Basle Convention (hazardous wastes)
- ISO 14000*
- World Bank voluntary guidelines
- Chemical industry voluntary guidelines (Responsible Care)*
- European Union Eco-Management and Audit Scheme

C. Finance and Corporate Governance

- System of multilateral surveillance of national financial, supervisory and regulatory systems encompassing banking and securities
- IMF's Special Data Dissemination Standards, Code of Good Practice on Fiscal Transparency and Code of Good Practice on Financial and Monetary Policy*
- Standards on qualitative descriptive information on financial systems, markets, institutions, laws, credit culture, skills and structure of the banking system, relations between banks, government and industrial sector*
- Prudential regulation and standards*
- Standards to monitor adequacy of foreign currency liquidity*
- Standards for supervision of large international financial groups and for cooperation and information sharing between national supervisors on the activities of such groups*
- Basle Core Principles on Effective Banking Supervision*
- Standards and guidelines on corporate governance*
- International standards for accounting, disclosure and auditing practices in the corporate sector*
- Standards and practices for governing exchange settlement risk, settlement arrangements for securities and derivatives and market liquidities in times of stress*
- Revision of the IMF agreement to provide for capital convertibility

Note: *Voluntary

In order to respond positively to these challenges, well-tuned, modern and effective domestic regulatory and incentive regimes are required. Weaknesses in the effectiveness of policy-making processes are heavily penalized. Accommodation to global change requires structural and administrative reform in many areas of public management through major investment in people and knowledge acquisition. The ensuing adjustment costs may be mitigated through the search for joint solutions to policy problems that governments cannot solve alone, for example, in the fields of environmental protection or regulation of global financial markets.

CONCLUSION: TOWARDS A NEW DEVELOPMENT PARADIGM

The manuscript versions of the chapters by the collaborating authors of this book were ready by early 1997. A few months later we witnessed the onset of the East Asian crisis, the Russian default and the collapse of the Brazilian currency – the real – in rather quick succession. The prospects for the world economy turned from cautiously optimistic to recessionary. Within this sharp change of orientation, a large number of developing and transition economies, including the most dynamic ones, suffered the consequences of drastic and massive reversals in capital flows, worsening terms of trade and record lows in development assistance, while their economic and social progress came to an abrupt halt. Recession, unemployment and social disruption ensued, appearing to make medium and long-term concerns, such as those of this book, recede into the background.[11]

Frequent, virulent and globally contagious financial crises have caused major discontinuities in economic and social progress in developing and transition economies throughout the late 1990s, with implications for these economies comparable to those of the Great Depression for developed countries. Although the results of the successful industrialization experience of the East Asian countries during the previous three decades will not be swept away even by several years of poor or non-existent growth, the key question is under what conditions these countries, along with the rest of the non-industrial world, may be expected to resume robust long-term growth.

The spread of globalization is outpacing the ability of non-developed societies to adjust to it. Globalization punishes factors of production that enjoy little mobility, such as labour, on which such societies largely rely, while it rewards factors of production that are highly mobile, such as know-how and financial capital, which are largely under the command of developed societies.

Not even the most unconditional supporters of East Asia's growth policies of relentless resource accumulation can afford to neglect the home-grown factors that underpinned the crisis, such as not enough attention paid to overcapacity build-up, core competencies, efficiency gains, risk management and prudential regulation. But this only added to severe weaknesses in global fundamentals.

The global institutional framework set up in 1945 has to deal with a world economy where, while nine out of ten dollars negotiated in world forex markets used to go to financing trade and long-term investment and the remainder to short-term capital movements, this proportion is now reversed. Meanwhile, normalized by global GDP, IMF resources amount today to a third of those they commanded in 1944. These traits go hand in hand with herd-like behaviour, moral hazard, proneness to panic and overshooting, and inadequate risk assessment resulting in unprecedented levels of volatility with a highly skewed impact.

By shattering conventional wisdom on development strategies and their place in the world economy, events of the late 1990s have defied conventional wisdom on economic development policy and catalysed the emergence of a new consensus on development, whose key features may be summarized as follows:

1. Economic stability requires congruence between domestic and global fundamentals and governance. Sound macroeconomic fundamentals do not immunize against contagion effects. No amount of macroeconomic excellence and mastery of the skills necessary to fight volatility suffices to offset systemic flaws in the global economy. Conversely, economic globalization is not consistent with highly vulnerable and exposed domestic financial and corporate structures.
2. Macroeconomic stability requires sound microeconomic fundamentals. While these need to be consistent with universally sound financial and prudential standards, they vary according to specific domestic institutions, practices and traditions.
3. Pursuance of sustained and substantially above-world-average long-term growth rates in developing and transition economies is highly risky in the absence of a sound mix of global/domestic and macro/micro fundamentals.
4. Domestic institutional, regulatory and governance frameworks need to be strengthened *pari passu* with or, preferably prior to, market liberali-

zation and deregulation, particularly in finance, irrespective of whether policies to foster resource accumulation are adopted or not.

5. Industrial development involves complex microeconomic and institutional transformations that markets alone, left to their own devices, cannot accomplish, even with the right macroeconomic fundamentals.
6. The economic, social and environmental dimensions of development need to be addressed in a complementary way. Policy reform requires a multidimensional approach. Institutional, regulatory, governance and social reforms need to be synchronized with macroeconomic stabilization, trade liberalization, privatization and deregulation. Policy reform should mark a continuum cutting across all areas of development.[12]
7. To succeed in developing dynamic comparative advantages it is not enough merely to fill gaps between policies such as those addressed to macroeconomics, education, environment, regional development and equity in an *ad hoc* manner. These policies need to be integrated with specific industrial development policies, since these various sets of policies do not substitute but complement one another.
8. Catching up through leapfrogging may be possible from time to time in selected areas, but is not viable as a general prescription, except at the cost of painful reversals and shocks in expectations. The time it takes to attain substantial economic and social progress may be somewhat compressed by supplementing domestic effort with policy lessons drawn from the experience of other countries, but there are no short cuts or quick fixes.
9. Flows of experience are not unidirectional but move in all directions: from North to South and South to North and from East to West and West to East. With globalization, learning in policy making increasingly relies on a global pool of experience which all countries share and on which all of them need to draw. Although such a pool should constitute an international public good, developing and transition economies are handicapped by asymmetries and imperfections in the market for information which tilt the global playing field.
10. Promoting competitive markets is not as simple as conventionally perceived. Opening up the economy, deregulating and privatizing are necessary, but far from sufficient, to attain a working market-driven economy. A clear understanding is also required of how to deal with non-performing markets, and of the relationships between markets, institutions and the state, as well as the structure of incentives that govern the implementation of public policy.

NOTES

1. Globalization is the process of growing interdependence among national economies as a result of ever more intense and varied commercial, financial and technological relationships among them.
2. 'Best practices' in this context means what, by general consensus, are regarded as 'superior' practices, rather than the 'optimum' practices of microeconomic theory.
3. Para. 3; Art. 5 on Notification and Transitional Arrangements of the TRIMs agreement reads: 'On request, the Council for Trade in Goods, may extend the transition period for the elimination of the TRIMs ... for a ... Member ... which demonstrates *particular difficulties* in implementing the provisions of this Agreement. In considering such request, the Council ... shall take into account the individual development, financial and trade needs of the Member in question' (emphasis added).
4. In addition to Adam Smith, David Ricardo and Thomas Malthus, economists of this century in the classical school include Frank Knight and Joseph Schumpeter.
5. The emergence of the new growth theory entails a Copernican break with the tradition – and irrelevance – of the neoclassical assumptions. Instead of perfect markets it posits that markets are imperfect; abundance of public goods constrains complete private appropriation; increasing returns replace decreasing returns; and endogenous technological change replaces exogenous technological change. Under these conditions, especially in the presence of monopolistic appropriation of the fruits of investment in R&D, the growth rate does not necessarily fall in conjunction with high levels of capital accumulation per person employed, while the influence of government policies on the growth rate gains in importance through their impact on the degree of openness of the economy, the rate of saving, the educational level and the spread of technology. Although, in many cases, it fails to provide answers, the new growth theory marks a reconciliation with reality. In an agnostic interpretation of their contribution, Nelson (1997) points out that much of the formal modelization of these theories takes place at the expense of their relevance and consists of the late adoption of already existing empirical findings. For example, they assume perfect foresight, or a correctly specified probability distribution of the occurrence of future events. Differences in corporate management and institutional organization are ignored, as is technological learning. An important methodological reason for these traits is that respective models remain close to the canons of general equilibrium theory.
6. See Abramovitz (1986), Barro (1991), Baumol et al. (1994), Bradford deLong and Summers (1991), Maddison (1991) and Verspagen (1993).
7. The crisis initiated in mid-1997 in South-East Asia translated into a reversal of historical trends. Although it is still uncertain exactly when South-East Asian countries will be able to resume robust industrial growth, there is little doubt that the fundamentals for such growth are very much in place (see Chapter 1). As to the pace of catching up, convergence among the economies in transition that are joining the European Union (EU), for instance, can be expected to proceed at a faster pace than among those which are not.
8. The feasibility, for instance, of coupling the German macroeconomic orthodoxy with the Anglo-American microeconomic *laissez-faire* is yet to be demonstrated. The delayed entry by the United Kingdom into the European single currency relates not just to divergences in economic cycle but also to institutional and governance issues (see Table 2.2 and source reference).
9. 'The real policy challenge is: how do we construct an international economic system that respects and best fulfills the aspirations of distinct national entities, including their desire for material advancement for which trade serves as a vehicle?' (Rodrik, 1998). Relying on Polanyi's (1957) insight that markets are sustainable only to the extent that they are embedded in social and political institutions, Rodrik reminds us that markets are not

self-regulating, self-stabilizing and self-legitimating, and that there is no single blueprint for embedding a market economy in society. Germany, Japan and the United States 'diverge greatly in their approach to social insurance, organization of labour markets, corporate governance, regulation of product markets, redistributive taxation, and intrusiveness of governments in the economy more broadly. These and other nations have developed various styles of national capitalism arising out of disparate historical trajectories and different sets of norms. There are as many working models of successful capitalism as there are advanced industrial countries' (Rodrik, 1998, p.16).

10. For example, ISO standards are not obligatory, but they are a *de facto* requisite to enter many advanced-country markets. The International Monetary Fund's (IMF) Special Data Dissemination Standards (SDDS) are voluntary. However, proposals have already been put forward to impose penalties on those IMF members which fail to subscribe and fully implement or remedy failures to meet the standards.
11. At the time the manuscript was submitted, a possible devaluation of the yuan was being openly debated in China, which might trigger a new series of competitive devaluations in Asia and beyond. This was taking place at a time when Japan's economy was experiencing its worst recession in modern times and the European economy was cooling down. Lack of consensus among industrial countries on how to stabilize the world economy – indeed, about whether anything should be done at all beyond further trade liberalization and improved financial surveillance and monitoring – only adds to the sense of uncertainty and perplexity. The global economy would appear to have entered uncharted territory without a compass. For a comprehensive listing of sources on recent crises see http://www.stern.nyu.edu/~nroubini/asia/AsiaHomepage.html.
12. See 'Industrial development policy: concepts and experience', Note by the Secretary-General to the General Assembly, A/53/254, 11 August 1998 (report submitted by UNIDO).

REFERENCES

Adams, F.G. (1993), *Transition Patterns: China versus Eastern Europe* (Internet: http://www.ssc.upenn.edu/east/fall94/Transition_Patterns.html).

Abramovitz, M. (1986), 'Catching up, forging ahead and falling behind', *Journal of Economic History*, 46, 386.

Barro, R.J. (1991), 'Economic growth in a cross-section of countries', *Quarterly Journal of Economics*, May, 407–43.

Barro, R.J. and Sala-í-Martin, X. (1995), Economic Growth, McGraw-Hill, New York, 3.

Baumol, W., R. Nelson and E. Wolff (1994), *Convergence of Productivity*, Oxford: Oxford University Press.

Benavente, J.M., G. Crespi, J. Katz and G. Stumpo (1996), 'Cambios en el desarrollo industrial de América Latina', *Revista de la CEPAL,* no. 60, Santiago, Chile, December.

Berger, S. and R. Dore (eds) (1996), *National Diversity and Global Capitalism*, Ithaca and London: Cornell University Press.

Boyer, R. (1996), 'The convergence hypothesis revisited: globalization but still the century of nations?', in Berger and Dore, 25–59.

Bradford deLong, J. and L. Summers (1991), 'Equipment, investment and economic growth', *Quarterly Journal of Economics*, May, 445–502.

Center for International Private Enterprise (1992), *The Economic Reform Survey 1992, Macroeconomic Dynamics through the Adjustment and Reform Process* (Internet: http://www.usis.usemb.se/ERT/e05/5REGION.HTML).

ECA (Economic Commission for Africa) (1994), *The African Economy in 1994,* Dar es Salaam.

ECA (1996), *Paris Declaration for the Least Developed Countries for the 1990s* (Internet: http://www.sas.upenn.edu/African_Studies/ECA/ECA_Pris15x.html).

Europa World Yearbook (1996), vol. II, London.

Hunter, B. (1996-97), *The Statesman's Year-Book,* 133rd edition, Berlin: De Gruyter.

Huntington, S.P. (1997), *The Clash of Civilizations and the Remaking of the World Order,* New York: Touchstone Books.

Klein, L.R. (1994), *The Economic Transition in the Former CMEA and Some Neighbours* (Internet: http://mcneil.sas.upenn.edu/east/winter94/text1.html).

Maddison, A. (1991), *Dynamic Forces in Capitalist Development*, Oxford: Oxford University Press.

Nelson, R. (1997), 'How new is new growth theory: a different point of view', *Challenge*, September–October.

OECD (1997), *Best Practice Policies for Small- and Medium-Sized Enterprises,* Paris: OECD.

Polanyi, K. (1957), *The Great Transformation,* Boston: Beacon Press.

Porter, M.E. (1990), *The Competitive Advantage of Nations,* New York: Free Press.

Przeworski, A. (1991), *Democracy and Market*, Cambridge: Cambridge University Press.

Ramos, J. (1996), 'Política industrial y competitividad en economías abiertas', *Serie Desarrollo Productivo* no. 34, Red de Reestructuración y Competitividad, CEPAL, Santiago, Chile.

Rodrik, D. (1998), 'Rethinking the world economy', http://www.ksg.harvard.edu/rodrik/TNRpiece.html.

Sachs, J.D. and A. Warner (1995), 'Economic reform and the process of global integration', in Brainard W.C. and Perry, G.L. (eds), *Brookings Papers on Economic Activity,* 1, 1–118.

Stabillon, C. (1997), *Policy Making for the Attainment of Fast and Sustained Economic Growth* (Internet: http://uni2a.unige.ch/~barras3/).

Szyrmer, J. and A. Vishnevsky (1994), *The Pattern of Economic Change* (Internet: http://mcneil.sas.upenn.edu/east/fall94/Pattern_of_EconomicChange.html).

United Nations (1996), 'The current economic situation in the ECE economies and the short-run outlook', *Economic Survey of Europe,* Geneva.

Verspagen, B. (1993), *Uneven Growth between Interdependent Economies,* Brookfield, VT: Avebury.

ANNEX 2A. THE SPREAD OF POLICY REFORM PROGRAMMES

Table 2A.1 Major economic policy reform processes: economies in transition

	Trade liberalization		Domestic economic policy reforms			
Country or territory	Year	Remarks	Year	Structural reform	Export-led strategy	Remarks
Albania	1991		1991–93	x		Financial reform; privatization
Armenia	Closed until end of 1994		1995	x		Privatization
Belarus	1994		1992–94	x		Inflation stabilization; financial reform; privatization
Bosnia and Herzegovina						
Bulgaria	1991		1991–93	x		Privatization; pension reform
Cambodia			1989			
China	Closed until end of 1994	Trade policies progressively liberalized since 1978, but trade still rife with quantitative restrictions (QRs) at least through 1994	1978	x	x	
Croatia	1992					
Cuba			1993	x	x	Trade liberalization; privatization
Czech Republic	1991		1989–90	x		Privatization

Estonia	1992	1990–91	x	x	Trade liberalization; financial reform; privatization
Georgia	Closed until end of 1994	1995	x		Privatization
Hungary	1990	1989–91	x	x	Trade liberalization; privatization
Kazakhstan	Closed until end of 1994	1993	x		Privatization
Kyrgyzstan	1994				
Lao People's Democratic Republic		1990	x		Privatization
Latvia	1993	1990–91	x	x	Trade liberalization; financial reform; privatization
Lithuania	1993	1990–91	x	x	Trade liberalization; financial reform; privatization
Mongolia		1991	x		Privatization
Myanmar	Closed until end of 1994	1990	x		Inflation stabilization
Poland	1990	1990	x	x	Trade liberalization; financial reform; privatization,
Republic of Moldova	1994	1993	x		Privatization
Romania	1992	1991	x		Inflation stabilization; financial reform; privatization

(continued)

Table 2A.1 continued

Country or territory	Trade liberalization: Year	Trade liberalization: Remarks	Domestic economic policy reforms: Year	Structural reform	Export-led strategy	Remarks
Russian Federation	Closed until end of 1994		1991	x		Privatization
Slovakia	1991		1989–90	x		Financial reform; privatization
Slovenia	1991		1992–93			
Tajikistan	Closed until end of 1994					
The former Yugoslav Republic of Macedonia	1994		1993	x		Privatization
Turkmenistan	Closed until end of 1994		1994	x		Privatization
Ukraine	Closed until end of 1994		1990	x		Privatization
Uzbekistan	Closed until end of 1994					
Viet Nam			1992	x		Financial reform; privatization
Yugoslavia	Closed until end of 1994					

Sources: Adams (1993), Hunter (1996–97), Klein (1994), Sachs and Warner (1995). Stabillon (1997), Szyrmer and Vishnevsky (1994), Center for International Private Enterprise (1992), *The Europa World Yearbook* (1996), and United Nations (1996).

Table 2A.2 Major economic policy reform processes: newly opened economies

	Trade liberalization		Domestic economic policy reforms			
Country or territory	Year	Remarks	Year	Structural reform	Export-led strategy	Remarks
Argentina	1991	Average nominal tariff level for manufacturing was 141 per cent in 1958; liberalization in 1976–80 did not sufficiently reduce effective rates of protection for all of manufacturing in 1980	1987–91	x	x	Inflation stabilization; trade liberalization; financial reform; privatization; tariffs reduced starting in 1988; import licensing abolished for most items
Bolivia	1985	Open 1956–79; closed 1979–84; open since 1985	1985	x	x	Inflation stabilization; trade liberalization; privatization; pension reform
Brazil	1991	Average effective protection rates in 1967 and 1973 exceeded 40 per cent; 1973 was most liberal year during period 1947–82	1988–91	x	x	Inflation stabilization; trade liberalization; privatization; major reforms announced in 1990; tariffs reduced to average 21 per cent. Almost all QRs phased out
Chile	1976	Until 1976 classified as closed due to import prohibitions, licensing, and multiple exchange rates	1973	x	x	Trade liberalization. Reform after 1973 eliminated QRs and a uniform tariff established (11 per cent)

(continued)

Table 2A.2 continued

	Trade liberalization		Domestic economic policy reforms			
Country or territory	Year	Remarks	Year	Structural reform	Export-led strategy	Remarks
Colombia	1991	Had complicated mixture of tariffs and QRs; average tariffs rates fell below 40 per cent in 1986 and stayed low up to present				
Costa Rica	1986	Open 1952–61; closed 1962–85; in the 1950s no exchange restrictions on foreign payments and no import licensing; imports could be obtained freely at exchange rate 17 per cent below rate at which exports had to be surrendered to central bank; joined Central American Common Market (CACM) in 1960; mean common external tariff (CET) 40 per cent in 1966 and 53 per cent before 1986; 1986 tariff liberalization reduced mean tariff to 26 per cent				

Dominican Republic	Closed until end of 1994	Liberalization during period 1981–86 did not go far enough; another liberalization begun in 1991, but not progressed significantly				
Ecuador	1991	Open 1950–82; closed 1983–90; extensive trade reform started in 1990; by 1991 virtually all the non-tariff restrictions (NTRs) eliminated. Maximum tariff: 35 per cent in 1990	1992–93	x		Privatization
Egypt	Closed until end of 1994	State-led development planning and import-substituting policies established in 1950s; in 1980s average effective import tariff was 49 per cent; assessment of recent reforms insufficient to qualify as open	1991	x	x	Inflation, stabilization; trade liberalization; privatization; new programme in 1991; QRs coverage of imports to 26 per cent; average tariff 42 per cent
El Salvador	1988	Open 1950–61; closed 1962–89; in 1950s and early 1960s, import licenses not required, and few restrictions on payments or transfers abroad; in 1960, joined the CACM; external tariff 53 per cent during 1966–86	1991		x	Trade liberalization

(continued)

Table 2A.2 continued

	Trade liberalization		Domestic economic policy reforms			
Country or territory	Year	Remarks	Year	Structural reform	Export-led strategy	Remarks
Guatemala	1988	Open 1950–61; closed 1962–88; in 1950s and early 1960s no import licensing or significant restrictions on payments or transfers abroad; in 1960, joined the CACM; election of civilian Government in 1985 started period of reform	1988			
India	1993	Until 1991 had very high tariffs and complex QRs	1991	x	x	Trade liberalization; privatization; labour market reform; maximum import duties cut from 355 per cent to 85 per cent in 1993 and to 65 per cent in most recent budgets; less than half of domestic manufacturing now protected by QRs compared with 90 per cent prior to 1991
Jamaica	1989	Open until 1973, closed 1973–89; in 1989, QRs eliminated and tariffs lowered to 20–30 per cent for most items				

Mexico	1986	Open 1956–64; closed 1964–84; imports could be made freely from French franc area countries up to 1964; mean unweighted tariff 47 per cent in 1980	1985–88	x	x	Inflation stabilization; trade liberalization; financial reform; privatization; substantial liberalization of QRs since 1985; tariffs reduced to average of 13 per cent; accession to GATT in 1986
Pakistan	Closed until end of 1994	In 1955 average import tariff exceeded 40 per cent; extensive import licensing through 1983; recent trade reforms have not gone far	1988	x	x	Trade liberalization; privatization; after 1988 import licensing abolished for wide range of items; maximum tariff reduced to 125 per cent
Paraguay	1989	Implementation of trade liberalization in 1989; simple average tariff was 16.2 per cent				
Peru	1991	Open 1948–67, followed by closure and then open since 1991	1990	x	x	Trade liberalization; privatization; non-tariff barriers (NTBs) eliminated and the tariff system simplified to two-tier rate structure (15 per cent and 25 per cent)
South Africa	1991	Traditionally followed an import-substitution and inward-looking development strategy; reinforced by externally imposed trade and financial sanctions in 1985; United States and several other countries began lifting trade sanctions in 1991	1994	x		Privatization; labour market reform

(continued)

Table 2A.2 continued

	Trade liberalization		Domestic economic policy reforms			
Country or territory	Year	Remarks	Year	Structural reform	Export-led strategy	Remarks
Trinidad and Tobago	Closed until end of 1994					
Uruguay	1990	Closed until 1982				
Venezuela	1989–92	Open 1950–59; closed 1960–89; open 1989–93; closed since 1993; in 1950s bound by a trade agreement with United States that kept protection low; in 1959 new Government used treaty's escape clause and sharply increased protection	1990	x	x	Trade liberalization; privatization; most QRs eliminated (10 per cent of tariff lines remain; tariff average 19 per cent with top rate of 50 per cent; accession to GATT in 1990

Sources: Economic Commission for Africa (1994, 1996), Hunter (1996–97), Klein (1994), Sachs and Warner (1995), Stabillon (1997), Szyrmer and Vishnevsky (1994), Center for International Private Enterprise (1992), *Europa World Yearbook* (1996) and United Nations (1996).

Table 2A.3 Major economic policy reform processes: newly industrializing economies

	Trade liberalization		Domestic economic policy reforms			
Country or territory	Year	Remarks	Year	Structural reform	Export-led strategy	Remarks
Hong Kong SAR	Always open				x	
Indonesia	1970	Until 1970 had dual exchange rate system; important trade liberalization measures were introduced between 1966 and 1967; import licensing eliminated in 1966; median tariff rate had fallen below 40 per cent by 1970	1990–94		x	
Malaysia	Open since 1963		1991	x	x	Trade liberalization; privatization
Philippines	1988	In 1960s average rate of protection exceeded 40 per cent	1992	x	x	Privatization

(continued)

Table 2A.3 continued

Country or territory	Trade liberalization		Domestic economic policy reforms			
	Year	Remarks	Year	Structural reform	Export-led strategy	Remarks
Republic of Korea	1968	Exchange rate unified by mid-1960s; gradual reduction in import tariffs started in mid-1960s; by 1968, average tariff was below 40 per cent	1992	x	x	Financial reform; privatization
Singapore	Open since 1965				x	
Taiwan Province	1963		1993	x	x	Trade liberalization; labour market reform
Thailand	Always essentially open		1992		x	

Sources: Hunter, (1996–97), Sachs and Warner (1995), Stabillon (1997), Center for International Private Enterprise (1992) and *Europa World Yearbook* (1996).

Table 2A.4 Major economic policy reform processes: less developed countries

	Trade liberalization		Domestic economic policy reforms			
Country or territory	Year	Remarks	Year	Structural reform	Export-led strategy	Remarks
Angola	Closed until end of 1994	Protracted civil war since independence	1995–96	x		Privatization
Bangladesh	Closed until end of 1994	Phased import liberalization is in progress but implementation very slow	1991–95			
Benin	1990		1991	x		Inflation stabilization; financial reform
Bhutan				x		Privatization
Burkina Faso	Closed until end of 1994	State-controlled export monopsony is in operation	1991	x		Inflation stabilization; financial reform; privatization
Burundi	Closed until end of 1994		1986–93	x		Inflation stabilization; financial reform
Cameroon	1993					
Cape Verde		Insufficient information on trade policy	1992–95	x		Privatization

(continued)

Table 2A.4 continued

Country or territory	Trade liberalization		Domestic economic policy reforms			
	Year	Remarks	Year	Structural reform	Export-led strategy	Remarks
Central African Republic	Closed until end of 1994					
Chad	Closed until end of 1994	Lack of progress on trade reforms				
Congo	Closed until end of 1994	Liberalization attempt in 1987, but did not go far enough	1994			
Côte d'Ivoire	Closed until end of 1994	Still extensive NTBs, scheduled to be phased out by 1995	1990	x	x	Trade liberalization; financial reform; privatization
Democratic Republic of the Congo	Closed until end of 1994	Never pursued open economic policies; no recent reform	1986			
Ethiopia	Closed until end of 1994	Civil war and devastating famines started in 1970s and continued through mid-1980s; transitional government assumed power in 1991; fragile truce prevailed in 1992	1992			

Gabon	Closed until end of 1994	Reform programme in 1994	1993		
Gambia	1985	In 1990, virtually no administrative controls on foreign exchange allocation	1986–93	x	Inflation stabilization; financial reform
Ghana	1985	In 1990, none of foreign exchange allocation controlled and only two items subject to NTRs	1988–92	x	Inflation stabilization; financial reform; privatization
Guinea	1986	Comprehensive dismantling of state-led development institutions, including external trade protection			
Guinea Bissau	1987				
Guyana	1988	Prior to 1988 extensive list of import prohibitions and restrictions, greatly reduced since then; in 1991 adopted Caribbean Community CET schedule with average rates well below 40 per cent	1991		

(continued)

Table 2A.4 continued

	Trade liberalization		Domestic economic policy reforms			
Country or territory	Year	Remarks	Year	Structural reform	Export-led strategy	Remarks
Haiti	Closed until end of 1994	Extensive tariffs and QRs protected domestic manufacturing during 1949–86; special export processing zones (EPZs) where firms are allowed to import intermediate products, assemble them and then export, but these represent small fraction of the economy; since 1986 liberalization extremely slow				
Honduras	1991	Open 1950–61; closed 1962–90; in 1950s and early 1960s no significant restrictions on payments or transfers abroad; in 1960, joined CACM; extensive trade reform between 1990 and 1992 included elimination of import permits and administrative foreign exchange allocation; import tariffs reduced to 5–20 per cent				

Kenya	1993	Open 1963–67, followed by closing, and then reform in 1993; in 1963, entered into customs union with the United Republic of Tanzania and Uganda with internal free trade and CET of 30 per cent for most goods, zero for equipment, and 75 per cent for luxuries; liberalization ended with Exchange Control Act of 1967 followed by gradual increase in licensing	1988–93	x	Inflation stabilization; financial reform; privatization
Lesotho	Not rated	Ambiguous case due to membership in Southern African Customs Union	1986–93	x	Inflation stabilization; financial reform
Madagascar	Closed until end of 1994	No significant reform	1989	x	Privatization
Malawi	Closed until end of 1994	Closed since early 1970s	1986–93	x	Inflation stabilization; financial reform
Mali	1988	State-led development during 1960–88; state export monopoly and extensive import licensing	1986–93	x	Inflation stabilization; financial reform

(continued)

Table 2A.4 continued

	Trade liberalization		Domestic economic policy reforms			
Country or territory	Year	Remarks	Year	Structural reform	Export-led strategy	Remarks
Mauritania	Closed until end of 1994	Closed during 1970–90; decisive intensification of reforms in 1992				
Mauritius	Open since 1968		1983	x	x	Trade liberalization; privatization
Mozambique	Closed until end of 1994	No major recent reform efforts	1990–93	x		Inflation stabilization; financial reform; privatization
Nepal	1991		1992			
Nicaragua	1991	Open 1950–60, closed 1961–90; import licensing and surcharges for acquiring foreign exchange in 1950s but licences were freely granted and average surcharge did not exceed 40 per cent. Adopted high CET of CACM in period 1966–86				
Niger	Closed until end of 1994	No sustained recent reform efforts	1986–93	x		Inflation stabilization; financial reform

Nigeria	Closed until end of 1994	Period 1986–1992 may qualify as liberalization	1985–90	x	x	Trade liberalization; financial reform; privatization; labour market reform
Rwanda	Closed until the end of 1994					
Sao Tome and Principe			1985	x	x	Trade liberalization; privatization
Senegal	Closed until end of 1994	No major recent reform efforts	1985–93	x	x	Inflation stabilization; trade liberalization; financial reform; privatization
Sierra Leone	Closed until end of 1994	State-controlled export monopsony still in operation; no recent major reform efforts				
Solomon Islands			1990–94			
Somalia	Closed until end of 1994					
Sri Lanka	1991	Open 1950–56; closed 1956–77; open 1977–83; closed 1983–91	1993			
Sudan			1991			
United Republic of Tanzania	Closed until end of 1994		1986–93	x		Inflation stabilization; financial reform

(continued)

Table 2A.4 continued

Country or territory	Trade liberalization		Domestic economic policy reforms			
	Year	Remarks	Year	Structural reform	Export-led strategy	Remarks
Togo	Closed until end of 1994			1991	x	Inflation stabilization; financial reform
Uganda	1988		1991	x		Inflation stabilization; financial reform; privatization
Zambia	1993					
Zimbabwe	Closed until end of 1994		1991–95	x	x	Inflation stabilization; trade liberalization; privatization; labour market reform

Sources: ECA (1994, 1996), Hunter (1996–97), Sachs and Warner (1995), Center for International Private Enterprise (1992), and *Europa World Yearbook* (1996).

3. Policy Benchmarking: Principles and Practice

INTRODUCTION

Policy makers in developing countries and economies in transition face the daunting challenge of coming forth with ever more relevant, focused and effective policies to achieve sustained growth, improve living standards and eliminate poverty and disease. As an unprecedented wave of policy reforms sweeps across developing countries and economies in transition, new ways are being sought to meet these demands.

Recent experience demonstrates that unilateral liberalization programmes in developing countries and economies in transition need to be coupled with policies aimed at assisting the economic structure to cope with unprecedented levels of exposure to international competition. This accommodation is neither instantaneous nor spontaneous. An overreliance on automatic mechanisms and the prompt reaction of markets and institutions may be as detrimental to policy success as the belief in the omniscience of the state.[1]

Framework policies to promote manufacturing competitiveness are particularly needed at a time of ever more intense competition in the world market, as well as offensive and defensive protectionist measures in the developed world.

As a result, levelling the playing field – seldom a concern for the closed economies of the past – has now come to the fore, along with capacity building, as an absolute policy priority since it affects growth and welfare through its impact on resource allocation. Although this priority is primarily country-specific, it is also common to most developing countries and economies in transition, thus calling for renewed multilateral action.

Cooperation among countries in the policy field may consist of harmonization, coordination or joint assessment, or benchmarking. A salient feature of these three levels of cooperation is the declining need for top-down intervention and centralized execution. In contrast to the first two, experience of policy benchmarking is very limited, especially across regions, where it offers the greatest potential.

POLICY HARMONIZATION

Steps towards policy harmonization often focus on compliance with international covenants and codes voluntarily adhered to on a bilateral or multilateral basis. Adherence in this case usually entails acceptance of some constraints on the scope for autonomous decision making in specific policy areas to gain access to markets, technology or finance. The most conspicuous example is the agreements reached in the Uruguay Round of trade negotiations.

The European Union (EU) and the Southern Common Market (MERCOSUR) are examples of highly formalized trade blocs. Harmonization may be focused on a common schedule of tariff and non-tariff reductions, as is the case with free trade agreements such as the American Free Trade Association (AFTA) and the North American Free Trade Agreement (NAFTA), and associations such as that between MERCOSUR and Chile. These normally also include an array of complementary deals in areas such as domestic content and clauses of origin. Conditionality represents yet another route towards policy harmonization. Multinational corporations (MNCs) favour policy harmonization as it helps them to reduce transaction costs.

POLICY COORDINATION

Policy coordination takes place when two or more countries decide to take a common stand in international fora. Examples are those of MERCOSUR and the Association of South-East Asian Nations (ASEAN) in their negotiations as blocs with the EU or ASEAN's common position in the World Trade Organization (WTO) on issues such as adoption of a multilateral agreement on investment (MAI) and labour clauses. The East Asian Economic Caucus (EAEC) is being enacted as a forum to discuss mutual problems and arrive at a common stand. Similar aims are pursued by groupings such as the G-15 and the Rio Group. Policy coordination is a more flexible and looser form of cooperation than policy harmonization since its scope, objectives and length may vary from case to case.

POLICY BENCHMARKING

Competitiveness policy benchmarking is a relatively new tool to monitor progress and to assess the situation against continuously improving best practice worldwide on an ongoing basis. Its effective use requires close consultation and joint work with the enterprise sector. It serves to assess not just how well or poorly firms, specific subsectors and entire sectors perform in a given country as compared with their counterparts in other countries, but also the factors that determine competitive performance. It goes beyond competitive analysis by providing an understanding of the processes, skills and capabilities that create superior performance. In doing so, policy benchmarking links up with the key medium- and long-term issues of concern to industrial development policy.

Economic performance results from the interplay between resources, institutions and policies catalysed by the action of economic agents. As globalization proceeds and capital and technology move ever more freely across borders, countries increasingly compete through policies ('policy competition') in order to take advantage of their natural and human resources, shaping their institutions, as best they can, continuously to raise their competitive performance standards. Roughly similar countries that do better provide the ideal yardstick for comparison.

Galvanized by the increasing globalization of the world economy, policy benchmarking presents a new frontier for multilateral cooperation. It offers a challenge to policy makers everywhere, especially in developing countries and economies in transition, to devise new and more practical and effective ways of mutual collaboration.

Although information flows across borders more freely than ever before, the variety and complexity of the information to be assessed also proliferates, leading to greater opacity rather than greater transparency. This is aptly illustrated by the growing web of often-overlapping international trade and investment agreements. Since 1947, 98 regional trade agreements have been notified to GATT under Article XXIV, with a further 11 under the 1979 Enabling Clause, which applies to developing countries and more than a third of them just during 1990-94. Likewise, by July 1996, there were 1160 bilateral investment agreements under way, two-thirds of which were signed since 1990 and 172 in 1995 alone.

Box 3.1 Best practices benchmarking in the Netherlands

In 1995 the Ministry of Economic Affairs of the Netherlands did an evaluation of the competitiveness of the Dutch economy. The dynamic international environment resulting from policy competition and ever shorter policy reaction times made it necessary to compare the Netherlands' position with that of other countries in terms of their performance, policy and institutions in a number of key areas. The method adopted was borrowed from industry's approach of looking at others in order to learn from them. In this case, the comparisons were with Belgium, Denmark, Germany, Japan and the United States.

The test was comprehensive, ranging from monetary and fiscal stability to research and training, and from physical infrastructure through the tax system to technological development. Strengths and weaknesses were identified and acted upon.

The social capability to combine cost efficiency with continual innovation was given special emphasis, on the grounds that it is the interplay between a dynamic, competitive market sector and strong government that creates the essential climate for competitiveness. The test adopted a private sector perspective by focusing on the conditions of the business environment.

The figure below describes the test methodology. Five infrastructural themes, two factor markets and the market for goods and services were distinguished. The impact of these on company costs, supply and the capacity to innovate and adjust was then assessed. The test did not factor in social infrastructure and elements of the welfare state.

The test results were summarized by means of high, average or low scores for each theme. In the main report, the findings are placed in perspective and discussed in detail, including, where possible, an assessment of the underlying institutions.

The general results pointed towards the need to create a modern economic structure, modernize education policy, strengthen the entrepreneurial climate, improve the functioning of the labour market and restore government finances.

Regarding *technological infrastructure,* the Netherlands scored high in public sector R&D and respective outputs, average in the extent to which public R&D and education met business needs, and low in

Test methodology

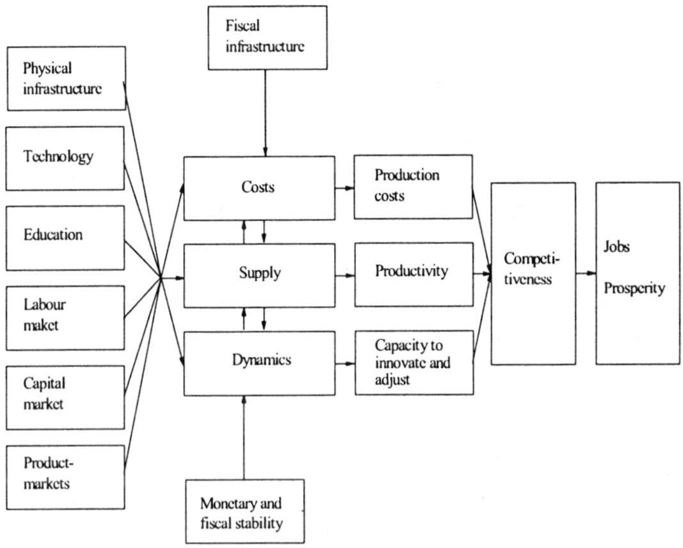

high-tech and private sector R&D performance. This points to the conclusion that incentives were needed to make the public research system address private sector requirements.

Some of the key findings in the field of *education and training* were that (i) value added by compulsory education scored high, (ii) training qualifications of higher secondary vocational and general education as well as university output scored average and (iii) the match between the qualifications of secondary and university graduates and the labour market needed improvement.

The results concerning environment revealed that the Netherlands held a leading position in sewage treatment and recycling while sulphur oxide emissions were being kept to a minimum. Nitrogen oxide emissions per capita, as well as waste generation, were found to be average. The main environmental weaknesses lay in excessive use of fertilizers, spread of pollutants and motor car emissions. The overall conclusion was that the environmental factor could stimulate innovation leading to comparative advantages.

Source: Netherlands Ministry of Foreign Affairs (1995).

Box 3.2 Productivity benchmarking in Malaysia

In its 1996 report the National Productivity Council warned that Malaysia's total factor productivity (TFP) growth had declined and would slide further if not checked. TFP is expected to account for some 30 per cent of overall economic growth for the next five to ten years. Malaysian workers, however, according to the report, displayed one of the lowest productivity levels when compared with the Republic of Korea, Taiwan Province, Hong Kong Special Administration Region and Singapore. Similarly, manufacturing productivity was lower than in Singapore, Taiwan Province and the Republic of Korea.

The findings suggest that Malaysia is losing out to its East Asian competitors, thus triggering a national debate on ways to address the problem. The Minister of International Trade and Industry, Datuk Seri Rafidah Aziz, admitted that Malaysia would have a tough time competing with its neighbours in the future. The government can provide the infrastructure, investment incentives, political stability and conducive investment climate. But the answer lies in the innovativeness, technological drive and competitiveness of Malaysian businessmen.

It was found that some two-thirds of manufacturing firms had barely reached low-level automation and an even greater share devoted little or no resources to R&D. Although often at the forefront of exports, Malaysian manufacturers appear reluctant to invest in cutting-edge technologies. According to Tan Sri Ramon Navaratman, an influential businessman, the key question is how to persuade them to phase out labour-intensive industries and move faster into more capital- and technology-intensive activities. Among the main bottlenecks are a low ratio of liberal arts to science students and the fact that R&D is perceived as highly risky, uncertain and costly.

Among other steps to address the problem, the Malaysian Government, through the Ministry of International Trade and Industry (MITI), is launching a *quality and productivity benchmarking service* under the National Productivity Corporation. The service will promote a continuous monitoring of productivity performance as a management tool to enhance and sustain competitiveness. MITI has also launched a *national productivity enhancement* campaign to counteract resistance to improving quality and investing resources in technology upgrading.

This resistance is seen as a serious problem in view of the coexistence of growing *external* competition and inadequate *internal* competition as well as a stumbling block in reaching the objectives of the Industrial Master Plan II. The National Productivity Corporation is advocating the adoption of policies with emphasis on TFP, increased added value content in manufacturing activities, improved capacity utilization and labour learning skills and higher R&D.

In addition, the Malaysian Government and Industry for High Technology, a government department under the Prime Minister's Office, has suggested a scheme whereby firms that do not spend enough on R&D be penalized. Firms exceeding a certain share capital would be required to contribute a small percentage of their earnings to a proposed R&D fund. Depending on how much R&D they perform, they would get their money back – eventually with a premium.

Benchmarking has been used as a management tool at the enterprise level for some time now. Yet policy benchmarking at the national level is still at the teething stage. European Governments have began to adopt it as a key tool only very recently. Likewise, the European Commission (EC) is also in the process of doing so in an effort to assist European manufacturing enterprises to match their United States and Japanese rivals in areas such as productivity and innovation. In this, the EC is relying on enthusiastic endorsement by the private sector as well as cooperation from Japan in the automobile and consumer electronics sectors. This cooperation is in the interest of Japanese enterprises with final assembly operations in EU countries to help upgrade the technical standards of their local suppliers as much as possible.

Originally developed as a management tool to assist individual enterprises to identify their weaknesses and strengths in relation to competitors and thus help them to identify ways of improving their relative performance, benchmarking was adopted by the Japanese, particularly through MITI, the Asian NICs, and somewhat reactively, the United States Department of Commerce, as a tool of national policy, followed later by the Europeans. Now the concept is gaining currency. The South-East Asian countries have become among the quickest to incorporate benchmarking, but the practice is spreading swiftly to a variety of institutions, including non-economic ones, in all regions and is being tentatively tested by a growing number of governments (for some examples see Boxes 3.1 to 3.4). To the extent that the latter's scope and objectives differ from – albeit they also embrace – those of enterprises, direct extrapolations from the enterprise management approach are not always appropriate.

To avoid the time lag of a decade or more usually involved in assimilating best practices in nearly all fields, developing countries and economies in transition can adopt – and profit from – this policy tool in order not to be too far behind most advanced industrial countries, particularly the Europeans. They can do so by moulding it according to their own needs and priorities rather than waiting until the benchmarking process fully matures and then having to acquire it on a turnkey basis. The idea is to use an approach of adopting by adapting, rather than trying to duplicate the experience of others.

Box 3.3 Competitiveness benchmarking in the EU

Europe's competitive position is under permanent review. Two aspects are considered critical: the impact and efficiency of the internal market and information technology and communications. Three dossiers have been produced recently on these matters: (i) a Commission document entitled *The Competitiveness of European Industry,* a working document of November 1996 that includes macroeconomic and sectoral comparisons of the main indicators of competitive strength revealing that European industry is in a less favourable position than that of the United States or Japan, (ii) the *Report on the Impact and Effectiveness of the Single Market*, an assessment of efforts to integrate the internal market which is meant to help strengthen the competitive position of European firms on world markets and (iii) *Benchmarking of the Performance of European Industry in the Area of Information and Communications Technologies* (ICT), which warns that, in terms of the competitive status of the sector, European policy is not taking sufficient account of the increasingly global nature of the ICT industry. The study, carried out by Booz-Allen and Hamilton, calls for 'dramatically accelerated' reform to help boost the position of Europe's US$350 billion ICT industry, which is seen as vital for creating future jobs and boosting economic growth.

It was found that, in general, European competitiveness in ICT lagged substantially behind that of the United States and Japan in all major subsectors except public telecommunications equipment. The fragmentation of ICT-related policies, standards and infrastructure was found to be a significant factor underlying Europe's fading competitiveness, expressed in a stagnating share of traditional mass market products and falling behind the United States in the critical growth areas of software and content. The United States was found to lead in software, consumer electronics, information technology hardware and private network equipment. One of Europe's major bottlenecks was shortage of skilled personnel, with European firms 50 per cent behind their United States rivals in value-added per employee. In emerging software markets that are key for multimedia services, Europe's competitive position was very weak, with 18 of the 20 top vendors coming from the United States. The European telecom sector was becoming increasingly competitive as liberalization proceeded, but varying stages of deregulation were causing a fragmented landscape. In the highly competitive semiconductor subsector, Europe has held a relatively stable position, but in information technology hardware and consumer electronics it experienced a small loss of market share.

As ways out of this predicament, it is recommended that a regulatory framework covering all ICT subsectors be established, along with an ICT-related R&D programme, a single European standardization agency for all subsectors concerned, and an initiative to boost skills. The cooperation scheme between government and industry implemented in the case of GSM mobile phone networks is recommended as a model.

Source: European Union, *The Competitiveness of European Industry*, November 1996.

Cooperation among countries in policy benchmarking consists of realizing the potential for learning from each other in policy making, as the industrial countries do through OECD. A UNIDO survey indicates a clear need in developing countries and economies in transition for this emerging form of cooperation (see Annex 3A).

Policy benchmarking needs to be undertaken in a methodical, systematic and organized way. While governments and decision makers in developing countries and economies in transition increasingly draw on international policy experience, they often do so either in an erratic, non-methodical way or by complete outsourcing, more often than not abroad, at above normal prices.

Box. 3.4 Skills benchmarking: the United Kingdom experience

The need to foster and improve vocational skills has been the driving force behind a unique benchmarking exercise undertaken recently in the United Kingdom*. Stemming from the Government's 1995 Competitiveness White Paper, *Forging Ahead*, the *Skills Audit* measured the United Kingdom's performance at the level of basic qualifications for employment against that of four competitor countries: France, Germany, Singapore and the United States.

The audit gauges the competitiveness of a country by the level and the rate of change of gross domestic product per head of population. Different types and levels of skills and qualifications were examined in terms of the following categories:

- basic skills (literacy and numeracy at a very low level)
- General Certificate of Secondary Education (GCSE) level two (the standard tested at the end of compulsory schooling)
- GCSE level three (intermediate skills)
- higher level qualifications (sub-degree, degree and postgraduate levels, including professional qualifications)
- core skills (numeracy, communication, information technology, learning ability and team working)
- lifetime learning (education and training after initial education, supplied either by employers or through individuals themselves).

The methodology for conducting the audit involved a review of existing research, new research on qualification levels and equivalences, sector benchmarking studies, a survey of MNCs operating in the countries of comparison and visits by researchers to these countries.

Overall, the audit revealed that the skill levels of young people were improving in all the countries studied, although the balance and speed of improvement varied. The United Kingdom continued to maintain a strong position in higher education, with its performance similar to that of France, Singapore and the United States. However, the German lead at this level was found to be striking. British performance at lower levels was improving but was not yet equal to that of the leaders.

At GCSE level three, the audit showed considerable improvement in France and the United Kingdom. As in the case of higher education, there was a very high and growing proportion of qualified Germans, including a significant number with vocational qualifications.

The United Kingdom's higher education system was found to be making a powerful contribution to national competitiveness through its range and diversity as well as its emphasis on quality and access. Since 1988, the proportion of young people enrolling for higher education doubled. At first degree or sub-degree level, 37 per cent of graduates followed science-related courses and more than 15 per cent received specific professional qualifications.

*Department of Trade and Industry/Department of Education and Employment (1996).

The need for a more rational, cost-effective and autonomous approach cannot be overstated. Because only sparse resources, if any, are usually allocated to benchmarking, it is frequently tackled by relying on information and advice from less than neutral third parties, rather than by drawing on applied analysis.

Indeed, a powerful economic rationale underlies such an approach. The important economies of scale and scope involved can hardly be reaped when the exercise is done at the individual country level. This is one of the reasons why the EC is launching its own work in this field – with Japanese cooperation.

As in so many other instances, outsourcing may appear natural to many developing countries and transition economies since other choices may not be available. Yet, when relying on specialized overseas suppliers, developing countries and economies in transition ought to be in a position to scrutinize rigorously the assumptions, methods and criteria used by the supplier. This is vital since the whole purpose of the exercise, as performed in the advanced industrial countries, is to foster the competitiveness of domestically located enterprises. The tool is designed to serve the specific needs of – and empower – business rather than to add glamour and clout to the work of government officials.

Benchmarking needs to be an ongoing exercise, simply because the shelf life of information on policies as well as of data on performance is usually rather short.

NORMATIVE VERSUS POSITIVE BENCHMARKING

Policy benchmarking can be approached either in a normative or in a positive manner. In the normative approach, the criterion for benchmarking may rest, for instance, on the assumption that markets do as good a job as can possibly be done at clearing themselves by matching supply and demand at the right prices. From this standpoint, the role of policy consists of removing whatever interferes with the working of the market, be it weak property rights or legislation which hinders resource mobility. For instance, if the aim is to determine how well an economy performs in the labour market, the standard to be used will be that of a country that comes the closest to conditions of entirely free entry and exit – that is, hire and fire – and to atomistic wage bargaining and that has the lowest possible wedge between labour costs and net wages. By defining best international practice in the labour market in this way, the closer a country comes to such a practice the better, in theory, it performs.

Policy benchmarking is intended to give governments an effective tool to foster enterprises' international competitiveness. Hence, highly valorative approaches are unlikely to help since they colour the exercise with views that, no matter how justified when it comes to setting goals, may be not that useful in understanding how outcomes are actually arrived at across countries.[2]

Positive benchmarking is about identifying which policies work best under specified conditions. The specificity clause is crucial. Without a thorough grasp of the conditions under which policies succeed, benchmarking exercises may lead to the wrong conclusions since similar policies cannot be expected to render similar results in different environments.

If, for instance, the South-East Asian industrializing countries are chosen as a standard, it is vital to account for such exogenous factors as the role of close economic relationships with Japan and China and reliance on Western countries' markets, along with domestic factors that influence the effectiveness of policy implementation.

Another important dimension concerns the complex interplay between macro- and microeconomic policies. When the ways in which gaps between these two are bridged are overlooked, a key link is missed in comparative exercises. One of the necessary conditions for a meaningful policy benchmarking exercise is a clear perception of how macro and micro policies relate to one another at national level. This is easier said than done: the relationship between the two is seldom addressed. Chapter 7 is devoted to this issue.

The positive approach is more likely to serve as a consensual tool than a normative one, since it rests on more widely shared criterion of what constitutes policy success, such as sustainable gains in welfare, growth, equity, jobs, earnings and quality of life.

One of the key objectives of positive policy benchmarking is to identify and remove bottlenecks on the supply side that make social and private returns to investment diverge either through underinvestment or through rent-seeking.

Using benchmarking as a policy tool is much harder than most other interventions. This can be illustrated by contrasting current with previous approaches to policy making. The skills and conditions required to formulate and implement policies designed to level the playing field in a competitive environment – insight, discernment, mastery of information and analytic method, consensus-building, focus, explicit and transparent standards of attainment and accountability – are more demanding and stringent than those involved in discretional allocation and redistribution of resources from the top, as was the case in the past.

It is much easier to appropriate the resources needed to subsidize a given activity or to concede to it a set of privileges and then simply await the results than to work proactively with enterprises in identifying their weaknesses and strengths in a competitive environment, devising an incentive system and playing an effective role as inducer, matchmaker, catalyser, enabler and sponsor. Furthermore, the latter approach often needs to be tailored to specific needs, as in the case of SMEs or specialized regional clusters. The task becomes even more daunting when it comes to capturing, let alone measuring, externalities and spinoffs. This should be added to objectives such as skill and capability creation and technological development as part of policy making, rather than merely relying on one-shot investment policy decisions.

BENCHMARKING IN DETAIL

To avoid a mass of inarticulate data of doubtful use for policy analysis, it is important to delineate carefully what is to be measured and how such results are to be used.

First, it is necessary to specify what the exercise comprises and what it does not. A way of doing this is suggested in Figure 3.1 and Table 3.1. Figure 3.1 provides an approximate idea of the overall analytical framework. Table 3.1 focuses on the core of the exercise itself.

Rather than assuming a hierarchical relationship between macro and micro policies, Figure 3.1 depicts one of interdependence, where both jointly contribute to define the incentive regime through such key relative prices as exchange and interest rates and level of effective protection. The incentive system thus arrived at, with the added influence of structural and superstructural factors such as political environment, rule of law, ownership and social structure, determine the functioning of factor and product markets and, through them, competitive performance. There is no one-way causality between many of these variables.

Table 3.1 depicts what is meant by functioning of markets. It does so by expanding the respective box in Figure 3.1. The table distinguishes between factor and product markets and provides broad performance appraisal criteria for them. Then the analysis is broken down according to level of aggregation – firms, subsectors, industry – and the relevant indicators of performance are specified.

Far from being a mechanical tool, unfortunately, there is considerable scope for uncertainty in this approach as a result of: (i) two-, or more-way causalities and interactions; (ii) difficulties inherent in factoring in institutional constraints; and (iii) varying time lags and response times.

In addition, there is no clear division between supply and demand of factors of production. Unlike in the past, when supply of scientific and technological knowledge, education, skills and public goods were supposed to come from government, firms are now increasingly being called on to contribute through their own knowledge-generating and skill-building activities. They are also becoming more involved in infrastructural supplies such as transportation, telecommunications and energy.

For these reasons, a rigorous distinction between inputs and outputs along sectoral lines becomes less relevant. The education system supplies skills inputs to industry, but has its own production function in generating skills from skills and other factors. Therefore its own proficiency needs to be benchmarked in terms of responsiveness, quality and relevance. The same applies to the science and technology infrastructure. On the other hand, although industry is a user of skills, it also produces them through formal training and on-the-job learning. Thus, it also has its own production function relating to skills.

So firms are increasingly involved in joint production of their core products and services, as well as of knowledge and skills. The latter's market value is directly correlated with their transfer potential. For this reason, the competence of a firm is not just relevant to the firm itself but also to its suppliers, customers and competitors, who may draw upon the information and skills it generates.

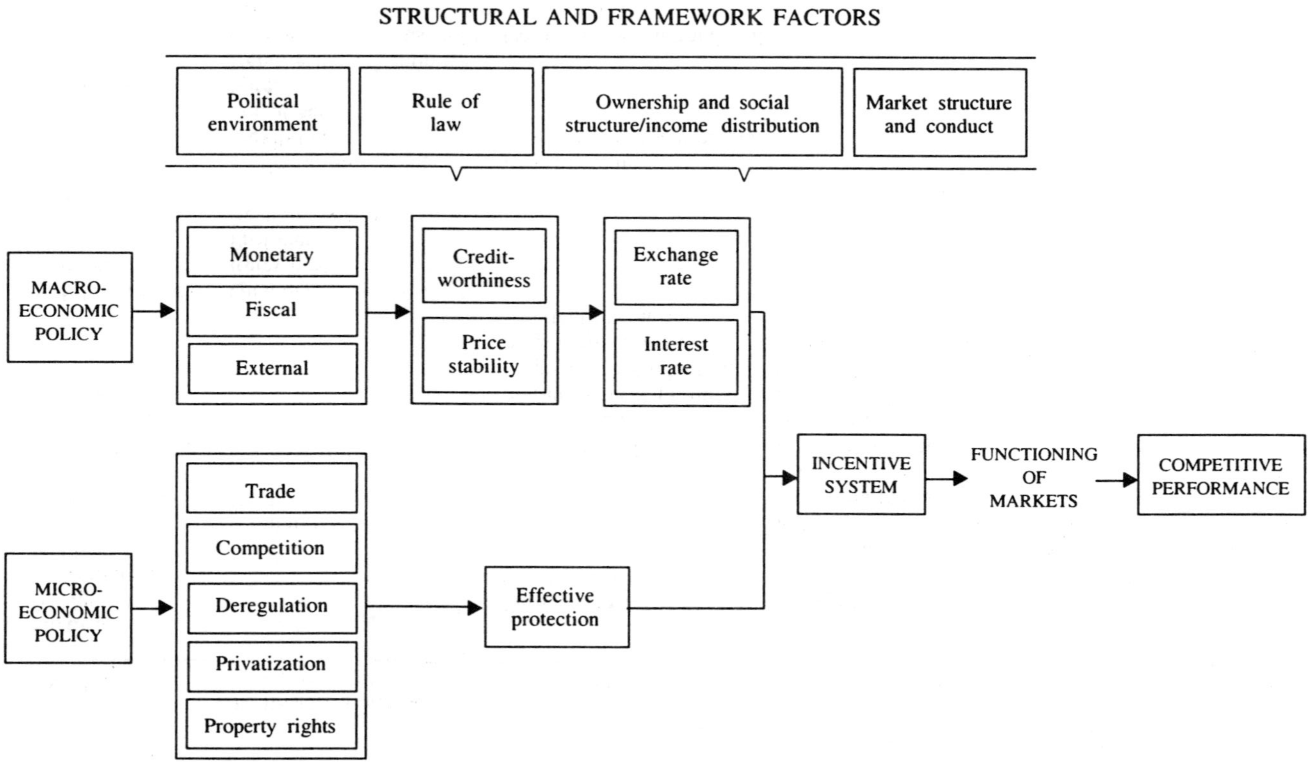

Figure 3.1 Benchmarking competitiveness policies

Table 3.1 Benchmarking manufacturing competitiveness policies

A. Markets	B. Broad performance appraisal criteria	Indicators of performance by level of aggregation		
		C. Firms	D. Subsectors	E. Industry-wide
I Factors				
i Natural resources		Formal and informal (on-the-job) training	As in C plus	As in D plus Total factor productivity
ii Physical and support infrastructure	Cost Availability Quality	Skill levels: cost and utilization	Relative unit labour costs Rate of growth of exports Export/output ratio Trade balance	Gross investment on MVA FDI in gross investment
iii Scientific and technological R&D		Innovative effort: • RDE/Sales • rate of new product/ process introduction • generic technology adoption rates	Revealed comparative advantage Ex-battery limits costs (infrastructure services, social security, taxes)	
iv Education and training	Quantity Relevance Proficiency Responsiveness			
v Skills				
vi Labour	Participation Flexibility Social security	Investment in – and vintage of – plant and equipment		
vii Capital	Spreads Venture capital supply Corporate and household savings	Domestic and international market shares		

		Profitability Retained profits Cash flow and indebtedness
II. Products		
Low, medium, high technology- and skill-intensive	Quality Variety Price Environmental friendliness and sustainability	

This highlights the importance of benchmarking exercises, particularly for SMIs as well as for manufacturing competitiveness strategy.

COMPETITIVENESS STRATEGY: INTERPLAY BETWEEN CAPACITY BUILDING AND LEVELLING THE PLAYING FIELD

SMIs can benefit most from benchmarking activities. They are usually unable to allocate resources to generating knowledge and skills, although they can greatly assist in raising overall productivity levels just by spreading best practices among themselves. Because of asymmetry of information and in access to resources, this is normally not favoured by the market. Benchmarking exercises assist in taking advantage of the benefits to be reaped by helping to unleash the immense potential inherent in the diffusion of information, knowledge and skills among SMIs. Advanced industrial countries and newly industrializing economies have been the first to develop and use techniques and institutions to tap this potential (see boxes in this chapter).

Benchmarking exercises are also intended for large enterprises and, among them, MNCs. Although the variety and quality of the available information do not always match their requirements in every respect, they can also draw important benefits. Their experience, in turn, can be drawn on by their specialized suppliers, whose awareness of best practices is thereby increased, such as in the case of Japanese automobile and electronics firms operating in Europe.

Bottom-up flows of initiatives and information, and decentralized execution as well as a sense of partnership between government and the private sector are key attributes of successful benchmarking exercises. These seek to increase competitiveness, flexibility and responsiveness of enterprises to changes in technology, relative prices and demand, thus fostering structural change.

These objectives involve permanent monitoring in order to level the playing field so that key requirements such as information, finance and institutional resources become accessible to all users. This involves enabling the weakest, yet potentially competitive, ones among them, such as SMIs, to draw on such resources. For this reason, policies aimed at factor and institutional development – including competence and capacity building, human resource development and technology diffusion – along with broader goals that concern overall development objectives are as important as those aiming to level the playing field. Structural change and competition need and feed each other.

Given the growing adherence by governments to rigorous standards of macroeconomic discipline, amounting to a narrower room for manoeuvre at this level, the above-mentioned strategy draws on better use of the greater scope for action available at more decentralized levels.

Skill building, for example, can be fostered without drawing on the national budget, through cooperation between the technical training institutions and enterprises along the line of the German dual system. Financial support to dynamic SMIs can be mobilized through institutional adaptations that enable them to become fully eligible for loans, for example by assessing the market value of their intangible assets. Examples of this kind can be multiplied with reference to technology diffusion. Their key commonality is that they do not involve resource transfers by taxing those who perform better. SMIs may, in some instances, require subsidies, which can be fully in line with current international codes and covenants in the trade and investment fields.

Despite their value as a means to allocate resources, markets are of little help when it comes to set goals for society. In times of rapid change, societies need to articulate a sense of direction. The most successful countries are those that are able to define a vision on which policies are predicated. As ever more developing countries and economies in transition come to this realization and, hence, endeavour to articulate or reformulate their own vision in an increasingly interdependent world economy, the need for reciprocal policy dialogue and learning in the policy field gains in priority.

NOTES

1. Lack of policy effectiveness may also be due to factors that are beyond the reach of policy makers and the skill and competence of policy practitioners, having less to do with intrinsic merits of policy itself than with lack of conditions that are necessary for policies to work, such as the ability to institutionalize and endogenize the policy-making process.
2. Market transparency is imperilled when there is imperfect and asymmetrical information, uncertainty and bounded rationality. But even under these conditions, some countries do better than others, for instance, in averting jobless growth and high unemployment, through the implementation of suitable offsetting policies. This involves a *positive*, as opposed to a *default* policy paradigm, which consists of defining manufacturing competitiveness and industrial development policies as a residual left over after other policies have been specified.

REFERENCES

Department of Trade and Industry/Department of Education and Employment (1996), *The Skills Audit* report from an interdepartmental group, London: Cabinet Office.
Netherlands Ministry of Foreign Affairs (1995), 'Benchmarking The Netherlands', Test of Dutch Competitiveness, The Hague, December.
UNIDO (1996), *Survey on Industrial Development Policy: Information Requirements, Priorities, Challenges and Constraints, Effectiveness and Private Responsiveness,* Vienna: UNIDO.

ANNEX 3A. RESULTS OF A UNIDO SURVEY ON INDUSTRIAL DEVELOPMENT POLICY[1]

Information Requirements, Priorities, Challenges and Constraints, Effectiveness and Private Responsiveness

During its fifty-first regular session, the United Nations General Assembly requested UNIDO to undertake an in-depth assessment and analysis of best practices in the field of industrial development policies and strategies as well as of their relevance for specific regions and countries. The aim was to provide practical insights and direction for developing countries and economies in transition.

The growing interdependence of the world economy underscores the need to benchmark domestic policies against international best practice on a continuous basis. This, in turn, requires access to information and analysis on policy trends and innovations worldwide, which is often not readily available. But little is known about precisely where, which kind of and by whom such information is needed.

To answer these questions, UNIDO undertook a survey during the second half of 1996 designed to help guide its research activities in the policy field.

Approach

Because the private sector shares increasingly in decisions on policy formulation throughout the world, the survey was addressed to leaders in this sector as well as to senior government officials involved in industrial development policy.

The key tool of the survey was a postal questionnaire comprising a combination of multiple-choice and open questions. The questionnaire was subdivided as follows:

- information requirements for industrial development and manufacturing competitiveness
- challenges and constraints to industrial development policy
- time-frame and policy assessment
- responsiveness of the private sector.

The overall rate of response was 29 per cent – nearly the same for both public and private sector - which is considered highly satisfactory for this type of survey. Sixty replies were received from 48 countries, with 32 of them, or 53 per cent, from public sector respondents and 28 of them, or 47 per cent, from private sector respondents (see Table 3A.1).

Table 3A.1 UNIDO's survey on industrial development policy: summary of results

	Number of questionnaires								
	Sent			Received			Response rate		
Region	PuS	PrS	T	PuS	PrS	T	PuS	PrS	T
Africa	28	21	49	7	5	12	0.25	0.24	0.24
Asia/Pacific	37	28	65	5	10	15	0.14	0.36	0.23
Latin America and the Caribbean	27	28	55	12	10	22	0.44	0.36	0.40
Eastern and Central Europe	22	19	41	8	3	11	0.36	0.16	0.29
Total	114	96	210	32	28	60	0.28	0.29	0.29

Note: PuS: Public sector responses
PrS: Private sector responses
T: Total responses

Source: UNIDO (IDPT/RPD/RES).

In terms of the response by country grouping (Table 3A.2), the greatest interest came from the public sector of newly opened economies and economies in transition as well as the private sector of less developed countries and of countries not included in these groupings (see Chapter 8).

Key Results

Based on the statistical responses received to the UNIDO questionnaire, the following summarizes the majority opinions on the main topics of the survey.

Need for sharing international industrial development policy experience

Prompt and timely access to information on and analysis of international industrial development policy experience is required on a routine basis in both the public and private sectors of developing countries and economies in transitions as vital inputs for their policy-making process.

Table 3A.2 Results of UNIDO's survey by country grouping

	Number of questionnaires								
	Sent			Received			Response rate		
Region	PuS	PrS	T	PuS	PrS	T	PuS	PrS	T
Newly opened economies	23	29	52	9	9	18	0.39	0.31	0.35
Less developed countries	30	25	55	7	10	17	0.23	0.40	0.31
Newly industrializing economies	6	5	11	2	–	2	2.00	0.33	0.18
Economies in transition	27	28	55	10	3	13	0.37	0.11	0.24
Rest	22	15	37	4	6	10	0.18	0.40	0.27
Total	108	102	210	32	28	60	0.28	0.29	0.29

Note: PuS: Public sector responses
PrS: Private sector responses
T: Total responses

Source: UNIDO (IDPT/RPD/RES).

Ways of meeting international information requirements

Most decision-makers involved in domestic industrial development policy processes still rely to only a minor extent on direct access to international data banks and assessments systems although the situation appears to be changing rapidly.

UNIDO's role as supplier of industrial development policy information and analysis

Most respondents concurred in attaching high priority to UNIDO setting up a data bank and information system on industrial development policy to serve Member States.

Generic versus beneficiary-centred industrial development policy

Respondents favoured generic and indirect policies akin to benchmarking, facilitation of access to information and decentralized support schemes in contrast to traditional beneficiary-focused industrial development policy.

Preferred channels of information and analysis

Public and private sector respondents assigned top priority to information and analysis about the interfaces between industrial development policy, on one hand, and investment incentives and competition policies in the product and factor markets, on the other.

The convergence between public and private views differed on information and analysis concerning specific areas of industrial development policy. Private sector respondents attached much higher priority to firm-centered rather than sector-specific policies whereas the opposite was the case for public sector respondents.

Although respondents tended to emphasize those areas where their own decisions mattered most, this was not always the case. In technology, public sector respondents ranked research, development and engineering near the top of the scale and technology extension services near the bottom, while private sector respondents did the opposite.

Key challenges and constraints

There was a significant degree of consensus between public and private sector respondents in their perception of supply-side factors. The case was different, however, when it came to demand-side factors.

The interaction of industrial development policy with macroeconomic policy stood out as the most important factor in the view of both private and public sector respondents, followed by that with policy on competition in factor markets and in the field of investment incentives (see Figure 3A.1.).

On the question of specific industrial development policy sub-areas, vocational training was seen as a key challenge by public sector respondents and as a key constraint by their private sector counterparts in terms of human resource development (HRD). In the area of SMIs both public and private sector respondents agreed that financing was the key constraint and entrepreneurship the key challenge. They also concurred in the area of technology, with technology extension and domestic research, development and engineering taking priority as both challenges and constraints. Regarding special promotional measures, the view was also shared that policies on quality and productivity posed the greatest challenge as well as representing key constraints.

Length of policy cycle

In the view of most respondents, the length of an industrial development policy cycle, during which the basic tenets of a particular policy were valid, tended to be either relatively short (up to three years) or relatively long (more than four years).

Assessing policy results

Nearly half the respondents considered that industrial development policy in their countries succeeded in meeting their goals to a considerable extent. Public sector respondents had a more positive view on this than those in the private sector.

Factors affecting policy effectiveness

Respondents' views were at variance concerning the factors accounting for industrial development policy effectiveness (Table 3A.3). Public sector respondents viewed exogenous factors such as external shocks, political instability and the like as the strongest influence on industrial development policy effectiveness whereas private sector respondents believed that the strongest influences were intrinsic to industrial

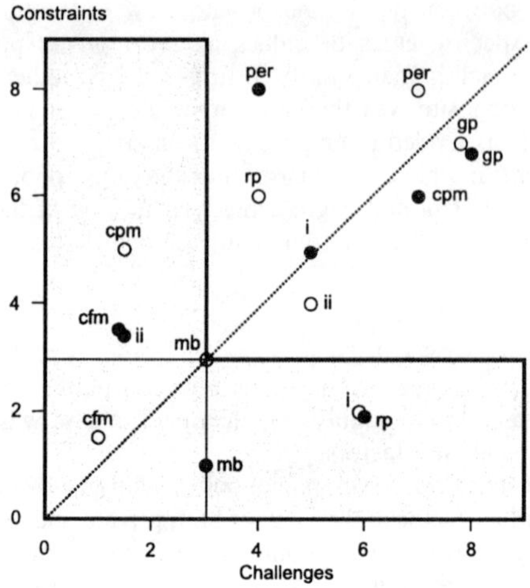

Key:
○ government sector
• private sector

cfm:	competition in factor markets	ii:	investment incentives
cpm:	competition in product markets	rp:	relative prices
mb:	macroeconomic balances	per:	privatization and enterprise restructuring
i:	infrastructure	gp:	government procurement

Constraints and challenges		Constraints		Challenges	
Public sector	Private sector	Public sector	Private sector	Public Sector	Private Sector
mb cfp	mb	cpm	cfm ii	i	rp

Figure 3A.1 Interfaces between industrial development and other policies

development policy-making. Key among these were lack of focus in policy priorities, weak capacity and vague time frames for implementation and imprecise specification of the intended impact of policies.

Private sector responsiveness

For private sector respondents, the overriding consideration in industrial development policy was the degree of participation in the policy-making process whereas, in the view of public sector respondents, the key influence on industrial development policy was exposure to competition.

Table 3A.3 Factors affecting the effectiveness of industrial development policy (average scores)

Factors	Public sector	Private sector	Total (weighted average)
Exogenous (external shocks, political instability, etc.)	3.6	3.92	3.75
Not enough consistency between different policy regimes	2.43	4.04	3.18
Other factors, making it necessary to:	2.93		
improve definition of objectives	3.50	4.19	3.82
focus priorities better	3.67	4.58	4.09
simplify implementation and monitoring	3.63	4.23	3.91
specify more precisely performance standards to be met by beneficiaries	3.30	4.12	3.67
increase transparency of costs and benefits	3.40	4.04	3.70
keep scope of intended impact:	2.34	4.46	2.29
– narrower	2.54	0.46	1.63
– wider	2.14	8.46	5.26
strengthen implementation capacity	3.60	4.46	4.02
implementation time frames:	2.80	4.60	3.14
– shorten	3.26	4.70	4.25
– lengthen	2.34	4.50	3.57

Source: UNIDO (IDPT/RPD/RES).

Conclusions

The findings of the UNIDO survey provide a focus for developing countries and economies in transition to gain access to valuable international experience as well as to develop the necessary research and technical co-operation agenda required for that purpose. Although private sector decision-makers have traditionally been considered passive partners in policy-making, their participation in the survey, along with their counterparts in the public sector, reflects the increasing role they are taking in determining industrial development policy.

The survey results demonstrate the acute awareness and growing need for access to international industrial development policy experience as an essential input for domestic policy-making in the developing countries and economies in transition. UNIDO is expected to play a role in serving this need.

The survey also identifies common concerns, as well as differences, in the views of decision-makers in the public and the private sectors. The needs expressed by such views tend to be highly complementary in the context of domestic policy-making processes in general.

NOTE

1. Further information on the Survey can be obtained for UNIDO.

PART II

THEMES

Overview of Part II

The main thrust of Part II is to place industrial development policy issues in the context of broader economic relationships. It does this by addressing three key generic themes: competitiveness, financial factors and micro/macroeconomic interactions.

Chapter 4 provides a detailed account of policies bearing upon manufacturing competitiveness at all levels, that is macroeconomic, subsector and firm-specific. These policies are discussed from the perspective of newly industrializing economies, newly opened economies, countries with economies in transition and less developed countries. This chapter provides a conceptual framework and some criteria for the measurement of competitiveness.

Chapter 5 addresses the differential impact of financial costs on the international competitiveness of manufacturing firms in selected developing and transition economies. One of the key findings of this chapter is that, because of weak domestic financial systems, there is a built-in bias by firms based in these countries in favour of borrowing abroad, irrespective of domestic savings rates. Nevertheless, most developing and transition economies are still deprived of access to international debt markets, particularly bond markets. The chapter also highlights the disruptive impact of a heavy concentration of banks from developing and transition economies on financing manufacturing enterprises through short-term financing.

Chapter 6 contains a comparative assessment of East Asia and Latin America from the perspective of the macro/micro policy dichotomy. It is argued there, among other things, that both regions have been at odds in the evolution of their respective macro- and microeconomic policies over the 1990s, with important implications in terms of effectiveness and sustainability. This discussion acquires particular interest in terms of vulnerability to the abrupt and vast swings in short-term capital movements that affected East Asia in 1996/97 and South America in 1998/99. For Indonesia, Malaysia, Republic of Korea, Thailand and the Philippines, the swing was, between 1996 and 1997, equivalent to 11 per cent of their combined pre-crisis dollar GDP, leading to a deep and protracted contraction of economic activity.

4. Manufacturing Competitiveness: Concept, Measurement and Policies

INTRODUCTION

This chapter discusses the concept and measurement of and the policies for manufacturing competitiveness. Although national competitiveness is not the main focus, it is a necessary point of departure in view of the controversies surrounding this notion and its policy implications.[1]

The idea of national competitiveness has attracted significant attention in the 1990s, as academics and policy makers debate if countries – as opposed to firms – are competitors in the international market or fundamentally complement each other; whether by purchasing goods and services they are at a comparative disadvantage; and if trading partners can raise their standards of living simultaneously or only at the expense of each other. In short, is international trade a zero or positive sum game? Generally, national competitiveness enthusiasts have tended to propose aggressive and often 'beggar thy neighbour' or protectionist trade policies which, if fully carried out, might eventually lead to the breakdown of the international trading system or at least arrest the trend towards a more open trading regime.

It is unquestionable that the involvement of countries in global markets affects their standards of living and that the quest of domestic firms for an expanded share of global trade generally brings economic benefits. However, it does not follow that a neo-mercantilist approach to trade makes economic sense or that countries should engage in protectionism to offset an inability to address domestic problems hampering their trade performance.[2] On the contrary, domestic economic problems should be addressed head-on through economic reforms. The success of such reforms is what will ultimately provide the basis for long-term productivity growth and a rise in living standards. Competitive advantage, it could be argued, ultimately results from an effective combination of national policies and company strategy.[3]

In this context, the broad definition of national competitiveness in the United States Competitiveness Policy Council's first report – 'the ability to produce goods and services that meet the test of international markets while our citizens earn a standard of living that is both rising and sustainable over the long run' – exemplifies a nation's primary economic objective as providing a rising standard of living for all its citizens while firms should aim at meeting the test of international markets.[4] Moreover, the report's emphasis on the role of domestic factors in ultimately determining the rate of productivity growth, such as investment in plant and equipment, education and training, knowledge and infrastructure, together with the overall economic incentive regime and business environment, as well as their overriding importance in determining manufacturing competitiveness, is fundamentally sound.

This highlights the fact that, in order to enhance manufacturing competitiveness, it is necessary to improve on the domestic factors that drive it. Many of these factors can be affected – for better or for worse – by policy. The proposition that competitiveness is domestically driven, with domestic policy and the business environment having more than a marginal role, is also applicable when competitiveness is examined from the perspective of a particular subsector or the manufacturing firm.

It could be argued that the fundamental difference between a manufacturing firm, a particular subsector and the manufacturing sector is one of levels of aggregation, with a subsector being just a set of firms producing a similar product and the industrial sector the aggregate of all subsectors. However, from a policy perspective, the focus on improving the competitive standing of a firm, a subsector or the industrial sector as a whole calls for different, though broadly complementary approaches.

To find the appropriate policies for manufacturing competitiveness, this chapter examines what constitutes a competitive firm, subsector or manufacturing sector. After establishing a concept of competitiveness, a set of accepted indicators or measures of competitiveness is identified. Although there is a multiplicity of such measures, as there are numerous alternative concepts of manufacturing competitiveness, the aim is to present those which are most useful for policy makers and practitioners from developing countries and economies in transition. Finally, this chapter discusses appropriate policy approaches, focus and priorities in view of the need for firms, subsectors and industrial sectors to improve their competitive position in domestic and international markets.

Finally, a taxonomy of policies for manufacturing competitiveness is suggested, grouping them according to which level they are targeted at and operated on, as well as to which country group they are most applicable:

- Firm-centred policies, including quality and productivity programmes, R&D incentives, promotion of training and skill acquisition, investment incentives and small-scale and micro-enterprise support.
- Subsector-specific policies, including trade and commercial policies, restructuring, targeted capacity creation, cluster support with a regional focus and networking efforts.
- Industry-wide policies focused on the reduction of country cost from macroeconomic mismanagement, poor social and physical infrastructure, including weak stewardship of the natural environment and adverse regulatory and business environment.

CONCEPT AND MEASUREMENT OF COMPETITIVENESS

What is manufacturing competitiveness? Many studies have argued that the manufacturing firm is the correct unit of analysis for competitiveness and its improvement.[5] Often these studies are guided by a presumption that in so far as the firm is the productive cell of a modern economy, the competitive standing of that economy is predicated ultimately on the competitive health of the individual firm. Thus, this section initially approaches the concept of manufacturing competitiveness from the perspective of the firm.[6]

A competitive firm is one that:

- stands at the best practice frontier, in terms of production and management, being cost-efficient, quality-oriented, dependable, flexible and innovative;
- has accumulated significant human and physical capital endowments, as well as intangibles, with demonstrated productive and technological capabilities;
- has a superior economic and financial performance.

A competitive subsector may be understood as one in which its representative firm is competitive, in the sense that firms, on average, produce a competitive output, as measured by the ability of the subsector competitively to supply domestic and international markets. A manufacturing sector must pass the same test if it is competitive. If it does, this constitutes *prima facie* evidence that the country's macroeconomic prices and systemic costs are in balance and that country is endowed with sufficient human, material and institutional resources to be competitive.

Once there is an acceptable basis for conceptualizing a competitive firm, a subsector and an industry, how can competitiveness be measured?[7] The measurement at firm level may be made on the basis of the following criteria:

1. At the best-practice frontier, the competitive firm must match the industry benchmark in terms of:
   - productivity levels (both in physical and value terms);
   - adoption of international total quality and environmental standards and norms, such as ISO 9000 and 14000;
   - rate of new product introduction in the market as generated by research, development and design activities and measured by the proportion of sales or employees devoted to R&D.
2. Accumulation of human, physical and intangible capital endowments by the firm is demonstrated by:
   - educational level of the labour force;
   - commitment to training, as measured by expenditures on training and proportion of employees engaged in training;
   - rate of investment in plant and equipment;
   - vintage of capital equipment;
   - extent of automation and diffusion of advanced manufacturing methods, such as flexible manufacturing systems (FMSs), robots, computer numerically controlled (CNC) machines.
3. The firm's competitive performance is made explicit in terms of:
   - domestic and international market share position;
   - profitability;
   - cash flow position and level of indebtedness.

Two measures of subsectoral competitiveness are implied here. First, an indicator of aggregate subsector efficiency, namely the relative unit labour costs (RULCs) are defined as the ratio of domestic to foreign labour costs adjusted for productivity differentials in the subsector. It reflects the relative movement of nominal wages, including social security charges; of the exchange rate against the currency of the country with the competitive subsector, or against a basket of currencies in case foreign subsectors are being aggregated; and levels of productivity. An improvement in the RULCs could be the outcome of a fall in nominal wages, a devaluation of the domestic currency or an improvement in productivity. As an index, or pure number, the RULC measure is most useful when charting longer-term trends in competitiveness of the subsector relative to that of other countries.

The second indicator of subsectoral competitiveness is performance-related and centred on trade measures. These include the rate of growth of subsectoral exports, export–output ratio, subsectoral trade balance, market share of the subsector in world exports and revealed comparative advantage indices for the subsector. When used to depict international competitiveness, these measures are a clear indication of where the subsector stands relative to the world industry.

Manufacturing competitiveness is expressed by the growth in TFP in comparison with other industrializing and developed countries. Other efficiency-related indicators at this level of aggregation focus on systemic costs:

- the sector's RULCs, which reflect the wage rate, including social security and related costs, and the real and effective exchange rate;
- real interest rates and other financing costs;
- tax rates and tax burden relative to GDP;
- infrastructure tariffs adjusted for quality and elasticity of supply;
- supply of natural resources and their absorption capability;
- level of pollution.

Manufacturing competitiveness is also a function of the accumulation of systemic capabilities, including:

- supply and quality of basic, secondary, professional and university education, as indicated by the degree of literacy in the population as a whole, dissemination of basic cognitive skills in the labour force and proportion of secondary school and university students in the relevant age cohort;
- proficiency and coverage of industrial training and skill-acquisition systems;
- supply elasticity and capillarity of technological and other industry support services provided by joint public–private undertakings, such as technological and productivity centres, as well as by private consulting firms;
- availability of technological endowments, as indicated by the ratio of

S&T expenditures and foreign technology purchases to GDP and degree of involvement of the private sector in R&D activities as measured by the proportion of private sector commitments – including contract research – in total R&D expenditures;
- vintage of the capital stock, as indicated by investment–GDP ratios;
- ratio of FDI in manufacturing to GDP and to the country's share of manufacturing FDI flows.

Finally, manufacturing competitiveness may be inferred from performance indicators. In this case, the same trade-related indicators used at the subsector level may be replicated at the level of the sector, namely: the rate of growth of sectoral exports, the export–output ratios, sectoral trade balance and an index of revealed comparative advantage. Market share indicators are less appropriate at this level of aggregation.

POLICY APPROACH, FOCUS AND PRIORITIES

A number of policy initiatives may be taken to improve the competitive position of manufacturing firms, subsectors or the industrial sector.[8] Their relative effectiveness varies depending on how well they are designed, implemented and coordinated with other policies and programmes; what human, physical and institutional resources they can deploy to attain predefined goals; and the incentive structure that ultimately affects the response of economic agents.

Table 4.1 lists key policies for manufacturing competitiveness according to their focus: firm-centred, subsector-specific or industry-wide. The level of priority for policy implementation varies depending on whether the country is a successful industrialized economy, turning towards outward-oriented strategies, among the least developed, or an economy in transition. The table presents stylized priorities, in the sense that there are significant variations among countries within a particular group. Nonetheless, it is arguable that, overall, there are enough commonalities within each group to warrant a common policy approach, a common focus and common priorities. Relative priorities have been established on the presumption that no major alterations take place in some key variables, such as relative prices. Significant macroeconomic shocks may alter the level of priorities and relative emphases of policies.

Table 4.1 *Policies for manufacturing competitiveness: a taxonomy and country group application*

Policies	Country groups A	B	C	D
A Firm-centred policies				
1. Quality and productivity programmes	+	++	+	++
2. Training and skill acquisition	+	++	++	+
3. Investment incentives	—	+	+	—
4. R&D incentives	++	+	—	—
5. Small-scale and micro-enterprise support	+	+	++	++
B Subsector-specific policies				
1. Trade and commercial policies	+	++	+	++
2. Subsector restructuring	+	++	+	++
3. Targeted capacity creation	++	+	—	—
4. Cluster support (with regional focus)	—	+	++	+
5. Government–private sector networking	++	++	++	++
C Industry-wide policies – reduction of country costs				
1. Macroeconomic and public finance costs	+	++	+	+
Exchange rate	++	++	++	++
Real interest rates	++	++	+	++
Tax rates	—	++	+	++
2. Physical infrastructure	—	++	++	+
Transportation	+	++	++	+
Telecommunications	—	+	++	+
Energy	—	+	++	+
Environment	+	+	+	++
3. Social infrastructure	—	++	++	+
Education and training	—	+	++	+
Health	—	++	++	++
4. Regulatory and business environment	+	+	++	++
Judicial system	+	+	++	++
FDI regulations	—	—	+	++
Competition policies	+	+	—	++

Notes: Country Groups
A: Newly industrializing economies
B: Newly opened economies (NOEs)
C: Less developed countries (LDCs)
D: Transition economies (TEs)

++ high priority
\+ moderate priority
— low priority

Firm-Centred Policies

Three sets of policies focus on the firm level. First, there are those that encourage producers towards the best-practice frontier, in particular, by:

- stimulating dissemination and adoption of total quality and productivity programmes; and by
- supporting research, development, design and engineering efforts through fiscal incentives, credit inducements and support infrastructure.

Although many countries practise both, recent evidence suggests that programmes for enhancing quality and productivity at firm level are particularly effective for economies turning towards outward-oriented strategies and for transition economies, where a protectionist strategy of industrialization has left a legacy of large, differentiated manufacturing bases combined with high levels of inefficiency, as in Brazil and India. From this perspective, effective management matters more than process technology, although the latter is still important. For resource-scarce economies, particularly, the application of continuous improvement, minimum waste of energy, materials and time, zero defects and other aspects of total quality can help make the competitive requirements of successful firms compatible with the resource restrictions of industrializing economies.

In those circumstances, efficiency gains can be significant and attained in a relatively short period if firms, under competitive pressure, adopt superior strategies in managing production, stimulated by quality and productivity programmes. The use of extension services and financial inducements can accelerate diffusion.[9]

The impact of R&D support on a manufacturing firm's competitive position is most acute for newly industrializing economies. This is not to say that countries turning towards outward-oriented strategies should refrain from enticing firms to engage in R&D, and to improve the design of their products and the engineering of their processes. On the contrary, productivity gains induced by quality and productivity programmes eventually peter out, and firms need to compete on the basis of product differentiation and innovation as well as cost and quality. In these circumstances, incentives that stimulate producers either to undertake R&D in-house or contract it out to university and other research centres are increasingly necessary.

The second set of firm-centred policies for manufacturing competitiveness concerns the build-up of capabilities by stimulating the accumulation of human and physical capital through:

- training and acquisition of industrial skills; and
- accelerated rate of capital accumulation and dissemination of automation equipment and techniques.

In the case of newly opened economies and for economies in transition, which have to use existing resources more efficiently, retraining and acquisition of skills should be a priority. In-firm training and skills acquisition is preferable and, therefore, justifies tax and other incentives that stimulate firms to invest in those activities. It is arguable that even among less developed countries that have a marked scarcity of individuals with basic skills, training incentives should be directed to firms. For those countries, however, it may be necessary to introduce extension services staffed by training agents able to assess the training needs of individual firms and propose programmes to meet their needs. As in the case of Brazil's Serviço Nacional de Aprendizgem Industrial (SENAI), experience suggests that those agents should be specialized in the requirements of individual subsectors.

For countries turning towards the international markets and for economies in transition, a critical bottleneck is the inability of firms to keep up with the required pace of capital accumulation and modernization of an ageing capital stock. In this regard, traditional instruments such as accelerated depreciation and long-term investment loans, and newer mechanisms such as venture capital funds help increase the supply of credit and equity for investment.

Policies that push firms towards the best-practice frontier and enhance their capabilities – by stimulating producers to increase productivity, reduce waste, improve product quality while accumulating the necessary resources to sustain their competitive position – contribute over the longer term to their financial and market performance. In addition, competitiveness can be improved by supporting SMIs' specific or different needs.

The third set of policies aimed at enhancing individual firms' manufacturing competitiveness centres on SMI and micro-enterprise development. Although the rationale for SMI support is often viewed in terms of employment, SMIs in less developed countries and economies in transition are possibly the most effective vehicles to facilitate firm entry and enhance market dynamism. This is so because in these economies markets are still thin and agents not well versed in the rules of the market. Moreover, these economies are often characterized by the presence of large state-owned enterprises (SOEs), which, effectively, deter entry of larger firms, unless through privatization.

SMI support is generally critical in two areas: finance, particularly in view of the difficulties that small-scale and micro-firms have in offering guarantees and the reluctance of financial institutions to supply credit otherwise; and managerial skills, from simple accounting to marketing expertise. The high costs of extension services and similar types of assistance that serve individual firms suggest that support services should be physically concentrated in a few high-visibility locations and that firms be able to access these services by phone, fax or Internet. The main role of such centres would be to provide information and answer direct inquiries regarding domestic and international market opportunities, problem-solving technologies, legislation and the like. SMIs are generally far more dependent on external sources of information, training and business support than larger, better-endowed firms, often not knowing where to find this information. The situation underlines the importance of a service-oriented, demand-driven institutional base attuned to the needs and requirements of SMIs.

Subsector-specific Policies

For many years, fostering capacity creation in specific subsectors was the central industrial development policy for countries attempting merely to substitute for imports or promote exports. Capacity creation was a successful long-term strategy in a few countries, but in most it proved uneconomic and unsustainable in increasingly open and competitive environments. Progressively horizontal, non-discriminatory policies – either centred on firms or applicable to manufacturing as a whole – gained favour over those with a subsector focus. They required less detailed information, while risk that policy makers would pursue the build-up of irrelevant projects was more limited. The probability of policy failure was in this sense smaller.

However, the practice of policy implementation has shown that many policies need, perforce, to be either targeted at or configured to specific subsectors. This applies to trade and commercial policies beyond an initial movement of trade liberalization and reform when universal rules are established, as well as to industrial restructuring and cluster support policies. Infant-industry arguments still hold for subsectors characterized by significant market failures, either from external economies or large technological economies of scale. They call for targeted support for capacity creation. In many countries, government–private sector networks are generally structured around subsector issues, demands and organizations. Subsector-specific policies are a natural response by governments in their partnership with businesses and other institutions to address issues of competitiveness.[10]

Trade and commercial policies

Trade liberalization, if properly managed, improves the competitive standing of industry and brings significant welfare gains to the population. The removal of NTBs, and the progressive reduction in the level and dispersion of tariffs, has now become a standard and fairly robust recipe for introducing the forces of import competition and reducing the anti-export bias of closed trade regimes.

As countries liberalize their trade regimes and adhere to WTO rules and conflict resolution mechanisms, it is essential that market-supporting instruments be in place to deter predatory dumping, offset unallowed subsidies and, whenever necessary, offer temporary relief as industry undertakes necessary restructuring steps. Trade liberalization is not, generally, a process that targets individual subsectors, though its effects vary according to subsector. However, commercial policies such as the imposition of anti-dumping or countervailing duties or other barriers to provide temporary support are more often than not applied to specific subsectors.

Of all country groups, the positive impact of trade reform is greatest among newly opened economies and economies in transition. These countries pursued import substitution policies with extreme vigour which, in many cases, led to gross resource misallocation and significant waste. The introduction of effective instruments to support trade liberalization, including procedures and institutions capable of dealing with unfair competition, is most critical among countries that have limited experience in dealing with the international trading system as a result of across-the-board import substitution policies.

Subsector restructuring

Import competition and requirements of the international market often constitute the most powerful inducements for restructuring and competitive enhancement of a subsector. In most economies in transition and newly opened economies, subsectors are under intense competitive stress, increased by adjustment programmes that reduce budgetary transfers to inefficient firms and subsectors and open the economy to the forces of competition. Effective response hinges on effective restructuring measures. Restructuring consists of a set of discrete, decisive measures to restore a firm's or a subsector's competitiveness. Efficiency-enhancing decisions face considerable hurdles. They can be classified into three categories: those that weaken discipline; those that hinder mobility; and those that limit the availability of resources.[11] Creating a regime conducive to efficient restructuring decisions requires government actions to overcome those hurdles, with the objective of:

- strengthening discipline, by establishing a competitive environment, tightening budget constraints and, for public enterprises, privatizing them or ensuring that the government exercises the state's ownership rights;
- enhancing labour mobility, by lifting restrictive labour regulations, introducing adequate unemployment compensation and supporting development of job placement and retraining agencies. Capital mobility, however, requires removal of legal and regulatory restrictions on asset transfers as well as provision of efficient bankruptcy procedures;
- augmenting resources, in particular, managerial skills, market and technology information flows and finance. Tapping foreign expertise, establishing management training programmes and promoting turnaround entities are basic measures to develop managerial skills. Restructuring can be facilitated through mechanisms that acquire and spread relevant subsector-specific information, possibly with the help of producers' associations and other groups that provide an interface with the private sector (see below). Increasing the availability of finance might require relaxing interest rate controls, restructuring financial institutions experiencing distress and creating an environment for efficient debtor–creditor transactions within which the asset and liability composition of debtor enterprises can be effectively restructured.

Government actions, therefore, need to be geared to the removal of policy distortions, for example, by eliminating fiscal and financial subsidies to tighten budget constraints, introducing rules to offset perceived market failures such as ownership reform and instituting an administrative and legal capacity to enforce such rules through, for instance, competition policy and employment agencies. Temporary subsector support or relief would be an acceptable policy if exchanged for a credible and explicit commitment by dominant firms to undertake significant restructuring measures, such as streamlining, cost cutting, hiving off intermediate activities and focusing on core business, so as to increase productivity and profits within a specific time-frame.

Targeted capacity creation

Historically, creation of new manufacturing capacity has been the key industrial development policy objective in most economies pursuing industrialization. Nowadays, most countries face the daunting job of improving the competitive standing of existing subsectors, being hard pressed to allocate scarce resources to entirely new ones. There may be scope for targeting new capacity in high-technology subsectors in newly industrializing economies with significant scientific and technological endowments and, to a lesser extent, in newly opened economies. Indeed, there is considerable effort among a few of those countries towards moving into new fields such as aerospace and biotechnology, but caution is needed since it is too early to know if they will succeed. In other country groups, this may not constitute a priority. Success often involves a fairly activist posture by governments, with all the risks that this entails. Many of these new subsectors are driven by university research; others are driven by government or public enterprises' orders. In most cases, significant S&T resources have to be mobilized, and returns are only visible in the long run. The instances of success have been characterized by a coordinated effort to achieve specific goals, responding to concrete needs, and meeting the market test sooner rather than later.

Cluster support

Firms belonging to the same industry often tend to cluster to take advantage of economies of agglomeration, including the presence of a dense network of suppliers and industrial service providers. A prime example of such clusters is found in northern Italy, with SMIs in subsectors such as shoes, furniture, certain types of garments and textiles, and specialized machinery concentrated in certain regions. Similar clusters exist in countries such as Denmark, Spain and Germany, as well as in the industrializing countries of Asia and Latin America.

The fact that firms in certain subsectors tend to be regionally concentrated to internalize particular externalities and improve their competitive standing suggests that regional and subsectoral clustering and specialization can be promoted as a means to improve manufacturing competitiveness. It also indicates that support can be extended to such clusters on a more effective basis than if firms were dispersed, particularly where markets are thinner, as in less developed countries. Insofar as such industrial clusters are made up of SMI producers, cluster support can be an effective instrument of SMI policy. The success of such policies depends on the presence of local professional and academic institutions capable of mobilizing producers and serving as their effective advocates, while directly or through third parties, disseminating information, providing training, technology and common facilities, and a bridge to the outside world.

Government–private sector networking

During the three decades following the end of the Second World War, governments in many developing countries functioned as a Schumpeterian engine of growth, assuming risks on the assumption that the private sector would not, creating capacity where none existed, guaranteeing the profitability of activities for which investment was required and micro-managing market forces for fear that, were the hand of the state not visible, market performance would be poor. In reaction to this brand of state activism, an opposite view of the role of government gained ground, starting in the mid-1970s, which assigned the state a passive and subsidiary role in economic development and the attainment of international competitiveness. This approach encapsulated the notion of a minimal state.

In practice, governments have been repositioning themselves as sponsors, catalysts and promoters of effective interaction with the private sector. The fundamental idea is that market failures and imperfections call for a non-passive role for government, but government bureaucratic and regulatory failures call for a limit on activism. In order to attain international competitiveness, governments in all country groups must ensure the flow of information, including relevant data for private decision making and, equally important, that good ideas and outstanding examples of competitive entrepreneurial and corporate practice become well known.[12]

Governments must also mobilize the private sector and other relevant groups to focus on specific, if long-term, goals. Together with the private sector, universities and other institutions, they must design a vision of the future for the manufacturing industry and specific subsectors for the next 10 to 15 years and find the means to accomplish it. Agencies and authorities should function as promoters willing to work with the private sector and others as appropriate. Redefining policy as vision and the basic implementation mechanisms as shared public–private efforts would, in essence, be the making of a new approach to industrial development policy.[13]

The United Kingdom illustrates this approach, where the Government found that working with business on a subsectoral basis was ‘a particularly effective way of addressing competitiveness' (UK Government, 1994, para. 4.2). In this context, Government agencies exchange information with subsectoral institutions with the aim of understanding the strengths and weaknesses of each subsector and assessing their overall competitive position. In partnership with the private sector, government provides support for firms to penetrate world markets, and acts to minimize unnecessary regulatory burdens while ensuring that enforcement is business-friendly and meets the needs of consumers, and ensures that policy and other decisions at all levels take into account their impact on business (ibid., para. 4.3).

Government sponsorship is not acting as an uncritical mouthpiece for a particular subsector, picking winners or subsidizing uncompetitive segments. Rather, it is working with the private sector to open communications channels, establish an effective partnership aimed at spreading best practice, benchmarking, assisting development of subsector export strategies, promoting SMIs in the context of supply chain development and, ultimately, attempting to address key determinants of competitiveness in partnership and cooperation with industry.

Industry-wide Policies: Reduction of Country Costs and Enhancement of the Business Environment

A central notion advanced here concerning policies target the competitiveness of the manufacturing sector as a whole is that the most effective means for improving competitiveness and living standards is to reduce country costs, broadly meaning the costs of mobilizing resources and doing business in the country.[14] Four sets of factors are considered: macroeconomic and public finance costs, costs related to provision of infrastructural services and the environment, costs related to social infrastructure and costs associated with the regulatory and business environment.

Macroeconomic and public finance costs

A stable macroeconomic environment is increasingly perceived as a *sine qua non* for manufacturing competitiveness in two distinct senses. Stability is a requirement for investment, in the sense that the less stable the environment and the higher the perception of risk, the less willing investors are to commit resources to update capital stock, modernize existing facilities and engage in extensive technological upgrading. By definition, the more volatile the environment, the less attractive investment projects become for a given level of return. Thus, after discounting for higher risk, more projects fail to reach an average risk–return threshold acceptable to investors.

Keeping macroeconomic prices – exchange rate, interest rates and tax rates – aligned is critical to stability. Large public sector finance requirements typical of governments that cannot or are unwilling to control expenditures – more commonly observed in newly opened economies and economies in transition – put an upward pressure on interest rates, damaging the productive sector. Moreover, high real interest rates end up attracting short-term capital and pushing the exchange rate upwards towards an overvaluation of domestic currency, further dampening growth and thereby investment, even though the cost of imported capital goods may become more attractive. In addition, a government's inability to control its accounts brings about either the monetization of the deficit, and hence, further inflation or more taxation, or a combination of the two. Both are highly damaging to the competitive standing of countries. A combination of relatively open borders to trade and an overvalued exchange rate brings about a large imbalance between the prices of traded and non-traded goods and services, further pushing up nominal and real wages as well as the costs of other services. The net result of these basic macroeconomic imbalances is, therefore, a high-cost, uncompetitive economy (see Chapters 5 and 6).

One important determinant of manufacturing competitiveness is the savings rate, both as a direct constraint on the rate of targeted accumulation and as an indirect restriction on investment projects, as a result of the interest rate. Countries with low savings rates tend, fundamentally, to finance investments at the cost of inflation taxes and external borrowing. Neither of these are sustainable. An increase in the rate of savings – and the development of financial and capital markets – is essential for economic as well as for modernization of the productive and institutional apparatus and, ultimately, for competitiveness.

Physical infrastructure

Manufacturing competitiveness presupposes an elastic supply of quality infrastructure services. The three critical elements of infrastructure are transportation, telecommunications and energy.

The importance of transportation to manufacturing competitiveness is self-evident. Nonetheless, it is worth stressing that while freight costs, including port charges, are dominant in bulk commodities, time and reliability become the preponderant factors for higher-value-added goods. Moreover, increasingly efficient manufacturing – not only assembly operations – presupposes rapid and timely delivery of inputs. Thus a flexible and efficient transportation network is essential, as is the need continuously to identify and overcome bottlenecks in the system. Like corporations, countries need to define and implement a logistical strategy consistent with the competitive requirements of the manufacturing sector. Although all country groups would profit from improvements in transportation networks, the largest transportation deficits can be found among newly opened economies and less developed countries, as well as the continental economies of China and the former Soviet Union. In newly opened economies, improvements can be achieved at a fairly rapid pace through establishment of a supportive regulatory framework for privatization and commercialization of existing transportation assets. This provides an environment where private capital flows into renewing and expanding the existing network. The same approach might fail among LDCs due to a combination of low economic density and a gross undersupply of infrastructure. Greenfield investment, therefore, will need to be financed and undertaken by the public sector, with the accompanying financing limitations most governments face for this type of investment, even though facility operations may be private. In many cases, only multi-country and multi-institutional support will enable highly attractive projects to be implemented, as is the case with the Southern Africa transportation initiative.

Telecommunications is undergoing what may be characterized as a revolution, as what was once thought of as a natural monopoly is now regarded as a competitive industry even at local level. Technological change – in the form of less expensive and far more powerful and flexible exchanges, new and highly efficient transmission media and less costly in-premise equipment – has been at the heart of this process. The combination of accelerated technical change and growing competition has allowed for a substantial fall in prices as well as the introduction of new telecommunications services.

The impact of these changes is unpredictable. It is clear, however, that countries with dense and efficient telecommunications networks will enable manufacturing to take advantage of globalization and regionalization trends in decisions on location. Moreover, insofar as clients increasingly demand rapid responses to inquiries and orders, electronic proximity to the client base becomes critical to competitiveness. The Internet already seems to be the most important of all networks to which firms need to be connected.

Despite the apparent ease of linking up to the Internet, the ability, speed and quality of access to the network depends, in large measure, on the availability and quality of the local phone lines and data transmission capabilities. In this sense, less developed countries remain farther behind and should assign high priority to a telecommunications policy that fosters modernization of existing plant and greenfield investments through the privatization of existing assets and the removal of regulatory barriers to private investment in all segments of the industry. This policy approach is applicable to all country groups, though the countries that would benefit most are those that are farthest behind in telecommunications infrastructure. They could take advantage of the technological breakthroughs of the last decade to leapfrog and intensify competition among service providers, enabling them to enter the market of countries with advanced telecoms services.

Availability, price, quality and reliability of supply of energy remains a major element of infrastructure-related country costs. Despite the fact that many new technologies are energy-saving and that complementary manufacturing services that are not energy-intensive play an increasingly dominant economic role, manufacturing production is still basically dependent on electricity and other sources of energy.

The organization of the electricity industry has changed significantly in the last few years. Technological change in generation has opened the possibility of competitive supply and a number of countries have, as a result, introduced major reforms in the industry with the aim of introducing competition and greater efficiency in generation, distribution and supply. As in telecommunications, regulatory reform to support private sector participation in the industry should be at the core of efforts to improve the supply of electricity. Although the impact of reform has proven to be most tangible in countries with relatively large systems, reform is particularly important in less developed countries, which often face continuous energy shortfalls that deter new investment and inhibit competitiveness of existing manufacturers.

A dimension of infrastructural considerations of concern to manufacturing competitiveness is the environment, in two distinct but related senses: first, in terms of the more traditional notion of regulatory and compliance costs associated with keeping up with environmental standards, which tend to be positive and growing in most countries; second, in terms of absorption capacity of the environment for the by-products of manufacturing activities, in the form of solid, liquid and gaseous wastes. The exhaustion of the latter is an indication of poor environmental stewardship as well as possible adverse living conditions for workers and managers in respect of pollution levels.

Strict regulatory and compliance costs are necessary in relation to zoning and other restrictions, enforcement of pollution standards and fines on violators, and the introduction of quantitative restrictions to deter environmental degradation. The cost of inaction is now clear to most countries in the form of marked environmental degradation, large clean-up costs and, in the extreme, transformation of large areas into barren wasteland. Moreover, higher environmental standards pose little impediment to competitiveness in environmentally sensitive goods. This suggests that compliance pays off and is not a hindrance to strong trade performance.[15]

In most countries improvements in the environment can be achieved by combining quantitative restrictions with market-based instruments, at a cost compatible with the competitive requirements of manufacturing. Pricing pollution and making polluters pay for the cost of pollution allows polluters to reallocate production, shift product lines and improve manufacturing methods to take into account a new set of relative prices. Forcing producers to face the cost of pollution by paying for it may achieve the same objectives as strict quantitative limits on pollution levels but at a lower cost to firms. The definition of property rights and exchange mechanisms for pollution has further allowed the emergence of markets for pollution permits in newly industrializing economies, which allocate rights optimally among plants and within an overall pollution envelope.

There is another set of market-based incentives which, at least for some countries, is even more effective in stopping environmental degradation. It is unquestionable that the consumption of energy and material inputs has been stimulated by subsidized prices, most particularly among economies in transition, leading to inefficiency, waste and significant environmental damage. The economic pricing of all inputs, in itself, already brings about a positive and very significant impact on environmental quality. As relative prices change, firms are compelled to produce more efficiently using methods to economize on scarce inputs reinforcing competitive standards. By improving their environmental record and practices, firms adhere to ISO 14000 and similar universal standards of environmental management. In the next few years, non-certification will effectively impede access to international markets.[16]

Social infrastructure

Education is now perceived as the primary or basic endowment for the competitive transformation of the economy. The higher the level of education of a country's labour force and, therefore, the larger the pool of educated workers available to the manufacturing sector, the better positioned will the pool of educated workers be able to generate skill-intensive, better remunerated activities. The educational requirements of a competitive economy focus on language and mathematics to understand, interpret, and solve problems, make decisions on the basis of new information and communicate. As firms move into the more demanding production methods, increasingly required for manufacturing competitiveness and involving most of the workforce –

total quality control (TQC) or total quality management (TQM) and the Japanese concept of *kaizen* (based on the principles of continuous improvements and introduction of minor innovations) – education demands expand significantly.

In addition to education, the health conditions of the population, in general, and the labour force, in particular, are important for the competitive standing of the manufacturing sector. This is often not fully appreciated. It is critical not only to the productivity of labour directly and the level of labour costs, but also to the attraction of new investment, insofar as living conditions are among the important variables in plant/firm location decision and subsequent reinvestment.

Although all country groups would profit from a more educated and healthier labour force, the less developed countries is the group in which lack of basic education and health impose the greatest costs to long-term development and the competitive standing of the sector. The shortcomings of basic education and health are also felt in some economies in transition, as in the former Soviet Union, where the health standards have deteriorated dramatically in the last decade, and in countries turning towards outward-oriented strategies.

Regulatory and business environment

An important element of country cost is the regulatory and business environment within which firms operate. The judicial system and rules and institutions that affect FDI and competition policy regulations shape the environment for manufacturing competitiveness.

Firms need to operate within a set of rules and institutions that frame and set the limits on the economic behaviour. These rules need to be stable, predictable and transparent to minimize regulatory risk and provide economic agents with the necessary horizon for productive activities. The less regulated an economic activity – manufacturing industry is a case in point – the more important is the rule of law and the presence of a strong judicial system. At the core of judicial enforcement is the establishment, recognition and respect of property rights. Closely connected is the enforcement of contracts. In the absence of either, markets do not emerge. In economies in transition, the resulting mobility barriers – from the lack of bankruptcy legislation, incipient contract laws, poorly developed labour, land and housing markets, an inability to pledge collateral to borrow money and other capital market imperfections – are extensive and not easily removable, as they relate ultimately to the creation of market institutions.

In all countries, the forces of competition, as well as the pressure exercised by informed and empowered consumers, are decisive in firms' efforts to improve their competitive standing. In many economies, government policies, by shielding firms from competition in domestic and international markets and softening their budget constraints through fiscal and financial subsidies, allowed them to survive on non-competitive bases. At the same time, the absence of effective competition policies and enforcement institutions to prevent anti-competitive conduct, the preservation of competitive market structures, the advocacy of competition within the deliberations of government and the education of the public were deterrents to competition.

In the absence of an effective competition agency, countries should introduce a precursor authority, draft appropriate legislation, and progressively accumulate the required technical capabilities for law enforcement. The latter should bring an initial emphasis on advocacy and education, clear cases of cartelization and vertical restraints by dominant firms.[17]

The absence of effective competition policy laws and institutions is felt most in economies in transition. This is partly because a legacy of socialism and of activist industrializing states is the presence of dominant or monopolistic enterprises in particular subsectors. In those subsectors where multiple enterprises were permitted, they were encouraged to cooperate rather than to compete. And it is partly because, in many of these countries, competition is less favoured culturally than the presence of a large state, characterized by extensive patronage and non-transparent and often promiscuous relations with the business community.

For a number of years, many countries had specific restrictions on FDI, on the assumption that such investment deterred the emergence of a class of national entrepreneurs, technologies used by foreign firms were in some sense inappropriate to the country's factor endowments, profit remittances were a significant drain on the country's foreign exchange, or foreign tastes and influence would corrupt local values and ultimately challenge national sovereignty.

In the last 15 years or so, this view has changed drastically.[18] A combination of intense competition among firms and nations, an accelerated rate of technical change and the simultaneous processes of globalization and regionalization have made MNCs possibly the most important force for redesigning the industrial landscape of the developing world. Particularly for economies in transition, but also for less developed countries, inward FDI came to be regarded as the centrepiece of any strategy that attempted to jump-start the industrial sector into world markets.[19]

Not only were entry restrictions lifted, but countries, and regions within countries, began competing for new investment flows with the help of fiscal incentives and, occasionally, financial support, in addition to providing guarantees against the political risk of expropriation and unfair compensation. Evidence suggests that the role of incentives, in particular, seemed quite limited.[20] Ultimately, the ability of countries to attract investment rests on a combination of market dynamism, availability of resources and an elastic supply of infrastructure services.

Along with the increasing openness of policy regimes, countries have engaged in active promotion programmes with the objective of differentiating themselves from alternative locations. The rationale for such programmes is strongest for the smaller economies among the less developed countries and economies in transition with a limited tradition of attracting FDI. The main investment promotion activities include: improving a country's image within the investment community through advertising, seminars and investment missions; attracting investment directly[21]; and providing services to prospective and current investors, including counselling, hosting prospective investors and accelerating various stages of approval processes.

Countries are generally interested not only in attracting FDI, encouraging sequential investment and retaining existing investment, but also in transferring technology. The transfer and dissemination of knowledge depends, in large measure, on the presence of a national innovation system, in the sense of policies and institutions that reward risk-taking and innovation, coupled with sufficient human resources educated to absorb technology.

NOTES

1. See the annual reports issued by the United States Competitiveness Policy Council; see United Kingdom Government (1995) and the Commission of the European Communities (1993).
2. See, for example, Krugman (1996), in particular ch. 6 and references therein. For a brief discussion on why competitiveness became a focal issue, see Ostry (1991).
3. See, for example, Dertouzos et al. (1989).
4. United States Competitiveness Policy Council (1994). This echoes Porter (1990) who noted that 'the principal goal of a nation is to provide a high and rising standard of living for its citizens. The ability to do so depends on the productivity with which a nation's labor and capital are employed.'
5. As noted by Porter (1990) 'firms, not nations compete in the international markets'. See also Hayes and Wheelwright (1984), and Hayes et al. (1988).
6. The validity of this perspective is attested to by the following statements extracted from the United Kingdom Department of Trade and Industry's 1995 report on competitiveness, *Forging Ahead*: 'In a market economy, the primary responsibility for improving competi-

tiveness must lie with firms ... by adopting best practice in all activities, benchmarking against the best in the world and striving to surpass the standard' (United Kingdom Government, 1995, para 1.21).

7. See the list of indicators of competitiveness in Coutinho and Ferraz (1994).
8. The scope for policy intervention is related to the extent to which market imperfections limit the scope for firms to improve competitively and, of course, the government's own limitations and failures. As noted in the United Kingdom's Governments (1995) report on competitiveness, 'the government creates the climate within which business can improve its performance by: providing a stable macroeconomic environment ['the most important contribution that the government can make to improving competitiveness'] based on low inflation, sound public finances and competitive tax rates, which is essential to give business confidence to invest; maintaining and developing open and competitive world markets and fighting to bring down barriers to trade; removing unnecessary burdens on business through deregulation, aimed particularly at small and medium-sized enterprises (SMEs); making markets work better through liberalization, sharpening incentives by the reform of personal and business taxation and extending markets through privatization; helping business help itself through better informed decision-making and the spread of best-practice; ensuring a favourable environment for inward investment; and improving value for money and standards in services, such as education, which are best provided by the public sector' (ibid., para. 1.22).
9. Examples of such extension centres are Canada's Industrial Liaison System, Taiwan Province's Productivity Centres and the Netherlands Innovation Centres, which provide high-quality advice, generally to SMIs, with technical personnel deployed to flag technological, engineering, marketing and organizational problems, propose specific solutions and monitor implementation as well as facilitate clients' contacts with universities and technical institutions.
10. Some of the policies described as firm-centred or industry-wide, such as training and skill acquisition or environmental stewardship, not only have a clear subsectoral dimension but are sometimes implemented with a strong focus on specific subsectors.
11. See Atiyas et al. (1992).
12. One important aspect of this information flow is country-wide competitive assessments. The United Kingdom Government, for example, published in 1994 an audit of the United Kingdom's competitive position, which identified the ten main factors influencing competitiveness, with special emphasis on education and training. This White Paper was widely welcomed by business. See United Kingdom Government (1994). See also Chapter 3.
13. See Frischtak (1994).
14. See, for example, Gonenc and Gassman (1984) and United Nations Economic Commission for Europe (1995), esp. pp. 3–7. The latter notes that industrial competitiveness refers 'to the quality of the business environment of a country and the factors which promote a propitious climate for the development of industry ... such as labour costs and conditions, corporate governance, the qualification of the workforce and investment in training, the state of the physical infrastructure – transport and telecommunications, the quality of public administration ... as well as competition policies, intellectual property protection' (p.7). For a discussion of the factors required to create an enabling environment, see also Marton (1995).
15. See Sorsa (1994).
16. For a fuller discussion of environmental policies see Kumar (1995). The report examines the impact of different environmental policies on industrial competitiveness and argues that 'in the medium to long term, the competitive position of efficient firms in export markets will most likely improve due to improved quality and environmental standards' (p. 3). The adverse impact of such standards is more likely to occur in small firms and natural-resource-intensive industries, though it is possible to mitigate those effects, particu-

larly for smaller units, if timely and appropriate measures are taken to access foreign regulations and standards and to adopt clean technologies and waste minimization at source (p.15). These conclusions reinforce the importance of countries engaging in an effective dissemination strategy for ISO 14000 standards, with a special emphasis on SMIs.

17. See Frischtak and Pittman (1996). See also Frischtak (1995), chs 2, 3 and 4.
18. As noted by UNCTAD (1995), 'the trend towards liberalization of national laws and policies regarding FDI (which began in the early 1980s) has continued and deepened during the early and mid-1990s. Of 102 new legislative measures adopted in 57 countries during 1993, 101 were in the direction of either liberalization of the promotion of FDI; during 1994, 108 out of 110 new norms adopted in 49 countries moved in the same direction' (p. 272).
19. If economic incentives are right, FDI often improves manufacturing export performance. The provision of export finance, insurance and information for direct and indirect exporters is particularly important for countries shifting towards outward-oriented strategies, which is already effectively done by newly industrializing economies. Yet, in the case of transition economies and the least developed countries, the weakness of domestic industrial exporters can only be effectively overcome by facilitating FDI directly into manufacturing and by facilitating the establishment of international trading companies, particularly in the case of agro-industrial exports.
20. Though competition among countries to attract FDI with the help of incentives is strong and pervasive, UNCTAD (1995), notes that 'relative to other factors, incentives are only a minor part in the locational decisions of TNCs [transnational corporations]. Factors such as market size and growth, production costs, skill levels, political and economic stability and the regulatory framework remain the most significant' (pp. 228–29). The same conclusion – that incentives do not seem to have much impact on the decisions of investors – is reached by Bergsman and Pirnia (1996). Still, the authors note that 'fiscal incentives tend to be effective: i. for foot-loose, export-oriented investments; ii. in countries or regions that are similar to neighboring countries or regions; iii. in places where the other aspects of the business climate are also favorable, and iv. where the incentives occur sooner in the project life and with more certainty' (p.272).
21. Investment-generating activities are most effective 'where a firm is already considering making an investment in a particular region of the world to produce for regional or global export markets … [it] requires extensive research [combined with investment promotion missions] to determine which firms are likely candidates not only to invest in the country but also what kind of investment they would bring ... [and] relies heavily on personal selling and direct contact with the prospective buyer. As a consequence, successful investment promoters need to have distinctive skills in marketing and in understanding the needs of diverse business operations' (Bergsman and Pirnia, 1996, pp. 276–7).

REFERENCES

Atiyas, I., M. Dutz and C. Frischtak (1992), 'Fundamental issues and policy approaches in industrial restructuring', Industry Series Papers 56, The World Bank, April.

Bergsman, J. and N. Pirnia (1996), 'Do Incentives Work?', *FDI News*, 1 (2), FIAS, March.

Commission of the European Communities (CEC), (1993), *White Paper on Growth, Competitiveness, and Employment – The Challenges and Ways forward into the 21st Century,* Brussels, December.

Coutinho, L. and J.C. Ferraz (1994), *Estudo da Competitividade da Industria Brasileira,* Papirus–UNICAMP, São Paulo, Annex I.

Dertouzos, M., R. Lester and R. Solow (1989), *Made in America – Regaining the Productive Edge*, Cambridge, MA: MIT Press.

Frischtak, C. (1994), 'O que é politica industrial', *Economia, Politica e Sociedade,* ILDEFES, March.

Frischtak, C. (ed.) (1995), *Regulatory Policies and Reform: A Comparative Perspective,* Washington, DC: World Bank, chs 2, 3 and 4.

Frischtak, C., and R. Pittman (1996), 'Relevance and implementation experiences of competition policies', in V. Thomas and S. Meyanathan (eds.), *The Practice of Regulatory Policy and Regulatory Reform in Reforming Economies,* Washington, DC: Economic Development Institute, World Bank..

Gonenc, R. and H. Gassman (1984) 'A new approach to industrial policy', *OECD Observer,* **187,** April–May.

Hayes, R. and S. Wheelwright (1984), *Restoring our competitive edge, competing through manufacturing*, New York: Wiley.

Hayes, R., S. Wheelwright and K. Clark (1988), *Dynamic Manufacturing – Creating the Learning Organization*, New York: Free Press.

Krugman, P. (1996), *Pop Internationalism,* Cambridge, MA: MIT Press.

Kumar, R. (1995), 'Environmental policies and industrial competitiveness', report prepared for UNIDO, Vienna, July.

Marton, K. (1995) 'Recent industrial policies in developing countries and economies in transition: trends and impact', background paper for Global Forum on Industry – Perspectives for 2000 and Beyond, UNIDO, 29 September.

Ostry, S. (1991), 'Lessons from the Triad', in I. Haque (ed.), *International Competitiveness – Interaction of the Public and Private Sectors,* EDI Seminar Series, Washington, DC: World Bank.

Porter, M.E. (1990), *The Competitive Advantage of Nations,* New York: Free Press.

Sorsa, P. (1994), 'Competitiveness and environmental standards: some explanatory results', Policy Research Working Paper 1249, World Bank, February.

United Kingdom Government (1994), *White Paper: Competitiveness: Helping Business to Win,* CM2563, London: HMSO.

United Kingdom Government (1995), *White Paper: Competitiveness – Forging Ahead,* London: HMSO, May.

UNCTAD (1995), World Investment report, Geneva.

United Nations Economic Commission for Europe (1995), *Industrial Restructuring in Selected Countries in Transition,* New York and Geneva: United Nations.

United States Competitiveness Policy Council (1994), *Promoting Long-term Prosperity*, Washington, DC: United States Government Printing Office.

5. Effect of Financial Factors on Manufacturing Competitiveness

INTRODUCTION

Costs of capital and their influence on firms' international competitive position have been a neglected subject of empirical analysis. This is surprising since the relative importance of these costs differs significantly among countries and costs of capital, therefore, have a differential impact on international competitiveness. For example, in some advanced industrial countries, costs of capital represent some 2 per cent of total sales of non-financial enterprises.[1] In economies in transition, however, costs of capital have, in general, a much higher relative importance. In Bulgaria, for example, their share in total sales of 530 large firms was 19 per cent in 1994, which was even higher than the share of labour costs. In Hungary and the Czech Republic the ratio of costs of capital to labour was much closer to the patterns in advanced industrial countries, but TEs' average ratio is at least twice as high as in advanced industrial countries.[2]

This chapter addresses the differential impact of financial costs on the international competitiveness of industrial firms in selected developing countries and economies in transition by: (i) identifying sources of financing for industrial firms; (ii) analysing conditions under which funds are raised from domestic sources, especially from banks; and (iii) assessing the availability of foreign debt-creating sources and respective conditions. The focus is on an analysis of costs at which developing country- and transition-economy-based firms raise debt financing, either at home or abroad.[3]

STRUCTURE OF CORPORATE FINANCING: A SURVEY OF SELECTED EMPIRICAL STUDIES

Firms have three main sources of capital: retentions on internally generated funds, bank loans, and financing raised on the capital market such as corporate debt or equity. The resulting mix of debt and equity determines a firm's capital structure. The literature in this area contains a relatively small number of empirical studies, and research is by and large confined to advanced industrial countries.

The most comprehensive empirical contribution on corporate finance in developing countries has been made by two International Finance Corporation (IFC) studies. The first one (Singh, 1992) examines corporate accounting and stock market information data for nine developing countries – India, Jordan, Republic of Korea, Malaysia, Mexico, Pakistan, Thailand, Turkey and Zimbabwe – in the 1980s. The sample consisted of the top 50 manufacturing companies quoted on the stock exchange in each country. Table 5.1 presents the summary findings of the study.

Table 5.1 Composition of financing of non-financial enterprises in selected developing countries (1980–88, as percentage of total investment)

Country	Internal	External		
		Total	Equity	Debt
India	34.9	65.1	14.0	51.1
Jordan	11.6	88.4	46.6	41.8
Malaysia	66.8	33.2	14.9	18.3
Mexico	26.3	73.7	69.4	4.3
Pakistan	42.0	58.0	20.4	37.6
Republic of Korea	21.0	79.0	44.3	34.6
Thailand	24.1	75.9	40.9	35.0
Turkey	17.5	82.6	60.9	21.7
Zimbabwe	42.9	57.1	35.2	21.9

Source: EBRD (1995) p. 97.

The second IFC study (Singh, 1995) extends the first one by substantially increasing the size of the corporate sample – 100 listed manufacturing companies in each country – and by including an additional country – Brazil. The chief conclusion of the study is that the enlargement of the corporate sample does not impair the two central findings of the 1992 study that developing countries' firms rely heavily on external funds and, especially, on equity financing through new issues of shares.[4]

The strong bias shown by the two IFC studies towards outside equity financing relates to the fact that their samples include only top stock-exchange-listed manufacturing firms from a small number of relatively well-developed emerging economies. The relative importance of debt *vis-à-vis* equity financing would be much higher if the sample were enlarged to include SMIs from the sample countries and enterprises from other developing countries, especially less developed ones.

By comparing the results of the IFC's studies on developing countries' corporate financing with stylized facts concerning corporate financing patterns in advanced industrial countries, one major difference can be identified.[5] Corporations from developing countries used both external finance and, particularly, outside equity finance, to a much greater extent than the corporate sector in advanced industrial countries (Singh, 1995, pp. 1–2).

There are no comprehensive empirical studies on corporate financing in economies in transition. Fragmented data (EBRD, 1995, ch. 6) lead to the tentative conclusion that, in contrast to developing countries, firms from economies in transition rely much more on self-financing. This pattern largely reflects the withdrawal of government from direct or indirect finance to firms in a context where the domestic financial sector is still in an early stage of development.

A survey of more than 800 fast-growing private enterprises in five countries – Czech Republic, Hungary, Poland, Slovakia and Slovenia – concludes that: (i) internal sources are by far the most important source of investment and working capital financing for all five countries, their share being between 49 and 80 per cent of total financial needs and (ii) bank loans are the only important source of external financing for investment and working capital purposes of the sample companies' financial needs, providing 13 to 38 per cent of their finances.[6]

With further financial sector development, external financing may be expected to become a more important source of corporate sector financing in economies in transition. With securities markets still in their early stages of development, bank lending will, for some time, continue to be the most important external source of corporate financing. Although the capacity of banks to direct savings into enterprise investment has increased over the last few years, it is still well below the need of economies in transition.

These studies lead to two main conclusions in regard to developing countries and economies in transition: first, external sources account for the bulk of corporate financing in developing countries while in economies in transition firms still rely more heavily on internally generated funds. With drastic reforms of financial sectors under way, it is fairly safe to project that in economies in transition external sources will also gain a much more prominent role.

Second, bank financing is a dominant source of external corporate financing in economies in transition, where capital markets either do not exist or are in very early stages of development. Bank lending also plays a more significant role than outside equity and debt issuance in corporate investment in a large majority of developing countries. The exceptions are a limited number of bigger firms in relatively few more advanced developing countries. These firms rely heavily on new issues of shares to finance their growth.

DEBT FINANCING FROM DOMESTIC SOURCES

In advanced industrial countries, corporate borrowers have in principle two main channels for domestic debt financing: borrowing from banks and raising financial resources on the primary market for corporate debt securities. In most developing countries and economies in transition, corporate debt markets do not exist at all, while in a relatively small number of emerging economies, such as Argentina, Brazil, Chile, India, Indonesia, Turkey and Venezuela, these markets have been established, but the volume of transactions is still very limited. This makes the banking sector by far the most important intermediator of financial resources between savers and investors. The role of the banking system is not just to mobilize funds and allocate them across sectors and individual firms, but it needs to perform this role efficiently. This is especially important for developing countries and economies in transition in which equity markets and markets for corporate debt financing are underdeveloped and do not provide alternative financial instruments.[7]

Interest Rates and Spreads

Table 5.2 shows that real lending rates (nominal rates adjusted for inflation) vary significantly among the countries in the sample. In 14 of 19 developing countries and economies in transition, real lending rates were higher in 1995 than was the unweighted average for interest rates in Japan and the United States. Lending rates also differ among developing countries and economies in transition. While firms from Argentina and Slovenia were raising funds from their domestic banks at real interest rates of 14 and 11 per cent respectively in 1995, their competitors from countries as diverse as Egypt, Malaysia, the Czech Republic and Hungary had access to domestic bank resources at a real rate of 3.5 per cent or less. Obviously the former were at a disadvantage.

Table 5.2 Real interest rates and real spread (%)

	Real lending rates		Real deposit rates		Real spreads	
Country	1992	1995	1992	1995	1992	1995
United States	3.2	5.8	0.6	3.0	2.6	2.8
Japan	4.4	3.5	1.7	0.8	2.7	2.7
Argentina	n.a.	14.0	–6.5	8.2	n.a.	5.8
Bangladesh	10.3	7.8	5.9	0.2	4.4	7.6
Chile	7.4	9.2	2.5	5.1	4.9	4.1
Czech Republic	–5.7	3.5	–11.6	–1.9	5.9	5.4
Egypt	5.9	0.7	–1.4	–4.1	7.3	4.8
Ghana	17.9	5.7	5.6	-0.6	12.3	6.3
Hungary	8.3	3.4	1.2	–1.7	7.1	5.1
India	4.7	5.7	–0.8	1.6	5.5	4.1
Indonesia	15.3	7.9	7.6	6.8	7.7	1.1
Kenya	4.3	27.8	–0.2	12.7	4.5	15.1
Malaysia	3.8	2.1	3.0	0.6	0.8	1.5
Mexico	2.9	7.1	0.1	3.1	2.8	4.0
Philippines	9.7	6.1	5	0.3	4.7	5.8
Poland	–4.3	5.2	–5.2	0.0	0.9	5.2
Republic of Korea,	3.7	4.3	3.7	4.1	0.0	0.2
Slovakia	-8.5	5.2	–13.6	–0.8	5.1	6.0
Slovenia	18.4	10.8	–2.0	2.4	20.4	8.4
Thailand	12.9	9.3	4.6	5.7	8.3	3.6
United Republic of Tanzania	7.8	16.2	–3.1	6.0	10.9	10.2

Source: Calculated from IMF, *International Financial Statistics*, various issues.

Note: The real lending rate is calculated as $((1+il)/(1+p))$ X 100, where *il* is the nominal lending rate and *p* is the Consumer Price Index (CPI) inflation rate; real deposit rate is calculated as $((1+id)/(1+p))$ X 100, where *id* is the nominal deposit rate and *p* is the CPI inflation rate.

Similarly, the spreads between lending and deposit rates also vary significantly across countries. In 1995, they were just less than 3 per cent for both advanced industrial countries in the sample, in contrast to not less than 5 per cent more commonly found in other parts of the world. In sub-Saharan Africa, for example, they were between 6.3 per cent for Ghana and 15.1 per cent for Kenya while, in economies in transition, they ranged between 5.1 per cent for Hungary and 8.4 per cent for Slovenia. A significant exception to this rule was provided by some Asian countries where spreads were less than 1.5 per cent, and in the case of Republic of Korea, only 0.2 per cent.

Several factors have been identified as reasons for the differences in lending rates and spreads across countries. Some of them are the following (IMF, 1996a):

Transaction costs

Transaction costs include, on the one hand, the costs of administering payments and, on the other hand, default costs. In developing countries and economies in transition, these costs tend to be significantly higher than in advanced industrial countries. Costs of administering the payments are higher, as payments systems are still evolving and have not reached the level of efficiency attained in advanced industrial countries. Default costs are also higher for developing countries and economies in transition than in the advanced industrial countries. This is primarily because of widespread macroeconomic instability, weak banking regulation and lack of technical expertise in the banking sector.

As a result, banks in many developing countries and practically all economies in transition are faced today with a high proportion of non-performing loans in their bank portfolios. To remain solvent, banks need to recover this loss by increasing lending rates for sound loans and, subsequently, by raising their spreads between lending and deposit rates. Table 5.3 provides information collected by the IMF on the quality of loan portfolios from among the sample countries that have experienced banking problems since 1980. For each of these countries, the Table gives the approximate date of the banking sector problems as well as the extent of the problem measured by the percentage of loans that were non-performing. In some African countries, such as United Republic of Tanzania, Ghana and Kenya, this percentage was more than 60 per cent in various years of the 1990s. Non-performing loans amounting to more than 15 per cent of total bank portfolio have also been registered over the last few years by the vast majority of economies in transition as well as by some countries in other regions, such as Argentina and Mexico in Latin America and Thailand and the Philippines in Asia. By contrast, annual loan losses are typically less than 1 per cent of loans outstanding in advanced industrial countries (Pohl et al., 1996, p. 15).

Table 5.3 Non-performing bank loans

Country	Period	Percentage of total loans
United States	1980s and early 1990s	4.1
Japan	1995	9.4
Argentina	1995	16
Bangladesh	1971 – present	high percentage of non-performing loans
Chile	1983	19
Czech Republic	1995	39
Ghana	1991	60
Hungary	1994	26
India	1991 – present	14.5[a]
Indonesia	1995	12
Kenya	1993	66[b]
Mexico	1994 – present	18
Philippines	1986	19
Poland	1995	15
Republic of Korea	1995	1.2
Slovakia	1995	32
Slovenia	1991	21
Thailand	1986	32
United Republic of Tanzania	1988 – present	60 – 80

Notes:
[a]Non-performing domestic assets of the 28 public sector banks.
[b]The percentage relates to one third of commercial banks.

Sources: IMF (1996a, pp. 22–4) and Borish et al. (1996), pp. 60–70.

Thin markets with high concentration

In most developing countries and economies in transition, the banking sector is poorly developed and highly concentrated. For example, the market share accounted for by the top five banks in selected economies in transition – Belarus, the Czech Republic, Hungary, Poland, Romania, Slovakia, Slovenia and Ukraine – ranged from 68 to 89 per cent of total banking assets in 1994 (EBRD, 1995, p. 161). High market concentration creates an oligopolistic environment in which banks may extract rents by increasing the fees and the spread and consequently the lending rates.

Government policies regarding the banking sector
These policies are another determinant of the spread between lending and deposit rates. Credit ceilings and selective credit policies erect walls in already thin markets reinforcing oligopolistic tendencies. The resulting lack of competition gives little incentive for development of strong banking skills such as analysing the credit-worthiness of prospective borrowers.

Access to Domestic Bank Credit

Data on average lending rates and spreads in a country provide important macroeconomic information about the cost of capital in a country. These data, however, do not give answers to some other important questions related to the relationship between enterprise and banking sectors at the micro-economic level. Two questions, therefore, deserve special attention: which companies have access to bank lending and to what extent do conditions at which companies tap banking sector resources in a country vary between more and less credit-worthy borrowers?[8]

There are no comprehensive data available for a reasonably large number of countries that would allow a systematic quantitative analysis of these questions. As a result, their analysis has to be qualitative and observed patterns and trends must be related in an intuitive manner.

Structure of companies with access to bank lending
A key pattern of banking operations in many countries is concentration of loans among larger firms while access by SMIs and individual entrepreneurs to bank loans is limited – when not beyond their reach. Banks are reluctant to lend to SMIs because they perceive such operations as excessively risky and costly. Moreover, the majority of entrepreneurs and SMIs are unable to provide the guarantees traditionally required by banks. Underreporting of profits and turnover for tax avoidance purposes also penalizes SMIs in some countries, as does their failure to register ownership of assets.

Manufacturing usually accounts for a significant share of total bank commitments. Although they vary among countries, reflecting differences in the structure of the economy, credits to industrial firms are not less than 22 per cent of the total in any of the Table 5.4 countries. In all but one country in the table, Egypt, manufacturing is the largest borrower from banks.

Table 5.4 Bank credits to manufacturing sector (% of total credits)

Bangladesh	End June 1995	32
Brazil	August 1995	22[b]
Czech Republic	End 1995	35[b]
Egypt	During 1995 – 96[a]	25[b]
Malaysia	End 1995	26
Thailand	During 1995	26

Notes:
[a]Preliminary
[b]Total industry

Source: IMF Country Reports, various years.

Differences in terms at which companies tap bank loans

There are significant differences across countries in interest rates charged to prime borrowers and other users of bank credits. In the United Republic of Tanzania, for example, nominal lending rates were between 30 and 46 per cent in June 1996 (IMF, 1996b, p. 63). In Argentina, the real interest rate on peso loans for prime borrowers was 9.5 per cent in mid-July 1996 but almost twice as high – 18 per cent – for non-prime borrowers. A much wider real interest rate gap between prime and ordinary borrowers has been reported in Brazil. While the former were able to borrow at an annual rate of 33.6 per cent in November 1996, access to credits for the latter was available at a rate as high as 133.2 per cent (Netto, 1997).

DEBT FINANCING FROM FOREIGN SOURCES

Interest rates reflect the cost of capital. If capital mobility is perfect – implying the absence of capital control – and domestic and foreign assets are perfect substitutes, then interest rates would represent the true opportunity costs of capital and would be determined by the world market rate. In these conditions, nominal interest rates among countries should differ only by expected exchange rate changes. In a situation where market imperfections prevail, interest rates may reflect high transaction costs, market structures and concerns over various risks as much as cost of capital. In this case, nominal interest rates are not closely related to world rates even if adjusted for exchange rate changes.

Table 5.5 Interest rate differentials and real cost of borrowing abroad (1995, in %)

Country	Nominal lending rates[a] (A)	International interest rate[b] (B)	Exchange rate depreciation[c] (C)	Inflation[a] (D)	Interest rate differential[d] (A–B–C)	Real cost of borrowing abroad[e] (B+C+D)
United States	8.8	6	3.5	2.8	-0.7	6.7
Japan	3.4	6	--5.6	–0.1	3.0	0.5
Argentina	17.9	6	5.3	3.4	6.6	7.9
Bangladesh	14.0	6	–0.5	5.8	8.5	–0.3
Chile	18.2	6	–5.7	8.2	17.9	–7.9
Czech Republic	12.8	6	–1.9	9.0	8.7	–4.9
Hungary	32.6	6	3.9	28.3	22.7	–18.4
India	16.5[b]	6	3.2	10.2	7.3	–1.0
Indonesia	17.1[c]	6	1.6	8.5[c]	9.5	–0.9
Malaysia	7.6	6	0.4	5.3	1.2	1.1
Mexico	45.1[a]	6	29.7	35.0	9.4	0.7
Philippines	14.7	6	1.0	8.1	7.7	–1.1
Poland	33.5	6	–4.2	26.8	31.7	–25
Republic of Korea	9.0	6	-0.4	4.5	7.0	–2.5
Slovakia	15.6	6	4.5	9.9	5.1	0.6
Slovenia	24.8	6	–10.7	12.6	29.5	–17.3
Thailand	15.5[d]	6	0.9	5.7	8.6	1.2

Notes:
[a]Rates for short-term and medium-term bank credits.
[b]Three month London Inter-Bank Offered Rate (LIBOR) on US deposits.
[c]Data collected from IMF and Morgan (1996).
[d]Difference between home and international market interest rate adjusted for exchange rate depreciation.
[e]Minus means that real costs of foreign loans are lower than loans raised from domestic banks.
Source: IMF, *International Financial* Statistics, various issues.

Table 5.5 shows interest rate differentials for most of the countries of the sample. They are calculated as the difference between nominal interest rates charged by the banking sector in each of the countries and a benchmark international interest rate adjusted for exchange rate depreciation. In comparison with advanced industrial countries, where interest rate differentials were rather small in 1995, indicating that domestic rates are very much in line with the world's benchmark rate, in all but two developing countries in the sample, as well as in all economies in transition, domestic rates were at least five percentage points above the international benchmark rate. In some of them, such as Chile, Hungary, Slovenia and Poland, interest rate differentials exceeded the 15 percentage point margin.

Even if the international benchmark interest rate is adjusted for exchange rate depreciation of the local currency and domestic inflation, the real cost of foreign loans is lower for most developing countries and for practically all economies in transition included in the sample, giving them an incentive to borrow abroad. As Table 5.5 shows, borrowing abroad was, in 1995, a very attractive proposition for most economies in transition, including Poland, Hungary, Slovenia and the Czech Republic, as well as for some developing countries, such as Chile, but real costs of foreign loans were also lower than domestic bank rates in countries such as the Republic of Korea, India and Indonesia. There was also, however, also a smaller group of countries, including Slovakia, Thailand, Malaysia and Mexico, where real costs of borrowing abroad were higher in 1995 than borrowing from domestic banks.

Access to Foreign Debt Flows

The late 1980s and early 1990s witnessed a dramatic revival and expansion of total net private capital flows to developing countries and economies in transition (Table 5.6).[9] Within this general framework, the volume of debt-creating flows also increased, from $2.6 billion in 1986 to $50.8 billion in 1995. Debt flows include two major instruments of financing: commercial bank credits and portfolio debt flows through bonds issued on international capital markets. Commercial bank lending, as practically the only source of debt financing for these groups of countries in the pre-1982 period, has throughout the 1990s lost in importance in relation to fast-growing bond financing.

Although global figures for developing countries and economies in transition indicate that as a group they have increasingly tapped foreign debt resources, the access to these resources varies enormously among countries. A sovereign state's ability to tap financial resources abroad and on what terms depends primarily on investors' perception of the country risk (Table 5.7).[10] Country rating assigned to a sovereign state by one of the major

Table 5.6 Total net private capital flows to developing countries and economies in transition (US$ billion)

	1986	1990	1992	1994	1995
Total private	20.0	44.0	100.3	158.8	167.1
Portfolio investment	1.4	6.7	27.3	67.1	55.7
Debt flows	(0.8)	(3.0)	(13.2)	(32.2)	(33.7)
Equity flows	(0.6)	(3.7)	(14.1)	(34.9)	(22.0)
Foreign direct investment	10.1	25.0	46.6	80.1	90.3
Commercial banks	1.8	1.7	13.8	9.2	17.1
Other	6.7	10.6	12.6	2.4	4.0

Sources: The World Bank, *World Debt Tables 1993–1994*, p. 10; *World Debt Tables 1996*, p. 3.

Table 5.7 Country risk assessment of the sample countries, by rating agencies and specialized journals

	Euromoney (September 1996)		Institutional Investor (September 1996)		Moody's[d] November 1996)	S&P[d] November 1996)	IBCA[d] November 1996)
Country	Rank[a]	Score[b]	Rank[c]	Score[b]			
United States	3	98.4	4	90.7	Aaa	AAA	AAA
Japan	12	94.0	2	91.1	Aaa	AAA	AAA
Argentina	54	57.3	59	38.9	B1	BB-	
Bangladesh	94	40.3	82	26.9	nr	nr	nr
Chile	29	77.4	30	61.2	Baa2	A-	A-
Czech Republic	35	73.7	29	62.0	Baa1	A	A-
Egypt	77	45.7	62	35.1	Ba2	no	no
Ghana	81	44.6	75	29.6	nr	nr	nr
Hungary	44	67.2	50	44.7	Ba1	BBB-	BBB-
India	46	63.7	47	46.3	Baa	BB+	no
Indonesia	41	70.8	39	52.2	Baa	BBB	no
Kenya	87	42.3	78	27.9	nr	nr	nr
Malaysia	27	80.2	25	67.7	A1	A+	no
Mexico	52	60.3	52	41.6	Ba2	BB	BB
Philippines	51	61.5	56	40.5	Ba2	BB	nr
Poland	55	57.1	51	44.0	Baa	BBB-	BBB

(continued)

Table 5.7 continued

	Euromoney (September 1996)		Institutional Investor (September 1996)		Moody's[d] November 1996)	S&P[d] November 1996)	IBCA[d] November 1996)
Country	Rank[a]	Score[b]	Rank[c]	Score[b]			
Republic of Korea	22	84.3	21	72.1	A1	AA-	AA-
Slovakia	49	62.2	53	41.2	Baa	BBB-	BBB-
Slovenia	34	73.8	43	49.9	A3	A	A-
Thailand	30	77.2	27	63.2	A2	A	no
United Republic of Tanzania	136	29.5	106	18.1	no	no	no

Notes:
[a]100 is maximum.
[b]178 countries were ranked.
[c]135 countries were ranked .
[d]Investment grade ratings and speculative grade ratings are as follows:

Investment grade ratings	
Moody's	S&P; IBCA
Aaa	AAA
Aa1	AA+
Aa2	AA
Aa3	AA-
A1	A+
A2	A
A3	A-
Baa1	BBB+
Baa2	BBB
Baa	BBB-

Speculative grade ratings	
Moody's	S&P; IBCA
Ba1	BB+
Ba2	BB
Ba3	BB-
B1	B+
B2	B
B3	B-

Source: *Euromoney*, September 1996; *Institutional Investor*, September 1996; Morgan (1996).

rating agencies has, *de facto*, became a precondition for its successful entrance into international capital markets. This rating is important for at least three reasons: (i) access of non-rated countries and, hence, also of their companies, to the international capital markets is either completely denied or accessible on a very limited basis; (ii) rating determines conditions at which the state can raise money on international capital markets, with the better the rating, the lower the costs of financing; and (iii) the rating assigned to a sovereign state creates a benchmark for borrowing conditions for all other entities from that particular state. Following the logic that entities operate within an environment created by the state, no entity from its territory can have a better rating than the state itself.

Some 50 developing countries and economies in transition were rated by at least one of the three world leading rating agencies, Moody's, S&P and IBCA by November 1996. The remaining 100 or so countries, including practically all African countries, many from Asia, Latin America and most of the former Soviet republics, have not been rated by these institutions. Raising money by non-sovereign borrowers involves additional risks. In the case of corporate borrowing, investors will usually look, in addition to the country risk, at least at the sector risk and risk of the borrower itself. As for sector risk, investors are interested in the sector's strategic importance, its prospects for growth, its international competitiveness and the like. An enterprise, in turn, must demonstrate a strong position in the local market, a proven track record of growth and managerial capacity and strategically convincing medium-term investment plans.

Bank lending

In contrast to the 1970s, the volume of commercial bank lending to developing countries and economies in transition was drastically reduced throughout the 1980s as a consequence of the debt crisis. At the end of the 1980s and the beginning of the 1990s, banks began to show a renewed interest in voluntary lending to this part of the world. The volume of lending started to grow again but has never recaptured the relative importance it had in the pre-1982 period.

Loan commitments to developing countries and economies in transition increased to US$112 billion in 1995, compared to US$73 billion in 1994. In the first nine months of 1996, loan commitments amounted to US$67.6 billion, 4 per cent less than in the same period of 1995. Of this total, 64 per cent were loans to the private sector, 32 per cent to the public sector and 4 per cent to sovereign borrowers (World Bank, *Financial Flows and Developing Countries*, various issues). Altogether, entities from more than 50 developing countries and economies in transition tapped into the international syndicated loan market in 1996 (data from Capital Data Loanware and *International Financing Review*). On a regional basis, Asian countries dominated accounting for US$42.7 billion of new loan commitments in the first nine months of 1996, which was equivalent to 64 per cent of the total. The other two important borrowing regions were the emerging economies in Europe, mainly economies in transition, and Latin America, with 14 and 13 per cent share respectively *(International Financing Review).*

Table 5.8 provides some basic information for a selected number of bank credits raised by industrial sector enterprises in the first half of 1996. The list is by no means complete and is prepared for illustrative purposes only. Based on the data contained in this table, the following major patterns of bank loans to industrial sector enterprises in developing countries and economies in transition can be identified.

Table 5.8 Selected commercial bank credits to industrial enterprises of developing countries and economies in transition (first half of 1996)

Company name	Country	Amount*	Signing date	Margin	Maturity
Yacimentos Petroliferos Fiscales (YPF)	Argentina	130.0	22/3	LIBOR: 175 b.p.	1977
Bahia Sul Celulose SA	Brazil	55.0	.../4	n.a.	1998
Petroleo Brasileiro SA	Brazil	100.0	26/6	LIBOR: 181.25 b.p.	1996
Petroleos Brasileiro	Brazil	250.0	19/4	n.a.	1997
Empresa Nacional de Minera	Chile	75.0	18/4	LIBOR: 55 b.p.	2001
Compania Minera Carmen de Andacollo	Chile	57.0	5/2	n.a.	2004
Anyang Henan Color Picture Tube Glass Bulb Co.	China	71.3	30/1	LIBOR: 130 b.p.	2001
Unitex Glass Co.	China	10.0	19/4	LIBOR: 100 b.p.	2001
Sinochem International Oil	China	45.0	2/2	LIBOR: 35.b.p.	1997
Empresa Colombiana de Petroleos	Colombia	5.3	29/2	6.93 per cent	2003
Czech Refinery Company	Czech Rep.	100.0	18/1	n.a.	
Teberebie Goldfields Ltd	Ghana	8.4	23/4	7.5 per cent	

Ashanti Goldmines Company	Ghana	185.0	. ./2	n.a.	
Indian Oil Corporation	India	45.0	6/1	LIBOR: 75 b.p.	2003
OCI Chemical Corp.	Rep. of Korea	40.0	18/1	LIBOR: 65 b.p.	1998
Steel Authority of India	India	45.0	24/6	LIBOR: 75 b.p.	2003
Indian Petrochemical Corp.	India	75.0	16/5	LIBOR: 98 b.p.	2004
SIV Industries Ltd	India	9.0	26/1	LIBOR: 150 b.p.	2003
PT Keramika Indonesia Assosiasi	Indonesia	9.8	18/4	LIBOR: 110 b.p.	1999
PT International Nickel Indonesia	Indonesia	421.5	29/2	n.a.	
PT Indah Kiat Pulp & Paper Corp.	Indonesia	5.6	22/5	n.a.	2001
PT Indo Aluminium Intikarsa Industri	Indonesia	8.0	25/3	LIBOR: 225 b.p.	2001
Tongyang Cement Corp.	Rep. of Korea	4.5	19/1	LIBOR: 87 b.p	1999
Hyosung Corp.	Rep. of Korea	6.2	5/6	LIBOR: 65 b.p.	2001
Korea Zinc Corporation	Rep. of Korea	19.5	. ./2	LIBOR: 73 b.p.	2003
Orion Hanel Picture Tube Corp.	Rep. of Korea	7.5	20/6	LIBOR: 80 b.p.	2003
Slanging Refining Co.	Rep. of Korea	10.0	12/3	LIBOR: 60 b.p.	1999
Samsung Electronics	Rep. of Korea	125.0	12/6	LIBOR: 26 b.p.	1997
Hyundai Precision & Industry	Rep. of Korea	10.2	7/5	LIBOR: 55 b.p.	2001
LG Engineering Corp. Ltd	Rep. of Korea	45.0	12/4	LIBOR: 45 b.p.	1999
Samsung Electonics Co.	Rep. of Korea	155.0	2/5	LIBOR: 40 b.p.	2001
Amsteel Mills Sdn Bhd	Malaysia	180.0	11/4	LIBOR: 137.7 b.p.	2001
Petroliam Nasional Bhd	Malaysia	149.8	18/4	n.a.	2002
Tan Chong Motor Holdings Bhd	Malaysia	59.3	21/3	GTCOMM: 65 b.p.	2002
Coca-Cola Femsa SA de CV	Mexico	165.0	14/2	LIBOR 325 b.p.	1999

(continued)

Table 5.8 continued

Company name	Country	Amount*	Signing date	Margin	Maturity
Embotelladores Mexicanos de Pepsi-Cola SA de CV	Mexico	35.0	22/4	n.a.	
Oil & Gas Development Corp.	Pakistan	30.0	3/5	n.a.	1999
Cerveceria Backus y Johnson	Peru	50.0	26/4	LIBOR: 275 b.p.	2000
Saudi Cable Company	Saudi Arabia	30.0	. ./5	n.a.	1997
Saudi Aramco Mobile Refining	Saudi Arabia	225.0	4/6	n.a.	2001
Flextronics Singapore Pte	Singapore	20.0	29/1	LIBOR: 137.5 b.p.	1996
Slovnaft AS	Slovakia	50.0	. ./6	LIBOR: 100 b.p.	1999
Caltex Oil	South Africa	100.0	28/2	n.a.	2001
Siam Cement Co.	Thailand	15.0	22/5	LIBOR: 30 b.p.	1997
Bangchak Petroleum Company	Thailand	120.0	14/2	LIBOR: 27.5 b.p.	1997
Siam Strip Mill	Thailand	120.0	4/3	LIBOR: 150 b.p.	2006
Delta Electronics	Thailand	75.0	8/3	LIBOR: 70 b.p.	2001
Siam Motor Company	Thailand	45.0	5/2	LIBOR: 87.5 b.p.	1999
Siam Guardian Glass Co. Ltd	Thailand	48.0	25/3	LIBOR: 67.5 b.p.	2002
Rayong Olefins Co.	Thailand	150.0	6/6	LIBOR: 40 b.p.	2006
Phoenix Pulp and Paper	Thailand	30.0	28/3	LIBOR: 70 b.p.	1999
Hai Van Cement	Viet Nam	7.8	. ./3	n.a.	2001
Poslilama Steel Structure Co.	Viet Nam	11.8	14/2	LIBOR: 60 b.p.	2002
Zambia Consolidated Copper Mines	Zambia	50.0	15/3	n.a.	1996

Notes:
*US$ equivalent; million.
b.p. Basis points.

Source: Extracted from the Capital Data Loanware.

First, the size of loans varies from very small ones (US$4.5 million in the case of Tongyang Cement Corporation) to very large ones (between US$225 and US$250 million in the cases of Saudi Arabian and Brazilian oil firms and US$421.5 million in the case of PT International Nickel Indonesia). Smaller credits tend to go to firms in various manufacturing branches while larger credits seem to be highly concentrated in oil and petrochemicals, mining and metals.

Second, spreads over LIBOR also vary significantly across companies.[11] On credits with maturity between years 2000 and 2003, margins range from 40 basis points, reflecting the excellent credit rating enjoyed at the time by a company from a country with high investment-grade rating – to 275 basis points, for a country that is at the lowest end of all rated economies.

Third, there are significant differences in loan maturities. This could be either a consequence of a borrower's preference or the relatively weak credit standing of the borrower.

Fourth, industrial firms from 21 countries raised money directly on international loan markets in the first half of 1996. Nine were from Asia (China, India, Indonesia, Republic of Korea, Malaysia, Pakistan, Singapore, Thailand and Viet Nam), six from Latin America (Argentina, Brazil, Chile, Colombia, Mexico and Peru), three from Africa (Ghana, South Africa and Zambia), two from Central Europe (Czech Republic and Slovakia) and one from the Middle East (Saudi Arabia). All but three of these countries, Viet Nam, Ghana and Zambia, have been rated by at least one of the world's three leading rating agencies.

Bond financing

Bond issuance by developing countries and economies in transition increased from US$6.3 billion in 1990 to an annual level of more than US$55 billion from 1993 to 1995. As Table 5.9 shows, these countries raised a record amount – US$65.7 billion – in the first nine months of 1996 compared with US$57.8 billion in the same period of the previous year (World Bank, *Financial Flows and Developing Countries,* various issues).[12]

The structure of total bond issues classified by issuers differs significantly from the comparable structure for bank lending. In the case of bond issues, private and public sector issuers accounted for 33 and 18 per cent respectively of the total in the first nine months of 1996. By far the largest share of all issues, 49 per cent, was made by sovereign issuers. The most active among them were Latin American States, accounting for some two thirds of total sovereign issues, especially Mexico and Argentina. Governments from this region issued large amounts of bonds primarily to refinance maturing obligations and to re-establish benchmarks in international markets (World Bank, *Financial Flows and Developing Countries,* various issues).

Table 5.9 International bond issues by selected countries and regions

Country or territory	1995 (in US$ billion)	Moody's	S&P
Africa	**2.0**		
Mauritius	0.2	Baa2	nr
South Africa	1.2	Baa3	BB+
Tunisia	0.6	Baa3	nr
Asia	**13.7**		
China	1.4	A3	BBB
Hong Kong SAR	2.9	A3	A
India	0.8	Baa3	BB+
Indonesia	2.3	Baa3	BBB
Malaysia	2.6	A1	A+
Philippines	1.1	Ba2	BB
Singapore	0.3	Aa1	AAA
Sri Lanka	0	nr	nr
Taiwan Province	2.3	Aa3	AA+
Europe	**6.6**		
Croatia	0	nr	nr
Hungary	3.3	Ba1	BBB–
Latvia	0	nr	nr
Lithuania	0.1	Ba2	nr
Poland	0.3	Baa3	BBB-
Russian Federation	0.3	Ba2	BB-
Slovakia	0.1	Baa3	BBB-
Turkey	2.5	Ba3	B+
Middle East	**0.9**		
Bahrain	0.1	Ba1	nr
Israel	0.3	A3	A-
Jordan	0.1	Ba3	BB-
Lebanon	0.4	nr	nr

Western Hemisphere	**23.5**		
Argentina	6.4	B1	BB-
Brazil	7.0	B1	B+
Chile	0.3	Baa1	A-
Colombia	1.1	Baa3	BBB-
Ecuador	0	nr	nr
Mexico	7.7	Ba2	BB
Panama	0.3	nr	nr
Trinidad and Tobago	0.1	Ba1	BB+
Uruguay	0.2	Ba1	BB+
Venezuela	0.4	Ba2	B
Total	**45.7**		

Note: n.r. not reported.

Source: Folkerts-Landau and Itô (1996) p. 93.

Because of strong sovereign issuers, Latin American borrowers accounted for some half of total bond volume in the first nine months of 1996. The next in line were borrowers from Asia with roughly a third, emerging European countries with some 10 per cent while Africa and the Middle East participated each with less than 2 per cent. Altogether, issuers from some 30 to 35 countries tapped international bond markets in 1995 and 1996. Table 5.9. shows that out of 33 countries with bond issuance in 1995, only five (Croatia, Latvia, Lebanon, Panama and Sri Lanka) did not have a rating from either Moody's or S&P. The combined volume of their 1995 issues was equivalent to less than 1.5 per cent of the total.

Issues of bonds by sovereign states accounted for some half of total bond issues in the first three quarters of the 1996. Data for the second and third quarters of that year suggest that issuers from the financial sector were the next most important with roughly a quarter of the total, while the remaining quarter was more or less equally distributed between issues from utilities and issues from the industrial sector. Manufacturing alone accounted for 10 and 9 per cent of total bond issues in the second and third quarter of the 1996 respectively (World Bank, *Financial Flows and Developing Countries,* various issues).

Table 5.10 reports on a sample of bond issues made by industrial sector enterprises from developing countries in 1996. Although the sample is not complete, it points out certain specific patterns.

Table 5.10 List of selected bond issues made by industrial enterprises of developing countries and economies in transition in 1996

Company name	Country	Amount (million)	Issue price	Coupon	Yield	Maturity
Bridas Corporation	Argentina	$100.0	99.71	10.25	10.66	1998
Industrias Metalúrgicas Pescarmona SAIC	Argentina	$75	99.58	11.75	12.35	
Yacimientos Petroliferos Fiscales	Argentina	LAIR 300 000	101.0	8.75	8.5	2001
Alcoa Aluminio Brazil	Brazil	$400	99.94	7.5	7.65	2008
Aracruz Celulose	Brazil	$200	99.54	8.75	8.84	2003
Bahia sul Celulosa SA	Brazil	$100.0	99.95	10.63	10.92	2004
Cementos Caue	Brazil	$20	100.0	13.0	13.0	2001
Ceval Alimentos	Brazil	$100.0	99.51	11.13	11.54	2004
Companhia Siderurgica Nacional	Brazil	$160	100.0	8.37	8.37	2003
Companhia Siderurgica Nacional	Brazil	$150	100.0	n.a.	n.a.	1999
Companhia Vale do Rio Doce	Brazil	$300	99.88	10.0	10.27	2004
Companhia Acos Especiais Itabira	Brazil	$150	99.6	11.13	11.52	2004
Ford Brazil Ltda	Brazil	$300	99.7	9.13	9.39	2008
Klabin Fabricadora de Papel e Celulose	Brazil	$70	99.71	11.0	11.36	2004
Metalurgica Gerdau SA	Brazil	$130	99.9	11.13	11.46	2004
OPP Petroquimica	Brazil	$125	99.74	11.5	11.88	2004
OPP Petroquimica	Brazil	$100.0	99.9	11.0	11.32	2004
Petroleo Brasileiro SA	Brazil	$125	99.88	8.75	8.97	2001
Petroleo Brasileiro SA	Brazil	$150	99.83	7.5	7.69	1997
Petroleo Brasileiro SA	Brazil	A 1250	99.86	9.0	9.02	2004
Petroleo Brasileiro SA	Brazil	$250	99.78	100.0	10.29	2006
Sinar Mas Multiartha	Brunei	$60	100.0	n.a	n.a.	1998
Industria Azucarera Nacional	Chile	$40	100.0	7.61	7.61	2003
Sociedad Química i Minera SA	Chile	$200	100.0	7.7	7.84	2006

ICICI	India	$150	99.4	7.13	7.37	2003
Reliance Industries	India	$100.0	99.3	10.5	10.85	2046
Reliance Industries	India	$100.0	99.79	10.38	10.67	2016
Reliance Industries	India	$100.0	99.96	9.38	9.6	2026
Indah Kiat Pulp & Paper Corp.	Indonesia	$100.0	84.26	n.a.	8.94	1998
Wijaya Karya	Indonesia	Rp 100 000	100.0	17.5	18.28	2003
Daewoo Corporation	Rep. of Korea	$150	100.0	n.a.	n.a.	2001
Samsung Electronics Co.	Rep. of Korea	$150	100.0	n.a.	n.a.	2006
Samsung Electronics	Rep. of Korea	$187[a]	100.0	3.3	n.a.	2003
Hong Leon Industries Bhd	Malaysia	$90	100.0	n.a.	n.a.	2001
Petroleum Nasional Berhad	Malaysia	$800	99.8	7.13	7.15	2006
Petroleum Nasional Berhad	Malaysia	$600	99.62	6.63	6.72	2001
Petroleum Nasional Berhad	Malaysia	Yen 14 000	100.0	3.6	3.63	2006
Petroleum Nasional Berhad	Malaysia	$500	98.65	7.63	7.74	2026
Rex Industry Berhad	Malaysia	SwF 11	100.9	4.0	3.76	2000
Bufete Industrial	Mexico	$100.0	99.62	11.38	11.86	1999
Cemex SA	Mexico	$300	100.0	12.75	13.16	2006
Cemex SA	Mexico	$300	99.85	10.75	11.09	2000
Coca-Cola Femsa	Mexico	$200	99.96	8.95	9.16	2006
Empresas la Moderna SA de CV	Mexico	$125	99.64	11.38	11.52	1999
Grupo Industrial Durango	Mexico	$250	100.0	12.63	13.02	
Panamerican Beverages, Inc.	Mexico	$150	99.45	8.13	8.4	2003
Petroleos Mexicanos	Mexico	LAIR 300 000	100.3	12.25	12.08	1998
Petroleos Mexicans	Mexico	$300	99.71	8	8.32	1998
Petroleos Mexicanos	Mexico	$300	99.8	7.75	7.98	1999

(continued)

Table 5.10 continued

Company name	Country	Amount (million)	Issue price	Coupon	Yield	Maturity
Grupo Empresarial Fenix	Paraguay	$100.0	99.73	12.75	12.83	2001
Philippine National Oil Co.	Philippines	$150	99.49	8.24	8.34	2001
Thai Petrochemical Industry	Thailand	B 3 000	100.0	11.86	12.23	2001
Thai Cars	Thailand	$250	100.0	n.a.	n.a.	2002
TPI Polene	Thailand	Yen 6000	100.0	n.a.	n.a.	2000

[a]Issue was made in yen.

Source: IFR Securities Data Base (without bond issues made by enterprises from the Republic of Korea) and The World Bank, *Financial Flows and Developing Countries* (various issues)

First, more than 80 per cent of bond issues covered in the table are for more than US$100 million each. Of these, there are nine jumbo issues, each larger than US$300 million, made by national oil firms in Malaysia and Mexico, a cement producer from Mexico and two Brazilian enterprises. This indicates that international bond markets have been tapped almost exclusively by large industrial companies and that SMIs are, *de facto*, excluded from this segment of international capital markets.

Second, the costs of borrowing vary significantly among enterprises from different countries. For example, while the 10-year bond issued on the dollar market by the Chilean company Sociedad Química y Minera SA has a yield of 7.84 per cent, the yield on a bond with similar characteristics issued by Cemex from Mexico is 13.16 per cent.[13]

Third, the majority of bonds issued by industrial sector enterprises have three to seven years to maturity, although two Indian firms stretched the maturity of their three bonds issued on the dollar market to 20, 30 and even 50 years.

Fourth, in 1996, industrial companies from only 12 developing countries raised financial resources directly on the international bond markets. These companies were from only two regions; 7 from Asia (India, Indonesia,

Republic of Korea, Thailand, Malaysia, the Philippines and Brunei) and 5 from Latin America (Argentina, Brazil, Chile, Mexico and Paraguay). To all of these countries with the exception of oil-rich Brunei, a rating has been assigned by at least one of the three rating agencies.

CONCLUSIONS

The costs of borrowing from domestic or foreign financial institutions are, in general, lower for industrial firms from advanced industrial countries than for those from developing countries and economies in transition. This puts enterprises from the latter countries into relatively worse international competitive position *vis-à-vis* companies from the developed world. In addition to this general conclusion, the following specific conclusions can be drawn:

First, although interest rates at which borrowers have access to bank credits from their domestic banking systems differ significantly from one country to another, real lending rates in the majority of developing countries and economies in transition were higher in 1995 than was the unweighted average lending rate for the two advanced industrial countries, the United States and Japan, in the sample. Differences in transaction costs across countries are an important reason not only for differences in real interest rates but also for differences in real interest rate spreads. In 1995, these spreads were generally at least twice as high in developing countries and economies in transition than in the industrialized world.

Second, the gap in lending rates charged by banks to prime and non-prime borrowers has not been below 50 per cent in any of the three sample countries for which data are available. The benchmark is usually that of government securities, and from there, the rates rise depending on the perceived credit-worthiness of a potential client. In addition to enterprises that do have access to banks, although at very unfavourable terms, there are many economic units to which the banks will deny access to financial resources as they are considered to be a high risk. Access of economic units to bank credits and financial resources from other formal financial institutions varies significantly among countries, and is, as a general tendency, more widespread for units in advanced industrial countries than for those in less developed parts of the world.

Third, some stylized facts have been identified as far as the access to domestic bank credits is concerned: (i) lending to the industrial sector usually accounts for between a quarter and a third of total bank lending, making the sector the most important borrower in most countries; (ii) banks tend to favour lending to existing customers, primarily among middle- and large-sized enterprises, while the access of small-scale entrepreneurs to bank credits is either very limited or even completely denied, often forcing them to rely on more costly informal financial sources; (iii) banking activity in developing countries and economies in transition is strongly concentrated in short-term loans for working capital while the banks are less willing to lend on a longer-term basis for investment purposes. This pattern of bank financing has a very disruptive impact on corporate financing in these countries, as there is, in contrast to advanced industrial countries, practically no alternative sources for long-term financing.

Fourth, differentials between nominal interest rates charged by banks in individual countries and a benchmark international interest rate adjusted for exchange rate depreciation are positive for all developing countries and economies in transition in the sample. In volume terms, these differentials are much greater than interest rate differentials for advanced industrial countries. Large positive interest rate differentials are, on the one hand, an important reason for the often disruptive capital inflows to developing countries and economies in transition and, on the other hand, an indication that banking sector distortions resulting in higher lending rates tend to be more severe in these countries than in advanced industrial countries. As a result of relatively higher domestic lending rates in developing countries and economies in transition, the real cost of foreign loans is lower than raising credits from domestic banks, making borrowing abroad an increasingly attractive funding alternative for these countries.

Fifth, although developing countries and economies in transition, as a group, have succeeded significantly in expanding their access to sources of external debt financing, syndicated loan markets and international bond markets, there are enormous differences between them in doing this. As a consequence of differences in country risks assigned to individual countries, access to international debt markets continues to be entirely, or almost entirely, denied to more than one half of developing countries and economies in transition and, consequently, to their companies. For the other half of these countries, the quality of their international market access varies considerably. There are countries and their companies for whom access is limited to only a few markets and borrowing terms are unfavourable, while, at the other end of the spectrum, there are countries and their companies that can raise financial resources from a variety of international debt markets on very favourable terms.

Sixth, foreign debt financing available to developing countries and transition economies includes two major instruments, bank lending and bond issuing. Syndicated loan markets are more easily accessible; entities from 50 emerging economies raised credits on these markets in 1996. Among these, industrial firms were some of the most active borrowers. Enterprises from this sector of the economy accounted for about a quarter to a third of total loan commitments to developing countries and economies in transition. Altogether, industrial sector firms from some 20 emerging economies raised money directly on international loan markets in 1996. The size of these credits varied from less than US$5 million to over US$100 million, as did the costs of borrowing. Interest rate spreads charged for prime industrial companies from investment-grade emerging countries were at the level of 40 b.p. while companies at the other end of the spectrum had to pay a spread of over 200 b.p. for dollar-denominated credits of the same maturity. To put these margins into perspective, they should be compared with the benchmark spread charged to top-rated industrial conglomerates from the highest-rated advanced industrial countries. Last year, these companies were charged less than 15 b.p. for credits with comparable maturity. This indicates that in 1996 their costs of borrowing from foreign banks were close to 200 b.p. or two percentage points lower than the costs of borrowing for poorly rated companies. This difference was equivalent to some 20 per cent of their total costs of borrowing on the syndicated loan market, taking into account that the LIBOR on dollars was around 6 per cent at that time.

Seventh, in contrast to international loan markets, access to international bond markets is even more restricted. Entities from only 30 to 35 countries tapped these markets in 1995 and 1996. All but a few bonds were issued by entities from the states with a country risk assigned to them by at least one of the world's three leading rating agencies. International bond markets are dominated by sovereign issuers while industrial companies participate with around 10 per cent in total volume. In 1996, their participation was limited to a small number of large-sized companies from less than 15 developing countries. On average, bond issues by industrial firms tend to be much larger than their borrowings from banks. As far as costs are concerned, yield on the bond issued by a top-rated company from a high investment-grade developing country was 5.3 percentage points lower than the yield for a comparable bond issued by a less credit-worthy borrower from a non-investment-grade country. It was, however, still some 0.5 percentage points above the benchmark yield on a comparable bond issued by a top-rated industrial sector company from a triple-A country. The difference in costs of bond issuance was, therefore, even higher than in the case of bank credits.

NOTES

1. See OECD (1995).
2. See Pohl et al. (1996), Annex 1.
3. The findings are based on a sample of 21 countries from different regions of the world: two advanced industrial countries (United States and Japan), three countries from Latin America (Argentina, Chile and Mexico), seven from developing Asia (Bangladesh, India, Indonesia, Republic of Korea, Malaysia, Philippines and Thailand), four African countries (Egypt, Ghana, Kenya and United Republic of Tanzania) and five economies in transition (Czech Republic, Hungary, Poland, Slovakia and Slovenia). The criteria for country choice were: (i) levels of economic development, especially financial sector development, (ii) relative economic stability during the last few years and (iii) availability of data. The total volume of corporate borrowing in these countries is not covered here – only debt financing arranged through formal financial institutions.
4. 'External' refers to funding sources outside the firm; 'foreign' denotes non-domestic external sources.
5. The most influential empirical work on corporate finance in advanced industrial countries has been done by Mayer (1988). Based on flow-of-funds data for the period 1970–85, he concluded (adapted from Singh, 1995): (i) Internally generated funds are the most significant source of finance. In general the self-financing ratios are higher in the Anglo-Saxon countries than elsewhere; (ii) banks are the dominant source of external financing in all countries, accounting for between 7.6 per cent in the United Kingdom and 50.4 per cent in Japan. Bank financing is also pronounced in France at 37.3 per cent, Finland at 28.1 per cent, Italy at 27.7 per cent and the United States at 24.4 per cent; (iii) bond financing is of marginal importance, at less than 3 per cent, in all countries, with exception of the United States (11.6 per cent) and Canada (8.6 per cent); (iv) outside equity financing plays only a minor role in enterprise financing, in the range of between –3.3 per cent for the United Kingdom and 8.2 per cent for Italy; (v) there is a strong inverse relation between the proportion of expenditures financed from the two most important sources of financing, retentions and bank credit; (vi) SMIs are considerably more reliant on external financing than large firms.
6. Zizek and von Liechenstein (1995), p. 30.
7. There are no systematic and regular data about the volume of transactions on primary markets for corporate debt in developing countries. According to a study published by IFC in 1994, the volume of these transactions was at an annual level of between US$4 and 7 billion in the years 1988–92 (Glen and Pinto, 1994, p. 19). Since then, primary markets for corporate debt have broadened, but this does not change two general conclusions: (i) primary markets for corporate debt are still of marginal or no importance in all but a few developing countries and economies in transition and (ii) credits from the banking sector are dominant source of domestic corporate debt financing in these countries.
8. The term-structure of banking sector loans is still another important point. Owing to macroeconomic factors and risk-aversion, commercial banks in many developing countries and economies in transition concentrate on short-term loans for working capital. In five Central European economies in transition, for example, short-term loans are about half of the banking sector's total stock, while flow figures indicate that new loans to firms are increasingly short-term (see Borish et al., 1996, pp. 46-47). Short-term loans also make up the bulk of credit extended by Ghana's banking system. Because of the short-term nature of banks' deposit liabilities and the uncertain macroeconomic environment, banks in that country have been reluctant to extend medium- and long-term credits for investment purposes. For long-term funds, Ghanaian banks depend primarily on external lines of credit (World Bank, 1996, p. 60).

9. Net private capital flows include debt financing (loan disbursement minus principle repayments), FDI flows, portfolio equity investment flows and official grants. Table 5A.6. reports on total volume and structure of net capital flows to developing countries and economies in transition. The new surge is due to: (i) sound macroeconomic fundamentals and strong economic in Asian economies; (ii) normalization of relationships with foreign creditors, Latin American major debtor countries and countries that initiated economic adjustment programmes and comprehensive structural reforms; (iii) similar adjustment and reform programmes in several economies in transition; (iv) improvements in the domestic economic climate as well as measures to strengthen and deregulate domestic financial systems which were introduced in a broad spectrum of developing countries.
10. Country risk is determined by political stability in the country as well as by its macroeconomic parameters and the thrust and rate of economic reform. Assessments of country risks are regularly prepared by a variety of financial institutions, including export credit agencies and commercial banks active in international finance as well as by some multilateral financial institutions. In all of them, country risk is used as an important component for defining an institution's lending policy, credit terms and limits towards potential borrowers from that particular country. Journals specializing in international finance are also active in country risk analyses. The two most widely circulated and opinion-influencing are *Euromoney* and *Institutional Investor*. Table 5A.7. presents the ranks and scores assigned to the 21 sample countries in the September 1996 issues of both journals (the ratings are published regularly, in the March and September issues). The most influential for potential investors are the country risk assessments made by the specialized rating agencies Moody's, Standard and Poor's (S&P) and International Rating Agency (IBCA). In contrast to bank lending, where creditors' decisions are usually based on their own country risk assessment, successful international bond placement depends primarily on the rating assigned to a prospective borrower by one or more of the three agencies. The purchasers of bonds are to a large extent institutional investors, such as pension funds, mutual funds and insurance companies. These investors do not usually produce their own in-house country risk assessments and, consequently, base their investment decisions on the risk evaluations made by the specialized rating agencies. In the context of their diversification of assets strategy, institutional investors are eager to invest in emerging markets portfolios, provided that these investments are made in bonds issued by reasonably credit-worthy borrowers. Many institutional investors are not allowed to buy papers from non-rated borrowers or from borrowers with the speculative-grade ratings. Table 5A.7 reports the sovereign ratings of the three rating agencies for the countries of the sample. Only four of them, all at the lower end of economic development, have not been rated by at least one of the rating agencies, while sovereign ratings for the remaining 17 countries vary from the highest investment-grade rating (AAA or Aaa), the United States and Japan, to the lowest speculative-grade rating among the sample countries, Argentina (BB– or B1).
11. Interest rate spread or margin is a proxy for the riskiness of a bank credit. It is measured as a difference between the interest rate paid by a debtor on that particular credit and reference interest rate, usually LIBOR, paid on the inter-bank market. Spread is usually defined in basis points, 100 basis points (b.p.) are equivalent to one percentage point. The intensified activity of developing countries and economies in transition in the syndicated loan market during the last two years has been accompanied by a narrowing of interest rate spreads. Data suggest that average spreads on Eurocredits for non-OECD countries declined from 118 b.p. in the second half of 1995 (37 b.p. for OECD countries) to 98 b.p. in the fourth quarter of the year (49 b.p. for OECD countries). Reduction of spreads is a consequence of intense competition among potential creditors, and many high-quality borrowers are obtaining credits at very favourable margins. Competitive pressures have

also resulted in a marked weakening of contract covenants (Folkerts-Landau and Ito, 1995, p. 74).

12. The considerable increase in bond issuance in the period 1990–96 is attributed, in addition to improved economic fundamentals in a large number of developing countries and economies in transition, to the entrance of the mainstream institutional investors in markets for emerging economies' papers. Investment opportunities in a number of Latin American countries and economies in transition that had previously appealed mainly to flight investors began to be transformed into investments acceptable to even the most conservative of the institutional investors. In this sense, they joined a group of Asian countries that have maintained access to international bond markets and that have been able to attract institutional investors from a broad spectrum of investor countries.
13. The yield spread is a proxy for the riskiness of a bond. It is measured as the difference between the yield on a particular bond and the yield on a risk-free asset, proxied by the yield on a United States Treasury security of comparable maturity. The terms of new issues by emerging economies improved significantly in the early 1990s. The average yield spread declined from over 400 b.p. in 1991 to 225 b.p. in 1994 (Folkerts-Landau and Ito, 1995, p. 35) and the positive trend of narrowing the spread continued thereafter. At any moment in time there are, however, significant differences among average spreads paid by individual countries, reflecting differences in countries' credit ratings. Sovereign borrowers continue to pay lower spreads than private sector borrowers, although private entities have achieved notable improvements in spreads in recent years.

REFERENCES

Borish, M., W. Ding, and M. Noel (1996): *On the Road to EU Accession: Financial Sector Development in Central Europe*, Washington, DC: World Bank.

EBRD (1995) *Transition Report 1995*, London: EBRD.

Euromoney (various issues).

Folkerts-Landau, D. and T. Itô (1995), *International Capital Markets.* Washington, DC: IMF, September.

Glen, J. and B. Pinto (1994): *Debt or Equity? How Firms in DCs Choose.* Washington, DC: IFC Discussion Paper no. 22.

IFC (1995), *Emerging Markets Factbook 1995,* Washington, DC: IFC.

IMF *International Financial Statistics,* Washington, DC.: IMF (various issues).

IMF (1996a): *Bank Soundness and Macroeconomic Policy,* Washington, DC: IMF (for internal use only).

IMF (1996b), *Tanzania – Selected Issues and Statistical Data,* Washington, DC: IMF

International Financing Review (various issues).

Mayer, C. (1988), New issues in corporate finance, *European Economic Review,* **32,** 1167–89.

Morgan, J.P. (1996), *Sovereign Ratings,* New York, December.

Netto, A.D. (1997), 'A tragedia dos juros' *Folha de São Paulo*, 15 January.

OECD (1996): *Financial Statistics Part 3,* Paris: OECD

Pohl, G., S. Djankov, and R. Anderson (1996), 'Restructuring large industrial firms in Central and Eastern Europe', World Bank Technical Paper no. 332.

Singh, A. (1995), 'Corporate financial patterns in industrializing economies: a comparative international study', IFC Technical Paper no. 2.

World Bank *Financial Flows and Developing Countries,* Washington, DC (various issues).

World Bank (1996), *Ghana – Financial Sector Review: Bringing Savers and Investors Together,* Washington, DC: World Bank

World Bank *World Debt Tables,* Washington, DC (various issues).

Žižek, J. and H. von Liechenstein (1995), *Venture Capital and Entrepreneurship in Central and East Europe: 750 Central and East European Dynamic Entrepreneurs Database Survey,* Phare, EFER and ECVA Final Report.

6. The Macro/Micro Policy Dichotomy: Implications for Cross-Country Replicability

Relationships between economic stability and have traditionally been surrounded by controversy. Policy makers keep the debate alive through their day-to-day macroeconomic and microeconomic interventions. Controversy is fed further by issues such as the macro/micro mix peculiar to the successful East Asian development experience, its subsequent breakdown and the scope for its replicability among developing countries.

One of the necessary attributes of a meaningful policy benchmarking exercise is a clear perception of how macro and micro policies relate to one another at national level. But much progress is still needed in this area if policy makers are to profit from shared experience.

CONCEPTUAL AND EMPIRICAL GAPS

Macroeconomics is about the external, fiscal and savings/investment equilibrium of the economy as a whole; microeconomics is about the organization and performance of the production system and its component units. Analytically they address quite different issues, such as price stability, on the one hand, and productivity, on the other. In actual practice, however, these variables interact in manifold and complex ways leading to differing perceptions and views.

Economic theory has not been of much help as a guide to sort out the difficulty. Macro and micro policies are often lumped together or treated as completely separate realms. This hampers understanding of their mutual interactions[1].

In turn, conceptual gaps lead to gaps in empirical analysis. Failures due to unsustainable macro policies or bureaucratic and institutional shortcomings are often mistakenly attributed to micro policies.

> The distinction between micro distortions and macro stability has made little impression on the development profession ... The literature on trade and growth is marred by severe analytical and conceptual confusions, with macro policies often confused with trade restrictions. The distinction between micro and macro is lost in many studies that attribute balance of payment crises to activist industrial policies, rather than the unwillingness or inability to balance budgets. (Rodrik, 1996, pp. 14–15)

The ultimate reason why the standard paradigm of economic theory has so far been unable to deal suitably with the macro/micro dichotomy is the adherence to postulates of perfect competition, which entail that the best thing for governments to do to promote growth is simply to get out of the way (Stiglitz, 1996).

This sort of perspective, in turn, has biased the understanding of the development experience of the East Asian countries and, with it, handicapped other developing countries in their ability to draw from that experience. For instance, the conclusions reached from the analysis of the sources of growth of the South-East Asian countries are critically affected by the assumption of perfect competition (Sarel, 1997), an issue elabourated in Chapter 7.

BRIDGING THE GAP: INTERPLAY BETWEEN MACRO AND MICRO POLICIES

Consensus on the need for macro stability is much greater than that on the nature of appropriate micro policy. The way different macro scenarios affect microeconomics (such as conduct of economic agents, market morphology, institutions, efficiency and growth) and the way structural reform influences macro stability are issues still far from settled.

Macro instability and its ensuing inflationary impact may bring about changes in economic structure, for example, through a permanent shortening of the length of contracts or the disappearance of certain types of contracts, which may make some activities infeasible (such as long-term financing). When economic agents sense that instability is more than just a transient event, they may change their conduct and thus provoke structural changes. Changes in micro structure and performance, such as in technology, capital/output ratio or propensity to innovate may outlive changes in macro conditions and so coexist with successive macro configurations (Frenkel, 1995).

Unanticipated and abrupt changes in macro variables lead to failures of coordination between individual and overall economic behaviour that spill over from market to market. For instance, macroeconomic disequilibrium may lead firms in imperfect markets to price adjustments that delay rather than prompt adjustments in quantities. It has been suggested that the key to the successful catching-up experiences of the Republic of Korea and Taiwan Province has been the ability to overcome coordination failures in investment (Rodrik, 1997).

Conversely, imbalances in the production system may lead to macroeconomic disequilibrium and instability. For instance, reliance on a narrow base of export products may have a direct impact on macroeconomic stability because of volatile terms of trade.

Differences in market and institutional maturity as well as in the degree of diversification of the economic structure produce sharp contrasts in macro/micro interactions between advanced industrial countries and developing countries and among developing countries. This entails much higher levels of economic and financial volatility in the last group.

The multiplier effect, a macro mechanism whereby an autonomous change in expenditure leads to a succession of induced changes, for instance, loses strength with the development of markets and institutions and the accumulation of wealth. With high savings capacity, unemployment insurance and access to credit, a transitory reduction in workers' income has a weaker effect on consumption than without them (Rodrik, 1997).[2]

The effects of devaluation is another example of how macro/micro interactions are affected by the structure of the economy. Other things being equal, when the most dynamic activities are export-oriented, a devaluation may have an expansive impact. When they are not, the impact may be recessive.

There are other ways in which institutional and market maturity and differences in economic structure make a difference. In advanced industrial countries, where the perceived risk of inflation is small, most debt is of relatively long maturity and denominated in the host currency. In developing countries and economies in transition, with a much shorter track record of sound monetary policy, shorter-dated debt denominated in hard currency tends to predominate (see Chapter 4). As a result, in the event of a financial crisis, a fixed exchange rate regime may force the government to raise interest rates to defend the currency, thus further damaging the banking sector. In developing countries and economies in transition a rise in short-term interest rates puts an almost immediate damper on demand. If a currency peg is abandoned, the cost of debt servicing rises dramatically, dampening demand and weakening enterprises' balance sheets. This is essentially what happened in the Mexican peso crisis of 1994–95, in Thailand in the summer of 1997 and in Brazil in January 1999. The triggering factors differed – fears of sovereign debt problems in Mexico, domestic banking difficulties in Thailand and domestic default in Brazil – but the sequence of the crises was similar: current account troubles and tumbling foreign-exchange reserves forced the currency to float.

The multiplicity of macro/micro feedback mechanisms means that their features are reciprocally determined. This precludes a clear-cut answer to the question of whether the causal link that goes from serious market failures to macro instability is stronger than the one that goes from macro instability to the lack of some key markets. This mutual causation explains why stabilization and economic reform tend to be components of an overall policy package. Rather than confusion, this circumstance calls for efforts to avoid lumping together such distinct policy areas, particularly in comparative analyses.

Key relative prices, such as exchange and interest rates, are important macro/micro transmission mechanisms. High real exchange and interest rates may hamper micro performance and, ultimately, undermine macro stability, for example through low export competitiveness leading to a growing trade deficit. Conversely, when export competitiveness is fostered through low real exchange and interest rates in the presence of fiscal profligacy and a low domestic savings rate, the ensuing macro instability may eventually trigger measures such as credit rationing and higher taxes that erode enterprises' competitiveness. Matters are made even worse if interest rates are high.

Because of this diverse macro/micro correspondence, micro policies that work under sound macro fundamentals may fail when such fundamentals are not in place; conversely, sound macro fundamentals may not be sustainable if coupled with wrong micro policies.

Failure to distinguish between macro and micro policies and their interactions leads to misattribution of causes. For example, import restrictions may cause resource misallocation but not necessarily lead to economic instability or a slow-down in long-term growth. Instead, overvalued exchange rates eventually lead to balance of payments crises, economic instability and deterioration in medium- to long-run economic performance. A negative relationship between exchange rate distortion and economic growth may hence have little or nothing to do with trade protection (Rodrik, 1997).

Micro distortions are often costly, as shown by the resource allocation costs of high protection. Yet positive externalities and absence of rent-seeking behaviour may warrant subsector specific subsidies. But large, sustained budget deficits are most likely to lead to balance of payments crises.

A benchmarking exercise that overlooks these key distinctions and links is bound to be of little value – when not plainly misleading.

LATIN AMERICA AND EAST ASIA: LEARNING FROM ONE ANOTHER

Differing paths

In 1965 Latin America and the Caribbean's average real per capita income (in terms of purchasing power) was almost twice that of East Asia. In 1997 it was about a quarter. In the 1960s, the average level of education in Latin America was slightly higher than that in other countries at a comparable stage of development. Today it is two years lower than average in similar developing countries and four years lower than in comparable East Asian countries.[3]

The comparison begs the question of what East Asian countries did right and Latin American countries did wrong. Is it an across-the-board contrast between orthodoxy and heterodoxy? Macro and micro orthodoxy – or the lack of them – may go hand in hand, but this is by no means always the case. One reason is that the meaning of microeconomic best practices is by no means as clear as that of macroeconomic best practices since the scope for institutional variety and policy discretion is far greater in the former case (see Chapter 2).

Conventional wisdom had it until recently that the foundation of the East Asian past success was market orientation and lean government.[4] The choice appeared to be simply between the failure of statist, inward-oriented policies, on the one hand, and the success of privately driven open-market policies, on the other. Yet, once the overall policy package is unbundled and the distinction between macro and micro policies drawn, explanations become less definitive as dichotomies internal to the respective models are revealed.

When Latin America was still questioning the benefits of trade during the 1960s and 1970s, East Asian countries were already on their way to showing that inward-oriented strategies were premised on an ill-founded export pessimism.

The persistence of macro imbalances probably played a larger role than micro inefficiencies in the failure of many import-substitution strategies pursued in Latin America. The debt crisis affected only those countries that lacked budget discipline (which is why it did not affect India and the Republic of Korea).

Doing the right things on the micro front did not prevent the Mexican crisis of December 1994 – January 1995, prompted by ill-managed macro policies: an overvalued exchange rate and domestic credit expansion. Yet the prevailing *ex post* rationalization of the debt crisis was that inward-oriented policies were to blame, rather than overspending and the erratic behaviour of the international capital markets (Rodrik, 1996, p. 15).

The pace of recent economic reform in Latin America has been quicker and its extent often gone considerably beyond that in East and South-East Asia to the extent that currently their respective courses are somewhat at odds (see Figure 6.1.).

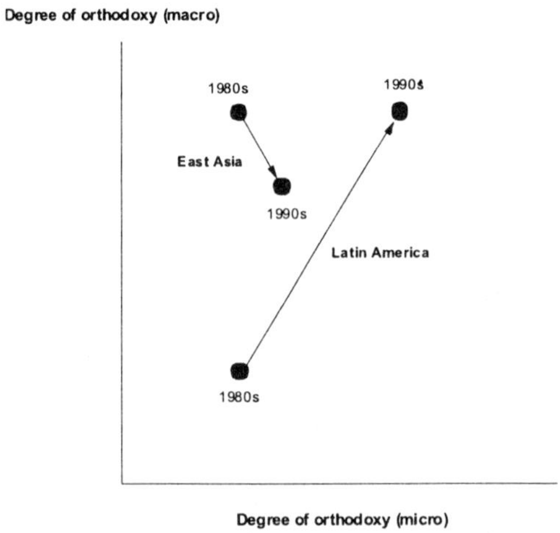

Figure 6.1 Stylized trends in macro- and microeconomic policies in East Asia and Latin America, 1980s–1990s

Before 1997, many of the policies that failed in Latin America succeeded in the Republic of Korea, Taiwan Province and Singapore. By the standards of the Washington consensus (see Box 6.1), the Republic of Korea and Taiwan Province scored high grades in macroeconomics and low in microeconomics. Although both employed fiscal restraint and competitive exchange rates, the Republic of Korea restricted FDI, restrained interest rates and subsidized credit while Taiwan Province gave priority to public enterprises in credit allocation. Neither liberalized imports until the 1980s. Both intervened in private investment decisions and relied heavily on SOEs during the 1960s. In short, although both countries practised macro orthodoxy on the fiscal and foreign exchange front and were thus able to avoid prolonged macroeconomic instability the 1980s, their micro experience diverged sharply from the orthodox path.[5]

Box 6.1 The 'Washington consensus'

Fiscal discipline

Budget deficits, properly measured to include those of provincial governments, state enterprises, and the central bank, should be small enough to be financed without recourse to inflation tax. This usually implies a primary surplus (that is, before adding debt service to expenditure) of several per cent of GDP, as well as an operational deficit, that is, disregarding that part of the interest bill that simply compensates for inflation, of up to about 2 per cent of GDP.

Public expenditure priorities

Policy reform consists in redirecting expenditure from politically sensitive areas, which typically receive more resources than their economic return can justify, such as administration, defence, indiscriminate subsidies and white elephants, towards neglected fields with high economic returns and potential to improve income distribution, such as primary health and education and infrastructure.

Tax reform

Tax reform involves broadening the tax base and cutting marginal tax rates. The aim is to sharpen incentives and improve horizontal equity without lowering realized progressivity. Improved tax administration, including subjecting interest income on assets held abroad – flight capital – to taxation, is an important aspect of broadening the base in the Latin American context.

Financial liberalization

The ultimate objective of financial liberalization is market-determined interest rates, but experience has shown that, under conditions of a chronic lack of confidence, such rates can be so high as to threaten the financial solvency of productive enterprises and government. Under such circumstances a sensible interim objective is the abolition of preferential interest rates for privileged borrowers and achievement of a moderately positive real interest rate.

Exchange rates
Countries need a unified exchange rate, at least for trade transactions, set at a level sufficiently competitive to induce a rapid growth in non-traditional exports and managed so as to assure exporters that this competitiveness will be maintained in the future.

Trade liberalization
Quantitative trade restrictions should be rapidly replaced by tariffs, and these should be progressively reduced until a uniform low tariff in the range of 10 per cent, or some 20 per cent at most, is achieved. There is, however, some disagreement about the speed with which tariffs should be reduced, with recommendations falling in a band between three and ten years, and about whether it is advisable to slow down the process of liberalization when macroeconomic conditions are adverse, such as with recession and payments deficit.

Foreign direct investment
Barriers impeding the entry of foreign firms should be abolished; foreign and domestic firms should be allowed to compete on equal terms.

Privatization
State enterprises should be privatized.

Deregulation
Governments should abolish regulations that impede the entry of new firms or restrict competition, as well as ensure that all regulations are justified by such criteria as safety, environmental protection, or prudential supervision of financial institutions.

Property rights
The legal system should provide secure property rights without excessive costs and make these available to the informal sector.

Source: Williamson (1994), pp. 26–28.

By contrast, the Latin American countries scored high in terms of the Washington Consensus during the last decade or so, on both accounts. In particular, Mexico, Bolivia and Argentina undertook more trade and financial liberalization and privatization within five years than the East Asian countries undertook in three decades (Rodrik, 1996).

Economic reform and relative prices: in search for sustainable success[6]

The potential for mutual learning between Latin America and East Asia in the area of macro/micro interactions is significant.

Economic reform programmes in Latin America are aimed at achieving and sustaining price stability and producing major structural reforms in the economy. Price-related measures include use of exchange rate as a nominal anchor of trade liberalization. This enables the government to keep a check on prices in markets exposed to import competition and reduce fiscal deficit to curb expansion in the money supply.

The key to structural reform is economic liberalization, used to enhance the efficiency and flexibility of the economy to allocate resources and achieve sustainable long-term growth. Though varying from country to country, trade policy is based on elimination of licences and other quantitative restrictions, substantial reduction of average tariffs and their range of variation, reduction or elimination of export taxes and deregulation and simplification of red tape in foreign trade.

Besides its open-door approach, the overall liberalization strategy includes privatization of inefficient, loss-making state-owned enterprises, elimination of restrictions on market entry or exit and removal of discretional tax and subsidy policies. It also comprises decisive steps towards the abolition of any kind of discrimination against foreign investment as a way of promoting capital accumulation as well as upgrading of organizational and technical practices.

Efficiency increases through these reform processes arise, on one hand, from static effects associated with better allocation of resources stemming from the removal of import-substitution policies and, on the other, from dynamic effects associated with the elimination of anti-export bias, which discourages innovation, cost rationalization, upgrading of technological skills and growth. Reform is also intended to discourage rent-seeking activities and improve the ability to absorb adverse exogenous shocks.

Significant achievements have already been attained. Thus, for instance, inflation rates have fallen dramatically, at a time of high growth by historical standards. In addition, the production system has been modernized and is now better able to cope with global competition.

Vulnerable points are not concealed, however, by the range of these achievements, particularly in those cases where success in reducing fiscal deficit has not been met. Among them, pride of place goes to distortions in relative prices associated with rises in real exchange rates and their impact on resource allocation. The trade-weighted real effective exchange rates of the eight largest Latin American countries appreciated steadily during the 1990s and by the mid-1990s were well below the 1986–89 average – except for Mexico, after the early 1995 devaluation (see Table 6.1).

Table 6.1 Latin America: trade-weighted real effective exchange rates in selected countries (1986–95; index 1990 = 100)

	1986-89 (average)	1990	1991	1992	1993	1994	1995
Argentina	126.6	100	73.4	64.6	59.0	58.1	57.7
Brazil	145.0	100	124.6	134.9	120.3	101.8	88.6
Chile	94.1	100	96.9	91.6	90.6	89.4	84.9
Colombia	82.2	100	96.7	88.6	84.4	75.4	74.6
Ecuador	85.5	100	95.3	94.7	82.3	77.7	79.1
Mexico	116.1	100	90.9	85.6	80.5	85.7	115.0
Peru	184.6	100	80.8	78.9	91.4	84.3	82.0
Uruguay	90.3	100	87.7	81.9	69.9	66.3	64.8

Source: Based on IDB (1996).

The objective of stabilization policies based on the use of the exchange rate as an anti-inflationary anchor is to make domestic and international inflation converge rapidly. Although feasible in certain circumstances, in practice this process takes a long time to work.

The domestic rate of inflation can be expressed as the weighted average of changes in the prices of two kinds of goods and services, that is tradable and non-tradable – whose relationship defines the real exchange rate. Since not all goods and services are equally exposed to external competition, an increase in demand, even if uniform, inclines relative prices in favour of those goods that are more protected.

Stabilization stimulates an increase in domestic demand in the short term. In an economy open to cross-border capital movements and where exchange parity is expected to remain unchanged, this process is fostered by capital inflows partly attracted by interest rate differentials. These differentials result from higher risk perceptions by international investors.

This type of expansion of domestic activity, characteristic of the first phases of anti-inflationary programmes, leads to a change in relative prices in favour of non-tradables. In economies with a history of high inflation, this change is accentuated by inertial price and wage indexation.[7]

The impact on relative prices is reflected in market shares. In Argentina, for example, the expansion of activity following the convertibility plan was coupled with a drop in the share of tradable in GDP at constant prices, from 37.2 per cent in 1990 to 34.3 per cent in 1994. Measured in relation to GDP at current prices, such a share went from 43.7 per cent in 1989 to 25.4 per cent in 1994. In both cases there was a slight recovery during the 1995 recession.[8]

With economic expansion, loss of international competitiveness in tradables eventually leads to a trade deficit – the flip side of increases in net external funding. Figure 6.2 shows the relatively import-driven opening up process in Argentina and Brazil in contrast to the relatively more export-driven strategies in East and South-East Asian countries.

A key component of this process at the micro level has been liberalization of capital good imports. Zero or near zero tariffs for capital goods, coupled with high social security charges, encouraged firms to substitute capital for labour in their investment plans.

If net external funding at low rates were to last indefinitely or were to be used to invest in the tradable sector of the economy, repayment capacity would be ensured and the problem of consistency not necessarily raised. However, since the former is unlikely and the latter is not the case, relative prices produce a mismatch in the distribution of profitability across sectors. The rates of return on non-tradables therefore well exceed tthose on tradables (ECOLATINA, 1997).

The 1990s have been, for the most part, a period of both rapid in consumption and decline in national savings in much of Latin America. The average share of savings in GDP declined from 20 per cent in the late 1980s to less than 17 per cent in 1993. Although there was some recovery in 1994 and 1995, the share remained below the rate recorded in the 1970s. Declines in private saving offset increases in public sector saving. Calculated in purchasing power parities, the average saving rate in Latin America is approximately half that in the East and South-East Asian countries, with Chile and the Philippines being exceptions in their respective subregions (see Table 6.2).

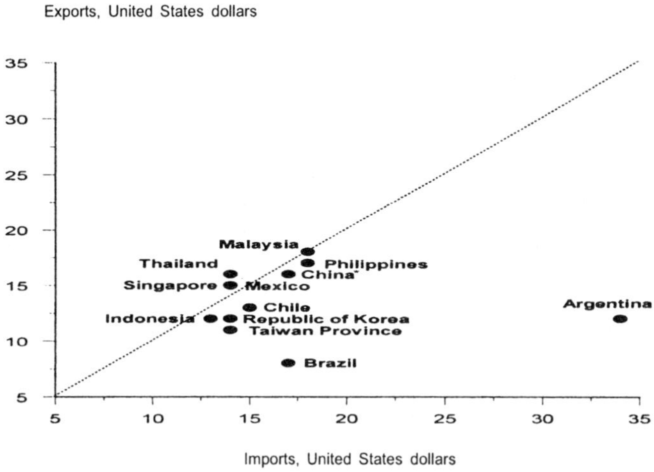

Notes: Annual average growth rates based on current United States dollars. Calculations for annual average growth rates for 1990–95: exports for Brazil and Chile; imports for Indonesia and Taiwan Province.
*For statistical purposes, data for China do not include those for Hong Kong Special Administration Region and Taiwan Province.

Source: UNIDO

Figure 6.2. Rates of growth in exports and imports in selected Latin American and South-East Asian countries, 1990–96

Table 6.2. Latin America and South-East Asia: investment share of GDP (1992, except indicated otherwise, at 1985 international prices)

Latin America			East and South-East Asia		
Argentina	11.5	(1990)	Indonesia	25.3	
Brazil	14.3		Malaysia	32.6	
Chile	27.0		Philippines	16.0	
Paraguay	17.2		Republic of Korea	39.1	(1991)
Uruguay	11.7		Singapore	36.2	
			Thailand	29.8	

Source: Penn World Tables Series Data.

Latin America's low and declining savings rates, coupled with increasing domestic investment, has led to a widening of current account deficits. Foreign investors have been called upon to finance the resulting shortfall (see Table 6.3).[9]

Table 6.3 Current account (CA) and capital account (KA) balances in selected Latin American countries (1990–95, in US$ billion)

	Argentina		Brazil		Chile		Colombia		Mexico		Total	
	CA	KA	CA	KA	CA	KA	CA	KA	CA	KA	CA	KA
1990	4.6	−1.9	−3.8	5.4	−0.5	3.0	0.5	. .*	−7.5	8.5	−6.4	15.0
1991	−0.6	3.6	−1.5	0.8	0.1	0.8	2.3	−0.8	−15.0	25.2	−15.0	29.0
1992	−6.5	11.0	6.1	10.4	−0.7	2.9	0.9	0.2	−24.0	27.0	−24.0	51.5
1993	−7.5	9.9	−7.5	10.0	−2.1	2.6	−2.1	2.7	−23.0	33.8	−35.0	59.0
1994	−9.3	9.9	−1.2	8.9	−0.8	4.4	−3.0	3.1	−29.0	12.8	−43.0	39.1
1995	−2.3	2.2	−18.0	29.3	0.2	1.2	−4.2	4.5	−0.7	15.3	−23.0	52.2

*Negligible amount.

Source: IDB, 1996.

Pegged exchange rates may be necessary for some time to keep domestic inflation in check. When coupled with low savings rates and heavy reliance on capital inflows, however, they are bound to exert increasing pressure on foreign accounts.

During 1990–95 more than two-thirds of FDI inflows to Brazil went to the service sector, thus generating little or no exports. In 1995–96 exports accounted for barely 10 per cent of sales by foreign manufacturing subsidiaries. For United States subsidiaries such a proportion represents some half of their worldwide average or 17 per cent compared with 30-40 per cent. It was higher than Mexico's in 1977 and about equal in 1982 and has remained half ever since 1986. FDI-related intermediate and capital goods imports and profit remittances abroad have increased five-fold from 1996 to 1997. Thus FDI is unlikely to help much to bridge the foreign account gap in the medium term, even in the absence of an international liquidity crisis (Ricupero, 1997). Policies to improve competitiveness by means other than devaluation has been the route chosen by Argentina in recent years and by Brazil until 13 January 1999. These policies are aimed at increasing productivity, changing the tax regime by switching from direct to indirect taxes and deregulating and privatizing in order to reduce costs. They are predicated, on the macro front, on a consolidation of fiscal equilibrium and, on the micro front, on the removal of long-standing inefficiencies in physical and social infrastructure.

At the beginning of the reform programmes it was expected that the wider and more rapid the opening of the economy to trade and financial flows, the greater its favourable impact on resource allocation, both from the static viewpoint and from the perspective of capital accumulation.

In practice, however, rapid economic opening up coupled with a lack of adequate financial instruments for the transition and in the context of anti-export bias in relative prices, has eliminated a large number of employment-intensive firms, particularly SMIs. Many of these might have proved viable, given time and the tools to restructure coupled with non-biased relative prices at the time of the opening of the economy. Policies often fell short of avoiding high adjustment costs, which markets by themselves could not prevent.[10]

High international liquidity in the early 1990s proved to be a double-edged sword. Although it did enhance the effectiveness of policy reform in reconciling stability and in the medium term, it also amplified potential sustainability problems, particularly on the external front.[11]

The recent experience of the Association of South-East Asian Nations (ASEAN) countries and that of Brazil invite us to focus attention on non-traumatic exit strategies for the relative price conundrum described above. A pegged exchange rate may be useful to stop intractable inflationary problems for some time, as in the MERCOSUR countries. Inflation has been consistently lower in countries with fixed exchange rates than floating ones, although no clear relationship with economic rates has been found (IMF, 1997).

Yet ASEAN countries' currency run in mid-1997 showed that volatility inherent in high cross-border capital mobility may lead to unwelcome adjustments when coupled with domestic demand, fiscal pressures and weak domestic banking systems. Slippages in micro fundamentals – resource misallocation and declining rates of return through a myopic perception of risks, excessive leverage and overinvestment – coupled with macro vulnerabilities are at the core of the problem.[12]

The ASEAN countries' deteriorating trade performance during 1996–97 was triggered by exogenous factors such as worsening conditions in key export markets, for example, increased competition from China in labour-intensive subsectors as well as in electronics, telecommunications equipment and machinery, and the strengthening of the United States dollar. Uncertainty about the overall economic outlook, in turn, had already prompted incipient short-term capital outflows in 1996.

Uncertainties on the external front, coupled with fiscal overruns, asset inflation and weaknesses in the banking system, eventually led to a turmoil in currency markets that region-wide interest rate hikes proved unable to offset. During the year ending 10 September 1997, the pegs were abandoned in one country after another with devaluations of 35 per cent in Thailand, 25 per cent in Indonesia, 23 per cent in the Philippines and 17 per cent in Malaysia. The solution was a renewed effort to keep fiscal accounts in line, consolidate the banking system and eventually accept a slowing-down in .[13]

One of the lessons from the recent ASEAN experience is that in times of great liquidity, investors' risk aversion relaxes a great deal and high-risk projects with high expected returns are flooded with capital. [14] This applies to foreign and domestic investors alike. For instance, during the recent currency crisis, many large Malaysian companies have run into heavy losses for not having hedged liabilities denominated in foreign currency.

In the face of exogenous events, such as an increase in the prime United States dollar lending rate, a sustained current account deficit of more than 3 per cent may put macroeconomic stability to the test. Excessive reliance on volatile short-term capital flows is inadvisable even, or rather particularly, in the era of globalization.

Avoiding the traumatic exit strategies from exchange pegs that plagued the ASEAN countries in 1997 is high on Latin America's agenda. This is ratified by the collapse of the Brazilian foreign exchange regime in 1999. If protectionism and a slow-down in growth are to be avoided, the only strategy is to continue increasing the overall productivity of the economies and, with it, export competitiveness in order to make an overvalued exchange rate unnecessary.

CLOSING REMARKS

By and large, the East Asian countries managed for a long period to avoid the failure of heterodox micro policies, which has proved unfeasible nearly everywhere else. Such policies largely avoided being undermined by rent-seeking behaviour and overcame constraints associated with the lack of disciplined bureaucracies and private sectors over a substantive period.

Part of the past success is owed to the imposition of strict performance standards that prevented individual rent-seeking from hindering enterprises' competitive performance to the extent often observed in Latin America (as revealed by the expression 'rich entrepreneurs, poor companies').

More basic, perhaps, were certain special initial conditions such as a labour force much better educated than would have been predicted on the basis of its income levels, and income and wealth distribution exceptionally equal by cross-country standards by the early 1960s. The first condition gave rise to a competent bureaucracy and enhanced the productivity of interventions aimed at boosting private investment. The second condition facilitated better governance by focusing on economic goals and avoiding redistributive policies.

Coupled with such favourable initial conditions, high savings rates and rapid physical and human capital formation and technological learning rates promoted by activist policies in a stable, market-oriented environment fostered a quick catching-up with the advanced industrial countries.

NOTES

1. Economics does not offer an integrated macro/micro theory. The macro/micro link is usually examined in the literature on the 'micro-foundations of macroeconomics' where, in the search for a unified theory, an effort is made to derive the most important propositions of macroeconomics from individual conduct within a given micro set-up (resources, technology, preferences and market structure). This approach, however, raises more doubts than it resolves. For instance, it does not account for unemployment or the influence of the money supply on the overall level of activity (Frenkel, 1995).
2. The multiplier effect was a distinct mechanism in the United States during the 1930s. Doubts were voiced in the early 1960s, however, as to whether it still operated at all.
3. The economic prospects of East Asian countries seemed dismal in the early 1960s. Saving and investment rates were very low and growth was slow. External assessments at the time were pessimistic relative to those for Latin America and Africa (Collins and Bosworth, 1966, p. 173).
4. Korea and Taiwan Province had already introduced vast reforms in the late 1950s and early 1960s. Abrupt financial liberalization in the absence of a sound regulatory and prudential framework facilitated the financial turmoil of 1997 by stimulating the mismatch between the of unhedged short-term borrowing abroad and that of long-term lending at home.
5. It has been pointed out that Hong Kong SAR is the only East Asian territory to have had an 'unadulterated laissez-faire attitude to microeconomic policy' (Rodrik, 1997). It has also been argued that the so-called Washington consensus (see Box 6.1) took privatization and trade liberalization as ends in themselves, rather than as means to more sustainable, equitable and democratic growth, and that it focused too much on price stability, rather than growth and output stability. It also overlooked the fact that strengthening financial institutions is as important to economic stability as controlling budget deficit and the money supply. While focusing on privatization, it paid too little attention to the institutional infrastructure required to make markets work and the importance of competition. See Stiglitz, (1998).

6. On the theme of this section see Machinea, 1996.
7. These trends were observed in the stabilization plans implemented by Latin American countries at the end of the 1970s, occurred again in Argentina, Brazil and Mexico in the mid-1980s, and have appeared once again in recent stabilization programmes. In contrast to the programmes of the 1980s, which had to cope with severe international liquidity shortages, those of the late 1970s and early 1990s took place in a context of high international liquidity, which gave rise to a greater exchange rate appreciation.
8. The drop in the share of tradables in GDP that follows a change in relative prices has little to do with the decreasing share of tradables in advanced industrial countries' GDP, where it results from maturing productive structures and high per capita income levels rather than abrupt appreciations of the exchange rate.
9. Preliminary findings suggest that domestic investment may have a closer correlation to foreign capital inflows than to the national savings rate (quoted in Pettis, 1996).
10. The other major problem of current policies lies in the social area. It is expressed in high unemployment, precarious employment and growing income and wealth differentials (including a skewed distribution of human capital). Some two-fifths of the labour force in many Latin American countries work in low-quality jobs. This is linked to negative employment growth due to the increasing substitution of capital for labour and a considerable decline in the number of employment-intensive SMIs. Being relatively free from pressures on income distribution is one of the major advantages of South-East Asia over Latin America in the search for macroeconomic stability.
11. Stanley Fisher recently observed: 'capital movements normally reflect correct perceptions on policy weaknesses (although) not always markets are right. There may be over-reactions owing to lack of information or the market's "herd spirit". Countries may be subject to sudden changes in market sentiment, sometimes without good reasons. The way to counteract these risks may consist of the use of capital controls. In some cases a selective restriction to certain types of capital may be justified although, preferably, market instruments should be used' (Fisher, 1997). Brazil failed to balance its public accounts and fell into domestic default. This, added to the wariness of international risk investors, the fall in the terms of trade and growing trade deterioration associated with the East Asian crisis, eventually led to the breakdown of the economic programme.
12. Structural problems such as skill shortages and excess capacity in automobiles, steel, chemicals and appliance industries are being addressed.
13. Large infrastructure projects deferred include: the M$ 20 billion (US$6.8 billion) new administrative capital of Malaysia (heart of the multimedia super-corridor), the M$ 13.6 billion (US$4.6 billion) Bakun Dam, the northern regional international airport in Kedah, and the KL linear city (a 2 km-long building over a river in Kuala Lumpur) in Malaysia, and the US$3.7 billion road and rail system through central Bangkok, and six power projects worth some US$6bn in Thailand. Indonesia also decided to postpone US$14.3 billion government spending, on power plants, toll roads and oil refineries.
14. It has been pointed out that, 'All Latin American booms have had in common the conditions of excess global liquidity resulting in capital inflows, and high or stable commodity prices. Whether the regime was pro-market or interventionist seems to have mattered less' (Pettis, 1996). In South-East Asia weak banks, poor supervisory controls and lax corporate governance amplified the consequences of exposing the economies to the vagaries of speculative international capital flows.

REFERENCES

Collins, S.M. and B.P. Bosworth (1996): 'Economic in East Asia: accumulation versus assimilation', Brookings Papers on Economic Activity, no. 2.

ECOLATINA (1997), private communication.

Fisher, S. (1997), quoted in *Folha de São Paulo*, digital issue, 13 September.

Frenkel, R. (1995), 'Macroeconomic sustainability and development prospects : Latin American performance in the 1990s', Discussion Paper no. 100, UNCTAD, August.

IDB (1996): *Inter-American Development Bank, Economic and Social Progress in Latin America – 1996 Report*, Washington. DC: IDB.

IMF (1997), *World Economic Outlook,* September.

Machinea, J.L. (1996), *Políticas de Desarrollo Industrial en la Era de la Globalización: Nuevos Desafíos y Oportunidades para los Países en Desarrollo,* Vienna: UNIDO, November.

Pettis, M. (1996), 'The liquidity trap – Latin America's free-market past', *Foreign Affairs*, November/December.

Ricupero, R. (1997), 'Carta aos leitores', *Folha de São Paolo,* 13 September.

Rodrik, D. (1996), 'Understanding economic policy reform', *Journal of Economic Literature*, **34,** March, 9–41.

Rodrik, D. (1997), 'TFPG controversies, institutions and economic performance in East Asia', CFPR Discussion Paper no. 1587, March.

Sarel, M. (1997), 'Growth and productivity in ASEAN countries', IMF Working Paper, August.

Stiglitz, J. (1996), 'Some lessons from the East Asian miracle', *World Bank Research Observer*, **11** (2), August, 151-177.

Stiglitz, J. (1998), 'More instruments and broader goals: moving towards the post-Washington consensus', WIDER Annual Lecture, Helsinki, January.

Williamson, J. (ed.) (1994), *The Political Economy of Policy Reform,* Washington, DC: Institute for International Economics.

PART III

COUNTRIES AND REGIONS

Overview of Part III

Part III provides overviews of the different country groupings examined in this book as well as country case studies for each grouping. As far as possible, the country chapters have followed a common approach in order to facilitate comparability. Basically, this common approach consists of placing the challenges and policies in the field of industrial development and manufacturing competitiveness in the context of macroeconomic and institutional conditions and reviewing their mutual interactions. As most of these chapters were completed by early 1997, emphases would have been different had they been written today. Yet risk elements are pointed out which, in a way, were pre-announcing underlying vulnerabilities. The medium and long-term issues on which this book is focused will no doubt return to the focus of attention of policy makers as soon as the heat of the shocks recedes, this time under a different light (see the conclusions to Chapter 2).

COMPARATIVE OVERVIEW

Chapter 7 examines the most distinctive features of the four country groupings. For example, it highlights the fact that up to the mid-1990s, the contribution of gains in total factor productivity growth to output per worker *vis-à-vis* that of increased physical capital and education per worker was, in most newly industrializing economies, considerably more substantial than in the industrial countries. This evidence goes to the core of the debate between those who place microeconomic policy on a rather low level in the policy hierarchy and those who see it as a vital ingredient of the policy mix. The changing effectiveness of specific policy instruments in the light of changing strategies among the newly opened economies is also discussed. Chapter 7 in addition underscores inter-country commonalities and differences in the process of economic and social transformation of countries with economies in transition in Central and Eastern Europe. It also deals with the low wage/low productivity trap in less developed countries as well as with the perhaps even more important dilemma of the existence of markets that are handicapped because the state is unable to strengthen them and a state that is handicapped because incomplete or absent markets prevent a rational allocation of resources. Chapter 7 closes by providing evidence on convergence and divergence between developing and transition economies, on the one hand, and advanced industrial countries, on the other.

NEWLY INDUSTRIALIZING ECONOMIES: THE REPUBLIC OF KOREA

The pre-1997 crisis period is now regarded in the Republic of Korea as 'the spendthrift era of the past'. In 1998 the economy fell into recession for the first time in 18 years. The US$58 billion IMF bail-out loan in late 1997 entailed steep rises in interest rates, stringent money markets and the start of a wholesale restructuring of the financial and corporate sectors. The economy started a fragile recovery in 1999 with an expected GDP growth of 2 per cent from a 5 per cent contraction in 1988.[1] Although a soft landing is expected for 2000, a long period of rehabilitation lies ahead. The onset of a new economic paradigm compatible with international standards is not expected to take place within less than five years.

The crisis has triggered a long-due redefinition of *chaebols'* core businesses in automobiles, electronics and semiconductors, including a radical scale-back in the number of subsidiaries. This includes the swap of Samsung Motors for Daewoo Electronics and Hyundai's takeover of KIA and LG Semicon, including one of the latter's two UK plants. Daewoo and Hyundai would become the only automobile producers in the Republic of Korea, with a capacity of 1.5 and 2 million vehicles per year, respectively. *Chaebols* are also in the process of drastically cutting the number of subsidiaries. These moves are being slowed down and at times arrested by inherent hurdles to such big deals and a tradition of corporate governance that is now under revision. The government is exerting strong pressure on *chaebols*' management to accomplish this.[2]

Chapter 8 is focused on Republic of Korea's industrial development policy up to 1996. However, it provides a number of hints on what might have gone – and did in fact go – wrong. These refer, in particular, to weaknesses in corporate governance and in the financial system and mismatches between microeconomic and macroeconomic policies. Chapter 8 highlights, for instance, how *chaebols*' rapid growth through diversification, cross-shareholding and mutual repayment guarantees among subsidiaries as well as government's implicit commitment to rescue failed target projects led to exceedingly high financial leverage and market distortions. The lack of transparency intrinsic to a highly asymmetrical and uncompetitive financial system, with the ensuing large backlog of actual and potential non-performing loans, is also stressed. Even the soundest macroeconomic fundamentals could not offset the harmful consequences of these distortions.

NEWLY OPENED ECONOMIES: THE CASE OF BRAZIL

After four successful years and with hyperinflation defeated, the plan for the Brazilian currency, the real, came to an end on 15 January 1999. By then, after having spent some US$30 billion in reserves to defend the currency, the government had little choice but to float it. As in the Republic of Korea, a policy of high interest rates to discourage capital outflows, in this case accompanied by severe fiscal restrain, led the Brazilian economy into a sharp recession. Brazil's economic plunge in 1999 is likely to trigger the sharpest Latin American downturn since 1982.[3] Indeed, 1998 was already the worst of the previous seven years for Brazilian industry.

In the context of a traditionally tightly closed economy, the crisis is likely to entail setbacks in an arduous process of economic integration with the world market. Yet pressures towards a return to self-reliance will be counteracted by a significant part of the economy that benefited from the diffusion of best international practices that took place over the 1990s throughout industry, as Chapter 9 vividly illustrates. This chapter also shows the dramatic improvements that Brazil made in microeconomic fundamentals as opposed to macroeconomic fundamentals. Thus, while productivity and quality improvements were being diffused across industry, the fiscal deficit became a major obstacle to efforts to ensure macroeconomic stability. Along with most of the developing world, the Brazilian economy also suffered the deleterious impact of historically low commodity prices and the aftershocks of the East Asian crisis in the shape of higher financial costs, worsening terms of trade and a deterioration of price competitiveness – partially offset by a steep devaluation.

Annex 9B briefly examines the policy reform experience in Argentina. Annex 9C discusses implementation bottlenecks in industrial competitiveness policies in Latin America.

HUNGARY

Chapter 10 deals with the pervasive interactions and rich interfaces between micro and macro policies in the light of the Hungarian experience. In particular, it probes the actual implications of policies that, although intended to be neutral across sectors, actually have differential effects owing to the varying specific weight of foreign investment, extent of reliance on domestic supplier networks and export propensity across sectors.

From the policy and institutional perspectives, Hungary is well on its way to overcoming the most difficult phases of the transition to a market economy and looks forward to its accession to the European Union. Yet, like the Republic of Korea and Brazil, Hungary has to pursue structural reform and macroeconomic stability within a highly adverse international economic environment. Despite a major modernization of its financial, trade and tax regimes, attaining macroeconomic equilibrium proved an elusive target over the 1990s, with negative spillovers on enterprise reform. Crisis management prevailed at the expense of emphasis on growth and productivity through industrial restructuring, regional development, SMI and technology promotion and upgraded standards of industrial development policy making.

Annex 10A reviews recent changes in Hungary's tax code.

UNITED REPUBLIC OF TANZANIA

Least developed countries are most exposed to the social costs resulting from external shocks and natural disasters, and this fact stresses the importance of domestic policies aimed at creating sustainable sources of livelihood for their populations by mobilizing domestic resources.

Commodity prices have reached record lows during the late 1990s. Sub-Saharan African countries are bearing the brunt of the ensuing damage since three-quarters of its export revenues depend on commodities. The fall owes a great deal to improved technologies in advanced countries. For this reason, global commodity prices may never fully recover. Commodity prices were already on their way down when the Asian crisis hit in mid-1997. The crises of the late 1990s have simply accelerated the decline.

The United Republic of Tanzania has made important strides towards economic reform. Levels of protection have been drastically lowered and privatization has been central to efforts aimed at reversing manufacturing decline and boosting economic growth. Chapter 11 provides important insights on the interaction between macro and micro policies in the United Republic of Tanzania over the 1990s, including original research results on the impact of trade liberalization on specific manufacturing activities. It also reviews the whole range of policies bearing upon the evolution of manufacturing competitiveness in Tanzanian enterprises.

Annex 11A provides an overview of success and failure in policy reform in the least developed countries.

ASEAN AND MERCOSUR

The dynamism of the two most vibrant cases of regional economic integration in the developing world, that is, ASEAN and MERCOSUR, has been stalled by successive East Asian, Russian and Brazilian crises. These regional schemes were not prepared to deal with abrupt changes in relative prices and the contagion effects from currency and financial runs. As a result trade flows were disrupted and defensive steps encouraged. The need for better coordination in both the micro- and the macroeconomic fields is one of the key lessons drawn. Chapter 12 highlights important dimensions of the remarkable progress made before the onset of the East Asian crisis.

NOTES

1. Inflation is expected to reach 3 per cent and the budget deficit 5 per cent in 1999. Some positive signs by early 1999 were: (i) stabilization of the currency and rising foreign reserves; (ii) low interest rates; (iii) record trade surplus, expected to exceed US$20 billion, due largely to low imports (the trade account went from a deficit of US$8.5 billion in 1997 to a surplus of US$39.9 billion in 1998, with a reduction in both imports and exports of 35.5 and 2.2 per cent, respectively); (iv) surge in foreign portfolio and FDI and (V) restoration of investment grade for sovereign debt. Negative signs include: (i) high unemployment (it may well go up from 8 per cent in 1998 to 10 per cent in 1999 as a result of company restructuring and consolidations; in 1998 alone 13 per cent of the total number of bank branches were closed down; the leading banks, most of them nationalized, experienced record losses and laid off 30 per cent of their personnel); (ii) falling real wages (the average Korean worker saw his or her salary drop from US$9624 per year to US$6400–US$6700 by the end of 1998). (iii) sluggish exports and consumer spending; and (iv) excessive corporate debt (in 1998 24 600 enterprises went bankrupt and 10 out of the top 30 conglomerates either declared insolvency or asked for government assistance).
2. A new code of corporate ethics is being promoted by the government which will feature recommendable corporate governance structures and business practices focused on the need for transparency.

3. By mid-February 1999 short-term interest rates in Brazil had shot up to about 40 per cent, and long-term debt carried a rate of 15.7 per cent. Concerns about Brazil pushed up interest rates elsewhere in Latin America as well. Unemployment, which reached 10 per cent in January 1999, was expected to increase substantially thereafter.

7. Overview of Countries and Regions

INTRODUCTION

Chapter 2 examined the impetus towards policy convergence stemming from globalization together with some contrasting trends towards differentiation among countries and regions. This chapter examines these trends in greater depth by assessing the widening gaps in economic performance among developing countries and economies in transition as well as respective policy challenges.

Taking into account initial conditions, past policy thrust and actual performance, sharply contrasting policy challenges can be identified among four groups of countries: (i) newly industrializing economies (NIEs), (ii) newly opened economies (NOEs), (iii) transition economies (TEs) and (iv) less developed countries (LDCs).[1]

Non-OECD countries increased their share of world GDP by a third between 1970 and 1995. Within this group of countries, as Table 7.1 and Figure 7.1 illustrate, the most dramatic increase was experienced by newly industrializing economies, whose share of the group rose from 10 per cent to almost a quarter. None the less, newly opened economies remained the largest non-OECD country grouping, followed by economies in transition. The share of less developed countries was static.

Figure 7.2 shows the frequency distribution of GDP growth among the four groupings during 1985–95. The statistical mode of the annual rate of growth among newly industrializing economies is 6–8 per cent, against 2–4 per cent for newly opened economies and less developed countries and negative for economies in transition. The performance gap across groupings from 1998 onwards will decrease as a result of the recession under way in East Asia and Latin America.

Figure 7.3 reports on the evolution of the share of MVA in GDP since 1970. Newly opened economies exhibit a declining trend since the mid-1970s. The opposite is the case among newly industrializing economies, where manufacturing became more important than among newly opened economies by the late 1970s, a gap that has kept widening. Manufacturing

Table 7.1 GDP by country grouping, 1970, 1980, 1990 and 1995

Country groupings or countries	GDP (million US$)				Average annual growth rates			Percentage share to total country groupings			
	1970	1980	1990	1995	1970–80	1980–90	1990–95	1970	1980	1990	1995
World	10 993 966	15 671 361	20 695 376	22 754 016	3.61	2.82	1.91	100.0	100.0	100.0	100.0
OECD	9 256 553	12 648 417	16 560 836	17 971 776	3.17	2.73	1.65	84.20	80.71	80.02	78.98
Non-OECD	1 737 413	3 022 944	4 134 540	4 782 240	5.69	3.18	2.95	15.80	19.29	19.98	21.02
Economies in transition	476 121	820 695	1 179 523	1 194 731	5.60	3.69	0.26	4.33	5.24	5.70	5.25
Newly opened economies	662 060	1 074 659	1 344 305	1 588 850	4.96	2.26	3.40	6.02	6.86	6.50	6.98
Newly industrializing economies	181 215	397 771	797 837	1 114 965	8.18	7.21	6.92	1.65	2.54	3.86	4.90
Less developed countries	160 223	232 954	330 323	370 141	3.81	3.55	2.30	1.46	1.49	1.60	1.63
Other	257 794	496 866	482 552	513 553	6.78	–0.29	1.25	2.34	3.17	2.33	2.26

Source: UNIDO database.

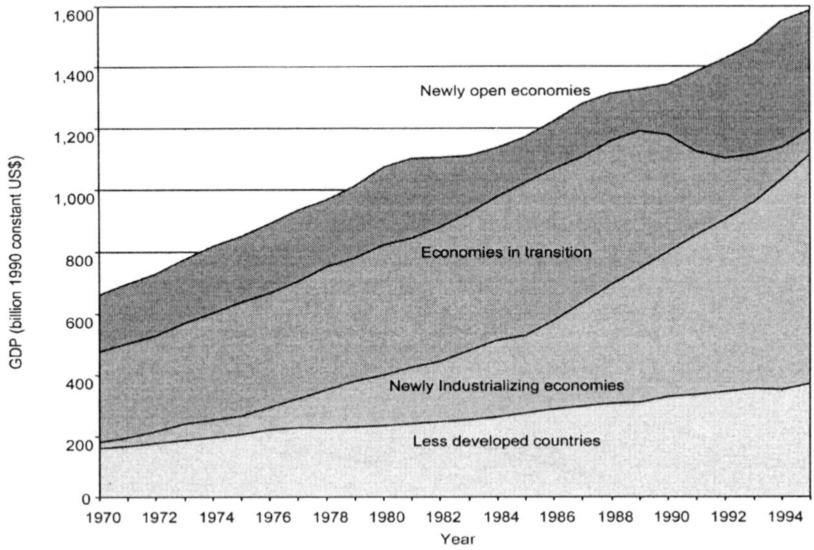

Source: UNIDO

Figure 7.1 GDP by country grouping, 1970-95

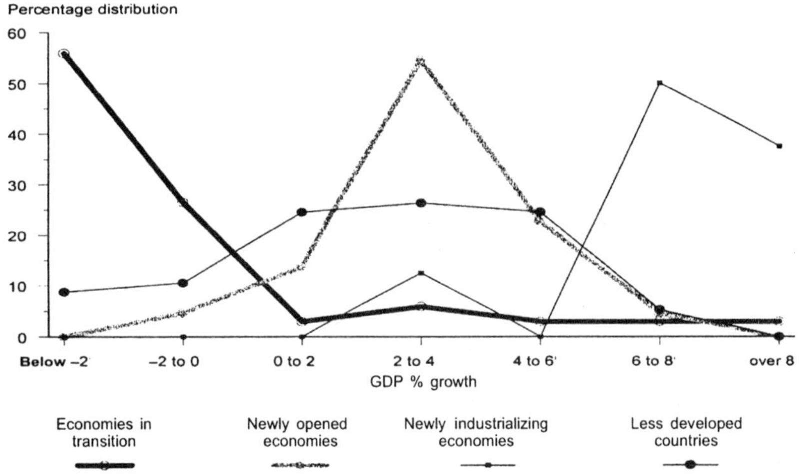

Note: Calculations based on 1990 constant US dollars.

Source: UNIDO database

Figure 7.2 Frequency distribution of GDP growth rates, 1985–95

remains most significant among economies in transition and least significant among less developed countries whose share actually declined during early 1990s.

These contrasts in performance are associated with differences in the efficiency of allocating resources. Trends in productivity provide the best comparative indicator on how the ability to generate wealth has evolved over time.

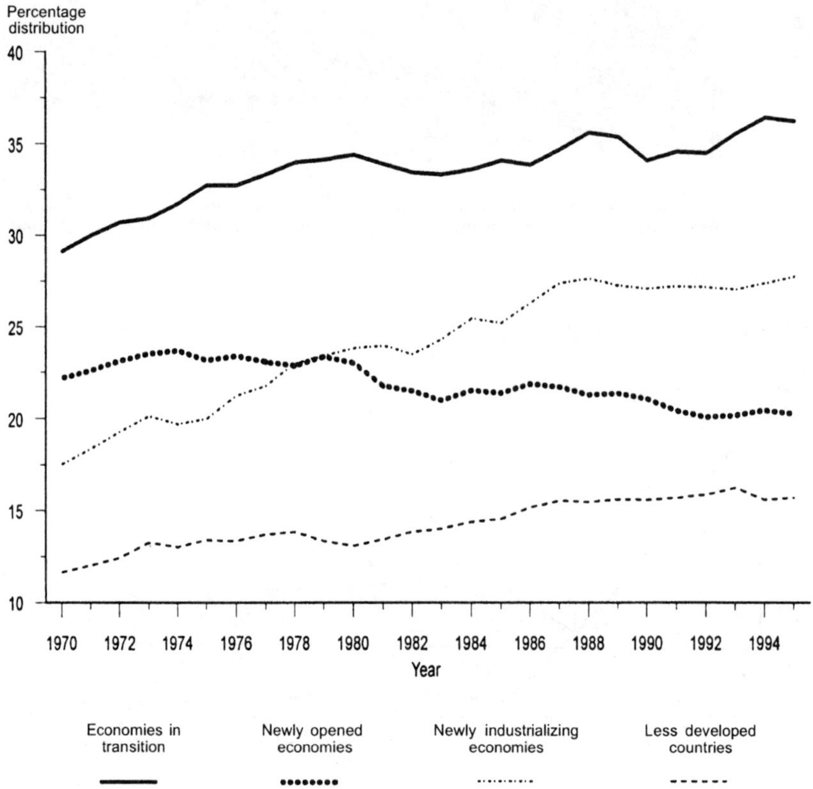

Note: Calculations are based on 1990 constant US$.

Source: UNIDO database.

Figure 7.3. MVA share in GDP, 1970–95

Figure 7.4 reports on the performance of output per worker and its components during 1973–85 and 1984–94 by region. East and South Asia, led by China, was the only region in the developing world that increased the rate of growth of output per worker between those two periods from a level already very high by world standards. By contrast, Latin America, Africa and the Middle East suffered negative or stagnated rates from relatively very low levels. As a result, interregional gaps in productivity performance broadened considerably between both periods. In comparison with East and South Asia, advanced industrial countries recorded a mediocre performance, with a substantial improvement in the United States and a slight deterioration in other advanced industrial countries.[2]

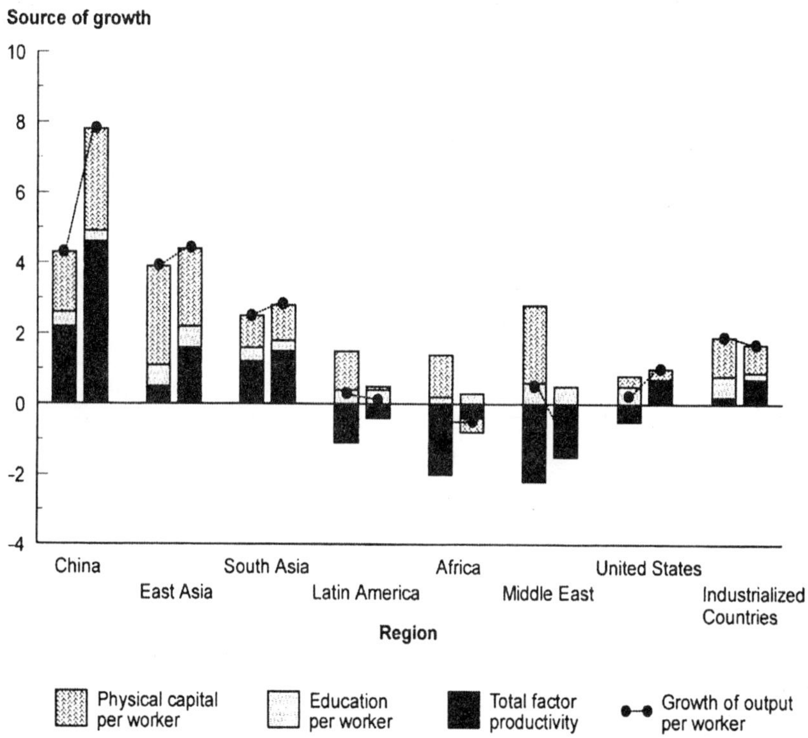

Source: Based on Collins and Bosworth (1996).

Figure 7.4 Sources of growth by region, 1973–84 and 1984–94

TFP growth played a significant role as a source of changes in output per worker among high performers during 1984–94. Its importance in East and South Asian countries was much lower than in the United States. Yet, compared with the contribution of physical and human capital, the role of TFP growth in those countries was similar to that for the average of advanced industrial nations, excluding the United States – 35–58 per cent as against 41 per cent. Furthermore, absolute TFP performance in East and South Asia has been substantially better than in advanced industrial nations and the United States, suggesting catching-up in productivity.

There are wide variations in the contribution of physical and human capital to growth in output per worker. Human capital accumulation has been less important than physical capital accumulation and TFP growth everywhere, except in Latin America, the Middle East and Africa, where physical capital accumulation and TFP growth were deterred by poor or negative overall performance. Physical capital accumulation is the major, and comparably important, single source of growth in output per worker in both East Asia and advanced industrial countries, except the United States. In absolute terms, physical and human capital accumulation are more important in East and South Asia and China, than in the United States and other advanced industrial countries (Table 7.2).

Table 7.2 World: growth in output, physical capital and education per worker (1984–94, annual averages)

Region	Output	Physical capital	Human capital
China	8.0	2.9	0.3
East Asia	4.4	2.2	0.6
South Asia	2.7	1.0	0.3
Africa	–0.6	–0.4	0.3
Middle East	–1.1	0	0.5
Latin America	0.1	0.1	0.4
United States	0.9	0.3	0
Other industrial countries	1.7	0.8	0.2

Source: Collins and Bosworth (1996).

Social conditions have deteriorated in a group of 30 countries comprising mostly less developed countries in sub-Saharan Africa and countries in

Eastern Europe and the Commonwealth of Independent States during the early 1990s. The social gap between this group and the rest has widened, largely as a result of significant falls in life expectancy or in real GDP per capita (UNDP, 1997, p. 46).[3]

Underlying this diversity in economic and social performance are fundamental differences in initial conditions and economic and social performance which, in turn, pose substantially diverse policy challenges. The following sections discuss the specific nature of these challenges from an industrial development perspective. Illustrative country case studies for each of the four groupings are presented in Chapters 8–11.

NEWLY INDUSTRIALIZING ECONOMIES

Key Characteristics

This group comprises the classic four Asian tigers – Republic of Korea, Hong Kong Special Administrative Region, Singapore and Taiwan Province – as well as the ASEAN-4 – Indonesia, Malaysia, Thailand and the Philippines. This section examines some important intra-group commonalities and differences and then discusses changes in endogenous and exogenous factors that led to the emergence of the new policy challenges faced by the members of the group.

Up to the 1997 crisis, newly industrializing economies were characterized by a blend of common elements unique in the developing world. These included:[4]

1. manufacturing-led, rapid, steady growth;
2. high saving and investment rates;
3. emphasis on physical and human capital accumulation;
4. high degree of government–private sector cooperation;
5. manufacturing export orientation favoured by absence of anti-export bias;
6. rapid structural change;[5]
7. relatively low incidence of redistributive pressures;
8. long record of sound macroeconomic/heterodox microeconomic policy mix;[6]
9. skilled and relatively insulated government bureaucracy;
10. performance-driven industrial policy.

In the early 1960s, most of these distinctive features did not exist. They were the outcome, to a large extent, of deliberate steps to switch towards a high growth pattern since that time. For instance, although the Republic of Korea and Taiwan Province started from a relatively advantageous base in terms of education and income distribution, in the early 1960s the share of exports and investment in GDP was 2 per cent and 10 per cent for the Republic of Korea and 10 per cent and 15 per cent for Taiwan Province, respectively. Their per capita income was comparable to that of several sub-Saharan countries at the time (see Rodrik, 1994 and Chapter 8 for the case of the Republic of Korea).

Along with the common features, several important contrasts, some of which have grown increasingly blurred, are evident in regard to policy approach and structural traits:

- emphasis on FDI-driven technological learning and skill formation as opposed to arm's-length acquisition and domestic R&D (Malaysia, Thailand and Singapore versus the Republic of Korea and Taiwan Province);
- use of SOEs to further industrial development policy as opposed to exclusive reliance on private enterprises (Indonesia and Malaysia versus Hong Kong Special Administrative Region);
- focus on large conglomerates, as opposed to SMIs (Republic of Korea versus Taiwan Province);
- emphasis on firm-centred as opposed to infrastructure-focused technological development (Republic of Korea versus Taiwan Province);
- reliance on domestic as opposed to international supplier networks (Republic of Korea versus Thailand);
- targeted versus free trade policies (Republic of Korea versus Hong Kong Special Administrative Region);
- first-tier newly industrializing economies enjoy a clear head start in human capital accumulation with respect to the ASEAN-4;
- resource endowment: Indonesia, Malaysia, Philippines – resource rich; Republic of Korea, Taiwan Province and Singapore – resource poor; Philippines – net emigration; Thailand and Malaysia – net immigration; Republic of Korea, Taiwan Province and Singapore – ethnically homogeneous; Malaysia, Philippines and Indonesia – ethnically heterogeneous; Indonesia and Malaysia – low initial education; Republic of Korea and Taiwan Province – high initial education.

By 1996, several countries in the grouping had already begun to show symptoms of growth fatigue, aggravated the following year by the onset of a major upheaval in exchange and financial markets whose long-term implications are still blurred. It is clear, none the less, that quite apart from the financial dimensions of the crisis, the abrupt reversal in long-term trends, and resulting downward revision in expected growth rates over the next few years, relate to underlying exogenous as well as endogenous causes affecting the manufacturing sector in a direct way.[7]

Endogenous causes include emerging skill shortages, strong upward pressures on unit labour costs and lagging investment efficiency, to which macroeconomic distortions such as overvaluation of local currencies and asset price inflation were added.[8]

Exogenous factors include increasing difficulty in obtaining technologies on arm's length basis (see Chapter 8), inadequacy of targeted policies in the emerging WTO order (see also Chapter 8) and new competitive challenges involving a squeeze between low-wage, labour-intensive product competition, on the one hand, and competition in technology and skill-intensive products from advanced industrial countries, on the other.

After more than two decades of sustained rapid growth, newly industrializing economies are now going through a painful adjustment to a new international environment less receptive to prior policy approaches. This entails an in-depth review of industrial development policies aimed at stimulating growth and transformation.

Foundations of a common policy predicament

Growth accounting exercises applied to East and South-East Asian economies have led to a controversy about sources of growth and alternative growth scenarios. Important in its own right, the debate also has policy implications. Although the controversy is far from settled, it already suggests some major conclusions on the role of initial conditions and emerging policy challenges.

Based on findings by Lau and Kim (1993 and 1994), and Young (1994a and 1994b), Krugman (1994) triggered the controversy by comparing the pattern of growth of newly industrializing economies with that of the former Soviet Union. Both would have been based on factor accumulation rather than on efficiency gains.[9]

Two major aspects can be distinguished in the controversy. First, the assumptions and models underlying measurement techniques and the interpretation of their results and second, the resulting policy inferences (see Table 7.3).[10]

Table 7.3 Contrasting views on the East Asian miracle

Growth engine	Measurement	Modelling	Policy inferences
Physical and human capital accumulation	Conventional growth accounting	Near-perfect competition	Market-driven policies
Technological catching up	Microeconomic evidence	Endogenous growth theory, evolutionary economics	Market-augmenting policies

The debate concerns, above all, the relative importance of the different sources of growth in output per worker. Based on assumptions of near perfect competition, some observers stress the unsustainability of an input-intensive growth pattern that relies heavily on rapid accumulation of physical and human capital and ensuing diminishing returns. Others, relying on evolutionary postulates and microeconomic evidence (see Nelson and Pack, 1995 and Nelson, 1997), emphasize the role of greater efficiency or productivity catch-up and derive less pessimistic prognoses.

The best available evidence suggests that capital deepening accounts for the bulk of growth in output per worker, with TFP growth a distant second. It also shows that TFP performance improved remarkably between 1973–84 and 1984–94 in all newly industrializing economies except the Philippines (see Figure 7.5).

As well as confirming that the contribution of TFP growth to growth in output per worker in newly industrializing economies is comparable to that of advanced industrial countries other than the United States, this evidence reveals that, in absolute terms, TFP performance has been better in the Republic of Korea, Singapore, Taiwan Province and Thailand than in the advanced industrial countries and the United States (see Figure 7.6).

In considering policy inferences and lessons learned, there is a polarization between those who place microeconomic policy at a lower level in the policy hierarchy and those who see it as a vital ingredient of the policy mix. Another controversy rages among those who hold the latter view, with some emphasizing policies addressed to productivity gains and some stressing policies aimed at fostering capital accumulation.

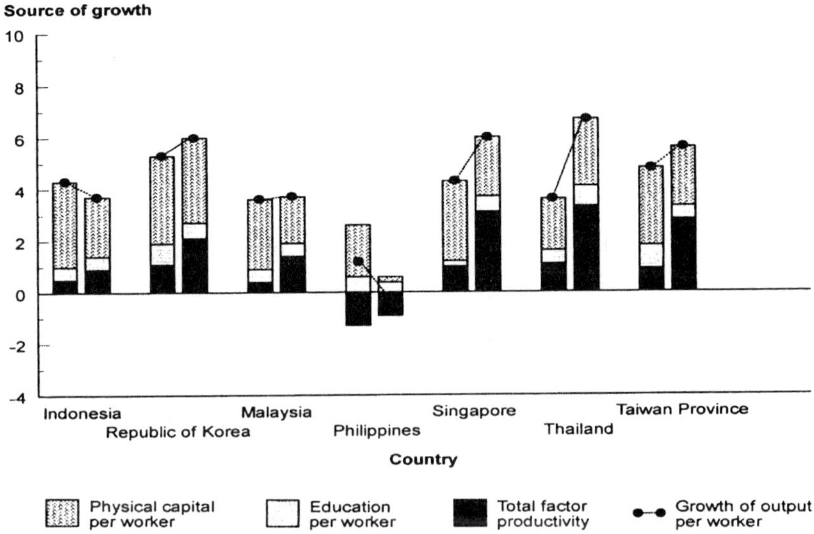

Source: Based on Collins and Bosworth (1996).

Figure 7.5 East Asia: sources of growth by country, 1973–84 and 1984–94

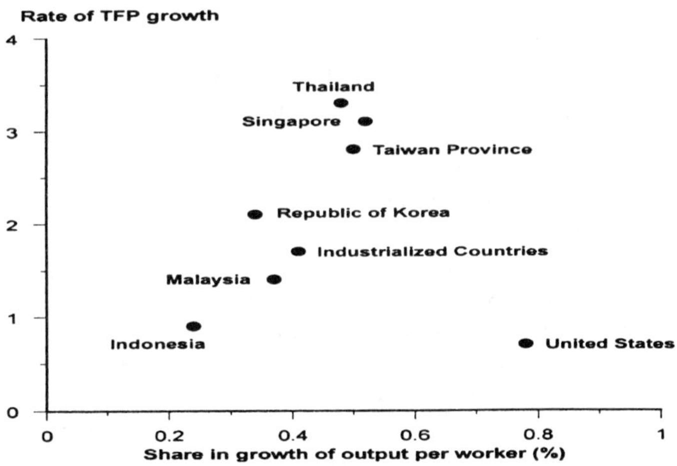

Source: Based on Collins and Bosworth (1996).

Figure 7.6 Total factor productivity in East Asia, 1984–94

At stake are both the interpretation of newly industrializing economies' recent industrial history and prognoses on which to base future policy thrust. The debate has evolved from a focus on the relative importance of market versus government intervention to the acceptance of such intervention and a focusing on the precise nature of interventions required to overcome pervasive market failures (Stiglitz, 1996).

Along with a compelling trend towards more upstream and functional policies, policy makers in newly industrializing economies face mounting demands on the extent of foresight required to allocate resources in the new innovation-driven stage that is gradually replacing the catching-up approach to industrialization. To set and monitor performance standards on phenomena that depend largely on uncertain spillover effects and externalities is incomparably harder than to set them on quantitative export or capacity targets, as in the past. It may be argued that performance standards are increasingly set and settled by the market itself. But to the extent that markets are pervaded by imperfections and asymmetries, as illustrated in Chapter 8, the problem reverts to the policy makers. They can draw heavily on advanced industrial countries' experience, since advanced industrial countries' governments still have an important say in the allocation of resources to innovation and technical change, both directly through government-sponsored programmes and subsidies and indirectly through special incentives (see OECD, 1996).

Irrespective of where progressive methodological refinements of growth accounting and other measurement tools may lead, a considerable degree of underlying consensus exists among newly industrializing economies. Although there is sufficient scope for physical and human capital accumulation and catching-up growth, there is also a growing need for policies to enhance TFP by increasing resources devoted to technological development, skill building and organizational improvements in a market-driven environment.

The comparison with advanced industrial countries suggests that, beyond a certain threshold and as the technological gap with advanced industrial countries progressively narrows, factor accumulation leads to increasing reliance on endogenous sources of growth. Whereas among poor-performing developing countries TFP inhibits rather than feeds growth in output per worker, the opposite is the case among newly industrializing economies. This is one of the key contrasts between them and the rest of developing countries observed in recent industrialization experience.

Policy advice to developing countries aspiring to learn from newly industrializing economies' experience has so far been highly influenced by divergent readings of the latter. Yet a coincidence is evolving on the need to ensure a suitable mix of macro- and microeconomic fundamentals. These include effective policy implementation and capacity-building, fiscal austerity, realistic exchange rate, high savings rate, skill building, quality upgrading, capital formation, competition, public-private co-operation and social equity, on the one hand, and appropriate government interventions to deal with market failures, on the other. This does not mean that simple, straightforward policy prescriptions can be derived. Beyond the realm of general and abstract principles, policies remain highly idiosyncratic, tailored to specific national environments.

NEWLY OPENED ECONOMIES

The newly opened economies are the largest of our four country groupings, accounting for one third of their total GDP in 1995 (see Table 7.1). Two countries, Brazil and India, account for almost half of newly opened economies' GDP. Adding the three next largest countries, Argentina, Mexico and South Africa, the share goes up to 77 per cent.

Since the mid-1980s, and especially during the 1990s, newly opened economies have embarked on the road of policy reform (see Annex 2A). Although results are positive in many respects, they cannot be considered an unqualified success. Productivity gains have gone hand in hand with a more open and competitive environment in a more stable macroeconomy. Yet growth rates are insufficient for these countries to catch up with advanced industrial countries within the next generation. Lack of social equity represents another important hurdle.

In most newly opened economies, the state traditionally played a key role in the promotion of economic activity. The dismantling of a complex regulatory maze of tariffs and NTBs, industrial investment licensing, capacity restrictions, strict rules on technology transfer, highly discretionary fiscal and financial incentives, price controls and barriers to resource mobility is still underway. In certain sectors, SOEs were key players and regarded as instruments of industrial, and often regional, development policy. In the early stages of industrialization such regimes were intended to support economic development by helping to mobilize resources and attract economic activity. Over time, however, they became less effective. Eventually, the same instruments that once stimulated investment and attracted entry became obstacles to resource mobility and competition.

Incumbent industries were generally favoured over new ones. Information asymmetries also played a role, with established producers having detailed knowledge of unwritten norms and those responsible for enforcing them. Relatively rigid market configurations emerged, as rents accruing to incumbents deterred them from penetrating new markets.

By reducing flexibility in resource allocation and use and limiting competition, such barriers resulted in losses in efficiency, both in a static and dynamic situation. In so far as such barriers tended to benefit incumbents, they contributed to an increase in income inequality and a decrease in social welfare.

Three major factors directly affecting the ability of newly opened economies to join global networks have been the focus of reform during the last decade and a half:

- the domestic regulatory arena, including rules governing FDI and technology transfer;
- the asset ownership structure of the economy;
- the international trade regime.

Most newly opened economies have moved to eliminate regulatory and trade barriers to integration into world markets, while changing – in some cases dramatically – the economy's ownership structure away from a predominance of SOEs in production of goods and services.

Such reforms aim to make resource allocation and use responsive to market signals of price and profitability, as well as to ensure that such signals follow relative scarcities and are as undisturbed as possible by market failures and imperfect forms of competition. To overcome these problems, the economy needs a regulatory regime that substitutes distortionary regulations for those that help minimize negative externalities and curb the effects of imperfect or missing markets.

Changes in the rules that guide economic activity and restructuring of regulatory systems and institutions seek to: (i) enhance firms' flexibility and speed in redeploying resources in response to changes in global markets and technologies; (ii) remove barriers to competition, factor mobility and firm growth; and (iii) simplify and increase transparency of rules. The ultimate aim is to improve the economy's operational efficiency and equity.

Because reform seeks to change or phase out instruments that have shaped the behaviour of markets and agents over the long term, it tends to be slow and subject to regression often involving difficult and protracted negotiations. Firms favoured by certain rules tend to view their decision to invest in a specific area as a response to government guarantees and guidance while government officials in the old regime tend to feel like stakeholders.[11]

Changes in the ownership structure of productive assets are intended to alleviate fiscal crisis as well as to inject greater competition and efficiency into markets dominated by SOEs. Before reform, the state had reached its fiscal limits in most newly opened economies, making it necessary to enact appropriate regulatory regimes to mobilize and support private investments essential for manufacturing competitiveness. Argentina and Brazil constitute two paradigmatic cases of NOE reform (see Chapter 9).

In South Asia, India, Pakistan and other newly opened economies in the region have also made significant strides in economic reform. Soon after independence, the Indian government imposed limits on competition. Trade and regulatory barriers were established as instruments of economic growth and social equity, with the objective of deepening and diversifying the industrial base. However, they became deterrents to competition and productivity gains. At an early stage in India's industrialization, competition was not perceived to be of critical importance to the attainment of major development goals.

In India, as in many other developing countries, however, dynamic efficiency losses from barely competitive markets tended to weigh ever more heavily and tip the balance against whatever short-term gains resulted from trade restrictions and regulatory controls. Challenge from imports, rivalry in international markets and entry of new firms gradually helped turn rent-seeking and technologically passive incumbent firms and groups into aggressive, productivity-oriented players.

In recent years, improvements in trade and regulatory policies have led to a significant supply response from Indian producers. Liberalization of exports was followed by a carefully planned process of trade reform and deregulation. The latter included price decontrol, removal of entry and expansion barriers in the form of restrictive capacity and technology licences and improved exit mechanisms.

Besides these developments, a large science and technology base, an increasingly educated labour force and a domestic market with a high potential for growth have made India a major new investment location on the Asian continent, together with China and Viet Nam. India is expected to make the transition to the group of newly industrializing economies in the not-too-distant future.

TRANSITION ECONOMIES

China alone accounts for over half of the total GDP of the economies in transition. This share rises to 87 per cent if the Commonwealth of Independent States is added, and to 97 per cent when considering the next three largest economies of the grouping (Poland, Hungary and Romania).[12]

Economies in transition in Central and Eastern Europe have gone through a far-reaching transformation process. In 1989–90 they initiated a radical change of their entire economic policy systems. By and large these reforms have been remarkably successful given the short time span since then. With the political system undergoing drastic changes, policy making for economic and industrial development has become a politically and legally complicated process. This is especially conspicuous in countries where resistance to government policies and an aversion to state intervention has developed after many years of central planning by state authorities.[13]

After abandoning the central planing system in 1989–90, most countries in Central and Eastern Europe embarked on a rapid process of transformation towards a market-oriented economic system. This presupposed a complete redefinition of the role of the state and of other economic actors such as enterprises and banks, together with the gradual creation of new institutions and mechanisms required for economic development in an open-market system.

The transformation has been historically unique in terms of the scope and complexity of tasks that needed to be undertaken in a short time span in economies that largely lacked the requisite experience and expertise. The tasks comprised:

- abandonment of a broad range of state planning and control mechanisms;
- gradual dismantling and redefinition of government functions and related administrative machinery;
- formulation and formal adoption of a wide range of new economic, property and regulatory laws to develop a private sector-driven, market-based and internationally integrated economic system; and
- establishment and operation of effective product, capital and labour markets with functioning price mechanisms, competition and privatization and restructuring of former SOEs.

Besides carrying out this reform process, it was imperative to ensure the continued operation of the social and infrastructure sectors as well as to limit as much as possible the severity and social impact of the economic crisis prompted by the collapse of the previous system.

Macroeconomic stabilization and resumption of overall constituted key goals for the medium term. These goals had to be pursued at a time of fierce international competition in product markets, competition for foreign investment resources and accelerating technological progress in the global economy. Integration into the global economy required establishment of new international agreements, membership of international bodies such as in the fields of trade and finance and compliance with a series of international codes and conventions. For these unprecedented tasks only limited international support was made available in terms of official financial assistance.[14]

The first major step towards international integration was marked by the collapse of the trading system established by the countries of the region under the Council for Mutual Economic Assistance (CMEA). This system had regulated trade among its member countries through complicated and generally inefficient mechanisms of central coordination and balancing of various bilateral trade agreements based on the transfer rouble. The international trade volume of the CMEA countries was, therefore, quite limited. By the mid-1980s it accounted for only 6 per cent of total world trade whereas CMEA's share in total world production was estimated at 30 per cent.

The system had, however, led to the establishment of very large producers in the member countries, specialized in well-defined product ranges and given, *de facto,* the monopoly on these products in CMEA as a whole. In mid-1991, after a previous virtual collapse, CMEA was formally dissolved, with no agreement reached for a successor arrangement. This meant that from the outset of the reform process the former large CMEA companies had to face an almost total disruption of sales to and purchases from previous trading partners. This forced them urgently to seek other markets and sources for inputs on the basis of convertible currencies without having had either the time or the resources necessary to adjust production to international competition.

Commonalities

Since the beginning of the transformation process, the economies in transition of Central and Eastern Europe have pursued systematic policy reforms. These have entailed price, financial and trade liberalization, privatization of SOEs, fiscal reforms and enhanced competition.

These economies shared a number of initial pre-reform commonalities. Important among them, as far as the industrial sector is concerned, were the following facts:

- the share of manufacturing in GDP and employment was higher than in advanced industrial countries, with heavy concentration on heavy and defence industries;
- manufacturing capacity was highly concentrated in large SOEs, with few SMIs;
- manufacturing processes were outdated, highly polluting and energy- and raw-material-intensive and with a very low degree of informatization and automation
- trade was heavily concentrated among themselves.

An important post-reform commonality has been the severe contraction in economic activity in early 1990s as a result of drastic reduction in domestic demand brought about by price liberalization, a collapse of the industrial enterprise and financial systems and the breakdown of the CMEA.

Differences

Although similar problems were encountered and similar policy reforms were initiated in the individual countries, a number of differences can be discerned as regards the approach and timing of reforms as well as the progress achieved so far. When reviewing these differences it should, however, be recalled that the transformation process is by no means complete and that many reforms are still under way or are yet to show their full impact. Moreover, the starting-point and general initial conditions for the transition differed widely between the various countries in the region.

First, there is a great difference in the size of market in terms of population. The Russian Federation alone accounts for almost half of the total population of the economies in transition of Central and Eastern Europe, which amounts to 330 million people. Then come three countries with middle-sized populations: Ukraine (52 million), Poland (39 million) and Romania (23 million). Hungary, the Czech Republic and Belarus have around 10 million people each. The remaining ten economies in transition of Central and Eastern Europe are small in terms of population.

Second, there is a wide difference in natural resource endowment. Whereas a few countries such as the Russian Federation, are rich in both petroleum and minerals, many others, such as Ukraine and the Baltic States, had based their previous industrial development on imported commodities. The agricultural sector was in some countries quite developed and effective while in others it was subject to major bottlenecks. For a number of countries heavily dependent on imports of oil, other raw materials or basic foodstuffs, the break-down of the CMEA system meant severe constraints on industrial production and consumer supplies.

Third, and perhaps most important, some countries, such as Poland and Hungary, had previous, recent experience with market-induced development and private ownership having already established, in some instances, significant private ownership and decentralized production systems in some sectors. Most other countries, such as many of the republics of the former Soviet Union, lacked this kind of experience. Thus both the experience and the actual degree of decentralization of decision making in the previous system varied among the countries of the region, creating different starting points for economic transformation. Some countries had already initiated and were well ahead in establishing the institutional infrastructure, including a basic statistical system, whereas others needed to create organizations and procedures required for the development of a national economy starting virtually from scratch.

Fourth, the industrial structure prevailing at the time of the initiation of the transition process differed widely across countries, largely as a result of the previous CMEA system of specialization. Some were much more tied into the CMEA structure than others. This meant significant adjustment burdens, especially for those countries with particularly one-sided and internationally less competitive industries.

Fifth, the countries in the region differed and still differ in the level of foreign indebtedness. Particularly indebted countries are Poland, Hungary and the Russian Federation.

Finally, there was a difference in the timing of reforms and policies such as those towards FDI. The newly independent states started their reform process much later than other countries in Central and Eastern Europe – just after the break-up of the Soviet Union in 1991. Moreover, they had to go through the difficult phase of gaining independence and subsequently that of nation building, before economic transformation could be initiated.

While most of the economies in transition of Eastern and Central Europe and the Baltic states began recovering in 1993–94, the countries of the Commonwealth of Independent States did not manage to revert their decline, although they did slow it down. Poland is the only country in this group that in 1996 had already fully recovered and even exceeded the level of GDP attained before reform. In countries such as Armenia, Azerbaijan, Georgia, Republic of Moldova and Tajikistan, real output in 1996 was still 40 per cent or lower than pre-reform levels.

Chapter 10 returns to the issues examined in this section in the light of the Hungarian experience.

LESS DEVELOPED COUNTRIES [15]

The group of less developed countries comprises 57 countries including 48 qualifying as least developed countries and nine other low-income countries. The GDP of this country grouping is the most evenly distributed of our four groupings, with only two members accounting for over 5 per cent of joint GDP, that is, Nigeria (11 per cent) and Bangladesh (7 per cent).

By definition, less developed countries are countries that confront serious impediments in their development process, start from a very low level and exhibit poor performance. To break this vicious circle, they have implemented far-reaching reforms since the mid-1980s with important variations in pace, extent, sequence, thrust and degree of success. On the whole, they have failed to avoid increasing marginalization of the world economy. The share of sub-Saharan Africa in world MVA went down from 0.6 per cent in 1970 to 0.3 per cent in 1995. A reversal of this trend is not yet in sight. As a group, they are suffering premature deindustrialization and obdurate difficulties in getting abreast of worldwide trends in technology and breaking the low wage/low productivity trap.

The quality and quantity of resource endowment plays a key role in accounting for their differences and commonalities, in particular in levels of socioeconomic development. Policy implementation, along with persistent structural rigidities and lack of adequate infrastructure, finance, managerial capabilities and skills, are also important in explaining less developed countries' poor record. Such constraints render them unable to compete in world markets and to advance their industrial development.

The lack of success in overcoming structural rigidities is a major obstacle to structural and framework reform. Weak and unpredictable governance erodes confidence in the legal and regulatory system, and credibility in macroeconomic policy, rendering it ineffectual and limiting the efficacy of complementary policy measures. This results in policy inconsistencies which add to the effect of past policy regimes that still linger on and hamper the smooth implementation of policy reforms aimed at enhancing competitive performance.

Since the mid-1980s most less developed countries have embarked upon a wide range of macroeconomic and structural reform programmes to address macroeconomic imbalances and foster market-oriented institutional change. The extent and quality of the reform pay-offs have been largely affected by differences in size, resource endowments and level of development. At least initially, the emphasis was on getting prices right, with less concern with structural rigidities.

Although all less developed countries face structural problems and confront difficulties in accessing product markets and external finance, the group has gained in heterogeneity over the years. Despite an overall bleak picture, several countries have recorded notable improvements while others have been critically affected by a range of non-economic factors such as civil conflicts, political instability, refugees, recurrent droughts, floods and devastating cyclones.[16]

At the same time, policy developments have been mixed. Some countries, such as those of the CFA zone, attempted to gain export profitability through devaluations while others decided to float their currencies.[17] More recently increasing efforts have been directed to institutional strengthening (for example, development of stock markets).

A major characteristic of manufacturing in less developed countries is its very narrow base. MVA accounts for less than 10 per cent of the combined GDP of less developed countries as compared to nearly 25 per cent in developing countries as a whole. Besides its small size, its relative importance has diminished in recent years.

Most less developed countries began implementing structural adjustment programmes (SAPs) during the middle or second half of the 1980s, though a few countries such as Malawi and Togo, began earlier, and others, such as Burkina Faso, Comoros, Ethiopia and Rwanda did not formally adopt SAPs until the 1990s. In a number of less developed countries, including Democratic Republic of the Congo, Sierra Leone, Sudan and Zambia, adjustment programmes were not implemented in a consistent and continuous way. Lack of consistent implementation of reform programmes has weakened belief in government capacity to manage change.

The primary objectives of the reform programmes include short-term economic stabilization, restoration of sustainable rates of economic growth and increased export orientation. In addition, the reform programmes comprise measures to reinforce macroeconomic management and reduce direct government involvement in and control over markets. The reforms were thus adopted in response to serious economic crises facing these countries during the first half of the 1980s and geared to a greater reliance on the price system. Differences still exist among the agriculture-based countries. The dilemma of price reform in agriculture for many less developed countries arises from the fact that governments, particularly those whose economies are dominated by traditional agricultural exports, have hesitated to carry out very comprehensive price and market reforms in the agriculture sector.

In addition to the low wage/low productivity trap, less developed countries confront another, perhaps more fundamental, dilemma: markets are handicapped because the state is unable to implement policies to strengthen them institutionally and offset their failures, whilst the state is disadvantaged because it cannot rely on an efficiently working market to make up for its own failures. This is probably the key issue to be addressed by international bilateral and multilateral economic and technical assistance.

Annex 7A provides further details on the composition of the country grouping. Chapter 11 examines the specific case of the United Republic of Tanzania.

CLOSING REMARKS

The previous sections have examined the wide variety of initial conditions, economic and social trajectories and policy challenges faced by developing countries and economies in transition. Contrasting policy and institutional legacies add to differences in resource endowment to inhibit mutual convergence.

If evidence of convergence among developing countries and economies in transition is less than persuasive, the case is even weaker with respect to advanced industrial countries. With the exception of East Asian countries, per capita income in developing countries in relation to per capita income in the advanced industrial countries has deteriorated, rather than improved, between 1960 and 1990 (see Figure 7.7). In contrast with China, where income remained about the same, Africa and South Asia suffered an acute deterioration by almost half. The worsening was substantial in Latin America and slight in the Middle East.

It might be argued that, without convergence of policies, differentiation among developing countries and economies in transition would be even greater than it is. Whether this is so or not is not just impossible to prove counterfactually, but it would say very little about the net social costs involved in pursuing policy convergence for the sake of maximization of static efficiency worldwide.

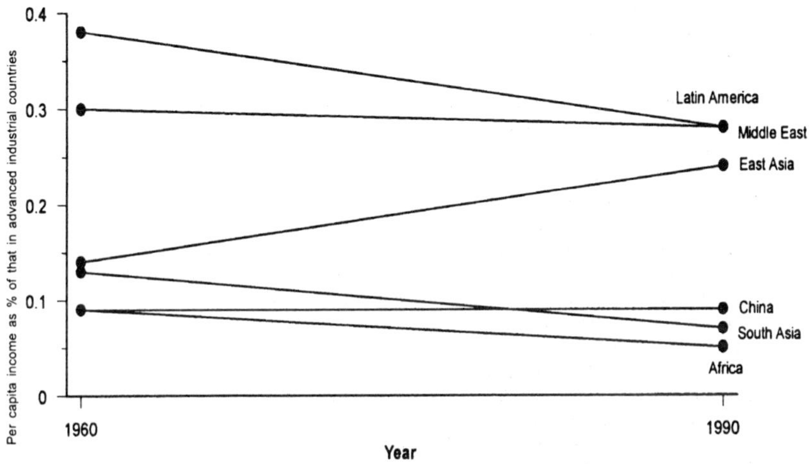

Source: Penn World Tables, mark 5.6.

Figure 7.7 Income position of developing countries and transition economies in relation to advanced industrial countries

NOTES

1. For a full list of the countries included under each grouping see Annex 7A. This classification follows economic rather than geographical criteria, although both are closely related. There is a large residual group made up of countries that do not meet the criteria chosen to classify these country groupings. It includes countries with very small domestic markets and heavily specialized in natural resources, notably oil, as well as a large number of small island economies. The geographical criterion is used in some cases owing to availability of data. Is the present classification of country groupings relevant after 1997? It is, in so far as changing conditions are factored in when discussing the nature of their differences and commonalities.
2. These figures are the best available to date. They are based on the Penn World Tables, mark 5.6 and a homogeneous cross-country methodology.
3. The South-East Asian recession, which began in the autumn of 1997, entailed a dramatic reversal of trends in social progress in the whole region, with a particularly acute impact in Indonesia.
4. The Philippines is an exception with respect to 1 and 2. None the less, it belongs to newly industrializing economies as a member of the flying geese flock (see Chapter 12). A break

in long-term trends among ASEAN countries took place in 1997, whose long-term implications are not yet quite clear. See, however, Chapter 4. Hong Kong Special Administrative Region is an exception with respect to 1 and 9, while Taiwan Province is relocating a good deal of its labour-intensive industrial capacity to the mainland.

5. The share of metal, machinery and equipment subsectors in manufacturing employment in South-East and East Asia rose from 21.5 per cent in 1975 to 28.2 per cent in 1990. For Latin America and the Caribbean, the corresponding figures were 25.1 per cent and 23.4 per cent and 12.8 per cent and 10.2 per cent for sub-Saharan Africa.
6. See Chapter 6.
7. One of the major uncertainties concerns the depth of the current slow-down which, in turn, depends on how quickly the health of local banking systems and capital markets is to be restored. Drastic budget cuts, interest rate hikes and massive bank closures accentuated the sharpness of the recessive adjustment. In contrast to Latin America a decade ago, however, ASEAN-4 countries have high savings, sound public finances, absence of wasteful public consumption, flexible labour markets and low taxation, although they did face a crisis of misallocation of investment in the private sector associated to guaranteed, although unsustainable, returns. Short-term foreign borrowing was used to support long-term investments in real-estate and other non-exporting sectors, with the consequent risk to borrowers, especially banks and finance companies. The impact of this mismatch was felt as soon as a weakening balance of trade led currencies to fall against the dollar: rentals on real estate developments were earned in local currency but debts had to be repaid in dollars. However, ASEAN-4's economic fundamentals, such as high savings, budget surpluses, flexible labour markets and low taxation remain in place and long-term prospects are solid. See Sachs (1997) and Hale (1997).
8. Deregulation programmes are under way, among other measures, to extend the use of competitive tenders.
9. A more recent strand of the debate concerns the relative importance of exports and investment to foster growth. Rodrik argues that strategic interventions to overcome co-ordination failures in investment were far more important than the role of export expansion in the Republic of Korea's and Taiwan Province's rapid industrial (Rodrik, 1994; see, however, Chapter 8).
10. Growth accounting decomposes growth in output per worker into its proximate causes. Such decomposition is *not* intended to explain the causes of growth. By postulating specific parameters and functional forms, however, it does make assumptions about the economic process, such as the elasticity of factor substitution or presence of externalities. Among such assumptions, the most frequent are that there is enough competition to ensure that earnings of factors of production are proportional to their respective productivity, that factors have fixed weights and that constant returns to scale prevail. In endogenous growth models, productivity gains, rather than capital formation *per se*, are perceived as the fundamental cause of growth. Rodrik (1997) questions the value of current TFP measurements in that, by ruling out the possibility of biased technical change, they fail to capture increases in TFP due to labour-saving technological change. By assuming that the productivity of all factors changes in equal proportions, reductions in capital share due to increases in capital per unit of labour are ruled out. In fact, such reductions may be cushioned either because of unitary elasticity of substitution or labour-saving technical change. Nelson and Pack (1995) also argue that diminishing returns to capital were offset by technical advances in East Asia. Sarel (1997) has elaborated more sophisticated measurements assuming that technological factor shares are determined by the industrial structure of the economy and its level of development. His estimates suggest that TFP growth is not systematically different in the ASEAN economies than in the United States.

11. This feature is, of course, also found among less developed countries with macroeconomic and structural reform programmes under way. See Chapter 11.
12. Since 1978, China has undergone a historic transformation and is becoming increasingly integrated into the world economy. Already the fifth largest trading power and recipient of some 40 per cent of world total FDI flows to developing countries and economies in transition, China accounts for over half of the GDP of the latter and is a category in itself. The special treatment it deserves is not within the scope of this chapter. What follows is focused on the economies in transition of Central and Eastern Europe.
13. Useful sources on Central and Eastern Europe include: EBRD, *Transition Report* (annual); The Economic Intelligence Unit (EIU), *Business Eastern Europe, Business Central Europe* and *Statistical Service* (various issues); UNCTAD/KOPINT-DATORG, *Privatization in the transition Process-recent Experiences in Eastern Europe,* UNCTAD/GID/7 (1995); UN Economic Commission for Europe, *Industrial Restructuring in Selected Countries in Transition – a Review* (Geneva, 1995); MOCT-MOST, *Economic Policy in Transitional Economies* Vol. 5, No. 2 (1995)
14. Official aid was provided in the form of bilateral grants, loans and other non-grant funds as well as multilateral programmes. From 1991 to 1993, for instance, total flows to Central and Eastern Europe and the newly independent states amounted to US$12–13 billion annually (see Murray, 1995).
15. The subgroup of least developed countries comprises 48 countries with a population of more than 585 million.
16. Bangladesh, Benin, Cambodia, Equatorial Guinea, Guinea-Bissau, Lao People's Democratic Republic, Lesotho, Mozambique, Myanmar, Sao Tome and Principe, the Solomon Islands and Sudan have improved their performance and most have had a notable increase in per capita income during the first half of the 1990s. Burundi, Democratic Republic of the Congo, Ethiopia, Liberia, Rwanda, Sierra Leone and Somalia belong to the second category.
17. CFA is the standard monetary unit of the African financial community, that is, Benin, Burkina Faso, Cameroon, Central African Republic, Chad, Congo, Côte d'Ivoire, Equatorial Guinea, Gabon, Mali, Niger, Senegal and Togo.

REFERENCES

Collins, S.M. and Bosworth, B.P. (1996), 'Economic in East Asia: accumulation versus assimilation', Brookings Papers on Economic Activity, 2.

Hale, D. (1997), 'The challenge now is trade', *Financial Times,* 7 November.

Krugman, P. (1994), 'The myth of Asia's miracle', *Foreign Affairs,* **73** (6), 62–78.

Lau, L. and J-I. Kim, (1993), 'The role of human capital in the economic growth of the East Asian newly industrialized countries', mimeo, Stanford University.

Lau, L. (1994), 'The source of growth of the East Asian newly industrialized countries', *Journal of the Japanese and International Economies,* 5, 3.

Murray, T. (1995), 'The international organizations: an overview', Table 1 (Annex), in MOCT-MOST, *Economic Policy in Transitional Economies,* **5**, (2).

Nelson, R. (1997), 'How new is new growth theory: a different point of view', *Challenge*, September-October.

Nelson, R. and H. Pack, (1995), 'The Asian Growth Miracle and Modern Growth Theory', unpublished paper, Colombia University and University of Pennsylvania, September.

OECD, (1996): *Public Support to Industry – Report by the Industry Committee to the Council at Ministerial Level,* OCDE/GD(96)82, Paris.

Rodrik, D. (1994), 'Getting interventions right: how much South Korea and Taiwan grew rich', Working Paper 4964, Cambridge, MA: National Bureau of Economic Research, December.

Rodrik, D. (1997), 'TFPG controversies, institutions and economic performance in East Asia', CEPR Discussion Paper No. 1587, March.

Sachs, J.D. (1997), 'The wrong medicine for Asia', *The New York Times,* 3 November.

Sarel, M. (1997), 'Growth and productivity in ASEAN countries', IMF Working Paper, August.

Stiglitz, J. (1996), 'Some lessons from the East Asian miracle", *World Bank Research Observer,* **11** (2), August, 151-77.

UNDP (1997), *Human Development Report,* New York: Oxford University Press.

Young, A. (1994a), 'The tyranny of numbers: confronting the statistical realities of the East Asian growth experience', NBER Working Paper no. 4680, March.

Young, A. (1994b), 'Lessons from the East Asian NICs: a contrarian view', *European Economic Review Papers and Proceedings,* May.

ANNEX 7A. COUNTRY GROUPINGS

Newly industrializing economies

This grouping includes higher industrial development performer countries and areas that share in the East Asian dynamic growth process. This 'strategic group' of countries and areas (Asian NICs and ASEAN countries) is characterized by having made manufacturing the key engine of economic growth for a substantive number of years.

Hong Kong Special Administrative Region of China
Indonesia
Malaysia
Philippines
Republic of Korea
Singapore
Taiwan Province
Thailand

Newly opened economies

This grouping include countries that have chosen to switch from inward- to outward-oriented regimes since the late 1980s

Argentina
Bolivia
Brazil
Chile
Colombia
Costa Rica
Dominican Republic
Ecuador
Egypt
El Salvador
Guatemala
India

Jamaica
Mexico
Pakistan
Panama
Paraguay
Peru
South Africa
Trinidad and Tobago
Uruguay
Venezuela

Economies in Transition

This grouping includes countries in transition from command to market economies. It includes countries in Central and Eastern Europe, Asia and Latin America (Cuba).

Albania
Armenia
Belarus
Bosnia and Herzegovina
Bulgaria
Cambodia
China
Croatia
Cuba
Czech Republic
Estonia
Georgia
Hungary
Kazakhstan
Kyrgyzstan
Lao People's Democratic Republic
Latvia
Lithuania
Mongolia
Myanmar
Poland
Republic of Moldova
Romania
Russian Federation
Slovakia
Slovenia
Tajikistan
The former Yugoslav Republic of Macedonia
Turkmenistan
Ukraine
Uzbekistan
Viet Nam
Yugoslavia

Less Developed Countries

This grouping comprises least developed countries based on the UN Economic and Social Council's Committee for Development Planning criteria and the low income countries as defined by the World Bank.

Afghanistan
Angola
Bangladesh
Benin
Bhutan
Burkina Faso
Burundi
Cameroon
Cape Verde
Central African Republic
Chad
Comoros
Congo
Côte d'Ivoire
Democratic Republic of the Congo
Djibouti
Equatorial Guinea
Ethiopia
Gabon
Gambia

- Ghana
- Guinea
- Guinea-Bissau
- Guyana
- Haiti
- Honduras
- Kenya
- Kiribati
- Lesotho
- Liberia
- Madagascar
- Malawi
- Maldives
- Mali
- Mauritania
- Mauritius
- Mozambique
- Nepal
- Nicaragua
- Niger
- Nigeria
- Rwanda
- Samoa
- Sao Tome and Principe
- Senegal
- Sierra Leone
- Solomon Islands
- Somalia
- Sri Lanka
- Sudan
- Togo
- Tuvalu
- Uganda
- United Republic of Tanzania
- Vanuatu
- Zambia
- Zimbabwe

Other Economies

This group includes economies which, although often export-oriented, rely most heavily on a few natural resources, such as oil, and/or countries with tiny domestic markets, such as the small-island economies in the Caribbean.

- Algeria
- Anguilla
- Antigua and Barbuda
- Bahamas
- Bahrain
- Barbados
- Belize
- Bermuda
- Botswana
- British Virgin Islands
- Brunei Darussalam
- Cyprus
- Dominica
- Democratic People's Republic of Korea
- Fiji
- French Guiana
- French Polynesia
- Grenada
- Guadeloupe
- Iran (Islamic Republic of)
- Iraq
- Jordan
- Kuwait
- Lebanon
- Libyan Arab Jamahiriya
- Macao
- Martinique
- Montserrat
- Morocco
- Namibia
- Netherlands Antilles
- New Caledonia
- Oman
- Papua New Guinea
- Puerto Rico
- Qatar
- Réunion
- St. Kitts and Nevis
- Saint Lucia

Saint Vincent and the Grenadines
Saudi Arabia
Seychelles
Suriname
Swaziland
Syrian Arab Republic
Tonga
Tunisia
Turks and Caicos Islands
United Arab Emirates
Virgin Islands
Yemen

8. Newly Industrializing Economies: The Case of the Republic of Korea

INTRODUCTION

Before 1997, industrial development and trade expansion went hand in hand in the Republic of Korea to give rise to what is often described as compressed growth and transformation. During the half-century up to then, the country pursued export-led industrialization and turned from one of the poorest agrarian societies in the world to a near-advanced industrial country, having joined the OECD in December 1996. The country dramatically shortened the usual phases of industrial transformation that took most of today's developed nations over a century.

Trade and industrial policies have evolved in a way that contrasts with that of many other developing countries. During the post-Korean War period, in the 1950s, industrial and trade policies pursued inward-looking import substitution to control postwar hyperinflation and to resolve the critical shortages of daily necessities. The Republic of Korea's modern industrial development began in 1962 based on a unique paradigm of an export-based industrialization strategy. The government involved itself in the industrial development process to varying degrees.

In the 1960s, various incentives and disincentives were introduced to encourage labour-intensive manufactured exports. In the 1970s, the government intervened to promote industrial deepening by targeting heavy and chemical industries (HCIs). The 1980s, however, witnessed the initial phases of liberalization in both industry and trade policies. Rapid industrial growth has also been accompanied by rapid political democratization and continued demand for new labour–management relations, which resulted in rapid wage hikes. With the advent of the WTO in 1995, during the 1990s liberalization and deregulation were emphasized in order to restructure the economy and generate high value-added products for export. In the 1990s the market became more transparent and competitive.

This chapter gives an overview of the dynamics of the export-based industrial development policies over the past half-century and their relative influence on the Republic of Korea's late catch-up industrialization, and a detailed description of adjustments in industrial development policies to the globalizing world economy before to the crisis of 1997.

From an overall perspective, the Republic of Korea's industrial and trade policies have complemented one another within an outward-looking trade regime that progressively enhanced the working of the market over time. Industrial deepening and trade expansion reinforced one another.

The first section sketches the evolution of industrial development policy from the early 1960s to the mid-1990s. The following section discusses the effectiveness of the country's export-oriented industrial development policy. After this a section focuses on innovation-driven industrial development policy, started in the early 1990s. The final section concludes by examining some challenges and policy implications for other developing countries.

EVOLUTION OF INDUSTRIAL DEVELOPMENT POLICY FROM THE EARLY 1960s TO THE MID-1990s

Export-led Industrialization Regime (1960s)

The Republic of Korea's modern industrial take-off began in early 1960 with the first Five-Year Development Plan (1962–66). The Plan dramatically shifted policy focus from a brief import-substitution regime in the 1950s to rapid export-led industrialization. The Park Chung-Hee Administration (1961–79) viewed increased foreign exchange earnings from manufactured exports as necessary to meet the rapidly rising import bill for energy and other daily necessities given the paucity of natural resource deposits.

The Republic of Korea was liberated in 1945 and then fought the Korean War from 1950 to 1953. In the war-devastated economy, the Government used a multifaceted import-substitution approach to reconstruct and stabilize the economy. Despite periodic devaluations, the official exchange rate was kept at an artificially high level throughout the 1950s. Other measures to protect domestic industries were prohibitively high tariffs, quota restrictions and prior approval for imports. By 1960, the country had completed its import-substitution phase for non-durable consumer goods and their inputs.[1] However, import-substitution policy clearly failed to make manufacturing a key sector.

Due to the shortage of natural resources and the small domestic market, the Park Government's industrial development policy was to make maximum use of the country's comparative advantage in labour-intensive manufactured goods for exports (Ahn, 1986). Given the centre–periphery development doctrines and resulting import-substitution policies prevailing at that time in developing countries, the Republic of Korea's export-based industrialization strategy, along with that of Taiwan Province, was quite exceptional.

Ever-increasing investment requirements were financed through heavy borrowing of foreign capital rather than FDI (Ahn, 1988). To facilitate this, the government provided the business sector with official repayment guarantees of foreign loans or borrowed directly to finance its own public projects. The proportion of foreign capital to total capital formation was approximately 40 per cent during the second half of the 1960s. It declined gradually, but was still 30.4 per cent in 1981 (Kwack, 1990). Several policy reforms or measures for export promotion are examined below.

Exchange rate and interest rate reforms

One of the first policy actions under the export-led industrialization regime was to devalue the local currency, the won, by nearly a 100 per cent. In 1964, the exchange rate went from 130 won/US$1 to 255 won/US$1. The Government also switched to a unitary floating exchange rate system so that a single rate could be applied to all transactions.

The government consistently attempted to provide realistic exchange rates for exports through a mixture of major devaluations and flexible adjustments. It also tried to compensate for periodic domestic currency overvaluation by means of financial and tax incentives for exporters. Through controlled exchange rates, exporters enjoyed the benefits of real exchange rate stability throughout the 1960s and 1970s, unlike most developing countries.

Following the exchange rate reform in September 1965, the interest rate was raised from 15 per cent to 30 per cent for one-year fixed deposits and loans to increase voluntary private savings and discourage unproductive use of bank credits. To encourage further private savings through financial intermediaries, transactions under false names were allowed until 1993 to give savers an incentive in the form of a tax shelter. These efforts to mobilize both domestic and foreign savings made possible a significant rise in the rate of investment. Both exchange reform and savings mobilization produced a highly favourable macroeconomic environment for export promotion.

Incentive schemes for export promotion

The incentive system for export-oriented industrialization in the 1960s and 1970s was basically designed to eliminate discrimination against production for export. Several writers concur in that such an incentive system was accurate enough to enable domestic firms to exploit the country's comparative advantage in export production.[2] Unlike the situation in most developing countries, in the Republic of Korea access to basic incentives in the 1960s was automatic for all production and commercial transactions related to exports. The system was industry-neutral and transparent for all exporters. The export bureaucracy functioned adequately to ensure that incentives and their access systems could be adjusted through continuous assessment of changing conditions at home and abroad.

There were two key systems for administering export promotion incentives. One consisted of unrestricted and tariff-free access to imported intermediate inputs and raw materials needed for export production. This system established a free trade regime for export activities and allowed producers to choose between domestic and foreign suppliers when purchasing inputs for export production. Exporters could buy those inputs at world prices, facing no disadvantage in prices paid for raw materials (Rhee et al., 1984).

The other system granted exporters automatic access to bank loans for working capital, often at preferential interest rates. One of the key requirements of exporting is readily available credit. Bank loans for working capital for export production were readily accessible because the central bank automatically rediscounted the export loans that commercial banks made to exporting firms without discriminating between large-sized conglomerates and SMIs. The system offset the case-by-case approach of bank managers and tax officials.

To prevent abuses, both direct and indirect exporters had to submit certificates of exports completed and their input coefficient. To ensure tariff-free import of intermediate goods for export production, exporters were required to pay tariffs on the intermediate goods and later received a rebate once proof of export was provided.[3]

Administrative support system

To complement the incentive system for export promotion, the Park Government also established key administrative support systems. Monthly export promotion meetings and export targeting worked to enhance the effectiveness of the various incentive systems for export. Progress was reviewed and measures designed to ensure attainment of export targets. Chaired by the President and attended by economic ministers and leaders from the business community, political parties and representatives from academia, the meetings brought the country's political leadership face to face with major economic agents.

To implement the government's industrial development and trade policies, the Economic Planning Board was created as a super-ministry with elite bureaucrats playing the pivotal role in development planning, budgeting and policy coordination. A transparent reward and punishment system based on performance criteria was instituted.

Government-led Heavy and Chemicals Industrialization (1970s)

Direct intervention of the 'hard state'

During the push towards industrial maturity, the most extensive government intervention took place when the Park Government announced the HCI Development Plan in 1973. The sudden shift from light manufacturing to HCI development was motivated by the need to improve national defence capabilities – after a one-third reduction of United States troops stationed in the Republic of Korea – and to upgrade the industrial structure ahead of newly emerging competitors.[4]

The HCI Plan outlined the need, scope and implementation programme for developing future strategic industries, consisting of shipbuilding, automobiles, steel products, machinery, non-ferrous metals, textiles and petrochemicals. The intention to shift from labour-intensive to capital-intensive industries had already been reflected in the seven special promotion bills enacted during the second Five-Year Plan (1967–71).[5]

Since the announcement of the HCI Development Plan in 1973, government's involvement became industry-specific and sometimes firm-specific by allocating business licences to some selected large-scale enterprises, the *chaebols*. The earlier industry-neutral incentives provided for exports as a whole were replaced by target industries or target firms for the promotion of these industries. The government provided those strategic HCIs with central bank credits, preferential interest rates, foreign loans, and tax incentives, including investment tax credits, accelerated depreciation allowances and tax holidays. They also constructed industrial parks such as the Changwon Machinery Complex and Yeochon Petrochemical Complex.

The industrial targeting strategy, with locked-in financial support from government, created and nurtured *chaebols* as engines of rapid industrial development. They generated the lion's share of production and exports and also accounted for the lion's share of loanable funds from financial institutions. One of the most serious consequences of the asymmetric promotion of *chaebols* was that they introduced impediments to the healthy growth of SMIs. On the positive side, the *chaebols* spearheaded the strongly expanding and deepening R&D activities, introducing the concept of technology-driven industrial development.

Despite the military and political objectives envisioned by the Park Government, the sudden HCI expansion led the economy to a crisis of major proportions in the late 1970s. On the eve of the first oil shock, targeted HCIs were extremely energy-intensive. The government provided virtually unlimited financial support with preferential credits in the 1970s, resulting in accelerated inflation, a growing balance of payments deficit and a large idle capacity.

Financial and other incentive schemes for HCIs

To finance the massive investment requirements of HCIs, a National Investment Fund was created through compulsory mobilization of private deposits from commercial banks. This single window of loanable funds allowed the government effectively to manage credit allocation based on standardized criteria. In addition, most concessionary loans were offered by specialized banks and other financial institutions, often under the direct control of the Ministry of Finance. Government intervention was also visible in other ways, such as high tariffs to protect infant HCI industries. Entry barriers were erected in certain industries to limit competition. Private firms were required to seek government authorization to borrow abroad.

Rationing of long-term domestic and foreign loans until the early 1980s was one of the most important instruments of control over private firms. The government also dominated domestic banks as the major shareholder, with power to appoint managers. Interest rates in the formal banking sector were set through government regulations.

The government used this leverage selectively to induce firms to focus on specific industries and exports. If firms did not comply with government policy, such as assigned export targets, long- or short-term bank loans could be suspended to force firms eventually into bankruptcy. In addition, a licensing procedure was used to block entry of firms into new lines of business whenever they did not adhere to the national export drive.

Economic consequences of HCI promotion

Early HCI promotion in the 1970s was affected most severely by the two oil shocks which substantially reduced the effectiveness of the export-led machinery. Due to HCIs' long gestation period, huge idle capacities and uncertain rates of return, distortions caused by government policy became increasingly apparent.

The HCI promotion policy fostered the growth of *chaebols* in order to reap economies of scale. The policy was reinforced by the government's implicit commitment to rescue failed target projects. This permitted the *chaebols* to grow very rapidly through diversification, cross-share holding and mutual repayment guarantees among subsidiary firms. Consequently, most big firms continued to register much higher debt-to-equity ratios than those in other newly industrializing economies and advanced industrial countries. As a result, the HCI drive during the high growth period resulted in a chronically excessive demand for financial resources.[6]

The expansion and increase in the number of *chaebols* created a monopolistic or oligopolistic market structure in major industries. The top 30 *chaebols* in mining and manufacturing were responsible for 34 per cent of shipments in 1978 and 41 per cent in 1982. In the early 1980s, the top ten *chaebols*, including Hyundai, Samsung, Daewoo and Lucky Goldstar, produced 20 per cent of manufacturing output. As a result, SMIs lagged behind in many areas.

The *chaebols*' economic power is reflected in the concentration of ownership. Founding families are estimated to own 60 per cent of the equity of the top 30 *chaebols*. Three-quarters of the member firms are not even listed on the stock market. Many observers wonder if the fruits of economic growth are distributed equitably despite a growing middle income bracket. In addition to the monopolistic or oligopolistic nature of major industries where *chaebols* are most visible, their sheer size and diversification also distort competition.

The government's use of the financial sector to achieve HCI targets deprived financial institutions of the role of intermediary between savers and investors. Interest rates ceased to be an indicator of savings and investment behaviour. Moreover, the rules of credit allocation by government were often not transparent. Some borrowers could easily obtain credit at preferential rates while others with worthy plans were denied it, even at a premium. This policy was burdened with ill-performing or dishonoured loans and the rate of profit became extremely low for those not favoured.

As a result, the financial sector failed to develop. Severe financial repression kept the banks from developing credit investigation functions to determine loan applicants' credit-worthiness. In this environment, financial entrepreneurship was largely discouraged. Despite recent liberalization efforts, deregulation of the financial sector has been slow, uneven and limited in scope. In the WTO era the financial sector needs to develop along with the rest of the economy. Financial liberalization and deregulation are also needed to bring in more competition. Whether the ever-diversifying *chaebols* should be allowed or constrained to manage commercial banks is another crucial question.

Despite the unfavourable economic consequences of HCI projects during the active promotion period and immediately afterwards, industrial deepening did take place. HCIs' share in total manufacturing output rose from 33 per cent in 1970 to 50 per cent in 1980. HCI products such as electronics, machinery, ships and iron and steel products began to appear in the export commodity list by the late 1970s.

With idle capacity and eroded competitiveness of HCI projects, domestic entrepreneurs began to realize the importance of a high value-added technological development as opposed to the traditional approach based on comparative advantage due to low wages (Kim, 1993).

Industrial Rationalization and Import Liberalization (1980s)

Industrial rationalization

Major HCI projects in such industries as power generation plants, automobiles and machinery became redundant. As a result, some HCI companies experienced severe financial losses mainly due to idle capacity and inadequate technology. To resolve the overcapacity problem, the Park Government launched the first phase of its investment coordination plan in 1979.

When the Chun Government came into office in the early 1980s, it gave top priority to stabilizing the economy and remedying distortions created by HCI promotion. The most important reform was related to the financial market. Both policy loans and government subsidies for such preferential loans were reduced. Most commercial banks were privatized and entry barriers to other financial markets were relaxed. Industrial targeting was gradually phased out and functional incentives emphasized.

The Chun Government replaced the seven individual industry promotion acts with a single Industrial Development Act in 1985. Under the new Act the Industrial Development Council, composed of representatives from various private sectors, was established to review and advise the Government on various industrial rationalization decisions. As a result, some unpromising projects were entirely cancelled or scaled down. Several projects were also merged into a single venture.

The Tax Exemption and Reduction Act was introduced to support those rationalized enterprises by exempting them from such obligations as capital transfer and property acquisition taxes. Between 1986 and 1988, 78 troubled enterprises benefited from the new legislation.

While providing the foundation for the industrial rationalization programmes, industrial development policy in the 1980s began to emphasize market functions by significantly reducing government intervention and encouraging private sector initiative. A fair and competitive market environment was encouraged by removing some import restrictions and entry barriers. The government provided temporary support only to those industries essential to the national economy but did not yet have an adequate supportive infrastructure for sustained .

Import liberalization

Policy makers recognized that import liberalization was an effective way of bringing in competition to protected but stagnant sectors of the economy. To maximize the benefits of market opening while protectionist measures continued, the government announced a five-year import liberalization schedule in the early 1980s, which gradually reduced tariff rates and eliminated NTBs. As a result, the import liberalization ratio of manufactured goods, measured by the ratio of automatic approval items to total tradable ones, rose from 37 per cent in 1965 to 95.4 per cent by 1988. Import surges and excessive bilateral trade imbalances were controlled by 39 special laws.

The motivation behind import liberalization was the search for international competitiveness of domestic industries rather than consumer welfare. To earn profits, domestic firms exposed to international competition had to do more than simply raise the market price and assemble imported parts. From 1984 onwards, comprehensive import liberalization reform measures had positive effects on import substitution in the fabricated metals and mechanical equipment industries. For example, the import dependence ratio of the metallic and machinery industry, measured by imports divided by total domestic demand, was 52 per cent in 1985 but dropped to 29.2 per cent in 1990.

The economic stabilization programme of the early 1980s was painful, but paid off later. The economy recovered gradually from its worst recession in 1980 and inflation shrank. The upturn in the economy owed much to favourable international conditions in 1986 characterized by the so-called three lows: low interest rates, low oil prices and low value of the dollar *vis-à-vis* the Japanese yen. The enhanced competitiveness of HCIs after some technological absorption also contributed to a great extent to recovery. The economy grew at annual rate of 12 per cent in 1986–87. During this period, the trade balance showed the first-ever surplus since the outset of economic modernization.

EFFECTIVENESS OF EXPORT-ORIENTED INDUSTRIALIZATION STRATEGY

The leading engine of the country's extraordinary economic expansion was the growth of manufactured exports.[7] Exports recorded a meagre US$52 million in 1962, when the export promotion programmes had just begun but exceeded US$100 million in 1964, US$1 billion in 1970, US$20 billion in 1981 and US$100 billion in 1995. The dramatic increase of exports was accompanied by a rapid change in export composition, which reflected a change in industrial structure. When export promotion began in the 1960s, wigs, plywood, footwear and low-quality textiles led the way. In the 1970s, they were replaced by shipbuilding, iron and steel. By the end of the 1980s, the country moved into the export of automobiles, semiconductors and machinery, which added to internationally competitive subsectors such as shipbuilding and iron and steel.

Effect of Neutral Exchange Rate Policy

Exchange rate policy is a crucial variable in explaining the main features of the trade regime in an outward-oriented economy. Since the exchange rate reforms of 1964–65, the export incentive system has been formulated to reduce trade-distorting effects on the export side. This is clearly reflected in the chronology of nominal and purchasing power parity (PPP)-adjusted effective exchange rates for exports and imports, as shown in Table 8.1.

Net export subsidies per United States dollar of exports have been gradually reduced so that the effective exchange rate for exports became identical to the official exchange rate. Despite a substantial inflationary trend, particularly before 1982, the anti-export bias index has been consistently near 1, indicating that the nominal exchange rate had been flexibly adjusted to prevent any significant overvaluation of the won.[8] The relative stability in the PPP-adjusted exchange rate since 1965 has significantly contributed to the rapid expansion of exports by removing the anti-export bias (Kim, 1995).

Table 8.1 *Republic of Korea: nominal and PPP-adjusted effective exchange rates, selected years*

	Nominal exchange rate (won/US$)			PPP-adjusted exchange rate (won/US$)			
		Effective			Effective		
Year	Official	Exports[a]	Imports[b]	Official[c]	Exports[a]	Imports[b]	Anti-export bias[a, b]
1965	265.4	275.3	293.1	265.4	275.3	293.1	0.94
1970	310.7	331.5	336.4	240.2	256.2	260.0	0.99
1973	398.3	407.0	417.7	320.6	327.6	336.2	0.97
1975	484.4	496.9	508.9	274.4	281.7	288.5	0.98
1978	484.0	495.0	526.9	272.0	278.2	296.1	0.94
1980	607.4	628.0	641.8	250.1	260.0	265.7	0.98
1983	775.8	775.8	831.7	264.5	264.5	283.6	0.93
1985	870.0	870.0	920.3	290.6	290.6	307.4	0.95
1988	730.6	730.6	780.3	319.3	319.3	341.0	0.94
1990	708.6	708.6	748.0	289.1	289.1	305.2	0.95

Notes: [a]Official exchange rate plus net export subsidies per US$ of exports.
[b]official exchange rate plus actual tariffs and tariff equivalents per US$ of imports;
[c]nominal official exchange rate multiplied by the PPP index and divided by 100. The PPP index is the average wholesale price index of the United States and Japan weighted by their respective average shares in the country's total trade volume.

Source: Kim (1995), pp. 1–131.

Effective Protection for Domestic Industries

While removing the anti-export bias, the government also protected strategic industries in the domestic market to ensure self-sustaining growth.[9]

Table 8.2 depicts some of the main aspects of the structure of protection and incentives between 1968 and 1988. First, the nominal and effective rates of protection were relatively low when compared with those in other developing countries, but much higher for the primary sector than for manufacturing. Second, within manufacturing, export incentives were much greater on average than incentives for import-substitution. Third, the nominal and effective rates for consumer durables, machinery and transport equipment were much higher than those for other industry groups for two decades, although this pattern of industrial protection had changed substantially by 1988.

Table 8.2 Republic of Korea: nominal and effective protection rates for domestic sales and effective subsidy rates for exports by industry groups, selected years (%)

Industry	Nominal protection rate (domestic sales) 1988	Effective protection rate (domestic sales) 1968	Effective protection rate (domestic sales) 1988
Agriculture*	100	19	159
Mining	24	4	32
Manufacturing	5	1	1
Processed foods	9	–18	–55
Beverages and tobacco	23	19	38
Construction materials	8	–11	–2
Intermediate production I	11	–25	–27
Intermediate production II	7	26	14
Non-durable goods	–2	–11	4
Consumer durables	3	64	22
Machinery	11	44	17
Transport equipment	14	163	54
Manufacturing total	5	1	1
All industries	13	11	16

*Includes forestry and fishery subsectors.

Source: Westphal (1978) for 1968 data; and Hong (1994) for 1988 data.

The Government also pursued import substitution for machinery, transport equipment and consumer durables while actively promoting export of finished goods from these manufacturing subsectors during the sample period. Based on the change in the export composition and subsequent gain in international competitiveness of the target industries, export promotion made use of existing comparative advantage while import substitution was used concurrently to nurture promising infant industries until they became internationally competitive.

Export-led Industrial Transformation

The leading role of exports is evident from the fact that the manufacturing sector grew at an average annual rate of nearly 15 per cent during 1965–90, compared with 9 per cent average GNP growth. The share of manufacturing in GNP rose from 18 per cent to 30 per cent during the same period.

Table 8.3 shows the relative contributions of such factors as domestic demand, exports, import substitution and technological change to industrial output growth for 1955–85. In the earlier part of the period growth in manufacturing output was mainly attributable to expansion in domestic demand and import substitution. However, domestic demand and export expansion made the chief contributions to industrial growth in the later part of the period. Export expansion to manufacturing growth went from 10.6 per cent

Table 8.3 Republic of Korea: contributions of autonomous factors to industrial growth and transformation

	Domestic demand expansion	Export expansion	Import substitution	Technological change
1955–63				
All industry total	78.0	9.2	15.9	–3.1
Manufacturing total	61.6	10.6	34.6	–6.8
Social overheads	136.1	14.9	23.9	74.9
Primary sector	97.8	7.2	–20.2	15.2
1963–75				
All industry total	64.4	32.4	6.3	–3.1
Manufacturing total	50.4	39.9	8.9	0.8
Social overheads	88.1	15.9	1.7	–5.8
Primary sector	119.9	26.2	–3.3	–42.9
1975–85				
All industry total	49.7	45.0	5.7	–0.4
Manufacturing total	36.6	56.4	8.1	–1.1
Social overheads	75.4	23.6	0.6	0.4
Primary sector	93.9	17.1	0.7	–11.7

Source: Economic Planning Board, *Yearbook of Major Economic Statistics*, various years.

during the first sub-period up to 39.9 per cent during the second and to 56.4 per cent in the third.

Table 8.4 shows that production and exports had a similar composition. Manufactured goods increased from some 61 per cent to about 94 per cent of total exports by 1990. Furthermore, in the category of manufactured exports, machinery and transport equipment increased from 3.1 per cent to nearly 40 per cent of the total between 1965 and 1990.

Table 8.4 Republic of Korea: production and export structure of manufacturing

	(1)	(2)	(3)	(4)	(5)	(6)
Production structure						
1963	27.8	15.4	18.0	30.0	8.8	100.0
1975	15.7	14.9	18.3	32.2	18.9	100.0
1985	10.5	12.1	16.8	40.8	13.6	100.0
Exports structure						
1963	20.7	20.8	13.9	38.6	6.0	100.0
1975	4.2	15.5	33.6	18.3	28.4	100.0
1985	1.5	9.6	20.7	27.9	40.3	100.0

Notes: (1) Food and agriculture
(2) Textiles and clothing
(3) Machinery and transport equipment
(4) Chemicals
(5) Other
(6) Total.

Source: Economic Planning Board, *Yearbook of Major Economic Statistics*, various years.

Two points stand out regarding the role of exports in the Republic of Korea's industrialization process. One is that structural change in manufacturing exports generally led to changes in manufacturing production. The second is that export expansion was more critical to rapid industrialization than import substitution, suggesting that the policy shift to export-led growth was quite effective in altering the pattern of industrialization. Given the export-oriented industrial strategy, changes in the country's industrial structure are closely related to changes in export trade structure, as shown in Table 8.5. Dominant industrial subsectors accounted for the leading items in the top ten export list.

Table 8.5 Republic of Korea's top ten exports, 1970-93

1970		1980		1993	
Item	Share	Item	Share	Item	Share
1. Textiles	40.8	Textiles	28.8	Electronics	29.5
2. Plywood	11.0	Electronics	11.4	Textiles	19.4
3. Wigs	10.8	Iron and steel	9.0	Iron and steel	8.0
4. Iron ore	5.9	Footwear	5.2	Chemicals	5.6
5. Electronics	3.5	Ships	3.5	Automobiles	5.5
6. Fruits	2.3	Synthetic fibres	3.3	Ships	4.5
7. Footwear	2.1	Metal production	2.3	Machinery	3.7
8. Tobacco	1.6	Plywood	2.0	Footwear	2.8
9. Iron and steel	1.5	Fish	2.0	Petrol production	2.2
10. Metal production	1.5	Electrical goods	1.9	Plastics and metal	1.8
Total (percentage)	81.1		69.3		83.0
Total exports (million US$)	835.2		17 505		82 236

Source: Korea Foreign Trade Association.

Role of Entrepreneurs and *Chaebols*

In a market economy, industrial development policy implementation operates through the private sector. It is essential to evaluate how private enterprise responds to policy directions. In the Republic of Korea, capital was borrowed internationally, technology and intermediate inputs were imported, and the government was ready to provide a host of export incentives. But these would only have led to indebtedness if they were not effectively combined with entrepreneurship. Jones and Il (1980) suggested that in the 1950s there was already a substantial stock of entrepreneurial talent. The country had gifted entrepreneurs who were willing to take risks and challenge international competitors well before the HCI drive. It was only in the 1960s, however, that entrepreneurial energies were tapped, largely through government efforts.

Most important, domestic entrepreneurs always emphasized indigenous efforts in mastering advanced technology and business practices in the world-market. The export orientation of national economic policy provided them with ready access to world class products. Entrepreneurial talents responded positively to various government incentives to build up indigenous technological capability. Both Lee Byung Churl, Chairman of the Samsung Group, and Chung Ju Young, Chairman of the Hyundai Group, who pioneered such new industries as shipbuilding, automobiles and semiconductors were ahead of their time in this regard.[10]

Despite the positive role played by both entrepreneurs and big business organizations, they concentrated economic power in the *chaebols,* in contrast with the relative weakness of SMIs, posing a threat to economic stability. Their growth has been financed primarily through debt instruments, which increases their vulnerability to market downturns. A sustained slump in sales could cause them to default on debt payments. The bankruptcy of large conglomerates could trigger a chain of bankruptcies, which would threaten the banking system. Under these circumstances, the government would be obliged to ensure *chaebols'* stability. This implicit guarantee encourages *chaebols* to continue diversification despite their precarious debt-to-equity ratio.

Performance-based Industrial Development and Trade Policy

During the past half-century the country has risen from virtually no exports to nearly tenth largest exporter in the world. Industrial development and trade policies kept evolving and adjusting to changing domestic and international market conditions. Since the early 1960s these policies shifted from interventionist to market-driven, as shown in Table 8.6. As a result, it is hard to generalize about the country's trade and industrial development policies. At each stage of industrial development different elements predominated, even under the outward-oriented development regime.

There are conflicting views on the nature of the country's industrialization model. From the neoclassical perspective, the 1987 *World Development Report* characterized the Republic of Korea's growth model as outward-oriented based on a free-market and free trade system. Scholars such as Alam (1989) and Kirkpatrick (1987) view it as completely interventionist, with a 'hard state', deviating little from an import-substitution growth strategy characterized by import licensing, high tariffs and investment targeting.

Several studies fall between the two extremes. For example, the 1991 *World Development Report* and the East Asian miracle study of the World Bank (1993) refer to 'a winning mix of fundamentals and interventions'. Amsden describes the Republic of Korea's industrial development model as

Table 8.6 Republic of Korea: macro and industrial development policy emphases and major export items, a summary

Period	Main policy direction	Major performance
1950s	Import substitution Price stabilization	Completion of easy import substitution of the three white industries, etc
1962–71	Policy shift to export promotion (EP) Expanding SOEs	Exports of goods and services: US$0.1 billion (1962) → US$1 billion (1971) GNP per capita: US$82 (1961) → US$289 (1971) Manufacturing/GNP: 17 per cent (1976)
1972–81	HCI under EP Administered credit allocation Import substitution of parts and components	Exports of goods and services: US$12 billion (1977) GNP per capita: US$1000 Manufacturing/GNP: 27.6 per cent (1976)
1982–91	Industrial rationalization Initial liberalization and opening up Shift to private sector initiatives	Exports of goods and services: US$83 billion (1991) GNP per capita: US$5000 (1990) Import liberalization ratio for manufactured goods: 99.9 per cent (1991)
1993–98	Deregulation Globalization (capital and foreign exchange liberalization) Technology-based industrial development policy	Exports of goods and services: US$151 billion (1995) GNP per capita: US$10 000 (1995) Application for OECD membership

a 'market augmenting paradigm of late industrialization' (Amsden, 1989, p. 150). Cho (1994) views it as 'market-conforming'.

The Republic of Korea's industrial development has mostly been associated with effective but carefully designed government activism that left exports largely free to follow market principles. The underlining spirit of this approach could be termed as a 'market-friendly', in which market solutions were sought whenever market functions were sound. However, the government intervened aggressively whenever market development was still at a rudimentary stage.

Export-driven industrialization strategy applied objective performance criteria aimed at rewarding or punishing subsidized industries since exporters had to compete in the world market. To win export orders abroad, the quality of manufactured goods had to be increased and production costs cut. Thus an export-promotion-type industrial development policy had a much better chance of succeeding and was consistent with market-guided resource allocation.

Since adopting an outward-oriented industrial development strategy in the early 1960s, the country has developed a general consensus to follow the export-first doctrine through cooperation between government, entrepreneurs and workers.

INNOVATION-DRIVEN INDUSTRIAL DEVELOPMENT POLICY (EARLY-1990s)

Motivation

When the Roh Government came to office in 1988, it lifted various bans on labour union activities while extending political democracy. As a result, a militant labour movement arose, which was accompanied by demands for rapid wage hikes and social welfare programmes since the economy, with a trade surplus, had been operating at almost full employment level. Since then, the country has undergone continuous rises in real wages. In recent years, the business sector has had difficulty in hiring workers for the so-called 'three-D jobs' – dirty, difficult and dangerous. By the late 1980s, wage increases outstripped labour productivity, as Table 8.7 shows.

A tightening labour market and wage increases also caused a rapid transformation of the manufacturing sector and industry relocation. Both ASEAN's aggressive bid for FDI and China's open-door policy helped accelerate this process. Labour-intensive industries like footwear, toys and textiles and clothing began to move to South-East Asia where workers were available at relatively low wages.

Rising labour costs and tight labour markets fostered industrial restructuring through investment in automation and labour-saving-technology. Many firms responded by starting capital-intensive industries to generate high value-added in manufacturing through applied technology and R&D.

The accelerated transformation of industry is apparent from Table 8.8. From 1975 to 1990, the clothing and textile industries, which had been the leading sectors, were replaced by the machinery and metals sectors. During this industrial transition, policy makers and industrialists realized that their industries were seriously boxed in between low-wage developing countries and advanced technology leaders in the global market.

Table 8.7 Republic of Korea: rate of nominal wage and labour productivity growth since the mid-1980s (annual changes)

Annual rate of growth	1984	1987	1988	1989	1990	1991	1992	1993	1994
Labour productivity	15.1	3.5	14.8	3.6	12.5	15.6	12.2	12.3	12.6
Nominal wage	7.9	11.9	19.5	25.2	20.1	16.8	15.8	10.8	15.5

Note: Labour productivity is defined by nominal GDP divided by total number of persons employed.

Source: Ministry of Labour and Korea Research Institute of Labour.

Table 8.8 Republic of Korea: structural transformation of industries (percentage of manufacturing)

Sector	1975	1980	1985	1990
Food and beverages	10.6	9.0	8.1	7.1
Clothing and textiles	35.6	30.9	28.1	22.1
Wood and furniture	3.7	3.3	2.7	2.9
Paper and printing	4.9	4.5	4.4	4.5
Petrochemicals and plastics	12.9	13.2	13.2	14.4
Non-ferrous metals	4.2	4.7	4.6	4.2
Primary metals	3.4	4.5	4.1	4.0
Machinery and metals	20.8	26.6	31.0	37.7
Others	4.0	3.5	3.9	3.1

Source: Republic of Korea Office of Statistics, *Manufacturing & Mining Census*, annual.

Drawing on Amsden's approach to the maturation of industry as a continuous diversification process,[11] the Republic of Korea can be said to be entering an advanced industrial stage after passing through two phases of industrial diversification. The first involved leading-sector diversification capitalizing on the country's abundance of labour by developing cotton spinning and weaving, garments and electronic assembly. The second phase centred on basic industry diversification into petroleum refining, fertilizers, cement, glass, tyres, more advanced electronic assembly, iron and steel, simple chemicals, shipbuilding, standard machinery, electrical machinery, integrated automobile manufacturing and commodity semiconductors. Post-industrial diversification still involves the same basic industries in which the country initially excelled, but scaled up into higher-quality mid-technology market niches.

Economic Liberalization under the WTO

The Republic of Korea took part in the seven-year-long Uruguay Round negotiations as part of its bid to become an active member of the globalized world economy. It also ardently supported making the Asia Pacific Economic Cooperation Forum an open, viable subregional economic cooperation body. In keeping with the WTO, direct subsidized support for export activities was abolished as well as some legacies of managed and controlled trade systems, which had often served as the main cause for trade disputes.

Instead, the government introduced an indirect functional support system for export activities, allowed under WTO rules. Special efforts have also been made to alter trading practices from a producer-oriented to a consumer-oriented system. Table 8.9 shows that the share of export financing in terms of total bank lending as well as its preferential interest rates, was sharply reduced after the mid-1980s.

Table 8.9 Republic of Korea: trends of export financing by deposit banks (percentage)

	1961–65	1966–72	1973–81	1982–86	1987–91
Export loans/total bank loans	4.5	7.6	13.3	10.2	3.1
Interest rates for:					
Export loans	9.3	6.1	9.7	10.0	10–11.0
General loans	18.2	23.2	17.3	10–11.5	10–13.0

Source: Bank of Korea, *Yearbook of Economic Statistics*, annual.

Having taken office in February 1993, the Kim Young Sam Government soon eliminated anonymous accounts in financial transactions in order to clean up the underground economy. A global income tax system, which included tax on financial incomes and compulsory use of real names in real-estate transactions, was also introduced. These reform measures were designed to eliminate various rent-seeking activities and to lay the foundations for a more transparent market economy.

As the Uruguay Round approached the final stage of negotiations, the government shifted the focus of economic policy to globalization by putting forward a timetable for opening the domestic economy, as well as by revising various rules and systems in compliance with international standards. With the WTO formally launched in 1995, open and fair competition became a new directional guideline in formulating industrial development policy. The new policy accelerated the industrial restructuring process. Labour-intensive industries continued to move abroad, especially to China, Indonesia, Thailand and Malaysia. For emerging industries, however, the country vigorously seeks foreign technology by encouraging FDI, which had largely been ignored in the past in favour of licensing, capital goods imports and foreign training.

FDI is being pursued, especially in high-technology areas, by simplifying government permission procedures and other regulations. Promotion of SMIs has become another important policy goal, along with the tightening of controls on *chaebols* to oligopolistic concentration of economic power. Regional industrial development policy has also taken high priority through the introduction of local autonomy.

The shift to a new paradigm is inevitable for various domestic reasons. The top three *chaebols'* gross sales now exceed the national budget. *Chaebols* operate their business on a global scale and are able to attract the best and brightest personnel. *Chaebols'* ability to gather international market information and introduce innovative practices appears to be far greater than government's. In these circumstances, government direct intervention is no longer feasible. As a result, the government–business interface needs to become more transparent and market-based.

Government intervention to achieve industrial targets is therefore being phased out. Instead, industrial development policy is focused on building infrastructure to promote technological innovation through private initiative.

Innovation-driven Industrial Policy

R&D-based industrial development policy in the imitation period

At the outset of its industrialization, the Republic of Korea relied on imports of foreign technology. At that time, technology was not a critical element and the mature technologies needed could easily be acquired through reverse engineering of imported capital goods. Domestic firms assimilated imported embodied technology so rapidly that they managed subsequent expansion and upgrading with little assistance from abroad (Ahn 1991, and Kim 1993).[12]

Both export orientation and reverse engineering techniques allowed Korean firms to adopt mature technology rather quickly. Formal R&D was not important when imitative reverse engineering proved an adequate substitute.

The government recognized the importance of S&T for industrial development, however, following completion of the first Five-Year Plan. President Park Chung-Hee initiated and monitored the S&T infrastructure in the 1960s and 1970s. The Korea Institute of Science and Technology (KIST), which was the country's first modern integrated technical research centre, was established in 1966 under his leadership. In the following year, the Republic of Korea became the first country to run a ministry-level administration for S&T by establishing the Ministry of Science and Technology (MOST). The Korea Advanced Institute was set up to offer high-calibre graduate programmes. The Technology Development Law and the Engineering Service Promotion Law were enacted in 1972. A number of specialized government-supported research institutes (GRIs) were also established.

During the imitation stage, the Government picked up a major portion of the S&T budget by allocating 0.18 per cent of GNP in 1964, 0.3 per cent in 1970 and 0.37 per cent in 1980. Although the percentages remained at almost the same level until the 1990s, they were relatively higher than those in other developing countries in the same years. Despite the marginal contribution of supply-side S&T policy to manufacturing competitiveness in its early stage, GRIs attracted high-calibre South Korean scientists and engineers from abroad who later on played a major role in developing HCIs and high-tech industries.

Although industrial development policy has been mainly the responsibility of the Ministry of Trade, Industry and Energy (MOTIE), which reacted to business cycles and the political situation, the S&T policy administered by MOST was able to maintain a considerable degree of consistency. In 1987, MOTIE launched the Industrial Generic Technology Development Programme, which was based on the Industrial Development Law and complemented MOST's R&D programme. In general, MOTIE focused on applied research and industrial technology designed to enhance the competitiveness and productivity of the manufacturing sector.

A new aspect of the industrial development policy was introduced as early as 1982, when the government conducted cabinet-wide S&T promotion meetings attended by representatives from industry, government-supported research institutes and academia. Similar to the export promotion meetings, their aim was to build a general consensus and set up new directional guidelines for S&T development to create an indigenous S&T base. Up to this point, R&D efforts were marginal and low-priority. In 1975, the share of R&D expenditure in GNP was only 0.42, but it increased to 1.88 by 1990. Despite the rapid increase of in R&D expenditures, the R&D expenditure ratio was still very low compared to that of the United States (2.68) and Japan (2.78) in the same year. In short, the government took initiatives in local R&D at a time when the private sector had neither the capability nor the market incentives to pursue such activities.

R&D-based industrial development policy in the globalization period

Rapidly rising wages and difficulties in obtaining sophisticated foreign technologies eventually induced firms, especially *chaebols*, to intensify their R&D efforts.[13] As firms moved on to higher technology, industrial development policy began to emphasize technology development, knowledge-creating activities and infrastructure requisite for an information society. It was widely agreed that industrial upgrading must come from development of high-technology industries such as microelectronics, biotechnology, new materials and information industries, along with both factory and office automation efforts.

However, policy makers realized that high-technology industries usually required large-scale investment but were risky due to the short life cycle of products. Furthermore, advanced industrial countries were very reluctant to transfer high technology because of fears of potential competition in new industries.

But as industrialization progressed and comparative advantage in labour-intensive industries deteriorated, the private sector took the leading role in domestic R&D (Kim, 1993). From 1980 to 1990, the bulk of R&D expenditures shifted from the government to the private sector (Table 8.10).

In due course, *chaebols* played a major role in expediting technological learning in industry during the recent decades. Most major firms set up in-house research institutes to develop various commercial technologies, while joining international networks through strategic alliances with foreign firms. The highly diversified but centrally controlled *chaebols* applied experiences in one field of business to another, achieving a rapid diffusion of technological capability to subsidiaries. These big business firms could afford to enter risky and expensive new areas of industry, as they were cushioned financially by their size and diversified portfolio.

Table 8.10 Republic of Korea: ratio of total R&D expenditure to GNP and relative R&D shares between the government and private sector (%)

	1980	1983	1986	1989	1992
R&D/GNP	0.77	1.11	1.77	1.99	2.09
Government versus private	64 : 36	34 : 66	23 : 77	20 : 80	18 : 82

Source: Industrial Technology Promotion Association, *Major Statistics of Industrial Technology*, annual.

Special loan programmes with preferential interest rates played an important role in promoting private R&D. Funds were provided to private firms through the Bank of Korea, commercial banks, venture capital and credit guarantee corporations.[14]

The technology-driven development strategy was given renewed priority in the late 1980s with the establishment of the Science and Technology Advisory Council, directly under the Office of the President, and of the Korea Industry Technology Institute, under the Ministry of Trade and Industry. Since the late 1980s, industrial development and technology policies have been closely related.

At the outset, the MOST R&D programme carried out two types of research. One consisted of government-initiated projects, which mainly dealt with high-risk research or research with important public externalities. These projects were entirely funded by the government. However, projects initiated by industry involved core industrial technologies that private firms could not develop alone owing to scarcity of investment funds and R&D capabilities, so both the government and industries shared funding costs.

In the 1990s, new technology-based industries began to emerge. For example, Republic of Korea firms started to participate in the international product network for information technology. Both the personal computer industry and the semiconductor industry gained recognition in the world market in the early 1990s. Other high-tech industries such as biotechnology, new materials, environmental technology and new energy sources were also identified as core technologies.

In response to new socio-economic needs, the MOST national R&D programme was enlarged to include six different projects, including the HAN, strategic national R&D, GRI, international R&D cooperative, nuclear R&D and research planning and evaluation projects. Table 8.11 shows that the government and the private sector shared almost equally the necessary funding for the MOST national R&D programme.

Table 8.11 Investment sources for the Republic of Korea Ministry of Science and Technology's national R&D programme (1993)

	Investment (100 million won)	
Project	Government	Private
HAN project	572	845
Strategic national R&D	338	334
GRI project	400	21
International cooperative R&D project	44	17
Nuclear R&D project	77	370
Research planning and Evaluation project	30	–
Total	1 461	1 587

Source: Republic of Korea Ministry of Science and Technology.

Among various components of the national R&D projects, the HAN project deserves special mention. Systematically prepared by various government agencies, it was launched in 1992 for a ten-year period. The aim is to strengthen industrial and technological capabilities in strategic areas in order to reach the level of advanced industrial countries in the twenty-first century. Designed as an interministerial programme, it embraces eleven fields of technology which are being intensively developed under the supervising ministries in collaboration with supporting ministries, as shown in Tables 8.12 and 8.13. The HAN project is broadly composed of two categories – product technology and fundamental technology development – to increase both the level of economic activity and the quality of human life.

Table 8.12 Republic of Korea: HAN project of product technology development

Project	Objective
New drugs and agro-chemicals	Development of new drugs from traditional oriental medicines by 1996 Discovery and development of two or three new drugs and agro-chemicals by 1997
Broadband integrated services and data network (B-ISDN)	Development of ATM (asynchronous transfer mode) by 1996 Development of B-ISDN by 2001
High-definition television (HDTV)	Establishment of HDTV monitor technology by 1993 Transmission and broadcasting technology by 1994 Flat panel display by 1997
Next-generation vehicle technology	Technologies related to next-generation automobiles and parts, including electrical vehicles to cope with environmental and energy problems as well as socio-economic change

Source: Republic of Korea Ministry of Science and Technology.

Under the HAN programme, the government supports individual projects in which the private sector is willing to fund at least 30 per cent of the cost. If the project succeeds commercially, firms have to reimburse the amount of public spending and, in turn, receive licensing fees based on their contributions. The HAN projects have helped increase the number of Republic of Korea patents issued in the United States. These went up from just a few to 537 in 1992 and 765 in 1993.

Financial reform and innovation-driven industrial development policy
Because the financial and industrial sectors reinforce one another, the government has continued to liberalize the financial market by eliminating

Table 8.13 Republic of Korea: HAN project of fundamental technology development

Project	Objective
Ultra-large-scale integrated circuits (ULSI)	Development and production of 256 megabyte DRAM by 1996 Development of 1 gigabyte DRAM by 2000
New advanced materials for information, electronics and energy	High value added new materials and synthesis of ultra pure materials that are important for the information industry and highly developed industrial society
Advanced manufacturing systems	Computer integrated manufacturing (CIM) by 2000 Research and development of intelligent manufacturing system (IMS) by 1996
New functional bio-materials	High quality biological resources expected to be important in 21st century industries
Environmental technology	Upgrading technology to solve national and global environmental problems and to provide better human and social environment
New energy	Highly efficient and clean energy
R&D on next generation	Design and verification study for a new reactor concept to secure stable energy resources in preparation for the exhaustion of fossil energy

Source: Republic of Korea Ministry of Science and Technology.

various regulations. One of the basic objectives of financial liberalization is to build up financial institutions' competitiveness through independent decision making and heightened competition. Deregulation of interest rates was accomplished in November 1995. As a result, the ratio of policy loans to total money loaned was reduced from 25.3 per cent to 19.8 per cent in September 1995.

At the time, a special presidential commission was set up to carry out a major reform of the financial sector. One of the ideas was to turn local financial institutions from supplier- into consumer-oriented. Short-term measures were to pursue further deregulation of the financial sector and consolidation of business lines by specialized lending-only financial firms. Mid- and long-term measures were to centre on making local financial firms bigger, encouraging them to specialize in self-selected business areas and reorganizing the domestic financial industry as a whole. It is estimated that the improved efficiency of local financial firms alone can contribute to driving down interest rates by 1 to 2 percentage points.

Another proposal for financial sector reform consisted of removing entry and exit barriers for firms engaged in finance. Foreign banks are also allowed to operate under competitive conditions. The panel recommended the transfer of monetary and credit policy from the Ministry of Finance and Economy to the central bank to ensure independence and neutrality.

The government also announced the promotion of venture capital as well as venture business to upgrade SMIs' technological capability. A Republic of Korea version of an angel fund would promote venture business under competitive financial market conditions. This is likely to become a new policy direction to promote innovation-driven industrial development.

SMEs' development and innovation-driven industrial development policy

As the Republic of Korea's manufacturing centres on mid-technology assembly-type industries such as automobiles, electronics and machinery, the parts and components industry needs to be developed in order to upgrade the quality of assembled goods.

The pro-HCIs policy was carried out to the neglect of SMEs in the 1970s and thereafter.[15] In recent years, the government's budget for functional support to SMEs has increased greatly, with focus on automation and collaboration in logistics, manpower development and information networks. To protect SMEs from unequal treatment *vis-à-vis* larger firms, the Korea Fair Trade Commission has revised the Fair Subcontract Trade Act of 1985. The revised Act prevents large firms from delaying payment to subcontractors. In February 1996, the government established the Small Business Administration, with 11 regional offices to assist SMEs by providing start-up financing, manpower, technological development and marketing.

A number of SMEs are regionally concentrated. As a result, localization policy has been very important, especially since the introduction of local autonomy in mid-1995. Jointly with the local government, the central government has also established assistance centres for SMEs in each region. Newly elected governors and mayors have given highest priority to promotion of local industries, which are basically SMEs. For the first time, local governments have authority to develop industrial sites and credit unions as well as to attract FDI.

Fostering both venture capital and venture business was to become a core part of current policy. In this regard, cooperation between academia and venture SMEs is being strengthened. Major universities instituted techno-valley concepts to attract venture businesses on to university campuses to work together with professors. After the introduction of the real-name financial and real-estate transaction legislation, some underground funds still held by the private sector were to be mobilized as venture capital by providing incentives such as tax credits or granting anonymity to the sources of funds.

Another way to strengthen SMEs' competitiveness relates to cooperative linkages between large-scale enterprises and parts and components industries along the lines of Japan's *keiretsu* cooperative relationships to minimize transaction costs and information asymmetries. To establish an efficient outsourcing system, the government has strengthened incentives for larger firms to share with SMEs capital, technology, market information and managerial know-how. In recent years, *chaebols* have also taken some affirmative actions in this respect on their own initiative.

FDI and innovation-driven industrial development policy

At the outset of industrialization, the country relied on foreign loans for capital formation, rather than FDI. To facilitate the inflow of foreign technology, FDI policy shifted from a negative list system to a positive list system in the early 1980s. However, more recently FDI has received renewed attention as a key source of technology and advanced managerial know-how. In line with this, an extensive and wide-ranging package of liberalization measures has been implemented. The FDI liberalization ratio reached 90.7 per cent in 1995, with 107 restricted business lines and is scheduled to increase to 97.2 per cent by 2000, with the number of restricted business lines reduced to 32.

In addition, FDI through mergers and acquisitions began to be allowed in 1997. Incentives to improve conditions under which foreign firms can operate were also introduced. One of the key objectives of inviting aggressive FDI is to encourage strategic alliances with local firms in high-technology areas and to benefit from quality requirements of investing firms.

High-powered HRD and innovation-driven industrial development policy

The Republic of Korea would never have been able to achieve high-level industrial development without a massive, well-educated and diligent workforce. In June 1995, the government announced important reforms in the education system. The main goal was to give schools more autonomy in order to encourage competition, making the education system more responsive to changing socio-economic demands.

In order to meet the increasing demand for skilled manpower, vocational schools were rapidly expanded to produce skilled students with practical knowledge. As of 1994, vocational schools' enrolment was 852 000, or 41.3 per cent of total school enrolment. At these schools, shop practice accounts for more than 50 per cent of total credit hours. The development of vocational high schools has been facilitated by cooperation between schools and industry so that the students are able to receive sufficient on-the-job training.

In order to produce middle-level technicians equipped with a solid theoretical base and proficient skills, several junior colleges were established in 1979, the number having grown to 135 by 1994. Enrolment increased from 165 000 in 1980 to 507 000 in 1994. Students at junior college are obliged to take the national certification examination, which guarantees excellent employment opportunities.

Recently, in-company technology colleges have also begun to play an important role in educating employees who wish to continue to gain academic knowledge together with technical skills. These colleges are designed to enhance the productivity and innovative capability of workers. The rapid increase in the number of trainees at in-plant institutes reflects the need to retrain lesser-skilled employees in new technologies. Firms employing more than 30 workers are required to reserve a certain amount of funding for vocational training, in the form of unemployment benefits, through a payroll tax.

While South Korean universities have an abundance of high-calibre scientists, R&D activities at university level have been sluggish due to heavy teaching loads as well as inadequate R&D funding for university professors.[16] To tackle this problem, the government created the Engineering Research Centre (ERC)/Scientific Research Centre (SRC) programme to improve capabilities for technology development by increasing the scientific staff available at universities. SRCs focus on new developments in basic science, while ERCs emphasize developing highly advanced technology for developing industries. In 1996, there were 20 SRCs and 25 ERCs, with the number expected to increase significantly. To ensure the quality of research activities at SRCs and ERCs, the government provides them with financial support for a period of nine years on the condition that they meet certain standards every three years.

Another important aspect of the innovation-driven strategy is the repatriation of South Korean scientists and engineers who were educated and who developed their professional careers abroad. The government offered financial support to 2178 scientists and engineers, including a small number of foreigners from overseas to work at research institutes, colleges and industries at home on a permanent or temporary basis. They have been instrumental in upgrading R&D capabilities.

CHALLENGES AND LESSONS

Challenges

The Republic of Korea's industrial development largely followed the flying geese pattern as a catch-up model. Declining industries from advanced industrial countries were introduced and forged into mature industries. As domestic wages increased, they were moved to other developing countries. This process continued until the country could no longer introduce declining industries from advanced industrial countries. As a result, the country now competes head-on with advanced industrial countries in such middle-level technology industries as semiconductors, automobiles, machinery, and information technology while searching for new frontiers. This raises a crucial question about to what extent the economic power concentrated in the *chaebols* is a plus or a minus for the international competitiveness of the Republic of Korea's economy in the post-WTO era.

Concentrated industrialization has created a number of structural problems in the economy. The sandwiched position of the country in the international dualistic structure of technology is still apparent. The rapid economic expansion of the *chaebols* in relation to SMIs has unbalanced the market. The financial sector is not competitive.

Although the dominant industries are currently capital- and technology-intensive, technological capability is still very weak relative to advanced industrial countries. As other developing countries increase their technological capabilities and advanced industrial countries maintain technical hegemony over global competition, the Republic of Korea is caught in a technology gap. Overcoming threshold factors in R&D is often as or more important than the ratio of R&D to GNP to compete in the global economy.

The Republic of Korea now faces the problem of creating fair and competitive market conditions in a globalizing world economy. In order to do so, it needs to dismantle existing rigidities and regulations on firms' entry and exit with more vigour. Other crucial questions include how to foster competition and cooperation between *chaebols* and SMEs as well as between local firms and MNCs, and how far may *chaebols'* R&D capabilities be optimized and integrated into a fair and competitive market environment.

The government–business interface has also changed. At the early stage of industrialization, the government was the dominant player but, in recent years, both have been on a relatively equal footing. Another challenge is to establish the private sector as a dominant economic player. To accomplish this, government's role will be to create conditions that facilitate and promote mobility of resources while increasing transparency and fair competition in the domestic market.

The legacies of hard-state intervention are still visible in many aspects of the economy. For example, a complicated system of permits from various government agencies still acts as an entry as well as an exit barrier. The economy still favours producers. A consumer-oriented society is still distant. Deregulation should proceed quite quickly so that Korean producers, especially *chaebols,* can operate in a far stronger open market environment while maximizing their existing R&D capabilities.

The Republic of Korea's industrial development policy in relation to the market has evolved over time. Neither industrial targeting nor a direct support mechanism are any longer in place. They have been replaced by functional support to foster world-class, high-technology products. Industrial development policy is essentially evolving into R&D promotion for the private and public sectors, with strategic alliances between Korean firms and high-technology MNCs and aggressive promotion of FDI and HRD as critical components.

The basic aim is to enhance competition by liberalizing the domestic market and to reduce interference in the micro-management of the economy and in private sector decisions. In this context, foreign residents will be allowed to buy South Korean companies' equities without limitations from 1999.[17] Previously closed sectors like automobiles will open to more domestic and foreign competition. The Government will also continue to privatize state-owned telephone, power and other companies to spur competition.

In short, export-led industrialization has essentially been designed to ensure that potential exporters are on an equal footing with international producers. The country used exports as the criterion to judge success. However, whenever market functions were beneficially performed, the policy was to let the market determine production. In general, Korean policy makers have been more concerned with dynamic efficiency gains than static efficiency.

Lessons

The Republic of Korea has drawn many benefits from the relative effectiveness of its export-based policy. The combination of a disciplined and reasonably educated labour force, dedicated national leadership, entrepreneurial talents and efficient bureaucratic capabilities, as demonstrated by the Economic Planning Board, has helped economic development.

Some general lessons can be drawn from the country's experience for other developing countries at various stages of industrial development. First, government incentive systems at the initial stages of industrialization need to be outward-looking to take advantage of export externalities and should be closely linked to quantifiable, transparent and performance-based criteria. Winning export orders from the competitive international market itself means that firms have passed an international efficiency test. Even during the HCI drive, the government penalized poor-performing *chaebols,* and rewarded good performers with new licences in more lucrative sectors. As a result, incentives reinforced efficiency.

Second, financial sector development should not be neglected in favour of tangible production. Evaluation of firms' credit-worthiness and monitoring of firms' risks should be transferred from the state to financial institutions in a framework of sound financial regulations and full accountability.

Third, entrepreneurship is essential in implementing government policies at all stages of industrialization. Therefore it is crucial to foster a critical mass of entrepreneurs with a business leadership function.

Fourth, a disciplined and motivated workforce and capable bureaucrats are fundamental in accelerating industrial development.

Last, national leadership should be able to build a national consensus to achieve developmental goals.

Above all, it is crucial that competition be fostered within regulatory and legal boundaries to ensure fair play and equal opportunities for all market participants as industrial deepening proceeds.

NOTES

1. The most notable non-durable consumer goods were cotton, sugar and flour.
2. Notably, Balassa (1976), Westphal (1978) and Rhee et al. (1984).
3. In 1965, the government also instituted the local letter-of-credit system to extend the same benefits to all firms that generated export value-added but did not export directly.
4. President Park's determination to ensure self-defence capability topped his regime's national priority in the wake of the ever-intensifying inter-Korean military hostilities in the 1970s, which often overshadowed economic rationality in the implementation of the HCI Plan.
5. Targeted subsectors were machinery (1967), shipbuilding (1967), textiles (1976), electronics (1969), petrochemicals (1970), iron and steel (1970) and non-ferrous metals (1971).
6. As a result of HCIs' preferential access to bank credit, nearly 60 per cent of total bank loans from 1975 to 1977 and close to 95 per cent of policy loans in 1978 were accounted for by HCIs. See Il, (1993).
7. The beneficial impact of the orientation towards labour-intensive exports can be seen in the factor proportions and the efficiency of factor use in manufacturing, which was characterized by a low capital–output ratio and a low capital–labour ratio as well as high rates of productivity growth. The unlagged incremental capital–output ratio for the manufacturing sector during 1965–76 was 1 : 3 in 1970 prices. There was no significant increase in this ratio during 1970–76 despite the newly emerging capital-intensive industries such as steel, shipbuilding and machinery. This demonstrates not only the emphasis on labour-intensive goods but also low construction costs and high rate of capacity utilization.
8. The direct tax reduction on export income was dropped in 1973, and the interest-rate subsidies implicit in preferential export credit significantly declined from 1972 and were completely eliminated after 1982.
9. When legal tariffs are the only instrument of trade restriction, they represent the nominal rate of protection. However, the effective protection rate defined as the percentage difference between domestic value-added under protection and the value-added in world market prices is normally used to measure the degree of protection extended to value-adding processes because it measures not only nominal protection of the product itself but also of traded inputs.
10. To name just a few of their business ventures: Lee Byung Churl had the foresight to develop semiconductors in the early 1970s. Samsung Electronics is currently a leading manufacturer of non-memory semiconductors. Chung Ju Young won international contracts to make large-scale ships, without even having the necessary shipyard, in the early 1970s. The Hyundai shipyard now builds the world's most competitive ships.
11. Amsden views the maturation of industry as a process of continuous diversification into industries requiring increasing amounts of physical and human capital and related technological and managerial capabilities. See Amsden (1995) pp. 17–18.
12. Entrepreneurs in the Republic of Korea lean towards management independence from MNCs as well as from other local firms.
13. The Republic of Korea's real wages increased a cumulative 62.5 per cent between 1987 and 1989. When adjusted in United States dollar terms, the increase amounts to 91.1 per cent, which is 2.8 times that of productivity (*Business Korea*, 1990).
14. There are three major government funds: the Industrial Development Fund, from the Ministry of Trade, Industry, and Energy; the S&T Promotion Fund, from the Ministry of Science and Technology; and the Information and Telecommunication Promotion Fund, from the Ministry of Information and Communication.

15. SMEs are defined as firms with fewer than 300 employees in manufacturing and fewer than 20 in services. At the moment the country has some 2.4 million such enterprises, including 300 000 in the manufacturing sector.
16. For example, in 1993, R&D expenditures in universities were only 7.2 per cent of total expenditures, whereas the figure for the government research institute was 21.3 per cent and, for industry, 71.5 per cent.
17. Up to 1996 they were allowed to buy a maximum of 25 per cent of a company's equity.

REFERENCES

Ahn, C.-Y. (1986), 'Economic development of South Korea, 1945–1985: strategies and performance', *Korea and World Affairs*, **10** (1), Spring.

Ahn, C.-Y. (1988), 'Foreign investment and trade promotion schemes: with some comparisons between Korea and Latin American countries', *Journal of Economic Development*, **13** (13), December.

Ahn, C.-Y. (1991a), 'Technology transfer and economic development: the case of Korea', Karen Minden (ed.), *Pacific Cooperation in Science and Technology*, Honolulu: East–West Center.

Alam, M. S. (1989), *Government and Market in Economic Development Strategies: Lessons from Korea, Taiwan, and Japan*, New York: Praeger.

Amsden, A.H. (1989), *Asia's Next Giant: South Korea and Late Industrialization*, New York: Oxford University Press.

Amsden, A.H. (1995), 'Post-industrial policy in East Asia', paper presented at the International Symposium on Political Economics of Korea's Industrial Development to commemorate the anniversary of national liberation, organized by Korea Institute for Industrial Economics and Trade, Seoul, 11 August.

Balassa, B. (1976), 'Reforming the system of incentives in developing countries', *World Development*, **3** (6), June.

Cho, S. (1994), 'Government and market in economic development', *Asian Development Review*, **12** (2).

Hong, S.-D. (1994), 'Analysis of factor contribution to Korea's economic growth', *Korea Development Review*, **16** (3), Korea Development Institute (in Korean).

Il, S.-K. (1993), *Korea in the World Economy*, Washington, DC: Institute for International Economics.

Jones, L.P. and S-K.Il, (1980), *Government, Business, and Entrepreneurship in Economic Development: The Korean Case*, Boston, MA: Harvard University Press.

Kim, K.-S. (1995), *Liberalizing Foreign Trade: Korea, the Philippines and Singapore*, Vol. 2, Cambridge, MA: Basil Blackwell.

Kim, L.-S. (1993), 'National system of industrial innovation: dynamics of capability building in Korea', in R. Nelson (ed.), *National Innovation Systems: A Comparative Analysis*, New York: Oxford University Press.

Kirkpatrick, C. (1987), 'Trade policy and industrialization in LDCs', in N. Gemmel (ed.), *Surveys in Development Economics*, Oxford: Basil Blackwell, pp.56–89.

Kwack, S.-Y. (1990), 'The economic development of the Republic of Korea, 1965–1981', in L.J. Lau (ed.), *Models of Development*, ICS Press.

Rhee, Y.-W., Ross-Larson, B. and Pursell, G. (1984), *Korea's Competitive Edge: Managing the Entry into World Markets*, Baltimore, MD: Johns Hopkins University Press.

World Bank (1993), *The East Asian Miracle: Economic Growth and Public Policy,* New York: Oxford University Press.

Westphal, L.E. (1978), 'The Republic of Korea's experience with export led industrial development', *World Development*, **6** (3).

9. Newly Opened Economies: The Case of Brazil

INTRODUCTION

Brazil has had a long history of industrial policy interventions. Since the Second World War, successive governments have been concerned with building up and developing an industrial base. After an initial period, when industrial development was founded on production of steel and few other intermediates, and construction of an infrastructure network, there were two important junctures in Brazil's industrial development policy formulation: in the mid-1950s, President Kubitchek's comprehensive Plano de Metas and, a few years later, the Second National Development Plan (1974–79), which provided a coherent framework for increasing import substitution, with emphasis on capital goods and intermediates industries.

Since the late 1970s, Brazil has not depended on industrial policy, in the strict sense of a set of instruments aimed at changing the sectoral allocation of resources in a systematic and purposeful way. Although, during the 1980s, successive governments made formal industrial policy announcements, the absence of effective mechanisms and, most important, the exhaustion of the import-substitution paradigm as a model of industrial development, translated into a *de facto* policy vacuum. It is only since 1990, after an 11-year hiatus, that a new government has redefined a new trade and industrial strategy. Trade liberalization has been most effective in changing the incentive regime for industry, where the competitive ability of firms became the basic determinant of success. The trade regime has been, therefore, at the core of the government's industrial strategy.

The transition towards a more open and competitive economy has been greatly helped by a quality- and productivity-enhancing programme launched in 1990, as part of the new policy regime, explicitly to strengthen firms in view of the new environment brought about by trade liberalization. While the latter, combined with a recessionary economy, imposed strict discipline upon firms, the Brazilian Programme for Quality and Productivity (PBQP) helped educate managers and workers as to the importance of total quality management (TQM), as well as reshape the internal organization of firms, with the introduction of new management concepts and tools. In this sense, the PBQP was instrumental in ensuring that Brazilian firms effectively reacted to the post-1990 open economy environment.

Institutional responsibility for industrial development policy formulation and implementation in Brazil rests with the Ministry of Industry, Commerce and Tourism (MICT). *De facto*, however, there is significant power fragmentation and lack of coordination, with only PBQP effectively in the Ministry's control. Thus trade policy is dictated by the Ministry of Finance, with considerable influence from Planning and Foreign Affairs. Export policies and associated fiscal and financial incentives come under the purview of Finance and Planning, with inputs from MICT and Foreign Affairs. The investment promotion regime, particularly that related to financial incentives, is under the Ministry of Planning, which is parent to the National Development Bank (BNDES). Technology and R&D policy is mostly concentrated in the Ministry of Science and Technology, although related fiscal incentives are filtered by the economic ministries. The direction of industrial development policy, therefore, oscillates, depending on which ministry has its share of control under the influence of political and short-term considerations.

BRAZILIAN INDUSTRIAL DEVELOPMENT POLICY IN ACTION

This section describes the main industrial development policy instruments in operation in the Brazilian economy and briefly assesses their impact.[1] Three categories of policies designed to enhance manufacturing competitiveness need to be singled out:

1. Firm-centred policies, including those directed towards dissemination of TQM, training and acquisition of skills; incentives that stimulate producers to undertake investment and R&D; and mechanisms that promote SMIs.
2. Subsector-specific policies, including trade reforms allowing for greater import competition, the impact of which tends to be differentiated across subsectors and programmes focused on creation, expansion or restructuring of individual industries.

3. Sector-wide policies, particularly those targeted at the reduction of manufacturing costs and promotion of exports.

Firm-centred policies

Among policies that focus on individual firms, BPQP is possibly the most important. Other support mechanisms include tax and financial incentives for investment and R&D as well as those targeted specifically at SMI development.

Brazilian quality and productivity programme

The ability of Brazilian firms to face the simultaneous challenges of recession and import liberalization in the early 1990s was a reflection of producers' commitment to cost-reducing and quality-enhancing measures. They led firms to subcontract or hive off the least economical activities; to reduce hierarchical levels in an attempt to improve intra-firm communication among employees, and between them and management; and to introduce *kaizen*, continuous improvement, quality circles, just in time (JIT) and other techniques of TQM and worker involvement, so as greatly to reduce the high levels of waste and inefficiency that have characterized Brazilian industry.

With liberalization of imports firms were faced with the choice between becoming internationally competitive, by adopting new standards of quality and productivity, or exiting the market. None the less, it is highly unlikely that the pace of dissemination of ISO standards and, in particular, the degree of awareness in society regarding the importance of TQM would have had the same impact were it not for the government's PBQP. The programme was launched in November 1990 to exert a 'decisive role in the competitive restructuring of national industry'.[2]

Although based on voluntary public and private actions, PBQP is considered, together with trade liberalization, the driving force behind the productive revolution experienced by Brazilian industry since the early 1990s. PBQP is based on both general and sectoral programmes. The former are focused on motivating agents and raising their level of awareness; disseminating information concerning the importance of improving the Q&P levels for all economic activities; and promoting development and diffusion of new managerial methods.[3] There are also 29 ongoing sectoral statewide programmes, involving 240 public and private institutions. The effectiveness of PBQP is based on large-scale training. By the end of 1994, 17 000 managers and specialists, known as quality multipliers, had been trained and, as a result, an additional 95 000 had been introduced to total quality management techniques.

The commitment to TQM is expressed in firms' adherence to international total quality standards, as codified in the International Standards Organization (ISO) 9000 series. Certification has become a major goal for industrial firms in Brazil. It has also developed into an effective marketing device, a signal to clients, suppliers, creditors, shareholders and the public that Brazilian quality standards are close to international norms. Moreover, the standards provide a common language and production methodology for producers of different countries and industrial cultures, critical at a time when firms are part of a globalized market. There are also gains from a global sourcing perspective, as commonality of standards, norms and practices lowers inspection and supervision costs.

Producers' perceptions confirm that standardization benefits are significant. In a survey of 93 ISO 9000 certified producers, undertaken by the National Confederation of Industry (CNI), in only four cases was there no positive impact from certification efforts (Table 9.1). This statistic eloquently illustrates the pace of adoption of ISO standards in Brazil. Moreover, as shown by anecdotal evidence, firms have benefited from reduced waste and overall higher levels of labour productivity since the start of the process.[4]

Table 9.1 Brazil: reported impact of adoption of ISO 9000, main results

Nature of impact	%
Productivity increases	54.9
Standardization of processes	35.2
Staff involvement with quality	31.9
Product quality improvement	25.3
Improvement in firms' external image	20.9
Increase in clients' satisfaction	20.9
Cost reduction	17.6
Improvement in quality system	9.9
Fulfil export requirements	6.6
Results still to come	4.4

Source: CNI, based on a sample of 93 firms.

The diffusion of ISO 9000 standards among industrial firms, and to a lesser extent, within service organizations, has been remarkably rapid (Table 9.2). Between 1990 and 1995, the number of certificates issued increased from 18 to 948, an average annual growth rate of 121 per cent. In each year between 1991 and 1994, the number of producers adopting TQM standards more than doubled. Since then, the number of firms and units certified has continued to grow but not at such a fast pace. None the less, by mid-1996, a total of some 1235 certificates had been issued and 1159 units certified in 853 firms, which compares favourably with all other industrializing economies, including Singapore (1003) and Taiwan Province (1060), with the exception of South Africa (1627 certificates issued).

Table 9.2 Brazil: evolution of ISO 9000 certification, 1990–96

Year	No. of firms certified	Cumulative no. of firms certified	No. of units certified	Cumulative no. of units certified	Cumulative no. of valid certificates issued
1990	13	13	17	17	18
1991	12	25	16	33	35
1992	44	69	60	93	96
1993	94	163	127	220	225
1994	270	433	366	586	595
1995	257	690	349	935	948
1996*	163	853	224	1159	1235

*Until June 1996.

Source: Comitê Brasileiro de Qualidade – Associação Brasileira de Normas Técnicas, *Certificações ISO 9000*, July 1996.

The sectoral distribution of the ISO 9000 is highly concentrated in manufacturing, with 84.1 per cent of all units certificated. Within manufacturing, the subsectors with the greatest number of certified units were electrical equipment and electronic and optical products (22.3 per cent); basic chemicals, other chemical products and synthetic and artificial fibres (16.0 per cent); basic metals and manufactured metal products (12.3 per cent) and general machinery and equipment (10.2 per cent) (Table 9.3). The concentration of ISO 9000 certificates in the more technology-intensive subsectors, – electronics, chemicals, metals and machinery – suggests both that the firms most capable of affording certification are concentrated in these subsectors and that the process of certification brings considerable competitive gains to such firms.

Table 9.3 Brazil: sectoral and subsectoral distribution of ISO 9000 certificates, June 1996

Sector and subsector	Certified units	%	9001	9002	9003
Manufacturing industry	1039	84.1	388	644	7
Electrical equip., electronic and optical products	275	22.3	137	137	1
Chemicals and synthetic and artificial fibres	198	16	69	128	1
Basic metals and fabricated metal products	152	12.3	24	127	1
General machinery and equipment	126	10.2	66	58	2
Transport equipment	104	8.4	54	50	–
Non-metallic products	59	4.8	6	53	–
Rubber and plastic products	39	3.1	14	25	–
Cellulose, pulp and paper, printing and publishing	28	2.3	4	23	1
Food products, beverages and tobacco	27	2.2	6	21	–
Other industry	31	2.5	8	22	1
Housing	81	6.6	35	45	1
Financial intermediation	22	1.8	2	20	–
Transportation, storage and telecommunication	20	1.6	–	20	–
Mining	17	1.4	–	17	–
Heavy construction	13	1.1	5	8	–
Other services and commerce	43	3.5	9	34	–
Total	1235	100.0	439	788	8

Source: Comitê Brasileiro de Qualidade – Associação Brasileira de Normas Técnicas, (1996).

Although certification tends to be spearheaded by larger firms, a comprehensive survey revealed that a considerable proportion of SMIs have been engaged in TQM and have successfully attempted certification (Table 9.4).[5] It reflects a trend captured by numerous surveys of the widespread adoption by manufacturing firms of some form of qualify- and productivity- (Q&P) enhancing programme, with a growing emphasis on training and upgrading of human resources.

Table 9.4 Brazil: programmes, techniques and methods oriented towards Q&P (percentage of responses from firms engaged at moderate and high intensities), 1994–95

Q&P programmes, techniques and methods	Firms' size				
	Micro	Small	Medium	Large	Average
Human resources training	79	87	96	99	89
Strategic planning	23	31	43	67	37
Work group organization	28	29	37	60	35
Subcontracting	23	31	37	50	33
Automation	18	23	45	58	33
Multifunctionality	28	29	34	41	32
Total quality management	18	25	31	58	31
Lead-time reduction	12	16	36	52	26
SPC	14	21	29	49	25
Just in time	15	21	28	41	24
ISO 9000	5	10	20	48	17
R&D programme	6	9	22	43	17

Source: CNI–SEBRAE (1996).

Producers have come to realize that the impact of the introduction of total quality programmes is dependent on the level of employees' basic cognitive skills and training. Although firms can deduct from their taxes twice their expenditures on training, either in-house or external, as an incentive to expand their knowledge base, training and acquisition of skills have been leveraged considerably by firms' commitment to improve managerial strategies and methods ultimately related to PBQP's effectiveness.

Quality gains An indirect assessment of firms' responses to PBQP's early efforts comes from a repeat survey of 950 firms undertaken in 1990 (year one of import liberalization and PBQP) and 1993 (Table 9.5). All indicators, except the one referring to training, showed a degree of improvement in the three-year period, some quite significant. Yet data also underscored the gap that remained between average international practice and world-class producers.[6] Though the best-practice frontier has also moved ahead in the intervening period, the intensified efforts by Brazilian producers in the last few years – centred on adoption of a differentiated set of quality systems with an emphasis on the ISO 9000 standards – have reduced still further the gap with international competitors.

Table 9.5 Key Q&P indicators: Brazil, EEC, the US and Japan

Indicator	Brazil 1990	Brazil 1993	World*	Japan
Rejections (defective parts per million)	23 000–28 000	11 000–15 000	200	10
Rework (% of products returning to process)	30	35783	2	0.001
Technical assistance expenses (% of sales)	2.7	2	0.1	< 0.05
Average delivery time (days)	35	20	2-4	2
Average lot size	1000	100–250	20–50	1-10
Inventory rotation (times per year)	8	8-14	60–70	150–200
Set-up time (in min.)	80	30–40	10	5
Machine downtime (as % of time idle)	40	21	15–20	5–8
R&D expenditures (as % of sales)	< 1	1–2	3–5	8–12
Training (% of hours/ employee/year)	< 1	< 1	5–7	10
Hierarchical levels	10–12	4–8	7	3

*'World' indicators reflect US and EEC firms' practices.

Source: IMAM Consultoria Ltda.

Training Over the last 50 years, the industry-led Serviço Nacional de Aprendizagem Industrial (SENAI) has provided training to the country´s industrial workforce through a network of extension units for professional and technical education. At the end of 1995, 956 units were in operation, covering more than 3000 municipalities, of which the majority were training facilities (329), centres for professional education (231) and relatively sophisticated and effective technology centres (24), in addition to 353 mobile units.

Aimed at primary and secondary school levels, SENAI´s professional education activities comprise the following:

- *Apprenticeship*: designed for 14- to 18-year-olds, employed or seeking employment, with at least four years of primary schooling.
- *Qualification*: targeted at workers over 14 and for specific occupations; provided at primary or secondary level.
- *Capacitation*: offered to primary school graduates at secondary level in specific occupations or occupational categories; these classes prepare workers for intermediate technical and support functions.
- *Technical formation*: professionalization at tertiary level for secondary school graduates.
- *Training:* targeted at improving knowledge of already qualified workers with courses structured to respond to the immediate requirements of firms and often offered at their premises.

In 1995, SENAI´s 956 units trained more than 2.3 million workers, a 61 per cent increase over 1991 (Table 9.6). Despite SENAI´s efforts to respond to the shifting training requirements of industry and its reputation as a model training institution in Latin America, its coverage is still relatively narrow, with only a fraction of the industrial workforce having access to its training resources. In particular, the level of training of workers in SMIs and in less developed areas of the country is still at an initial stage.

Investment and R&D incentives Since the early 1990s, most productivity gains in manufacturing were achieved by enhancing the efficiency of existing capital assets.[7] A combination of more robust growth and high levels of capacity utilization provided a major stimulus for the expansion of investment in 1993–95. Nevertheless, government investment incentives play a subsidiary, though non-marginal, role. BNDES is the only domestic source of long-term finance, at rates which generally do not compare favourably with those quoted internationally for projects with similar risk–return profiles. The

Table 9.6 Workers trained by SENAI, 1991–95

Type of professional education	1991	1992	1993	1994	1995
Apprenticeship	97 240	96 216	92 344	90 500	88 402
Qualification	106 072	152 581	226 564	282 000	292 730
Training	1 209 200	1 494 073	1 780 830	1 841 000	1 899 578
Capacitation	19 192	18 306	19 755	21 000	23 098
Technical formation	16	37	36	40	387
Total	1 431 720	1 761 213	2 119 529	2 234 540	2 304 195

Source: SENAI.

current government-determined long-term interest rate is in the order of the London Inter-Bank Offered Rate (LIBOR) plus approximately 6 per cent in addition to other BNDES service charges. Still, demand for BNDES resources has grown considerably. Disbursements rose from an average of US$3.1 billion in 1991–93 to US$5.5 billion in 1994, of which US$3.2 billion went to machinery and equipment.[8] BNDES is responsible for financing some 8 per cent of gross fixed capital formation in the Brazilian economy, where most firms are low-leveraged and generally finance investment out of retained earnings.

Federal tax incentives are only available for investments located in the north-east and Amazon regions. Most states and many municipalities compete quite fiercely, however, for new investments through a mixture of explicit sales and property tax reductions and rebates and increasingly scarce state bank loans, as well as through supply of infrastructure services on a preferential basis. The fiscal cost of state and municipal subsidies has not been estimated with any degree of precision, although the amount of revenue foregone is a source of concern to the federal government in view of the dire fiscal ill-health of most states.

R&D and design activities These activities – the basis of product innovation and differentiation – are in their infancy in Brazil.[9] The government's R&D policy is aimed at:

- increasing R&D activities, with total S&T expenditures in Brazil in the order of 0.9 per cent of GDP in 1995, comparing unfavourably with other rapidly industrializing countries, which spend 1–2 per cent of GDP on these activities;

- expanding involvement of the private sector, since 80–90 per cent of expenditures are still financed and undertaken by the government; and
- improving the interface between the productive sector and university and research institutions.

Current legislation allows firms to charge R&D expenditures, including expenses paid to third parties, against a maximum of 8 per cent of owed income tax. In addition, capital goods and instruments dedicated to R&D may be imported without federal value-added tax and are subject to accelerated depreciation, at twice the normal rate, while expenditures associated with intangibles are amortized at an accelerated rate. Firms are also allowed a 50 per cent credit against income and financial transaction taxes on expenses associated with the payment of royalties, technical assistance and specialized services to foreign parties. These incentives are non-automatic, being awarded after assessment by organizations accredited by the Ministry of Science and Technology. The implied fiscal cost of these incentives since they became operational in early 1994 and until mid-1995 was reales 492.5 million, generating reales 1.2 billion in R&D and technology modernization outlays.[10] By the end of the decade, the government expects firms to become responsible for 30–40 per cent of S&T outlays, which would then correspond to 1.5 per cent of GDP.

R&D term finance is available from the government agency FINEP. FINEP's ADTEN programme is the agency's key instrument for financing innovation and design-related activities of industrial firms. In the period 1992–94, the agency financed an annual average of US$130 million at significantly positive interest rates. Before December 1994, the modal real interest rate charged for ADTEN loans was 12 per cent. Thereafter, firms paid the above-mentioned long-term interest rate, a variable risk factor and an ADTEN-specific interest charge varying from 4 to 10 per cent annually. On a smaller scale, R&D resources are also available from BNDESpar, a BNDES subsidiary, on a venture capital basis. Since 1988, a total of US$30 million has been approved, averaging four projects annually for the period 1992–94, for product development in telecommunications, software, industrial equipment and other areas.

SMI Development SMIs in Brazil, which make up 95 per cent of industrial establishments, are responsible for 23 per cent of total sales and 42 per cent of employment, while contributing approximately 9 per cent to GDP. Backing for SMIs is codified in a special statute, which differentiates them from larger firms for tax, regulatory and other purposes. It specifies income and payroll tax exemptions, in addition to a more flexible treatment with regard to labour laws. The detailed regulations that make the statute operational in some key areas are to be approved by Congress, including a drastic tax reduction and simplification for SMIs.[11]

SEBRAE is the focal point for most SME support in Brazil. SEBRAE is a privately managed agency, represented in 27 states. It is financed through a payroll tax, currently amounting to 0.6 per cent of the wage bill, which corresponds to approximately US$500 million in 1995 and concentrates on the provision of information and other support services to SMEs on a decentralized basis. SEBRAE's network of over 400 windows generates approximately 30 000 queries daily regarding tax, regulatory, market demand and other issues, in addition to flagging new business opportunities for SMEs.[12] Considerable resources are employed in dissemination of information through mass media, publications, seminars and the like. SEBRAE also promotes and funds a credit insurance scheme to alleviate the lack of guarantees that constitute the major barrier for SMEs to finance at competitive rates. A pilot scheme was established with FINEP, which has been operational since March 1994, on the basis of a US$5 million fund. SEBRAE's Fundo de Aval de Apoio as Pequenas e Médias Empresas guarantees as much as 50 per cent of the amount borrowed, for which firms pay a 2 per cent fee for 24-month loans and 3 per cent for 36-month loans.

Access to credit is also facilitated by SEBRAE and BNDES' R$ 500 million credit line for SMEs created in June 1996. The resources are directed to the acquisition of machinery and equipment and to fund operating capital requirements. Enterprises may borrow up to R$ 90 000 for payment in 36 months with a 6-month grace period at non-commercial interest rates. SEBRAE estimates that 16 000 firms will benefit from the credit line.

Subsector-specific Policies

Among subsector-specific policies for competitiveness enhancement, trade liberalization has had the most impact. Although the process was not specifically targeted at any individual subsector, stronger competition from imports was not felt uniformly across subsectors. Just as the impact of imports was non-neutral, so was the government response. Defence against unfair trade practices, such as dumping and subsidies on import flows that threatened the existence of individual subsectors became part of broader restructuring programmes aimed at helping individual subsectors regain competitiveness, as in the case of shoes, textiles and toys. In addition, other subsectoral programmes have been aimed at promoting capacity expansion and investments for modernization with a view to making the country a regional and global competitor. In this context, a good example is the automotive industry. In a few instances, subsectoral policies are targeted at technology-intensive areas, with expected long-term economic results, a paradigmatic case being the space programme.

Trade policy

In the last few years, Brazil has become an increasingly open and competitive economy. The 1988 tariff rationalization efforts, which reduced both average tariffs and their standard deviation, were followed by a comprehensive trade reform. Starting in March 1990, the process of trade liberalization involved the immediate removal of explicit NTBs and the announcement of a time-bound decrease in the level and dispersion of tariffs (Table 9.7). From 1 January 1995, MERCOSUR countries have shared a CET with 11 tariff levels, ranging from 0 per cent to 20 per cent, in increments of 2 per cent.

Table 9.7 Brazil: evolution of tariff structure, 1987–93 (percentages)

Tariff	1987	1988	1989	1990	15 Feb. 1991	1 Jan. 1992	1 Oct. 1992	Jul. 1993
Average	55.6	35.0	31.2	31.5	23.6	19.7	17.1	16.1
Mode	30.0	40.0	40.0	40.0	20.0	20.0	20.0	20.0
St. dev.	26.0	17.0	20.0	19.6	17.4	14.2	10.7	7.9
Range	0–105	0–105	0–105	0–105	0–85	0–65	0–55	0–35

Source: IPEA, 'Perspectivas da Economia Brasileira, 1992' Government of Brazil and FUNCEX.

A more detailed examination by major product groups reveals significant decreases in tariff levels in the period 1990–94, affecting a broad spectrum of tradables, intermediates, durables and non-durables (Table 9.8). Particularly striking are the tariff reductions for products vulnerable to import competition, namely, synthetic fibres, tools, electrical machinery, vehicles and toys. Although the figures displayed refer to nominal rates of protection, the overall reduction in the levels of variance, as indicated by data on standard deviations from Table 9.7, suggests that effective rates of protection must have also moved down substantially.

Table 9.8 Brazil: tariff levels by major product groups (%)

Subsector	1990	Sept. 1994	Difference
Cotton	30.6	13.9	16.7
Wool	14.7	11.4	3.3
Synthetic fibres	30.0	15.1	14.9
Garments and accessories	50.0	20.0	30.0
Shoes	50.0	19.6	31.4
Iron and steel	21.9	11.2	10.7
Aluminium	22.5	12.3	10.2
Tools	43.4	17.8	25.6
Electrical machinery	38.8	16.5	22.3
Vehicles	63.3	18.0	45.3
Boats	35.8	16.8	19.0
Furniture	41.8	17.8	24.0
Meat	18.5	10.0	8.5
Cereals	20.7	6.7	14.0
Beverages	75.1	19.7	55.4
Organic chemicals	24.3	6.3	18.0
Drugs	22.8	10.1	12.7

Source: CNI.

Pressured not only by actual import penetration but also by the threat that customers could look for alternative foreign suppliers in order to obtain better purchasing terms, industrial firms responded by undertaking the most drastic defensive restructuring actions seen in Brazil since the beginning of industrialization. They greatly improved productivity and reduced costs. Between 1990 and 1994, the rate of labour productivity growth for the manufacturing industry averaged 9.15 per cent per year (Table 9.9), compared to –0.5 per cent between 1985 and 1990.[13]

Table 9.9 Brazil: output, employment and labour productivity growth in manufacturing industry, 1990–94 (in percentages)

Subsector	Industrial production	Employment	Hours worked	Productivity/ hour
Food	1.73	–4.79	–5.62	7.79
Beverages	4.11	–5.22	–6.4	11.22
Rubber	3.28	–13.87	–11.74	17.01
Electrical and comm. equip.	3.18	–8.4	–8.46	12.71
Pharmaceuticals	–0.73	–0.87	–1.81	1.1
Tobacco	4.43	–5.77	–6.3	11.45
Plastic material	0.25	–4.81	–4.73	5.23
Transport equipment	8.49	–2.67	–3.13	12
Mechanical equip.	4.16	–4.13	–5.25	9.92
Metallurgy	3.05	–8.51	–4.9	8.36
Non-metallic minerals	0.34	–6.15	–6.52	7.34
Pulp and paper	3.2	–6.55	–6.35	10.2
Cosmetics	3.52	–3.01	–3.94	7.77
Chemicals	1.14	–6.12	–7.15	8.93
Textiles	0.66	–7.43	–8.32	9.79
Clothes/garments	–3.18	–7.73	–6.77	3.86
Average	2.55	–5.9	–6.05	9.15

Source: Cacciamali and Bezerra (1995).

The rapid increase in industrial productivity allowed prices to fall. As a result of the 1990 trade reform, the pressure from import competition, combined with the 1990–92 recession, was sufficiently strong for industrial prices to fall in real terms for major product categories, with the exception of foodstuff and drugs. In both cases, firms benefited from removal of price controls, using the opportunity to recover their target profit margins through the exercise of monopoly power.

Since the stabilization plan for the real (Plano Real) and the monetary reform of 1 July 1994, relative prices have shifted considerably. While industrial prices, particularly for tradables, have remained under competitive pressure, prices of services and other non-tradables, including labour but excluding public utilities, rose by 18.9 per cent during the first year of the plan. Thus, while the aggregate price index increased by 28.7 per cent, retail prices by 38.5 per cent and industrial wages by 44.1 per cent in the period July 1994–June 1995, prices of inputs of an industrial nature from 39 subsectors rose by just 12.7 per cent, while prices of imported inputs contracted by 0.5 per cent (Table 9.10).

Table 9.10 Brazil: price changes for selected products, December 1989 – July 1994 (in percentages)

Industrial inputs	Share	Variation	Cost changes
Domestic inputs	68.8	12.7	8.7
Imported inputs	7.9	–0.5	–0.4
Hourly wages	15.4	44.1	6.8
Public utilities	1.4	–6.5	–0.9
Other	6.5	18.9	1.2
Total	100	–	15.4

Source: Fundação Centro de Comércio Exterior (FUNCEX).

The gains in productivity and the shift in relative prices attest to the impact of trade liberalization on productivity, costs and prices. Yet the growing pressure from imports and balance of payment difficulties has led to a number of *ad hoc* protectionist measures. The MERCOSUR tariff agreement includes a list of exceptions for 300 product codes whose tariff levels will converge to the CET, some by the year 2001, including vehicles and capital goods, others by 2006, in the case of informatics and telecommunications. The agreement also includes a rotating list of some 20 products with tariffs above or below pre-agreed levels at the Government's policy convenience.[14] The underlying reasons why products were included or deleted from this latter list are related to:

- balance of payments difficulties, as exemplified by the 70 per cent tariff increase of March 1995 affecting some 109 consumer durables and vehicles;
- apparent undersupply of foodstuff or industrial inputs, which led to tariffs being reduced to zero, as in the case of corn, tomatoes and certain chemical and textile inputs or to an intermediate level;
- temporary industrial relief, as in the case of shoes and textiles, among others.

Subsectoral programmes

For many years, industrial policy in Brazil was characterized by a profusion of subsectoral policies and incentives aimed at substituting imports and protecting domestic production of capital goods, consumer durables and intermediates. Although most trade- and investment-related import-substitution policies have been phased out and emphasis is now on the attainment of international competitiveness across subsectors, there remains a limited, though growing, number of subsectoral policies and programmes. The apparent economic rationale is, alternatively, the restructuring needs of the subsector, its expansion requirements or its infant status.

Subsectoral relief and restructuring: textiles, toys and footwear Trade liberalization and the pressure from imports led the government to re-erect protective barriers and establish subsector-based relief programmes with a restructuring component managed by BNDES. This was targeted to specific subsectors, including textiles, toys and shoes. These traditional subsectors suffered from significant increases in imports, fall in production, reduction in capacity and rising unemployment.

In the case of textiles, the domestic market was penetrated by imported synthetic products and low-cost garments from China, other East Asian countries and Ireland. While in 1990–92, subsector exports averaged nearly three times the level of imports, out of a total trade volume of US$1.5–2.0 billion, by mid-1995 the ratio of imports to exports was 2 : 1. Imports expanded from US$557 million to US$2.3 billion between 1991 and 1995, an average annual growth of 42 per cent per year. Garment imports, in particular, rose from US$47 million to US$351 million; and synthetic textile imports climbed from US$67 million to US$351 million between 1993 and 1995. In Americana, the country's most important textile centre, the number of plants shrank by 12 per cent, from 5319 to 4682, between 1989 and 1995, while the subsector workforce was reduced by 50 per cent, shrinking from 1 094 000 to some 500 000 workers.

The toy industry faced similar difficulties. Imports expanded from US$44 million in 1993 to US$75 million in 1994 and soared to US$164.6 million in 1995, an increase of 117.7 per cent in one year. The share of the imports market moved from 10.5 per cent to 33.3 per cent in the post-liberalization period of 1991/95, while revenues dropped by 23.9 per cent between 1994 and 1995 and production by 5.4 per cent between 1992 and 1995. Excess capacity increased from 15.7 per cent to 44.1 per cent between 1993 and 1995. Of the 450 industrial plants, 110, or 24 per cent, closed their doors or failed, and as much as 45.3 per cent of the labour force was dismissed between 1991 and 1995, with 1994 alone seeing a reduction of 38 per cent.

In the footwear industry, competition from Asia has posed a major threat to the domestic industry. Exports dropped from US$1932 million to US$1499 million between 1993 and 1995. Since 1993, three-quarters of the 4000 plants in the Vale dos Sinos region, which is the largest footwear production area, shut down, while the workforce was reduced by 47 per cent.[15] In 1995, the subsector's excess capacity was some 40 per cent.[16] The government responded by imposing quotas, increasing tariffs and establishing subsectoral restructuring programmes (Table 9.11 and Annex 9A). In the case of textiles, tariffs for 13 items increased from 18–20 per cent to 70 per cent until December 1996, while importers of 40 other items had to settle their balances within a 30-day period in order to avoid the large domestic–international interest rate differentials. For toys, tariffs were increased from 20 per cent to 70 per cent, while the tariff increase in case of footwear went up from 20 per cent to 40 per cent.

The protectionist measures were not uncontested. Tariff protection for the toy industry, for example, generated unfavourable reactions. Some observers wondered why the government did not use a specific anti-dumping instrument for the toy industry instead of increasing the tariff indiscriminately to the maximum of 70 per cent for all countries, since the supposedly predatory imports came from China. The EU, responsible for 27 per cent of toys exported to Brazil, sent a note to the Ministry of Foreign Affairs alleging that the measure was not in accordance with the WTO Safeguards Code and claiming that protection was given comprehensively by not distinguishing the degree of similarity of the products affected. United States and Hong Kong representatives also criticized the Brazilian decision. The Brazilian Association of Toy Resellers also contested the Government's decision, arguing that there was no significant harm to the local toy industry. Industry sales expanded by 53.3 per cent based on an increase from US$2.89 in 1994 to US$4.43 in 1995 of the average unit price.[17]

The weakness of these subsectors is related to the low levels of investment and limited efforts at modernization as well as to unfair trade practices. Although few doubt the importance of, and the Government's commitment to, an open economy, the process of liberalization has actually unleashed pressure from numerous interest groups seeking protection from competition. In some cases, this is legitimate and economically justifiable, as predatory dumping and a significant use of subsidies are still pervasive in some

Table 9.11 Brazil: subsectoral programmes

Sectoral incentives	Firm's commitments
Textiles	
Introduction of import quotas, starting June 1996 and valid for 3 years, for products from China, Hong Kong Territory, Republic of Korea and Taiwan Province (1997 values ranging from 49 300 to 20.16 million kg)	No formal commitments
BNDES created credit lines for fixed investment and operating capital and capital goods imports and exports (pre-shipment) for the whole sector	
Toys	
Increase in import tax from 20 to 70 per cent; introduction of temporary safeguards from July to 31 December 1996 (not applicable to MERCOSUR imports)*	Restructuring programmes and creation of 12 000 jobs Price stability in 1996, with possibility of 5–6 per cent price reduction U$335 million investments in quality, productivity and design until year 2000 Price reduction between 5 per cent and 10 per cent per year starting in 1997
Footwear	
Products included in CET's exception list and tariff increase from 20 to 40 per cent BNDES created credit lines for fixed investments and operating capital, capital goods imports and exports (pre-shipment)	No formal commitments

*The tariff evolution was 85 per cent in 1991, 40 per cent in 1993 and 20 per cent in 1994.

Source: *Gazeta Mercantil*, various issues.

markets. At the same time, smuggling, particularly from Paraguay, estimated at US$12 billion, represents unfair competition. In other instances, however, there is no economic justification for renewed protection since lack of competitiveness is a product of accommodative behaviour. In any case, the dissent introduced by frequent changes in the trade regime constitutes an unwanted source of policy instability, with an adverse effect on investment and other long-term decisions.

Globalization with a regional base: the automotive industry In the period 1980–92, the Brazilian automotive industry stagnated. Production hovered around million units, with one-quarter going to export markets; the rate of new model introduction slowed considerably, and entry of new manufacturers came to a halt, with Fiat the last to enter the market, in the mid-1970s. The liberalization of imports in March 1990 and subsequent policy initiatives introduced major changes to this picture.

Liberalization led to a fall in industrial prices and rapid expansion of domestic production, from 1073 million units in 1992 to 1581 million in 1994. With the removal of NTBs and the progressive reduction in tariffs, which reached a low of 18 per cent in September 1994, there was an upsurge in imports, at a rate the Government considered unsustainable from a balance of payments perspective and highly damaging to domestic industry. In March 1995, the government restored tariffs to 32 per cent and in June to 70 per cent, in addition to imposing quotas.[18] In December 1995, the quotas were modified to include agreements reached with MERCOSUR governments and the private sector. These agreements and their subsequent re-editions, which have been in effect since 1 January 1996 and will last until the end of 1999, provide the frame for the country's automotive industry transition regime to the MERCOSUR common regime in the year 2000.[19] The programme's intrinsic importance is related to the economic weight of the subsector, which accounts for nearly 10 per cent of GDP, and the fact that it is the object of dispute with Brazil's trading partners, Japan, the EU and the Republic of Korea. It possibly constitutes the only policy that effectively targets an industry to become a major regional and international player by promoting its expansion, modernization, intraregional specialization and outward orientation. By the year 2000, the industry was expected, before to the 1999 crisis, to produce at least 2.5 million vehicles, becoming the largest producer in Latin American and the fifth or sixth largest in the world.

The programme offers sharp tariff reductions for imports of parts, components, capital equipment and vehicles for those producers willing to commit themselves to specific export and investment targets (Table 9.12). For every dollar of exports or purchase of domestically manufactured capital goods, producers will be able to import inputs – intermediates, parts and components – as well as fully assembled vehicles, with tariffs reduced by 90 per cent and 50 per cent respectively. However, the CET remains binding at 20 per cent as a floor for vehicles. The value of imports favoured by reduced tariffs would be limited to 100 per cent of exports and 140 per cent of capital goods purchases, the latter progressively reduced to 70 per cent by 1999, converging with Argentina's incentive rates, which will increase gradually from the current 40 per cent of investment outlays. To provide flexibility to new assemblers, domestic inputs for entrants will need to average just 50 per cent for the first year of operation and 60 per cent thereafter. For assemblers to benefit from zero tariffs in intra-MERCOSUR trade, the domestic content of vehicles would need to reach 70 per cent.

Provisional Measure 1235 provoked criticism in Argentina and a formal complaint from Japan. Argentina argued that it is was not in agreement with the tariff rate of only up to 2 per cent for inputs, particularly rolled steel and autoparts. Japan condemned the entire Brazilian regime, arguing that it created privileges for assemblers already installed in Brazil and made competition very difficult for Japanese exports. Together with the EU and the Republic of Korea, Japan planned to present a formal complaint to the WTO.

The liberalization of imports, allowing foreign producers to test Brazil's market and establish a network of dealers and service providers and, later, the introduction of the new automotive industry regime, stimulated investment and led to structural change in the industry. Competitive behaviour became the norm in an industry accustomed to quasi-cartelist conduct. Better-quality models were introduced, allowed by more flexible domestic content rules. New entrants were attracted, including Renault, Mercedes-Benz (for autos), as well Kia Motors and Asia Motors, among other Republic of Korea automakers. All traditional players and newcomers have announced significant investments – US$10 billion to US$12 billion until 1999 – in projects ranging from assembly lines to building of facilities for full production, 84 companies having signed agreements with the government by October 1996. Most of these developments are summarized in Table 9.13, which presents the sector´s investments, strategies, plans and projects for the short- and medium-term in MERCOSUR as formally announced by the companies.

Table 9.12 Brazil: summary of the automotive industry incentives of Provisional Measure 1235, of 15 December 1995, and amendments

Benefits – tariff reductions

Capital goods – 90 per cent reduction until 1999

Inputs (includes raw material and autoparts) – tariff reductions of 85 per cent in 1996, 70 per cent in 1997, 55 per cent in 1998 and 40 per cent in 1999, subject to a 2 per cent tariff floor

Assembled vehicles – 50 per cent reduction (only for assemblers) limited to CET's tariff floor, resulting in the following tariff levels: 35 per cent in 1996, 31 per cent in 1997 and 20 per cent in 1998

Beneficiaries

Firms manufacturing and assembling vehicles in general; bodies, parts, pieces and components; finished and semi-finished sets and subsets; and tyres

Firm's commitments

1. Ratio of local capital goods acquisitions to tariff-reduced imports of capital goods: 1 : 1 in 1996–97 and 1.5 : 1 in 1998–99
2. Ratio of acquisitions of local raw material to tariff-reduced imports of raw material: 1 : 1 in 1996–99
3. Ratio of MERCOSUR imports + tariff-reduced imports of inputs and vehicles to net exports: 1 : 1
4. Ratio of tariff-reduced imports of autoparts to net exports: limited to 2 : 3

Additional investment bonus: 140 per cent in 1996, 120 per cent in 1997, 95 per cent in 1998 and 70 per cent in 1999 (for every $1 spent in the acquisition of local capital goods, the firm is authorized to import $1.4 at reduced tariff in 1996, $1.2 in 1997, $0.95 in 1998 and $0.70 in 1999

Additional exports bonus: 20 per cent (for every $1 exported the firm is authorized to import $1.2 at reduced tariff)

Rate of local content: 50 per cent in the first year and 60 per cent thereafter (inputs acquired in MERCOSUR when balanced with exports are taken into account for calculating local content)

Other incentives: newcomers are allowed 3 years to fulfil commitments and meet the local content requirements; accelerated depreciation is allowed

Fines for the non-observance of the conditions agreed to import at reduced tariffs: ranging from 60 per cent to 120 per cent of incentives

Source: *Gazeta Mercantil*, various issues.

Table 9.13 Investment plans and strategies for the MERCOSUR automotive sector

Investments	Strategies, projects and plans
Asia Motors (Brazil)	
Initial: $100 million Until 1999: $500 million	New unit for production of Topic van starting 1999, with capacity for 60 000 units/year in 1997
Audi (Brazil)	
US$500 million	New unit in partnership with Volkswagen for producing Golf (VW) and A3 (Audi) models from a shared platform, with a capacity for 150 000 units/ year
Chrysler (Brazil)	
US$150 million	New unit for production of intermediate sedan, possibly Neon; plans to produce motors for the Brazilian and Argentinian markets
Chrysler (Argentina)	
US$150 million	New unit to manufacture Cherokee pick-up
Fiat (Brazil)	
US$1 billion (95–97)	$500 million – expand capacity to build Palio 2, pick-up and van versions $500 million – Engine unit for Brazilian market $1 million – Tempra´s successor project (1997–99); production to be concentrated in Brazil
US$1 billion (98–99)	Plans to specialize units to build a few models from 2 platforms; old models will be gradually replaced by Palio's and Tempra´s successor; Brazil to become the base for Palio production, responsible for 2/3 of global output; Plans to build 3 million cars/year, of which 1 million Palios, up to year 2000, as well as to manufacture heavy trucks
Fiat (Argentina)	
US$600 million	Building plant to manufacture Palio 3 (sedan) for both markets, to replace the Tipo (180 000 units/ year) starting at end of 1997; plans to build engines and gears for the Palio and the Brazilian-manufactured Tempra and to build Iveco light and intermediate trucks

Ford (Brazil)	
US$2.5 billion until 1999	Expand capacity for production of compact Fiesta and its derivatives from 1996, exclusively in Brazil; assembly line for Fiesta and Escort gears to be inaugurated shortly; plans to build heavy trucks starting from 1997 and to integrate operations of both countries; will transfer the production nucleus of F1000 and F4000 pick-ups from Argentina to Brazil; plans to produce the Mondeo (CKD) to replace Versailles and Royale; will build a new model, Ka, starting from 1997 and Zetec engine for Mondeo $350 million investment in modernization as part of the company's strategy of integrating local manufacturing units with the European ones
Ford (Argentina)	
US$1 billion	Modernize plant and expand capacity; plans to transfer the entire Escort and Verona production lines to the country
GM (Brazil)	
US$2.6 billion until 1999	Will expand capacity to concentrate production of Corsa (Chevrolet) line exclusively in Brazil; plans to manufacture a wide range of models from the Vectra to S-10 pick-ups; starting from the inauguration of new Argentine plant, intends to divide lines between Brazil and Argentina US$70 million investment in unit modernization for manufacture of 10 000 light trucks in Brazil in 1997; full capacity (15 000 units/year) in 1998
GM (Argentina)	
US$1 billion	Building plant for cars and light trucks assembly starting in 1998; will keep the manufacture of intermediate and light trucks 6–100 and 6–150 in Argentina and will manufacture C20 and D20 pick-ups for both markets (D20 produced exclusively in Argentina); other GM models are built in both countries

(continued)

Table 9.13 continued

Investments	Strategies, projects and plans
Honda (Brazil) US$100 million initial, could reach US$600 million	Building assembly line for production of the Civic (sedan) starting in 1997; initial production: 15 000 units/year for MERCOSUR and other Latin America countries, with production to be doubled by 1999; initial local content: 50 per cent; will import engines, gears and electronic components; will build engine plant to achieve 80 per cent of local content by 1999
Hyundai (Brazil) US$900 million	New plant for production of different models, among which H100 starting in 1997
Kia (Brazil) US$100 million (to be confirmed)	New plant (30 000 units/year capacity); level of investment still undefined; production to start with Besta and Bongo models (15 000 units/year) by the beginning of 1998
Mercedes-Benz (Brazil) US$400 million US$800 million until 1999	New plant or manufacture of new generation of hatchback cars with high local content; currently produces truck and bus bodies, with activity to be phased out in 1997; will concentrate on truck and bus engines
Renault (Brazil) US$1 billion	US$750 million in the first 7 years of project, which will start operating in 1999 with production of 4-door coupé hatch Mégane (100 000 units/year)
Renault (Argentina) $500 million	Undefined
Scania (Brazil and Argentina) US$200 million in both countries until 1977	Will integrate operations in Latin America and will build buses, engines, cabins and axles in Brazil; will build heavy and light trucks in Argentina as well as gear boxes

Toyota (Brazil) $150 million	New plant for manufacture of Corolla model (15 000 units/year) starting in 1998
Toyota (Argentina) $150 million	New plant to manufacture HiLux utility (20 000 units/year) starting end 1998 for both markets
Volkswagen (Brazil) US$500 million in 1996 US$2.5 billion until 1999	Plans to concentrate production of popular cars in Brazil (Golf) and to reduce platforms from 16 to 4; will build a production unit for the assembly of Volkswagen, Seat and Audi from a shared platform; currently investing US$550 million to expand capacity for the Latin American and European markets, with US$250 million in a bus and truck plant (40 000 units/year) and US$250 million in an engine unit (1200/ day)
Volkswagen (Argentina) US$500 million until the year 2000	Plans to concentrate production of intermediate cars (e.g. Voyage) in Argentina; recently started production of Golf in Argentina; started manufacturing the Polo Classic for both markets (Brazilian version of the model, named Voyage, will not be manufactured before 1997); has units producing Golf, Pointer, Quantum, Saveiro and diesel/units

Sources: *Gazeta Mercantil*, *Jornal do Brasil*, *O Globo*, various issues from December 1995 to July 1996.

The MERCOSUR automotive industry has attained a considerable degree of integration. Both assemblers and autoparts producers are directing their investments with a view to the common market and setting up complementary production lines in order to achieve the considerable economies of scale and product differentiation that characterize the industry. Brazil is becoming the focus of production of compact and sub-compact cars, as well as trucks and buses. The country will concentrate on the production of new models, similar in technology and quality to those launched in the United States and Europe, being positioned as the launching platform for exports of compact cars such as the Ford Fiesta, the Fiat (Palio) and a new Mercedes world car. Based on the size of Brazil's domestic market[20], production will capitalize on the country's advantage in having the most modern and largest autoparts and components plants in Latin America. Production lines of some vehicles that were manufactured and exported from Brazil have already been shifted to Argentina. Argentina is expected to concentrate on the production of intermediate models and older vehicles belonging to specific niches. This intra-bloc specialization pattern is depicted in Table 9.14.

Table 9.14 Intra-bloc integration and specialization of car models

Carmaker	Argentina	Brazil
Chrysler	Cherokee pick-up	Possibly Neon (intermediate sedan)
Fiat	Palio 3 (Tipo's substitute)	Palio 2 (pick-up and van)
	Engines and gears for Brazilian Palio and Tempra	Tempra substitute
	Light and intermediate trucks	Heavy trucks
Ford	Escort and Verona	Fiesta, F1000 and F4000
		Mondeo and Ka (new model)
		Zetec engine
GM	Pick-up C-20 and D-20 and others	Corsa and others
Peugeot	Peugeot 40S, 40S Break and 504	
Renault	Renault 19, Clio and Traffic	Mégane
Scania	Heavy and light trucks, transmission gears and differentials	Buses, engines, cabins and axles
Toyota	Hilux	Corolla sedan
VW	Voyage	Golf
	Polo Classic	Polo Classic (1997)
	Also produces Golf, Pointer, Quantum and Saveiro	Also produces Parati, Santana, Fusca and Kombi

Sources: *Gazeta Mercantil, O Globo, Jornal do Brasil*, various issues from December 1995 to July 1996.

Intra-industry trade has been growing considerably as a result of intra-bloc specialization, having reached US$1.14 billion in 1994, including autoparts. Brazilian exports to MERCOSUR amounted to US$765.4 million and Brazilian imports US$375.4 million. The intra-industry trade coefficient for

Argentina and Brazil reached 39 per cent of total trade for 1993, 51.3 per cent for trade in manufactures and 77.3 per cent in the case of the automotive industry.[21]

These policies have also provoked major changes in the Brazilian autoparts industry, weakened by underinvestment and poor, frequently family-run management. The industry has been facing an increasing wave of mergers and acquisitions in the last three years, especially from the second half of 1995 onwards. According to the manufacturers' union, Sindipeças, by the end of the decade there will be a 35 per cent reduction in the number of firms. Only 350 of the current 540 are expected to remain, mostly foreign-controlled, while 33 per cent of the labour force will have lost their jobs as a result of mergers and acquisitions. The lack of competitiveness of the subsector, which underlies those changes, is evident from a recent survey, which showed that only 86, or 16 per cent of the firms were internationally competitive, while 44 per cent had not even adopted the modernization programmes.[22]

Trade reform and the advent of MERCOSUR have been major forces in the modernization of the automotive industry. In this respect, policy makers had few choices other than to introduce a more open and competitive regime so as not to risk condemning the industry to an irreversible state of backwardness. As in the case of the informatics industry, which was protected from the challenge of imports and the entry of foreign producers for more than 15 years, technological progress and the forces of globalization forced a reassessment of subsectoral policies. Although the new regime is far from neutral, it is more in line with the requirements of an internationally integrated industry, where both sourcing and production are undertaken on a global scale.

Targeting high technology: the Brazilian space programme Brazil has had a relatively long tradition of space-related activities. Embraer, privatized in December 1994, is one of the two major aircraft producers in industrializing countries, catering both for the civilian and military markets.[23] The Brazilian space programme is the other major government initiative in the field, comprising the development by the Instituto Nacional de Pesquisas Espaciais (INPE) of data collection and remote sensing satellites, as well as earth stations, while the Centro Tecnológico da Aeronáutica (CTA) became responsible for development and launching of the satellite launch vehicle as well as the establishment and operation of the launch base of Alcantara.[24]

The US$1.1 billion programme was created to exploit the country's scientific and technological potential, as well as its favourable geographical position for satellite launching purposes in terms of its proximity to the equator and climatic conditions. The idea was to enable Brazil to take advantage of the emerging market for small satellites, particularly in the communications area. Although at its launch, in 1979, the space programme considered using both military and civilian technologies, the long-term objective came to centre on commercial civilian applications. Initially, Alcantara was to become an alternative to France's Kourou base in French Guiana as a vehicle assembly and testing ground and launch site, open to non-traditional customers, particularly the Chinese and the Russians, in addition to American firms looking for less expensive alternatives. In the medium to long term, Brazil was to offer satellite imaging and geosensoring services as well as launch vehicles. The creation of the Brazilian Space Agency in 1994, modelled after NASA, was a significant step towards consolidating the approach that the programme's success was linked to its commercial applications and orientation.

The space programme represents a systematic endeavour by a multiplicity of civilian and military agencies to achieve an ambitious objective by developing-country standards. It has involved numerous industries with significant technological spin-offs for producers involved in:

- the development of new and more resistant materials, such as high-quality steels, bronze and aluminium special alloys and high-precision engineering plastics, for the launch vehicle;
- the production of solid fuel, which led to new plastic resins currently exported by Petrobras and related combustion systems; and
- development of the guidance system for the launch vehicle and earth control station systems.

In addition, INPE, CTA and the new agency have developed the capacity to assemble and test satellites and their launch vehicles, activities essential for the country to enter the commercial launch business.[25] To justify the government's initial involvement in these infant, high-technology industries, these ventures must become commercially viable, without continuation of public subsidies.

In contrast to the recently introduced subsectoral restructuring programmes, those for the automotive and space industries are examples of more comprehensive and forward-looking government efforts. The space programme, in particular, though *de facto* the major subsectoral programme undertaken in Brazil in a frontier area, has been overlooked, because its industrial dimension, long-term economic impact and commercial applications are only now emerging.

Industry-wide Policies

The key set of industry-wide policies to make Brazilian manufacturing more competitive is embodied in the goal of reducing manufacturing costs. There are a number of dimensions that determine such costs:

- macroeconomic prices: the exchange rate, interest rates and tax rates;
- cost, reliability and elasticity of supply of infrastructure services;
- level of education, skills and health of the population;
- regulatory regime and business environment;
- a reduction in manufacturing costs would be *ipso facto* an improvement in the sector's competitive position and, thus, an important element in increasing market share.

Between 1988 and 1995, Brazilian exports as a percentage of world exports contracted from 1.2 to 0.8 per cent, while the country's export to GDP ratio decreased from 10.4 per cent to 8.7 per cent, slightly more than a third of the Republic of Korea's and less than traditionally inward-looking India, at 9.6 per cent. Although the effective exchange rate-adjusted incentive rate varies considerably across product groups, the domestic market is generally more profitable than export markets. Exports remain, for the most part, a countercyclical activity. So far, Brasil's manufacturing costs seem to exceed the benefits from competitive export financing and other export support policies and initiatives.

Reduction of manufacturing costs

The relatively high cost of doing business in the country has damaged the competitiveness of the productive sector. The excessive taxation of production, social and physical infrastructure deficiencies and the government's inefficiencies and excessive bureaucracy have hampered investments and job creation, offsetting the size and dynamism of the domestic market as a source of competitive advantage.

Post-stabilization exchange rate appreciation, estimated at 15 per cent, and high real interest rates combined with large spreads charged by the banking system in financing firms' operations have contributed to inflating manufacturing costs.[26] The impact of these factors would have been even more adverse had they not been balanced by the significant growth in productivity and decrease of business uncertainty since the start of the Plano Real. In addition, high real interest rates have contributed decisively to the growth of manufacturing costs.

Taxation

The country's tax system constitutes the major component in manufacturing costs.[27] While the tax burden is not high compared with international standards, its unevenness creates distortions which fall heavily on production. A CNI study indicates that the total burden amounts to 25 per cent of GDP, whereas industry's contribution is 36 per cent of value-added. Brazilian income tax averages 48 per cent, which compares unfavourably with the United States and Europe, at 38 per cent, and other Latin American countries, at 31 per cent. Indirect taxes amount to 28.7 per cent in Brazil, 21.8 per cent in Latin American countries and 15 per cent in the United States and Europe. Furthermore, basic non-wage costs, including social security contributions, leave periods, holidays and thirteenth (extra monthly) salary, amount to 102 per cent.[28]

Except for dividend tax, Brazilian corporate taxation is 48.2 per cent whereas the Latin American average is 31.5 per cent, Asia's 31.4 per cent and the United States', Canada's and Germany's 38.5 per cent. Domestic social insurance costs, at some 37.4 per cent of the payroll, are also high compared to other countries. The average for several Latin American countries and the United States, Canada, Germany and France, known for their high taxation systems, is around 20 per cent. Furthermore, Brazil is the only country to tax value-added on a regional basis and, as result, it is unable fully to eliminate taxation on exports, as is done in the EU and other countries adopting a value-added tax. According to 1990 estimates, the indirect burden falling on Brazilian exports averaged 11.7 per cent for manufactured products while in industrialized economies the rate is zero.[29]

Manufactured exports are exempted from federal and state value-added sales taxes, in addition to the 2 per cent sales-related Cofins tax. Tax credit is available for the finished goods tax as well as for the social integration programme and Cofins taxes paid on purchases of domestic inputs for export-oriented production. In addition, a drawback regime is available for direct and indirect exporters, in the form of import duty exemption, restitution or suspension. Income derived from manufactured and services exports is taxed at a maximum rate of 30 per cent and exempted from Brazil's 10 per cent social contribution on profits. Payments of interest and service charges for export financing as well as for export logistics and marketing are exempt from income and financial operations taxes. Finally, 18 tax-sheltered export processing zones (EPZs) have been approved; four were slated to begin operations in 1996. Different from their MERCOSUR partners, Brazilian EPZs must direct all of their production to the external market, which might require harmonization of current legislation.[30]

Tax reform is high on the policy agenda of the government. A number of proposals are currently in Congress to simplify the tax system, lower its cost and make it more efficient and equitable. Although there is near consensus that the system as it currently stands penalizes the manufacturing sector, there is wide disagreement on how should it be reformed and on the redistribution of the tax burden.

Infrastructure

Inadequate physical infrastructure is another major factor contributing to manufacturing costs. Public investment in transportation, ports, telecommunications and energy has decreased continuously since the beginning of the 1980s. According to recent estimates, SOEs' total investments in energy, transportation and communications in 1993 were 44 per cent of the 1980s' level. In 1993, investment in transportation was slightly more than 10 per cent of what was invested in the 1980s. The deterioration of roads and railways contributed significantly to increased transportation costs.[31] In addition, the performance of Brazilian ports is worse when compared to those of other Latin American countries. Some estimates put the cost of Brazilian ports at least three times higher than those of its major competitors.[32]

Policies to reduce the infrastructure component of manufacturing costs focus on attracting investment through privatization of services and the introduction of competition in infrastructure markets, whenever feasible. Major changes are being introduced in transportation, telecommunications and the electricity industry in the form of privatization. By the end of the decade, the infrastructure landscape is likely to have been drastically transformed, with major private-led initiatives to improve operational efficiency and invest in new facilities and equipment, contributing to significantly lower manufacturing costs.

Privatization

Privatization is now regarded as the major instrument of the government to reduce infrastructure costs. Yet, at the beginning of the programme, the sale of SOEs was undertaken in response to other imperatives, most importantly the disposal of industrial assets as a means of phasing out government´s involvement in business activities with large accumulated deficits.

Between 1981 and 1989, there were no governmental programmes for large-scale privatization. During this period 38 small companies were privatized for US$700 million. Starting in 1990, the magnitude and scope of the privatization process were significantly widened, with the sale of 34 SOEs of the industrial sector and 32 other enterprises with minority government participation. Between 1991 and 1994, the government concentrated its efforts on the privatization of the steel, petrochemical and fertilizers sectors, in their entirety (Table 9.15). Since then, major capital goods firms still in the hands of the government and two large utilities were sold. A fairly decisive programme of infrastructure concessions, some of them critical to the enhancement of the competitive standing of the industrial sector, was structured allowing significant portions of the highway system, 36 ports and the railway system to be privately operated by late 1997/early 1998. Thus, while the western and eastern portions of the rail network have been privatized, the southern portion was expected to go private by the end of 1996. In addition, 841 kilometres of federal roads, which represents a future investment of US$1.1 billion by private operators, have been privatized and another 15 000 kilometres are included in the programme, representing 30 per cent of the federal network and an investments of US$6 billion.

Post-privatization performance of SOEs privatized between 1990 and 1994, which were mostly industrial enterprises, has been impressive. They gained in efficiency, increased output, sales and profits and substantially expanded investments (Table 9.16). It is arguable that such clear improvements in performance are not as easily replicable in sectors demanding regulatory oversight, such as public services. Yet the economy-wide impact of this later phase of the privatization process cannot be overstated. To a large measure, the decrease in the manufacturing costs is predicated on how well private operators manage large chunks of the public service infrastructure in the country, and the extent to which they will provide an elastic, high-quality supply of infrastructure services at competitive tariffs.

Education

Severe deficiencies in the country's education system hinder the supply of an educated and skilled labour force. The high levels of illiteracy, at 19 per cent in 1990, coupled with the poor quality of basic education, have a significant impact on the acquisition of knowledge and long-term growth in labour

Table 9.15 Brazil: companies privatized in the period 1991–96

Steel	Petrochemicals and chemicals		Fertilizers	Public services	Capital goods
Acesita	Acrinor	Oxiteno	Arafértil	Escelsa	Celma
Açominas	CBE	Petroflex	Fosfértil	Light	Embraer
Cosinor	CBP	Polialden	Goiásfertil	RFFSA	Koppol
Cosipa	Ciquine	Poliolefinas	Indag	SNBP	Mafersa
CSN	Compania	Polipropileno	Ultrafértil		
CST	de Alcalis	Polisul			
Metais	Copene	Politeno			
Caraiba	Coperbo	PPH			
Piratini	Copesul	PQU			
Usiminas	CPC	Pronor			
	CQR	Salgema			
	Nitriflex				
	Nitrocarbono				

Notes: Total number of companies: 45. Total revenue collected: US$11 billion.

Table 9.16 Brazil: performance indicators of privatized SOEs

Variable	Average before privatization	Average after privatization
Sales	1.25	1.4
Production	0.97	1.16
Sales/employee	0.86	1.7
Profit/employee	0.32	1.29
Production/employee	0.76	1.39
Number of employees	1.65	0.85
Profit/assets	−1.77	0.2
Investments	0.57	25.4
Debits	1.48	1.12

Source: BNDES.

productivity.[33] Firms are forced to spend large sums in order to guarantee minimum levels of education and health for their workforce. Although the government is trying to improve basic education and there is growing awareness of the enormous costs to the country and to the manufacturing sector of not having an educated labour force, not enough is being done to reverse the current situation.

Finance

Once macroeconomic stability is consolidated, it is expected that term finance will progressively become available from private sources, while as real interest rates fall firms will be more willing to tap finance for working capital. Currently, only BNDES offers long-term investment credit. In the case of exports, direct finance is available from the Banco do Brasil´s Programa de Financiamento às Exportações (PROEX) and BNDES´s Programa de Financiamento à Produção e Exportação de Máquinas e Equipamentos (FINAMEX).

The former programme was originally for a restricted list of goods and services, basically focused on capital goods and engineering services. Having been extended since December 1995, it now includes consumer goods such as food, footwear, perfumes, ceramics and textiles. More recently, the programme was extended to the services sector. The programme finances up to 85 per cent of the FOB value of exports, at LIBOR plus rates, for a period of ten years. Interest rate equalization is also available for exporters to offer competitive post-shipment supplier's credit.[34] By the end of 1995, the programme had started equalizing the interest rates of 100 per cent of exports, which were previously limited to 85 per cent, and extended payment terms as well as grace periods.

Pre- and post-shipment finance of capital goods exports is available from FINAMEX, with PROEX funds, as much as 100 per cent of the value of the exported goods, depending on degree of domestic value-added.[35] In 1995, the Government allocated US$840 million for interest rate equalization, so that finance provided by Brazilian exporters was competitive, and US$200 million for direct finance of capital goods and services exports. Because of an excess supply of funds, the 1996 budget was reduced to US$500 million and US$120 million respectively, equal to about 1.2 per cent of total exports.[36]

In June 1996, a new programme was created by BNDES, Programa de Apoio às Exportações, to benefit industrial subsectors weakened by the liberalization process and by the appreciation of the currency. It was also aimed at subsectors with export potential, including textiles, garments, footwear, furniture, marble and granite products, household appliances, cutlery, plastic products and autoparts. Its R$ 1 billion funds are operated by financial agents and used to equalize the terms of finance provided domestically to those available in the international market. Pre-shipment finance is available at 5.5 per cent annually, plus LIBOR and BNDES´s spread, ranging from 2 per cent to 3 per cent per year. The payment term is 15 months, with a 9-month grace period, and credit is limited to US$10 million per company.[37] Since the programme's launch, BNDES has been criticized for not demanding the availability of finance for the restructuring commitments from selected subsectors.

Legal and regulatory environment

Brazil's manufacturing costs are affected by frequent changes in legislation, sluggishness of the judicial system and the excessive number of laws. Despite these hurdles there have been, in the last decade, considerable efforts at deregulation, some of them successful, as in the case of price deregulation and lowering of policy-induced entry barriers. To improve the competitive standing of manufacturing industry will now require major reforms in the judiciary system, which are unlikely to come about in the short to medium term.

To develop exports, in particular, the government is in the process of submitting to Congress a comprehensive foreign trade law as well as an export credit insurance scheme.[38] There are currently more than 150 decrees orienting and disciplining foreign trade, many of which are outdated. Their irrational regulation of foreign trade hampers the understanding of the legal framework, impairs business and generates excessive bureaucracy. The new foreign trade law has the following objectives:

- to provide a clear vision of the strategic objectives and supporting instruments for the sector, with revision of hundreds of decrees, resolutions, notes and instructions;
- to define clearly and objectively the intervening agencies and their role in coordination and execution of policies;
- to build an effective trade promotion system, with creation of a strategic commercial information centre; and
- to adapt foreign trade policies and actions to international rules and agreements, notably, those of MERCOSUR, the Latin American Integration Association (ALADI) and WTO.

Intellectual property rights

An important aspect of the regulatory environment is the intellectual property right (IPR) regime. A new intellectual property code was approved by the Brazilian Congress in 1996, which is broadly consistent with the TRIP agreement, to which the country is a signatory. The IPR system is managed by the Instituto Nacional de Propriedade Intelectual (INPI), the agency responsible for processing patent and trademark applications, issuing them and ensuring their protection, together with the court system. Processing of patent applications by INPI is quite sluggish, as is the justice system, while the penalty structure does not constitute a sufficient deterrent to the infringement of property rights. Unless the system is improved – in terms both of human resource capabilities and procedures – and enforcement enhanced, the positive impact of the new, more modern legislation may be limited to a few subsectors for which patent protection is critical and which did not enjoy such protection in the past, such as pharmaceuticals. Moreover, the public must be educated about the importance of intellectual property rights protection for the enhancement of competitiveness of Brazilian industry, as well as for the capacity of the country to attract foreign investment and for development and transfer of technology.

Although reductions in manufacturing costs are critical to competitiveness, over the longer term, the competitive position of firms depends on their incorporating new technologies, investing in plant and equipment, and benchmarking themselves against leading producers. At a more aggregate level, the country´s competitive performance in the world economy will depend much on the accumulation of private and social capital, the limitations on which are imposed by savings. Besides the Brazilian economy having relatively low rates of savings, the still incipient recovery in private savings rates has been offset by a significant deterioration in the public sector (Table 9.17).

Table 9.17 Brazil: Savings in GDP ratio

	Domestic			
Year	Public	Private	Foreign	Total
1985–1989	–0.4	21	0.1	20.7
1990–1994	4	12.8	–0.1	16.7
1994	3.9	12.4	0.2	16.6
1995	–0.8	14.7	2.5	16.4

Sources: IBGE and Central Bank.

Over the longer term, a sustained improvement in the competitive position of the country will depend, therefore, on the ability of the public sector to attain a surplus over the next years, as a basis for recovery of public investment in social infrastructure, and a significant increase in private savings. Even assuming a relatively long-term low capital–output ratio of 4, an aggregate savings ratio of 24 per cent would be needed to sustain an annual growth rate of 6 per cent. Although this is achievable, it will take a strong measure of macroeconomic stability, predictability of rules and strong economic incentives for growth before such levels are reached.

NOTES

1. For a detailed description of some of the main industrial development policy instruments for the four MERCOSUR countries see Bosco and Machado (1995). See also Guimarães (1995).
2. See Government of Brazil (1991).
3. It encompassed, among other actions, instituting the National Quality Prize, patterned after the Japanese and American Edward Demming and Malcom Balbridge Prizes, established in 1951 and 1988, respectively. In Brazil, the prize is awarded under relatively rigid criteria by a private foundation, set up in October 1991 and financed by 75 firms. In 1994, competitors for the Quality Prize were judged by 160 volunteers, from the 350 managers who were trained in total quality management by the foundation in 1994.
4. Sade Vigesa, for instance, reduced 75 per cent of electricity transmission tower fabrication defects in the process of adapting the firm to ISO standards; Freios Varga lowered by 50 per cent casting defects during the ISO implementation period (see *O Globo*, 13 November 1994). Phillips Lighting, the first producer of light bulbs in Latin America to be certified, reduced its defect ratio from 322 lamps per million to 26 per million during and after conforming to ISO 9002 standards; similarly for Castrol, a producer of motor oils, which saw input rejection rates drop from 8 per cent to 0.5 per cent and rework from 13 per cent to 1 per cent between 1990 and 1995, with results already appearing while the firm was in the process of attaining the ISO 9001 certification (*Gazeta Mercantil*, 10 May 1995, p.12).
5. CNI–SEBRAE (1996). This survey included firms of various sizes from different industrial subsectors. It was conducted jointly by BNDES, CNI and the Brazilian SME Support Service (SEBRAE). Of the 1356 firms surveyed, 459 (33.8 per cent) were micro (5 to 19 employees), 294 (21.7 per cent) small (20 to 99 employees), 364 (26.8 per cent) medium-sized (100 to 499 employees) and 212 (15.6 per cent) large (500 or more employees). Together they employed some 530 000 people with annual revenues of nearly US$54 billion. Most replies came from firms belonging to metal–mechanics (341), garments, footwear and textiles (162), food products (142), non-metallic minerals (106) and electrical and communications equipment (81).
6. Still, it is important to stress that of the 950 producers surveyed, 33 per cent were firms with fewer than 100 employees; 45 per cent had between 100 and 500 employees; 12 per cent between 500 and 1000 employees; and 10 per cent had more than 1000 employees. In so far as smaller producers generally remain farther away from the best-practice frontier, the survey results may not be directly comparable with international frontier indicators, which are defined by the practices of large-scale, world-class producers.

7. In 1992, the rate of capital accumulation or investment reached, according to the government's Institute of Economic and Social Planning (IPEA) reached its nadir, with just 13.7 per cent of GDP compared to 16.6 per cent in 1989. This climbed to 14.4 per cent in 1993 and reached 17 per cent in the last quarter of 1994. Although it reached close to 18 per cent in 1995, these levels are still low compared with other fast-growing industrializing countries.
8. See *Jornal do Brasil*, 15 February 1995.
9. Very little is known about design in Brazilian industry except that managers are still unaware of its importance as a means of differentiating products and creating value. As a result, most graduates of the oldest and best-known industrial design school in Brazil, Escola Superior de Desenho Industrial, have either abandoned the profession or entered the marketing and visual programming fields.
10. See *Gazeta Mercantil*, 10 October 1995.
11. Neither Paraguay nor Uruguay has a differential treatment of firms by size. In Argentina, a specific statute for SMEs was approved by Congress in March 1995, conferring fiscal incentives, making the application of labour laws more flexible and facilitating access to credit. SMIs are encouraged to invest in low- and high-unemployment areas. These incentives apply for producers with fewer than 40 employees. A maximum eligibility-related turnover amount may be defined when the operational details of the statute are approved by Congress.
12. Information and technical assistance to SMIs are also provided quite effectively by university-based dual-technology services. The University of São Paulo inaugurated the programme in late 1991, and since then it has carried out 8000 consultations, 90 per cent of which were from SMIs, while spawning 14 other equivalent programmes in other parts of the country.
13. See Cacciamali and Bezerra (1995). Starting in 1994, there was considerable contraction in the rate of industrial productivity growth, which dropped to 3.6 per cent in 1995 and 3.7 per cent in the first quarter of 1996. This slow-down was the result of, on the one hand, the reduction of activity after 1994 and, on the other, the inability of Brazil to sustain high levels of productivity gains through reduction of the workforce without significant investments in technology and changes in the productive processes (see *Gazeta Mercantil*, 26 July 1996 – based on a study conducted by Paulo Gonzaga M. de Carvalho).
14. See Decree 69/96.
15. The Vale dos Sinos cluster encompasses 18 towns, which are responsible for some 40 per cent of domestic production and 80 per cent of footwear exports.
16. The industry is reacting. Labour cooperatives created recently are helping to reduce costs. Firms that invested in technological modernization, such as Azaléa, remained highly competitive. In 1995, it had the best results since its foundation 37 years earlier.
17. See *Gazeta Mercantil*, 19 July 1996.
18. In the first half of 1995, 300 000 vehicles were imported; for the remainder of the year, the government allowed in an additional 150 000. Yet a combination of high interest rates and other credit restrictions, as well as an increase in tariff levels to 70 per cent, led to a sharp fall in demand for imported vehicles. In early October 1995, the vehicle quotas were condemned by the WTO, which rejected the balance of payments rationale argued by the Brazilian government. They were subsequently suspended. See *Gazeta Mercantil*, 9 October 1995.
19. The Argentine automotive industry regime was established on 20 December 1991 and is valid until the end of the decade. It allows local assemblers to import, at a reduced tariff rate of 2 per cent, parts, components and vehicles against actual exports or investment commitments. Those benefits were extended to producers of auto parts contracted by car manufacturers. According to the Ouro Preto agreement – which established the opera-

tional basis of the free trade area – a common automotive industry regime was to be negotiated by 1997, to take effect as of 1 January 2000. It will be characterized by intra-bloc free trade, a CET (20 per cent for cars) and absence of distortionary incentives that might steer investment across MERCOSUR countries.

20. Emerging Asian countries' sales in year 2000 are expected to reach approximately 4.6 million vehicles compared with an estimated market of 2.5–3 million in Brazil alone (See *Jornal do Brasil,* 5 February 1996).
21. See Lucangeli (1995). The intra-industry trade coefficient (ITC) reflects the proportion of intra-industry trade within a particular segment relative to total trade volume in that segment. Thus, when the exports and imports within a segment are equal, the coefficient is 100; when to positive exports (imports) there are no imports (exports), the coefficient is zero. Or, algebraically, ITC = 1 – [abs.($X - M$)]/[$X + M$] times 100 per cent.
22. See *Jornal do Brasil,* 21 June 1996, which reported the Roland Berger Associates' survey results.
23. See Frischtak (1994).
24. See Cavagnari Filho (1993).
25. Within the framework of the Sino-Brazilian Programme of Spatial Cooperation (CBERS), two earth-resources observation satellites will be built in the period 1996–2000.
26. In 1991, the spread was some 2.3 per cent; the following year it dropped to 0.6 per cent; and, by the end of 1995, it reached 3.82 per cent. Indeed, the World Bank's evaluation of Custo Brasil (June 1996) pointed to a 20 per cent increase since 1992, mostly due to exchange rate appreciation and the high level of interest rates. Other variables, such as the high costs of ports operations and excess of bureaucracy, were also significant (World Bank, 1996).
27. A recent study conducted by Buzalen & Hamilton Consultoria for the automotive industry concluded that manufacturing costs create a 15 per cent disadvantage for domestic automobiles when compared to imported ones. This is mostly due to the share of taxes, which represents 23 per cent to 35 per cent of the consumer prices in Brazil, whereas in Italy, France and Argentina the share amounts to 16 per cent, in Germany to 25 per cent, in Japan to 8 per cent and in the United States to 6 per cent.
28. It has been estimated that steel exports are taxed at a rate of 26.9 per cent, in comparison with 15 per cent in Argentina and Japan and 10 per cent in the Republic of Korea.
29. At the beginning of 1995, the government decided the restitution of some 5 per cent of Cofins and PIS-PASEP taxes on exports.
30. Twenty-seven EPZs – one for each province – have been approved in Argentina, in addition to the Tierra del Fuego Free Zone. In Uruguay there are nine EPZs, five of them operational.
31. The poor maintenance of roads increased the costs of freight by 38 per cent on average and the consumption of fuel by 35 per cent (road transportation is responsible for almost 60 per cent of domestic freight).
32. For example, the number of containers per crane/hour for the port of Rio de Janeiro is about 10, while for Hamburg it is nearly 30.
33. See Confederação Nacional da Indústria (1995).
34. In an operation for ten years and at 10 per cent interest rates, the importer would typically pay 8 per cent, with the remaining 2 per cent covered by PROEX. Currently, the maximum interest rate differential absorbed under the programme is 3.5 per cent.
35. Among 1445 operations undertaken between January 1993 and July 1995, 1166 were requested under BNDES's FINAMEX programme.
36. The programme is considered by exporters to be bureaucratized and quite restrictive in terms of its positive list and financing terms. The Central Bank plans to introduce major changes, including expansion of the list of goods to include consumer durables, textiles and ceramics, among others; increase of the maximum rate of interest rate equalization

and making it available for shorter-term (3–5 years) operations, where demand is concentrated; and establishment of simpler rules and operational norms. See *O Globo*, 14 October 1995.

37. The beneficiaries the Programme complain of excessive bureaucracy and lack of interest of the banking system in intermediation. The operating agents are accused of selectivity, asking for guarantees of as much as 150 per cent of the value negotiated, limiting their ordinary capacity of obtaining credits.
38. Brazil has not had a system of export credits insurance since 1991. With the objective of reinstituting the system from January 1997 onwards, the government began a search for partners to constitute a private export credit insurance company, with minor participation by Banco do Brasil and domestic banks and insurance companies. The company will use its own resources to cover commercial risks, whereas political and other non-commercial risks will be taken on by the National Treasury. The government expects to stimulate exports with the increase of credit. For 1997, insurance demand is estimated at US$1.63 billion, equivalent to 3 per cent of total exports, while, by 2005, credit insurance demand is estimated at US$12 billion, or 12 per cent of total exports for that year.

REFERENCES

Bosco, M. and João Machado (1995) 'Política Industrial no Mercosul', mimeo, FUNCEX, Rio de Janeiro.

Cacciamali, M.C. and L.L. Bezerra (1995) 'Produtividade e Emprego Industrial no Brasil', mimeo.

Cavagnari Filho, Carlos L. (1993), 'P&D Militar: situação, avaliação e perspectivas', *Série Ciência e Tecnologia no Brasil,* Fundação Getúlio Vargas, April.

CNI–SEBRAE (1996), 'Qualidade e Produtividade na Indústria Brasileira', Rio de Janeiro.

Comitê Brasileiro de Qualidade– Associação Brasileira de Normas Técnicas (1996); *Certificações ISO 9000,* May and July.

Confederação Nacional da Indústria (1995), *Custo Brasil;* Rio de Janeiro.

De Band, J. (1994), 'Policy mix and industrial strategies', in P. Bianchi, K. Cowling and R. Sugden (eds), *Europe's Economic Challenge: Analyses of Industrial Strategy and Agenda for the 1990s*, London: Routledge.

Dini, M. and W. Peres (1995), 'Sistemas de innovación en América Latina: Experiencias locales y apoyo institucional', in Pontificia Universidad Javeriana (ed.), *Política Industrial y Desarrollo Tecnológico: Lecciones para el caso colombiano*, Centro Editorial Javeriano, Santafé de Bogotá.

Frischtak, C. (1993), 'Learning and technical progress in the Brazilian aircraft industry: the experience of Embraer', CEPR Discussion Paper no. 356, Stanford University.

Gassmann, H. (1994), 'From industrial policy to competitiveness policies', *OECD Observer*, no. 187, April–May.

Gazeta Mercantil (various issues).

Government of Brazil (1991), 'Programa Brasileiro de Qualidade e Produtividade', Brasilia.

Guimarães, E.A. (1995), 'A experiência recente de poliíica industrial no Brasil: uma avaliação', Texto Para Discussão no. 326, Instituto de Economia Industrial, Universidade Federal do Rio de Janeiro, March.

IPEA (1992), 'Perspectivas da Economia Brasileira', Rio de Janeiro: Government of Brazil and FUNCEX.

Jornal do Brasil (various issues).

Katz, J. (1996), 'Interacciones entre lo micro y lo macro y su manifestación en el ámbito de la producción industrial', in J. Katz (ed.), *Estabilización macroeconómica, reforma estructural y comportamiento industrial: estructura y funcionamiento del sector manufacturero latinoamericano en los años 90*, Buenos Aires: ECLAC/IDRC and Alianza Editorial.

Lahera, E. (1996), *Aspectos económicos de la gobernabilidad*, Santiago de Chile: ECLAC.

León, L.V. (1995), *Fortalecimiento de gremios empresariales en América Latina*, Serie Desarrollo Productivo, 29, Santiago de Chile: ECLAC.

Lucangeli, Jorge (1996) 'El Intercambio Argentino–Brasileño en 1994: se consolida un padrón de comercio maduro', mimeo.

Macario, C. (1996), *Experiencias exitosas de exportación: las principales lecciones de Brasil, Chile, Colombia y México*, Santiago de Chile: ECLAC, Division of Production, Productivity and Management.

Monitor Company (1995), *Construyendo las ventajas competitivas del Perú: Región Arequipa*, Boston, MA: Monitor.

O Globo (various issues)

Peres, W. (1994), 'Policies for competitiveness', *CEPAL Review*, 53, Santiago de Chile

Peres, W. (ed.) (1997), *Políticas de Competitividad Industrial*, Mexico: Siglo XXI editores.

Ramos, J. (1996), *Política industrial y competitividad en economía abiertas*, Santiago de Chile: ECLAC, Division of Production, Productivity and Management.

Robbio, J. (1995), 'Algunos comentarios sobre el grado de apertura de la economia', Instituto para el Desarrollo Industrial, Nota N. 39, Table 1.

World Bank (1996), Report No. 15.663-BR, Washington DC, 26 July.

ANNEX 9A. BRAZIL: SUBSECTORAL PROGRAMMES

Textiles

1. Introduction of import quotas, starting June 1996 and valid for three years, for products from China, Hong Kong Special Administrative Region, Republic of Korea and Taiwan Province (values ranging from 49 300 kg. to 20 160 000 kg in 1997)
2. For the short term, BNDES created credit lines for the whole subsector including spinning and weaving, fit and finish and garments for:

- fixed investments and operating capital: value: less than R$ 3 million; payback period: 3–8 years; BNDES participation: 80 per cent; cost of money: TJLP + LIBOR + spread of 5–7 per cent per annually[a]

- fixed investments and operating capital (operated by bank's agents): value: less than R$ 5 million; grace period: 6–24 months; payback period: 26–96 months; BNDES participation: 80 per cent; cost of money: TJLP + spread of 5–7 per cent annually
- exports (pre-shipment): value: less than R$10 million per firm; grace period: 9 months; payback period: 15 months; BNDES participation: 85 per cent; cost of money: United States dollar variation + LIBOR + spread of 5.5 per cent annually
- acquisition of machinery and equipment (operated by BNDES agents); payback period: 96 months; BNDES participation: 80 per cent; cost of money: TJLP + spread of 5 per cent annually
- imports of machinery and equipment: grace period: 8 years; BNDES participation: 80 per cent; cost of money: TJLP + spread of 5 per cent annually[b]

3. For the long term, BNDES incentives will be established based on diagnoses of the subsector´s weaknesses and strategies

Toys

1. Increase in tariffs from 20 per cent to 70 per cent: temporary safeguard starting July 1996 and valid until 31 December 1996 (not applicable to MERCOSUR imports).
2. Commitments by industry representatives: must be engaged in restructuring programmes – stable prices to year–end with possibility of price reduction between 5 per cent to 6 per cent; US$ 335 million investments in quality, productivity and design until year 2000; creation of 12 000 jobs; price reduction between 5 per cent and 10 per cent annually starting in 1997

Footwear

1. Products included in ECT's exception list and a tariff increase from 20 per cent to 40 per cent
2. BNDES´s Programme for Support of the Footwear Industry, valid from April 1995 to June 1996, included: participation in 80 per cent of fixed investments; payback period of 8 years; operating capital limited to 100 per cent of investment
3. BNDES´s support for the short term, valid until December 1996, included new credit lines for:

   - fixed investments and operating capital: value; less than R$ 5 million; payback period: 3–8 years; participation: 80 per cent, cost of money: TJLP or LIBOR + spread of 5–7 per cent annually
   - fixed investments and operating capital (operated by financing agents): value: R$ 5 million and more; grace period: 6–24 months; payback period: 36–96 months; participation: 80 per cent; cost of money: TJLP + spread of 5–7 per cent annually
   - exports (pre-shipment), value: less than R$ 10 000 per firm; grace period: 9 months; payback period: 15 months; participation: 85 per cent; cost of money: United States dollar variation + LIBOR + spread of 5.5 per cent per year
   - acquisition of machinery and equipment (operated by bank's agents): payback period: 96 months; participation: 80 per cent; cost of money: TJLP + spread of 5 per cent annually

- machinery and equipment imports: payback period: 8 years; participation: 80 per cent; cost of money: TJLP + spread of 5 per cent annually
- guarantees available for acquisition of equipment; conditions to be defined

4. Shareholders' finance: same conditions as those for fixed investments and operating capital
5. For the long term, BNDES incentives to be established based on diagnoses of the sector's segments, identifying weaknesses and strategies

Notes:
[a]TJLP – long-term interest rate.
[b]BNDES credit lines for textiles and footwear also include Japan Eximbank's line for the finance of capital goods, spare parts and intermediates as well as services imports from Japan.
[c]Tariff evolution: 85 per cent in 1991, 40 per cent in 1993 and 20 per cent in 1994).

Sources: *Gazeta Mercantil, Jornal do Brasil* and *O Globo,* various issues, and BNDES.

ANNEX 9B. THE CASE OF ARGENTINA

After nearly half a century of inward-oriented economic regimes, a brief episode of ill-fated trade liberalization (1976–81) and the ensuing re-erection of protective barriers, the Argentine economy remained relatively closed during the 1980s (Table 9B.1). On a cross-country comparative basis, and using international trade/GDP ratios as indicators of the degree of integration into world markets, Argentina was considerably less open than East Asian, European and other Latin American economies and nearly as autarkic as Brazil, with an economy one-third as large. As a result, the country remained largely detached from international trade, investment and information networks and, consequently, unresponsive to global changes.

Table 9B.1 Trade indicators – selected countries (percentages)

	Average, 1980–1990		
Country	X/GDP	M/GDP	(X+M)/GDP
Republic of Korea	35.93	33.81	70.21
Chile	31.27	31.89	63.16
Germany	28.75	23.48	52.23
Italy	19.45	18.08	37.52
Spain	18.13	17.77	35.89
Mexico	17.26	16.92	34.19
Japan	10.78	7.3	18.07
Argentina	8.85	7.22	16.07
Brazil	9.13	6.85	15.98

Note: X: exports; M: imports.

Source: Robbio, (1995).

In Argentina, the dominant economic phenomena of the 1980s were pervasive macroeconomic instability and repeated policy shocks, which rendered the economic environment particularly volatile, as expressed by rates of inflation, real exchange rate, interest rates and other key economic indicators. Faced by increased variance in key prices and policy rules, domestic producers reacted defensively by consolidating their positions and buying out competitors, while diversifying away from directly productive activities into financial assets at home and abroad.

The volatility of the environment, combined with a stagnant domestic market, caused investment rates to fall sharply during the decade, contracting to just 7.3 per cent of GDP in 1990, after a brief recovery occasioned by the Austral Plan, and in the immediate aftermath of a hyperinflationary bout. At such low levels, the capital stock in Argentina was being depreciated at a rate faster than it was accumulating.

The steep reduction in investment rates affected both domestic investment and FDI, while the limited investment activity of the 1980s was, to a great extent, driven by an investment promotion regime that transferred significant rents to dominant firms and major groups. Practically all major investment projects undertaken by national groups during the 1980s were supported by the promotion system, which stimulated investment by raising profitability through lowering both the resource requirements of new projects and the tax burden after start-up. Absorbing an estimated 1.9 per cent of GDP in 1986 alone, the system, which has since been drastically curbed, introduced major distortions in resource allocation, industry structure and firm behaviour. It offered substantial cost advantages to those firms that were generally powerful incumbent industries belonging to major economic groups and often operating in protected sectors.

By the mid-1980s, levels of protection were formidable. In 1987, for example, nominal tariff rates for manufacturing industry, calculated as a percentage of *ad valorem,* were 31.9 per cent and, when weighted by production, 37.3 per cent. Moreover, only 54.1 per cent of tariff positions were not covered by NTBs in the form of import licensing, a proportion that amounted to 42.9 per cent if calculated on a share-of-production basis. Despite the profitability cushion provided by promotion- and protection-generated rents, by the late 1980s, investment remained inhibited by the instability of the economic environment and a stagnant domestic market. The economic turning point can be traced to the 1988 removal of most NTBs, which lowered the anti-export bias of the trade regime and was instrumental in the ensuing export response, reinforced by the reforms of the 1990s.

Reforms of the Early 1990s and their Impact on Industry

A policy drive comprising macro stability, deregulation, privatization and a more neutral incentive regime was aggressively pursued by the government elected in 1989. Although the country is still quite far from achieving a balanced macro regime, particularly in view of the exchange rate rigidity introduced by the Convertibility Law, the changes introduced by structural reform have taken root and become, in large measure, irreversible.

A major incentive was the deregulation of domestic markets for goods and services. By the end of the last decade, the Argentine economy was gripped by a regulatory maze, which functioned as a barrier to competition by constraining the mobility of factors, segmenting markets, and distorting or impeding their operation, particularly in their price-setting and allocative role. Firms also faced a multiplicity of internal and external tax wedges, mostly inefficient and growth-inhibiting, but easy to collect. They combined to dampen efforts to improve efficiency and added to the costs of doing business in the country.

The State Reform and the Economic Emergency Laws of 1989 provided the legal basis for the encompassing Deregulation Decree 2284 of 1991 as well as for the macroeconomic and fiscal programme, and trade reforms. They allowed the government to intervene, change the legal status or organizational framework of, sell, liquidate or dissolve, any state entity, including public enterprises and regulatory agencies.

In the period 1991–93, a number of markets were deregulated: port and transportation services for cargo (including mail) and passengers (road, air, sea and river); wholesale marketing of fruits, vegetables and other fresh food; services of the medical and teaching professions; import and sale of pharmaceuticals; insurance; cement; and oil and gas. The removal of regulatory barriers in these activities was complemented and reinforced by the dissolution of ten key regulatory authorities, including the National Grain Board, the National Meat Board and the Special Tobacco Fund, and the abolition of special funds that supported their functioning.

The deregulation programme stimulated production and commercialization of non-tradable goods and services by lowering mobility and competition barriers. All legal norms, including price controls, entry and operation restrictions, that interfered with the free functioning of markets were removed, with the exception of natural monopolies or privatized activities, while legislation curbing the exercise of monopoly power was strengthened. Most importantly, deregulation allowed Argentine firms far greater flexibility, thereby lowering their response times and moving them closer to their international competitors.[1] The process of deregulation during the first half of the 1990s, reinforced by more recent changes in labour legislation, significantly lowered production costs for most critical items, with the exception of post and telecommunications tariffs and, as a result, improved in a very substantial way the competitive standing of Argentine firms (Table 9B.2).

The lowering of regulatory barriers to mobility and competition was reinforced by trade reform, with the removal of most remaining QRs and reduction in tariff levels. While QRs were reduced to 7 per cent of domestic production coverage by late 1990, automobiles and electronics being important exceptions, the *ad valorem* tariff band was narrowed from 0–115 per cent to 0–24 per cent, with an average rate of some 18 per cent.

In February 1991, the government announced that specific duties would be converted to *ad valorem* tariffs, while the number of tariff rates was to be reduced to three: 0, 11 and 22 per cent. Most export restrictions were lifted, customs procedures simplified and related taxes unified, the production coverage of industrial export taxes was reduced to 30 per cent and the statistical tax on exports eliminated.

Import competition and export rivalry stimulated by trade liberalization became powerful instruments for the structural transformation of industry. They led to greater horizontal specialization, with firms focusing on areas of advantage; vertical disintegration, with parts and components becoming more accessible; and exploitation of

Table 9B.2 Argentina: evolution of critical costs, 1991 and 1996 (in constant US$)

	1991	1996
Labour costs (1990=100)	108.2	92.7
Social security	100.0	58.8
Wages	120.5	127.7
Productivity	111.3	137.8
Energy tariffs (1991=100)		
Electricity		
Mid–large	100.0	72.5
SME	100.0	79.8
Natural gas		
Mid–large	100.0	110.0
SME	100.0	125.2
Other costs		
Port costs (1990=100)		
Containers		
Short stay	100.0	23.3
Long stay	100.0	41.9
Port tariffs		
Exports	100.0	40.4
Imports	100.0	64.3
Freights (1991=100)		
Containers		
Exports	100.0	54.0
Imports	100.0	54.3
Bulk		
Imports	100.0	64.3
Post and telecom (1990=100)		
Post charges	127.8	142.6
Telephone charges	138.2	175.2

Sources: Union Industrial Argentina.

scales of economy, in so far as, in an open economy, the market potentially encompasses the entire world. With the consolidation of the MERCOSUR integration process, firms started to incorporate in their calculations both the opportunities offered by the Brazilian market and the competitive threat from, as well as the opportunities for cooperation with, other domestic firms.

Trade and the stability of the exchange rate also became important for the modernization of the Argentine economy. The relatively low tariffs on capital goods, which have fluctuated until recently between 0 per cent and 5 per cent together with the absence of NTBs, facilitated modernization and stimulated technological upgrading by firms. As investment recovered, capital goods imports expanded at a fast rate. The share of capital goods imports in gross domestic investment, for example, more than doubled in the early years of reform (1991–93), reaching 34 per cent as compared with 10 per cent in 1985.

In most countries, the major force for integration in the global economy is foreign firms investing directly in the country. The regime regulating FDI in Argentina is relatively open and generally does not create artificial obstacles to the inflow of capital. Foreign investors are not required to obtain prior approval for their investments, and the Foreign Investment Law and supplementary rules ensure the principle of equal treatment, with Argentine and foreign investors enjoying the same rights and duties. This unrestricted policy, which also applies to 100 per cent foreign-owned companies, extends to investment in the manufacturing, mining, commercial and service sectors, as well as to such areas as defence, telecommunications, power, gas and insurance.

The intellectual property rights (IPR) regime also underwent significant changes in 1995–96, with the approval of new legislation that ensures the broad consistency of Argentina's IPR system with the TRIPs agreement and with legislation enacted in Brazil in the same year. Remaining major gaps in the legislation include the absence of effective protection for computer software and trade secrets, as well as a degree of uncertainty concerning the enforceability of ill-defined provisions (as in the case of compulsory licences).

Sustainability of reforms

Argentina faces three critical challenges in improving the competitive position of its manufacturing sector. First, a significant change in domestic relative prices and profitability in relation to industrial goods and in favour of services and other non-tradables has induced major groups to move progressively into the latter (see Chapter 6). In many ways, this reflects differing conditions of competition across markets, quite intense in industrial tradables to limited for non-tradables, particularly for recently privatized firms. The rededication of the economic groups and large firms to the production of tradables, which they pursued very effectively in the late 1980s, and a reallocation of investment flows accordingly, will require the readdressing of relative prices and profit rates in favour of manufactured production and exports. To a greater extent than they are now, investment funds will need to be allocated to the tradable goods sector, particularly to the competitive production of industrial goods.

Second, the competitiveness of the industrial sector needs to be based on continuous modernization. Gross domestic investment is expanding, and so are capital goods imports. These trends are positive and need to be maintained if the country is to modernize its productive sector. If the market for Argentine goods and services continues to expand, and investors remain confident, there is no reason for the current modernization process to suffer a reversal, as long as an open trade regime is maintained and investment funds are made available.

Although there has been a degree of backsliding with respect to trade reforms and term credit is still quite limited, access to investment goods and an increase in investment rates may be ultimately constrained by the rate of savings in the economy. As recovery continues, the country will have to rely increasingly on domestic savings, in view of growing investment requirements and volatility of external sources. Yet domestic savings remain a modest proportion of national income, having amounted to less than an average of 5 per cent in the first half of the 1990s.

Third, firms generally need to focus increasingly on the international market, incorporating its parameters in their calculations. The essential challenge for all Argentine industrial firms is to reduce costs and create value so as to become internationally competitive. This implies that producers need to move beyond rationalization efforts typical of defensive restructuring into total quality management, while building the capability for product differentiation, innovation and design. This applies to the mass of SMIs – which are the focus of not always effective support initiatives – as well as to large firms.

NOTE

1. The evolution of freight and port costs, which fell considerably within a year or two after deregulation – by as much as 35–40 per cent – illustrates the importance of regulatory reform to the integration of the Argentine economy into world markets. The simplification of customs and other related bureaucratic procedures, with savings estimated at 1 per cent of the FOB value of exports, has further facilitated integration.

ANNEX 9C. INDUSTRIAL COMPETITIVENESS POLICY IN LATIN AMERICA AND THE CARIBBEAN: IMPLEMENTATION BOTTLENECKS

The Latin American and Caribbean countries (LACCs) have improved significantly their capability of designing manufacturing competitiveness policies, and have also adjusted such policies to the new characteristics of the international marketplace.

Manufacturing competitiveness policies reappeared with great strength in most LACCs in the 1990s because the economic context generated by hands-off policies did not fulfil the expectations it had promised, or, at least, not with the speed that some analysts and politicians expected. In this sense, one of the most important lessons from the Chilean experience had not been understood; that is, the long period of business and institutional learning needed to get positive results regarding growth and employment once the structural changes began. Moreover, Mexico's 1996 industrial and foreign trade programme shows very clearly that it is feasible to make important changes in the main competitiveness policies of the country while keeping within the framework of orthodox macroeconomic policy. Thus reality has proved wrong the assumption that, given an orthodox macroeconomic policy, there is only one possible industrial strategy: no policy at all.

The strengthening of competitiveness policies in Chile also deserves special consideration. In this case, it did not result as a reaction to slow growth, but from the government's perception that the factors behind fast growth in the previous decade could not be replicated in the future and that, in some cases, they are already becoming exhausted. Among the forces difficult to replicate are all those that had a 'once and for all' impact, for example, the opening up of the economy from a previous situation in which extreme protectionism prevailed, or a fast privatization process. Among the factors that are becoming exhausted, the most relevant is the possibility of maintaining a strongly undervalued exchange rate in the long term, as well as low real wages. So the Chilean government decided to put in place competitiveness policies in the fields of technology promotion and human resource development to develop competitive advantages other than those derived from relatively abundant natural resources and cheap labour.

Moreover, export promotion policies in Chile are mostly the result of a persistent belief, prevailing since the late 1970s, that the new external markets – particularly for non-traditional products – are not already opened, but that they should be opened in a joint effort of private entrepreneurs with governmental support (Macario, 1996).

The most important weakness in policy design in the region lies in the link between the new market-driven policy context and the will of several countries to pursue subsectoral policies. It is difficult to imagine a mid-term scenario where comprehensive sectoral programmes – with goals, action lines and financial resources directly attached – will again be designed in the region. However, progress in this field is still possible if future policy design recognizes that horizontal policy lines have *ex post* heterogeneous subsectoral impacts, since not all industrial sectors require new technologies and qualified human resources with similar intensity.

Thus the design of instruments of horizontal scope should incorporate an *ex ante* evaluation of their potential subsectoral impact, or, conversely, those instruments may be designed with the purpose of supporting the industrial sectors that use them more intensively and frequently.

Although competitiveness policies are stronger in those countries where no quick results were obtained from structural changes, they do not aim at reverting those changes or slowing their speed. In spite of this, there has been a strong tendency to subordinate manufacturing competitiveness policies to macroeconomic stabilization policies, in terms of their perceived relevance and in the timing of their implementation.

Several implicit components of competitiveness policy are involved in the fact that stabilization itself is only feasible in the mid-term if structural change also takes place. Beyond the political impacts on the legitimacy of the governments associated with every success or failure in each stabilization effort, competitiveness policies contribute to it. This is so because a stabilized environment has a strong impact on competitiveness, while only strong and sustained productivity growth in the long term makes the stabilization process structurally feasible and sustainable. To advance in this field it is necessary to integrate microeconomic and macroeconomic perspectives (Katz, 1996). To focus the attention on the institutional changes required by competitiveness policies – the reform of the savings and investment system, for example – may be an efficient option to reduce this complexity.

In spite of progress achieved in policy design, implementation capabilities in LACCs are still meagre, as shown by programmes that are never implemented, or by programmes that have not had any relevant impact in spite of, or perhaps because of, their ambitious objectives. Poor implementation capability is a bottleneck which results from the following factors (Peres, 1994):[1]

(i) Gap between design and implementation, characteristic of most of LACCs. This gap has at least two dimensions. On one hand, ministries responsible for the design of industrial policy do not normally control the policy instruments necessary for their execution. This is especially clear in the cases related to tariffs, fiscal incentives, and industrial or export financing, which tend to be in the orbit of the Treasury, while policy design lies within the Ministry of Industry. This gap explains why programmes in the region are so ambiguous and why often they read more as research reports than as actual policy documents.[2] Similar problems related to poor coordination and bureaucratic rivalry emerge also in other areas, such as S&T, international economic negotiations and competition policies.

   Besides bureaucratic inefficiency, these conflicts also lead to considering the necessary balance between objectives and constraints only *ex post*. This allows policy makers to present highly ambitious objectives (for example, competitive integration into the world markets) while the budget restrictions of policy implementing agencies impede them from achieving these objectives. This problem is particularly apparent in policy designs which include many objectives, but no goals – a frequent case in the region.

(ii) Institutional failures in policy implementation are also caused by the lack of a policy *operator*, that is to say, an institution (not necessarily a state agency) able to lead the policy process. It is quite usual in the region to overestimate the importance of systemic or structural determinants, thus neglecting the role of leaders, both individuals or institutions. To improve policy implementation it is necessary to promote the development of the leadership capabilities and the political will of people and institutions which are in charge of policy making or have to apply policy instruments.

(iii) Policy implementation is always more difficult and complex than policy design – and more expensive. It is during implementation when problems such as uncertainty, lack of information and the operator's bounded rationality surface. Thus, it is relatively easy to 'pick winners' when designing policies but extremely difficult to use that selection as a sound basis for actual policy implementation. After more than a decade of budget reductions and in a context where government policy agencies have lost a significant part of their technical capabilities, policy complexity is particularly difficult to handle.

The progress the region has made regarding the transfer of successful policy design experiences seldom gives rise to the requisite institutional development. It is relatively easy to replicate a successful policy design; it is far more difficult to replicate the institutional learning necessary to carry it out. Sometimes, even in the same country, it is hard to replicate successful experiences in order to extend their impact so as to reach more than a few enterprises.[3]

In a general perspective, implementation bottlenecks may be understood as a governance problem, that is to say a problem related to the power and the rules used in the management of economic resources for development. Implementation, as well as governance, is determined by several factors: (i) degree of social consensus behind the policies; (ii) transparency and fairness of the rules the game; (iii) quality of the government's actions, and (iv) the responsiveness and accountability of those actions (Lahera, 1996). In the particular case of industrial development policies, lack of consensus, poor accuracy of the rules and absence of impact evaluations diminish the quality of the government's actions.

The most important improvements in this field so far have been the agreements on policy design reached by the private and public sectors. These agreements took place through different institutional arrangements. The following two are among the most significant ones.

First, there are the mechanisms for negotiation between business chambers (generally at their highest level) and the public agencies in charge of the industrial policies. Two recent examples are: (i) collaboration between the Ministry of Trade and Industrial Promotion and the Mexican Confederation of Industrial Chambers in the elaboration of the Programme of Industrial Policy and Foreign Trade of May 1996; and (ii) cooperation between the Ministry of Industry and Trade and the Venezuelan Confederation of Industry in the design of New Guidelines for a Negotiated Industrial Strategy, announced in June of the same year. The dialogue that took place in these collaborative experiences has given the private sector a sense of ownership and commitment that it would otherwise have lacked.

Second, there are the formal organizations, councils or boards for policy negotiation. These organizations have different institutional arrangements, but they always respond to the need of an arena to negotiate competitiveness issues, particularly regarding the industrial sector. Examples of these organizations, which have developed since 1992, are the Brazilian industry negotiation boards (*camaras sectoriais*), the Industrial Policy Council in Costa Rica, the National Competitiveness Board in Colombia and the Chilean Production Development Board. Other examples are some 1996 initiatives such as the creation of an Industrial Competitiveness Council in Bolivia and an Industrial Development Council in Venezuela; as well as the implementation of a Competitiveness and Productivity National Council in Ecuador.[4]

A brief review of these experiences shows the variety of conditions that policy implementation must face in the region. The boards are different in their functions, institutional insertion, membership and their members' power. In the case of Chile and Colombia, the functions of the boards are those of a consulting organization. In Brazil, the industry negotiation chambers are oriented towards decision making. Naturally, in the first case their members can be individuals with no formal representation of business or labour organizations, while in the second case such representation is essential as the agreements reached should be binding on all the members of those organizations.

Even when the boards of different countries may have similar functions, their institutional insertion and membership composition differ. Thus, for example, the Chilean Production Development Board exists within the framework of the Industry

Ministry, while the National Competitiveness Council of Colombia is integrated into the Presidency of the Republic. The boards always include as main actors the private and public sectors, while the labour participation differs remarkably (from the strong activity of the Brazilian chambers to a reluctant participation as in Chile). The presence of the academic sector (universities) is formally included only in Colombia.

Although the private sector considers the competitiveness boards as adequate communication channels with the authorities and also as a good source of information, it is still too early to reach general conclusions from the experiences of the boards.

Small boards or councils can create working committees for specific tasks, meet frequently, have clearly spelt-out missions within a predetermined time frame and be connected to the highest decision level possible.[5] In this way they may avoid being seen as favouring particular ministries.

As to the academic and labour sectors, there are two main aspects worth discussing. On the one hand, the involvement of intellectuals is very useful in organizations that must constantly compare different experiences, present conclusions and prepare documents. Yet, on the other, labour participation, although essential in competitiveness matters, has faced two types of problems: (i) lack of representatives with technical capability, and (ii) difficulties in councils with employer delegates during conflicts (strikes, for example).

The advantage of having boards with decision-making, or at least consulting, capability strictly depends on the disposition of the parties to share power. Doubtless, granting decision-making capacity motivates the private sector to assume a shared responsibility in policy management.[6]

Competitiveness boards have had a significant impact on competitiveness policy design in the region; however, social agreements required for policy design do not always suffice. The assumption that policies will not always be implemented, which is quite often made in the region, eases the way to social agreements at the policy design level since these tend to be supported by only very weak implementation commitments. The management rule according to which the *quasi* resolution of conflicts can be attained through non-operational agreements which postpone difficult decisions is largely applied. Ambitious competitiveness policies often tend to be based on formal (empty) social agreements even if they are non-operational. In this framework, frequent renegotiations of policy design agreements are the rule more often than not.

Competitiveness policy boards have helped to legitimize policies and have at least partially worked to improve their efficiency. This combination of legitimacy and efficiency is the boards' most important contribution to policy implementation and economic governance. The boards have supported the substitution of a procedural approach to rationality (De Band, 1994) by a substantive rationality approach to policy decisions – difficult to achieve due to the dynamism and uncertainty prevailing in the marketplace. Thus the application of the right policy-making mechanism becomes a means to reach a right decision, that is to say a decision that may be implemented. This logic may not be perfect, but it seems to work efficiently.

This procedural rationality also leads competitiveness policies to return managerial capabilities and power to the states, provinces and counties. Also in this case, the rightness of the policies is a result not only of their substantive contents, but also of the fact that implementation agents and direct beneficiaries participate in their design. There are important reasons why competitiveness policies should no longer be limited to the national dimension, but should become authentic decentralized policies. Two of them are: (i) to facilitate a country's adaptation to a new international trade environment by fostering a set of comparative advantages different from the one prevailing in the past, and (ii) to be able to grant subsidies that are admissible (green) for the WTO regime. However, the potential impact of decentralization on policies' legitimacy and efficiency, in the sense previously used, must not be underestimated.

This might not be the ideal approach to the subject; but it implies real progress from past approaches to industrial decentralization – or industrial deconcentration without any transfer of power to the local levels – which were above all an instrument to correct or reduce economic concentration in few development poles.

Mechanisms to foster policy consensus and promote decentralization open a real possibility of progress in policy implementation. They can become efficient parts of a work agenda (or road map) rather than elements of a formal plan or programme. Such agendas specify strategies and favour instruments and policies – some of which are not necessarily defined in the policy documents – that will be determined by negotiation during implementation, sometimes at a decentralized level. The 1996 industrial development policies of Brazil and Mexico may be interpreted in this way, as indeed they are considered by their public and private stakeholders.

Progress of policy design in the region must be accompanied by progress in implementation and evaluation of policy impacts sooner rather than later. Concentration of the best human resources of government in planning and designing policies has already yielded results. Most countries of the region need seriously to consider deploying such resources in the implementation and evaluation areas, where the government's actions are weakest. The equivalent for the private sector is to advance in strengthening business chambers as intermediate-level organizations capable of participating in the policy implementation process. A modern competitiveness policy is one that provides information, supports business efforts regarding technology diffusion and HRD, and facilitates the export process. And, as a modern business chamber is one that provides services to its members in the same areas, the possibility of achieving synergy in both efforts is very high.[7] However, it is necessary to strengthen the technical capabilities of these chambers so that they can provide useful services to their members, overcoming their traditional role of lobbying for trade protection and public contracts for their members (León, 1995).

Blending public efforts to make more efficient the policy implementation and evaluation processes with private efforts to strengthen its chambers in order to participate actively in the working of competitiveness policies will help overcome situations where consensus about policies does not result in actions. Put another way, it will help to close the enormous gap between theoretical strategies and applied strategies that prevails in the region (Monitor Company, 1995).

Although a window of opportunity has been opened, it will not last for ever (Ramos, 1996). While the revival of competitiveness policies owes much to the unfulfilled promises of *laissez-faire,* fast and concrete results are expected from them – all the more so when they are still considered by many analysts and politicians as a 'necessary evil'. To keep this window of opportunity open demands impact and action; once again implementation is of the essence.

NOTES

1. For an analysis of the differences between industrial and competitiveness policies, see Gassmann (1994).
2. Often such documents are filled with considerations like 'mechanisms will be studied for ...'. Sometimes, considerations of this type are more frequent than actual policy commitments.
3. This is particularly true regarding the most successful institutions of the national systems for innovation in the region. Many countries are interested in replicating experiences as, for example, the Chile Foundation or the Electric Research Institute of Mexico. However, it has been extremely difficult to reproduce these experiences, even though their most relevant features are well known (Dini and Peres, 1995).
4. The National Agreement for the Advancement of Productivity and Quality (Acuerdo Nacional para la Productividad y la Calidad) in Mexico in 1992 could also have been included in this list, but lack of implementation made it almost irrelevant.
5. The National Competitiveness Council of Colombia had these characteristics. This entity seems to have been the more efficient and has the lowest conflict level of those analysed here.
6. While in Colombia the private sector, particularly the large enterprises, was the force behind the creation of the National Competitiveness Council, in Brazil the sectoral chambers resulted from government initiatives strongly supported by proactive business and labour sectors. In the Chilean Production Development Board, the government has been the initial and permanent force, facing difficulties to obtain a stable labour presence and spontaneous business participation.
7. The experiences of the Association of Manufacturing Exporters in the implementation of projects to promote SMIs in Chile, and the Colombian Association of Plastic Industries in establishing a sectoral technology and training centre teach valuable lessons. On the other side, the experience of the Brazilian labour unions confederation indicates that it is possible to expect a similar synergy if labour is also integrated into the national efforts towards competitiveness.

10. Economies in Transition: The Case of Hungary

INTRODUCTION

This chapter reports on industrial development policies in place or under consideration in Hungary. Since 1989 the country has undergone a transformation from a centrally planned to a market-based, internationally integrated economic system. The process includes major economic policy reforms, creation of supporting institutions and a change-over to modern, competitive structures of production. The transformation is gradually evolving and subject to recurrent policy changes and refinements as well as occasional set-backs in terms of impact and economic achievements. A review of industrial development policies in Hungary at any given point in time can, therefore, only provide an indication of the direction this process is taking and a broad description of the currently prevailing policy framework and debate.

RECENT ECONOMIC AND INDUSTRIAL DEVELOPMENT POLICIES AND PERFORMANCE IN HUNGARY

Overview

Hungary's transformation from a centrally planned to a market economy system in recent years has encompassed three distinct phases: (i) 1988–89: initial transition period characterized by a gradual decline in production; (ii) 1990–93: breakdown of productive sectors with drastic economic decline and (iii) 1994 onwards: beginning of partial economic recovery.

While it may seem somewhat simplistic to analyse Hungary's complex transition process by breaking it up into distinct phases, this approach illustrates the pattern of change, provided that some important facts are borne in mind.

Hungary initiated economic reforms at an early stage. In 1968, attempts were made to soften the rigid system of centralized planning and resource allocation. The State Act of 1977 was intended to limit state intervention in enterprises and allow them greater autonomy. Although these initiatives did not immediately lead to non-interference by the state in the operation and investment decisions of industrial enterprises, and later had to be curtailed due to political pressures, they created a sense of collective memory in Hungary. The existence of privately owned plots was, in any case, an important element of the relative decentralization. Subsequently, in the early 1980s, a number of other, more elaborate, economic reforms were introduced. The possibility of establishing industrial cooperatives in the late 1980s implied a move away from strictly SOEs and facilitated the acceptance of the role of independent producers.

These reforms were pursued and accelerated over the years. Most importantly, they paved the way for the application of the far-reaching policy change introduced in 1989. At this time, the early transformation of the economy could be built on the experience gained, including that through established international business contacts. The industrial culture, contacts and partnerships with Western companies, as well as knowledge of foreign markets and business practices, were certainly far more advanced than in other Central and East European countries (CEECs) at that time. Long-standing international business contacts, in particular, contributed greatly to considerable FDI inflows in the years following the opening of the economy. Foreign firms were ready to invest and establish either joint ventures or wholly owned production and distribution companies in a market with which they had already been closely associated for several years through licensing, distribution and various other cooperation arrangements.

Although the collapse of the previously dominating CMEA trading system meant the need for a complete and rapid reorientation of exports and imports and, thus, a radical change of products and quality, the long-standing use of relatively advanced Western technology and associated skills made these changes considerably easier.

Previous adjustments – including the partial de-linking from the rouble system – meant that the forint was overvalued by only some 10 per cent at the start of political and economic transformation. Unlike other CEECs, Hungary was able to avoid a drastic devaluation of its currency at that time.

At the time of its participation in CMEA, Hungary had been allocated a special role within that trading system to act as intermediary between Western markets and CMEA in the field of technology, by importing Western technology and supplying it to CMEA countries. This arrangement yielded benefits for the Hungarian economy but, since imported technology had to be purchased with hard currency, it also contributed significantly to the country's large foreign debt, which still constitutes a major burden on the economy.[1]

Although macroeconomic indicators do seem to strengthen the argument for a distinct phasing of the transition process, the Hungarian economy underwent a somewhat different type of phasing than is normally associated with such a process (see below). At this point, it is important to underline the special features and complexity of Hungary's transition process and, hence, the need for special policy responses.

A brief review of the growth rates of GDP and gross industrial production shows that the rapid and deep decline of the economy reached its bottom in 1991/92. Industrial output picked up in 1993 and has since been growing. This growth must be contrasted, though, with the previous drastic decline in production, which, during 1989–92, reached 45.4 per cent. The level of industrial output and GDP in 1994 barely reached that of 16 years previously. The investment level corresponded to that of 20 years earlier.

Table 10.1 reports on the development over the transition period. It shows the overall economic and industrial recovery by the mid-1990s. The question in this context is how sustainable these trends are, and to what extent their driving forces can ensure medium- and long-term economic and industrial growth. The effectiveness and relevance of industrial development policy will subsequently be discussed against this background.

Table 10.1 Trends in the Hungarian economy: selected indicators (deflated values, yearly changes in percentages)

	1990	1991	1992	1993	1994	1995
GDP	−3.3	−10.2	−3.0	−0.8	2.9	2.0
Domestic investment	−9.6	−12.1	−1.3	2.7	12.3	0
Industrial output	−11.1	−24.7	−18.4	4.7	8.3	4.8
Industrial export	−17.7	−24.7	−4.7	3.8	20.0	19.1
Industrial productivity	−6.2	−8.8	−3.8	13.4	15.7	10.5
Investments in industry	−8.4	−11.8	4.0	−11.2	11.4	10.6

Note: Food processing is not included in industry output data.

Source: Ministry of Industry and Trade (1996).

Understanding the various policies affecting industrial development in Hungary is more complex than may at first appear. First, explicit industrial development in Hungary in recent years is hard to discern. Second, since the beginning of the transformation process, the Hungarian government and legislative bodies have designed a large number of laws, decrees and regulations relevant to industrial restructuring and investment[2]. To single out and assess accurately the effects of all these policies on the performance of manufacturing is not an easy task, especially since many have been or are being amended. The impact of the various economic policies and regulations on industrial firms and new investments can only be measured over longer time frames.

Industrial restructuring and achievements in terms of industrial growth and export performance during the first half of the 1990s cannot be directly attributed to explicit industrial development policies. Rather, macroeconomic and trade liberalization policies, as well as FDI and privatization programmes and promotional measures, have resulted in the *de facto* emergence of Hungary's current industrial structure. Only by examining the policy reform process and the way it has affected economic transformation in Hungary is it possible to discern the current pattern of industrial development and recent initiatives for more explicit industrial development policies.

The Ministry of Industry and Trade has recently issued a series of official documents which outline the new industrial development policy for the coming years. Although it is not clear when this policy will be applied in full, it forms the basis of the following section.

Foreign Trade and Restructuring

Trade liberalization

The shocks that affected the Hungarian economy most during the transformation process were the collapse of the CMEA trading system, liberalization of foreign trade and abrupt discontinuation of subsidies to the often large industrial enterprises. Trade liberalization was initiated in 1989, when import-licensing requirements and quotas were abolished for 40 per cent of imports, by value. This was increased to 65 per cent in 1990, 90 per cent in 1991 and 92 per cent in 1994. Government decree 112/1990, which came into force in January 1991, is the basis for regulating foreign trade and is updated annually. In January 1995, through the GATT agreement, the licensing of food product imports was replaced by protection through customs duties. As a result, 92 per cent of industrial and food production was opened to international competition. Besides some specific products such as arms and material for nuclear power stations, sensitive industrial and agricultural goods remain for the time being subject to import licensing, including textiles and clothing, footwear, cars, finished pharmaceuticals for human consumption, telecommunication equipment and detergents. An overall import surcharge of 8 per cent was introduced in 1995, except for capital goods for investment and primary energy.

Hungary signed an agreement with the largest trading partner, the EU, which came into force on 1 February 1994 and was subsequently supplemented by further protocols and agreements. The trade regulations, as of January 1996, stipulate that exports of all Hungarian industrial products should be exempt from customs and quantitative restrictions, with the exception of textiles and textile clothing. Previously duties on EU imports of Hungarian iron and steel products were also eliminated.

While protection of imports from the EU will gradually be abolished, the question can be raised to what extent import protection in recent years may have influenced the structure of industry. Due to frequent changes in trade policy, it is, however, difficult to assess actual import protection over a number of years. Table 10.2 reports on the structure of nominal and effective tariff protection for imports from EU in selected industrial subsectors in 1994.

Table 10.2 Hungary: nominal and effective protection (selected industrial subsectors, 1994)

Subsector	Average nominal rates	Effective protection rates
Metallurgy	6.00	19.52
Machinery	10.14	18.68
Construction material	3.47	3.99
Chemicals	7.77	19.63
Light industry	10.45	16.01
Food industry	25.96	111.52
Other industries	9.82	13.35

Source: *Newsletter Hungary*, 1996.

The ongoing liberalization of imports from the EU will exert further considerable pressures on the structure of industry inherited from the past, particularly for more protected industries. During 1990–93 the food industry, the most protected subsector, not only retained its position as the largest industrial activity but also slightly increased its share in total industrial output, from 21 to 24 per cent. Although no comparable data are available for 1994 and 1995, the food industry grew by 4 per cent solely due to export sales. These increased by 21.1 per cent whereas the rate for domestic sales was −1.4 per cent. This shows the heterogeneity of this large subsector in which domestically oriented business declined while export-oriented, foreign-dominated business expanded considerably.

Price liberalization meant that the prices of 90 per cent of consumer goods were freed, with only electricity and gas prices remaining regulated by law. The new law on foreign exchange of 1 January 1996 made the forint convertible. Some restrictions prevail only for capital transactions. The previous exchange rate policy had resulted in a gradual real appreciation of the forint. In early 1993 and until early 1995, when the devaluation policy was introduced, the real exchange rate measured by consumer price levels exceeded the 1990 level by 35 per cent.[3] With the new policy, a pre-announced devaluation of 29 per cent, as calculated from the beginning of the year, was carried out in early 1995. On the basis of a comparison of unit labour costs (ULCs) in identical currency, this generated an improvement of some 15 per cent in the cost competitiveness of domestic producers.[4] Devaluation was followed by a programme of daily changes of exchange rate, the monthly devaluation rate being 1.8 per cent during 1995. The new system of exchange rate policy was based on a crawling peg linked to a basket of currencies. This pre-announced system of daily devaluation made it possible not only to ensure Hungarian competitiveness on a continuous basis but also to dampen uncertainties and speculation regarding devaluation and inflation.

From CMEA to EU trade

The importance of the CMEA market for Hungarian industry was especially pronounced in certain industries, above all, bus manufacture, shipbuilding, food processing, machine tools, telecommunication equipment and instruments. Since the output of these industries was predominantly aimed at supplying CMEA countries, in particular the former Soviet Union, they were the ones most affected by the sudden collapse of the CMEA trading system during the initial stage of the transformation process. Dwindling domestic demand and disruption of CMEA trade forced Hungary to seek new export markets, primarily in the EU countries.

Having already established some trade relations with countries of the EU, Hungary built up its trade volumes with these countries through rapid reorientation of production and significant inflows of FDI made possible by policy reforms, so that they soon became Hungary's largest collective partner. The recovery in 1994–95 was primarily attributable to the rapid growth of exports, and the trend is continuing. During 1993–95, the share of Hungary's exports to EU countries grew from 58.8 to 62.7 per cent and the import share from 54.8 to 61.5 per cent. Meanwhile, the trade with former socialist countries declined further, the share of exports dropping from 25.5 to 24.4 per cent and the share of imports from 29.4 to 24.0 per cent.[5]

Hungary has been largely successful in transforming its production and trade structures in a rather short period of time in spite of severe overall resource constraints. In this process, the industrial sector became the predominant recipient of FDI, allowing major restructuring and expansion of production. Hungarian firms faced drastic adjustment pressures without, however, having access to the substantial investment capital required to reorient production and build up new competitive production systems. With increasing foreign competition in the limited and shrinking domestic market, a large number of Hungarian industrial firms became non-viable. By contrast, foreign investors in Hungary introduced not only up-to-date know-how and market access but, above all, foreign capital resources on better terms than their Hungarian counterparts. They were thus in a position to restructure existing companies, develop modern, competitive production capacities and expand both domestic and export markets, thereby, in effect, contributing to a further phasing out of local companies in some areas. The very strict bankruptcy law of October 1991 finally forced many Hungarian firms out of business. Only those firms that managed to adjust quickly to the competitive conditions of a liberalized market system survived this shock treatment. In September 1993, this law was significantly amended, providing for the possibility of a qualified majority of creditors to reach agreement out of court.

As a reflection of the crisis and the subsequent rapid economic restructuring during the recovery, the share of agricultural exports to EU countries declined from 27 per cent in 1989 to 15 per cent in 1995. However, it can be assumed that EU agricultural policies restrained Hungary's exports of its traditional agricultural produce, in which Hungary otherwise had competitive advantages. The agricultural sector lost much of its former strength and supply capacity primarily as a consequence of policy reforms, including land ownership and size changes. The redistribution of land led to the break-up of agricultural and forest areas into plots that were far too small. With the new and growing competitive environment, these proved not to be viable for modern, efficient production. In some cases, these reduced plots were, therefore, used for housing. In pursuing its reform process, Hungary did not adequately restructure and modernize the agricultural sector to enable it to sustain or re-establish its competitiveness. So far, the sector has not been able to shift significantly its production towards higher levels of productivity as well as to higher-value segments of domestic and foreign markets nor to ensure that agriculture be linked to the modernization process in the industry. Some modernized food industries have reported that deliveries of critical agricultural inputs have been disrupted due to deteriorating agricultural supply capacities. While economic policies have brought about significant industrial restructuring, prospects for agro-industrial linkages seem not to have been developed substantially.

During the time of the CMEA trade system; machinery constituted nearly a third of Hungary's total export volumes. The collapse of CMEA trade resulted initially in a sharp decline in machinery exports. Nevertheless, the subsequent rebuilding and rerouting of exports in the machinery and transport equipment industry has been quite successful. The share of this subsector in total exports grew rapidly, reaching 25.6 per cent in 1995. At the same time, though, the share in imports reached 30.8 per cent, reflecting major investment modernizing the industry. FDI has, thereby, contributed significantly to trade expansion in this subsector through acquisition of large, former SOEs and greenfield investments and production for exports on the one hand, and through substantial inputs of modern imported production equipment, on the other.

Overall, companies with foreign interests have played a leading role in trade growth, accounting for more than 40 per cent of Hungarian trade in 1994, up from 25 per cent three years earlier. Within the framework of the liberalized trade system, FDI has been using Hungary, to a large extent, as an export base while also catering to domestic demand. This development has relied significantly on imported equipment and production inputs.

Privatization

Privatization of SOEs advanced rapidly through market-conforming policy schemes and opening to FDI. By mid-1995, the private sector accounted for some 60 per cent of GDP and more than a million private firms had been registered. The initial target of the privatization programme was the SME sector. More than 10 000 of these enterprises are now in private hands. The SME sector now comprises some one million entrepreneurs and 200 000 business organizations. Privatization of large-scale enterprises started later but was expected to be completed by 1997.

Under the law of May 1995, a new privatization programme was established to bring greater transparency and clearer timing into the legal framework. The law differentiates between various categories of SOEs and includes a programme for complete or partial privatization. Under this law, 46 enterprises will remain fully state-owned, such as the railway and postal service. The State will retain majority ownership of the electric grid and nuclear power plants as well as keeping a 25 per cent stake in the larger banks. The state will have minority ownership of the main oil and gas company (MOL), main electricity company (MVM) and five regional gas companies. A stake of 10 per cent will be held in the large, by now already privatized telecommunication company (Matàv). To safeguard competition and avoid the emergence of new monopolies, the Law on the Prohibition of Unfair Market Practices was introduced in 1990. An anti-monopoly office was also set up.

Recent Hungarian strategy and the privatization programme are being judged favourably. The logic of the plan to retain minority holdings in certain areas is, however, questioned, and further clarification is sought. Selectivity and careful monitoring are being suggested in imposing special employment and investment commitments. Clarification of the terms for the exchange of vouchers for assets and improvements in asset backing for compensation vouchers are also being advised.[6]

Foreign Direct Investment (FDI)

The inflow of FDI has been substantial during the transition years, averaging an annual US$1–2 billion. In 1995, FDI amounted to more than US$4.5 billion, while the stock of FDI reached a value of US$11.9 billion. The total number of enterprises operating with foreign interest totalled 24 000.

Since embarking on its transformation, Hungary has, in spite of its relatively small domestic market, attracted 37 per cent of total FDI destined to CEECs, making it the largest single recipient. This is due to several factors.

First, Hungary had already developed close contacts with firms in Western European and other leading OECD countries before transformation began. These long-standing business contacts created confidence among MNCs in Hungary's industry and paved the way for an initial wave of FDI once legal and policy framework conditions made it possible. Many foreign companies considered it quite logical at this time to strengthen and formalize their business arrangements and establish production facilities. Initially, this took place primarily through joint venture agreements which, as laws permitted, were often subsequently turned into wholly foreign-owned enterprises.

Second, privatization of large SOEs constituted a crucial basis for many FDIs. The cases of Tungsram, taken over by General Electric for some US$500 million, the airline Malév, acquired by Alitalia, and German/United States investment in the large telecommunication company Matáv are cases in point, each involving substantial capital investment. Foreign capital investment in Matáv in 1993 alone accounted for some one-third of total FDI inflows that year. In 1995, US$2.8 billion, or 70 per cent of total FDI flows resulted directly from privatization transactions. Privatization of large-scale Hungarian enterprises brought in 35 of the world's 50 largest corporations into the country's economy accounting for nearly half of FDI stock. As a result, a number of industrial subsectors are dominated by firms with foreign interest, particularly in the manufacturing sector. Measured in terms of registered capital and net revenues from sales, in 1994 majority foreign-owned manufacturing firms accounted for 79.2 per cent of the market in motor vehicles, 85.2 per cent in electrical machinery and equipment and 69.9 per cent in telecommunications equipment. The share is lower in basic metals (35.6 per cent) and in chemicals and pharmaceuticals (40.7 per cent).[7]

Third, Hungary has become a very attractive location for export-oriented industrial FDI due to its skilled, low-wage labour and its proximity to EU markets.

Fourth, overall economic policy and, in particular, foreign investment laws and regulations are conducive to FDI. The Hungarian economic system has proved to be a solid basis for partnerships with international business.

Fifth, Hungary started to attract FDI at an early stage, well before other CEECs had the opportunity to do so. With this head start, Hungary managed to attract a significant first wave of FDI, which, in turn, paved the way for further, continued flows into industry.

Policy Implementation: Concerns of the Business Community

Since the initiation of the reform process, the Hungarian government had to formulate and pass swiftly new laws and regulations in order to move as fast as possible towards a market-based economic system as well as to foster and support the restructuring of industry. These far-reaching, rapid-paced policy reforms proved to be indispensable for the effectiveness of the transformation process. Concerns by the business community referred partly to issues of implementation and partly to the policy-making process.

One concern of industrialists is the content and style of the new laws and regulations, including rules for their application, often hard to understand and comply with. Another major concern is that changes in laws and regulations affecting investment, taxes, foreign trade transactions and the like occur too frequently and abruptly. The rapidly changing conditions for investment, production and trade are creating uncertainties in the business community and hampering timely adjustment by private industry. Retroactive application of some new regulations aggravated the situation. Enterprises need to receive full information and explanation about new laws and regulations well ahead of time so as to be able to understand their implications and applicability. On this basis, they can then plan investments, adjust production and market strategies and take other decisions crucial to the enterprise. That advance notification would have been important but not always possible was apparent in the case of changes in foreign exchange rate policies. Sudden and drastic devaluations have caused severe disruptions of sales and production in many enterprises. However, it would not have been opportune to announce these in advance.

In a radical and quick process of economic transformation, the rapid introduction and application of large numbers of new laws, policies, regulations and related amendments is unavoidable. An inherent problem of such a policy reform process is that it leads to economic uncertainty and disruptions. In these conditions, it is essential for government to ensure that the policy-making process forms an integral part of the policy package. The preparation and formulation of policy instruments and other measures that affect industrial development need to include exchange of information, advance clarification and, possibly, joint analyses and consultations with private sector enterprises and foreign investors. Greater transparency allows the business community to better prepare for new policies and adapt to emerging conditions. Government would benefit from gaining insights into the constraints and perspectives of industry as perceived by industrialists. To this end, industrialists have suggested that strengthening of public information systems, designation of ministerial contact desks for private industry, and other measures to enhance communication be pursued. On the other hand, government authorities have pointed out that various industrial firms and their associations have not always communicated their views, concerns and suggestions to relevant government authorities in a consistent and coordinated way. This suggests the need for increased and improved coordination by industrial organizations.

A related issue concerns the constrained capacity of government offices to handle the difficult and complex work of policy formulation and application of new regulations and measures as well as related analytical, administrative and monitoring tasks. The business community is critical of lengthy administrative delays in receiving authorizations, re-export rebates and registration of property. In the period of crucial policy work and development of new productive and institutional structures, it is of the utmost importance that authorities have requisite human and technical resources at their disposal. Effective and rapid administrative processes are as important as many policies *per se*.

Yet the precarious state budget situation limits these possibilities, and has led to cuts in allocations, with a corresponding reduction of crucial capacities in the ministries as well as of resources for commissioning economic analyses by research institutes.

The business community is also wary of poor coordination between ministries and authorities at central and local levels in matters concerning policies and regulations. Proposals have been made for the continued improvement and restructuring of the state administration at central and local levels to foster greater transparency and efficiency in the transformation process. Arrangements need to be made for recurrent information and special training programmes for civil servants entrusted with the tasks of economic and industrial development policy making and application.

As in most other economies in transition, high taxation and other social costs as well as royalties, tariffs and the like charged to private enterprises often invite some SMEs to avoid legal registration. With the high tax burden and various trade and other regulations in Hungary, there has apparently been a surge in illegal production and trade practices in recent years. Besides a significant loss in revenues for the state budget, the market becomes distorted and legitimate enterprises are seriously affected.[8] The international acceptance and credibility of the industrial system suffers from such discrepancies in tax payments, especially if prosecution is hampered by bottlenecks in the legal system. The domestic and foreign investment climate, especially in the industrial sector, would be greatly improved if the informal economy could be curtailed.

The business community demands adherence to regulations and tax laws as well as explicit disincentives for irregularities of this sort. It also stresses that the government needs to pay more attention to efficient control in parallel with the application of market-oriented reform policies. The administrative machinery and judicial system need to be reviewed and restructured. Information campaigns may help to increase transparency and help both the business sector and the public to understand the functioning of laws and administrative and legal systems related to economic transformation. Besides tax evasion, key problem areas to be addressed in this connection are the privatization programme, public procurement, consumer legislation and product-related environmental standards. Regulations and procedures need to be scrutinized as to their correctness, non-discriminatory effects and transparency. Hungarian authorities' acceptance of certification from other EU countries is another issue raised by the business community.

The privatization programme is an essential component for both the preparation for EU membership and the industrial restructuring process. Industrialists have emphasized the importance of full transparency in tendering and proper access to company information. Efficient and proactive co-ownership by the state must be ensured in those cases where the state is to retain part of the ownership. There should be a clear differentiation between privatization processes and temporary holding functions.

Financing of investments constitutes a crucial issue for industrial restructuring in Hungary. If macroeconomic and fiscal fundamentals do not improve drastically, they will dampen mobilization of domestic investment in the near future. So far, domestic entrepreneurs have had difficulty in obtaining sufficient local investment funds at reasonable cost. Foreign investors, on the other hand, have easier access to cheaper international capital, thus enjoying a favoured position. Concerns have arisen that domestic enterprises might be crowded out by foreign capital.

Loans in foreign currencies could be used to substitute local currency loans under the new currency law. Securing of claims represents another issue that raises concerns in the business community and will require attention in the near future, in particular the enforcement of mortgages.

A feature common to the transformation process in CEECs is that laws and regulations affecting the labour market have changed radically and that labour disputes arise frequently due to these rapid changes and different interpretations of these laws and their applicability. The Hungarian Labour Code constitutes an important basis for organization of the labour market. However, the complexity of the text, lack of flexibility of regulations and difficulties encountered by the labour courts in handling the large volume of disputes are among the main concerns put forward by foreign business in Hungary. These issues will have to be addressed in the medium term as they are among the key determinants for FDI and other business decisions as well as for the international competitiveness of industry in general.

The concerns of the business community confirm, first, that government policies and regulations affecting industrial development are not confined to industrial development policies *per se* but cover a wide range of general laws, regulations and measures. Second, the concept of transformation is not only applicable to industry and the economy but also to restructuring and modernization of legislative and administrative machinery.

CURRENT INDUSTRIAL DEVELOPMENT POLICY TASKS AND CONCEPTS

Overview

The Hungarian transition to market- and private sector-led growth and towards international integration has been largely successful. After the virtual breakdown of industrial production during the initial phase of transformation, the economy started to recover, prompted by considerable structural change and shifts in ownership. Industrial growth and adjustment have been spurred on by large inflows of FDI. These, in turn, have been attracted by privatization of large SOEs.

Such high levels of FDI inflow are unlikely to be sustainable, especially since the government's privatization programme was due to be completed in 1997. In the medium- and long-term, other countries are likely to emerge as more attractive destinations due to larger markets and lower labour costs unless initiatives are taken to enhance Hungarian industry's skill- and technology-intensiveness using the abundant human capital available.

Rather than being all-embracing, economic and industrial recovery took place hand in hand with major imbalances, in particular in the current account and the state budget. Although the current account deficit decreased from US$3.9 billion in 1994 to US$2.5 billion in 1995, it still accounts for more than 5 per cent of GDP. Gross foreign debt amounts to US$30.5 billion. In spite of severe budget restraints, the government budget deficit reached Ft 134 billion in 1995. Inflation runs at 29 per cent and the unemployment rate has climbed to 10.6 per cent. Structural imbalances also prevail within the industrial sector, between economic sectors and between the various regions in the country.

Policy makers need to undertake major efforts to address macroeconomic imbalances and enable industry to pursue restructuring and growth. While macroeconomic stabilization is a priority for the immediate future, Hungarian industry needs to increase competitiveness as a basis for sustainable growth. The Ministry of Industry and Trade is responsible for monitoring the restructuring process of the industrial sector as well as designing and formulating industrial policies.[9]

The manoeuvrability and leverage of industrial development policy making is limited in Hungary by: (i) stringent economic and fiscal policies; (ii) a restrictive monetary policy and other austerity measures; and (iii) international trade policy commitments laid down in the GATT and EU agreements.

At least for some time, macroeconomic and trade policies will continue to dominate industrial performance, competitiveness and structural patterns. Industrial development policy concepts and instruments need to be embedded in the overall economic policy framework. This is taking place through emphasis on the horizontal nature of Hungary's industrial development policies.

The main principles and goals for the Hungarian industrial development policy are contained in the report *Hungarian Industrial Policy* (Ministry of Industry and Trade, 1996). It states that, after the years of contraction, Hungarian industry and industrial development policy will face new challenges during the second half of the 1990s, such as the speeding up of modernization with a view to catching up and integrating with the EU countries. The following points are also made: (i) industry will have to be restructured so as to produce higher added-value goods in production and exports; (ii) conditions will have to be set for legal harmonization with Europe; (iii) links within industry for joint work and cooperation will have to be rebuilt and widened both at home and abroad; and (iv) emphasis must be placed on exports and increasing the share of domestic products in the domestic market, contributing thereby to macroeconomic balance and growth of exports at a rate faster than that of imports.

The need for an active industrial development policy is also put forward. It is emphasized that, although a sound macroeconomic policy and improvements in the business climate can provide general conditions for sustainable industrial growth, they are not a sufficient condition. Improvement of international competitiveness demands promotional initiatives by the state.

The new policy addresses, first, steps towards European integration such as harmonizing Hungarian policies and regulations with established EU policies. Second, eight horizontal policy programmes are to be pursued:

1. Stimulation of investments;
2. Support for corporate R&D and innovation;
3. Reinforcement of the modernization role of FDI;
4. Development of supplier networks;
5. Export incentives;

6. Market protection;
7. Labour costs as factors of manufacturing competitiveness;
8. Representation of interests and cooperation in industrial development policy.

The government has emphasized the horizontal character of its policies. This rules out industry-specific interventions at enterprise or subsector level and stresses policies to provide an overall environment and general industry-wide framework for decision makers in industry to operate according to market principles. This would mean no preferences to particular industrial subsectors.

A review of Hungarian industrial development policy statements from 1991 and subsequent revisions of those from 1993 and 1995 shows an emphasis on non-interventionist and neutral policies.[10] This was particularly evident in the 1991 statement. In the first few years of reform, though, the government did provide some direct support to selected enterprises. These were mainly large, export-oriented and threatened by closure during the initial economic crisis. Assistance was given primarily through state debt purchasing and partial forgiveness. It also entailed restructuring of enterprises' debts and reduction of certain state claims such as those on outstanding obligations for social charges. The government also provided regional support mainly to the crisis-ridden steel industry. With the establishment of the privatization programme, such direct interventions were discontinued.

The 1993 policy statement contained an explicit differentiation between short-term crisis management and medium- and long-term structural development. It included suggestions for specific treatment of a few large SOEs, mainly in the engineering, food and light industries so as to cushion the effects of trade liberalization and the CMEA's breakdown. In the end, however, these attempts failed to have specific, long-term structural effects.[11] In the 1995 policy statement, horizontal policies are aimed at gaining longer-term manufacturing competitiveness by means of an overall environment conducive to investment and domestic industrial integration in conformity with EU policy approaches. Also, mention is made of strategic growth industries. Yet, rather than singling out specific industrial activities, inhibiting factors to and requirements for developing overall technological and skill-creation capacities as well as for formulating general incentives in these fields are identified. The statement stresses the role of enterprises' independent decision making within the general policy framework.

It is still too early to assess the actual degree of neutrality of the envisaged policy instruments. For instance, financial, technical and other measures are to be used to develop domestic sub-delivery systems but they might also be applied selectively to sub-industry systems. Likewise, regional development support could have an implicit bias towards certain subsectors, such as the steel industry. Even in this sense, though, Hungary would be in broad compliance with both EU and OECD policy principles and practice.

Preparations for European integration

To achieve the goal of full EU membership, the government is committed to pursue an industrial development policy in harmony with the ensuing obligations.[12] The policy harmonization issue primarily concerns compliance with competition rules and avoidance of market-distorting policies. Thus, restrictions are stipulated on state aid to reduce capital cost, with a ceiling of ECU 3 500 per job and a maximum of 20 per cent of capital costs, as well as on any discriminatory measures.

No major incompatibilities are apparent between Hungarian policies and EU principles. Hungary has established an open state aid system within the prescribed limits. Similarly, the importance attached to development of infrastructure, product-related environmental standards and policies governing FDI follow EU principles.

The government has adopted a three-year programme of legal harmonization. The quality system is being reformed so as to make regulations for product certification and procedures and institutions for certification comply with EU directives. The product liability law will extend the adoption of quality assurance systems in industry. In 1995, the Hungarian Parliament also passed legislation on national standardization so as to ensure the adoption of EU technical rules and standards. In the same year the Act on Public Procurement was passed with the aim of adjusting to EU rules. Within this framework, Hungary may, however, give preferences to domestic suppliers during a transition period.

Institutional mechanisms and structures are required, along with laws and regulations, for entry into the EU. Constrained by fragile industrial structures and institutions and a stringent state budget, hurdles are faced by Hungarian policy makers to advance along these lines. Industrial restructuring needs to proceed alongside with major efforts to attain a macroeconomic balance. Public finance must be consolidated while enhancing public sector efficiency and skills.

In this context, Hungary's recent entry into the OECD may be seen as an endorsement by the international community of the country's legislative and policy framework. For Hungary, this is part of its international integration policy as well as an important step towards EU accession negotiations, expected to start in the near future. Other advantages of OECD membership are: (i) expansion of the framework of cooperation with non-European OECD member states; ii) access to information on pertinent international developments; (iii) better conditions for bonds and other securities to be issued; (iv) a more favourable rating from other OECD countries in the areas of export credit insurance and guarantees; and (v) a channel to share experience gained in the transition process with other CEECs.[13]

Stimulating Investments

Overall investment in Hungary continues to be low, some 21 per cent of GDP, in relation to the substantial requirements for industrial modernization and growth and the need to adjust the economy for EU membership. Although the investment ratio is higher than that of other Visegrad countries,[14] the government has set the goal of continuously increasing it during the coming years to attain a level comparable to that of EU countries – around 25 per cent. The promotion of both domestic and foreign investment, especially to industry, continues to be one of the prime tasks for Hungarian policy makers.

During the transition period, FDI has been substantial and has played a major role in industrial recovery. By 1988 the government had already established basic tax laws, as well as two specific laws, in support of FDI.[15]

FDI incentives have been regularly refined and expanded. Recent changes have included the introduction of guarantees for foreign investors covering repatriation of profits in the currency of original investment and full and immediate indemnification for any loss resulting from nationalization or expropriation. Production equipment as contributions in kind to the equity of the company are free of customs duty. Companies with foreign participation can declare their premises a bonded, customs-free area. For more recent changes in the tax code see Annex 10A.

In addition to the standard package of incentives, the government offers special advantages to investors in industrial parks. Several parks are currently in operation and more are under construction. For both, domestic and foreign investors, they offer full physical infrastructure – water supply, electric power, drainage, telephone and fax lines, and road and rail connections as well as various services, cheap or free land, local tax preferences and direct contact with relevant public authorities. Most of these parks are aimed at entrepreneurial and innovative development. In Szeged, for example, the Talent Centre Entrepreneurial Incubator House focuses on biotechnology and the Székesfehérvár Entrepreneurial Centre is based on the town's specialization in electronic and precision engineering, and the vehicle and aluminium industries. Several custom-free zones have been established that qualify for treatment as if they are outside Hungary for purposes of customs, foreign exchange and other legal regulations. These zones are either commercial for warehousing, or industrial, for export production. Only recently did Hungary establish its first functioning science park that could be used to attract domestic and foreign scientists and innovators, and contribute to industry-related research work.

Hungary's success in attracting FDI attests to the effectiveness of the country's policy framework. Besides laws and regulations directly applicable to FDI, broader macroeconomic and trade and foreign exchange rate policies have had a major role in bringing FDI into Hungary, as have policies and programmes for privatization of large-scale industrial SOEs. Rather than vouchers or other forms of direct transfer, privatization policies in Hungary were conceived as market-oriented measures offering exceptionally favourable conditions for FDI. Some 50 per cent of FDI have been greenfield investments. Political and economic stability, geographical location with direct, easy connections to the EU market, quality of labour and low cost of skilled labour are some of the other key determinants that have attracted FDI. With wages in Hungary some one tenth of those in Germany, conditions for investment in Hungary are seen as very favourable, although productivity is somewhat lower. Investors praise the reliability and technical skills of the Hungarian labour force. Policy makers are addressing the issue of how to ensure that FDI flows are sustainable so that modernization of industry can continue and its international competitiveness be built up in the coming years.

Policy makers are aware that, to maintain the momentum of FDI, current constraints need to be alleviated and further foreign participation in future industrial development facilitated. Hungary is confronted with comparable countries that offer highly competitive FDI incentives while its own initial advantages in terms of policies and market development seem to be eroding. Wages may become less competitive and the small domestic market prove a limiting factor. On the other hand, the substantial FDI stock in Hungary may have reached a momentum at which multiplier effects will become noticeable.

Macroeconomic imbalances, including high inflation and declining domestic income, represent the most crucial constraints to be tackled. Continued price hikes hamper stabilization and have a negative impact on exports, despite the announced crawl of the forint and of real wages, resulting in a further decline in domestic consumption. As yet, other barriers confronting FDI, such as inadequate business infrastructure and information systems, lack of predictability of key parameters for strategic decision making and a degree of inefficiency of the public administration have not been fully overcome. At the same time, the privatization process is gradually winding down and will lose its influence in stimulating FDI flows. In addition to emphasizing macroeconomic stabilization as the prime condition for stimulating investment in general, the following special investment incentives are envisaged:

- tax incentives to strengthen generation of internal funds in companies;
- stimulation of restructuring and exports through favourable loan arrangements;
- strengthening the role of development banks and setting up a bank for restructuring; and
- support measures for investments in SMEs through a guarantee system, access to favourable credits and internal fund generation.

Total spending by the government on direct aid to industry is said to be limited to 2 per cent of industrial value-added.[16] Envisaged support to SMEs certainly also conforms with EU directives. In its policy statement, the government stressed the use of indirect methods for attracting FDI, but 'positive discrimination in favour of specific structural policy goals' is also mentioned, which may need to be further elaborated to ensure EU conformity.[17]

In its endeavours to pursue these policy changes, Government authorities need to establish close and continuous contacts with private industry. The role of industrial associations is to be reviewed to ensure that they are working effectively with contact points in the public administration. Training of civil servants and ensuring compatible resources and salaries in the public administration are further issues under consideration.

Besides these endeavours to increase foreign and domestic investment, the government is aware of the need to optimize the ensuing developmental impact through technological development, stimulation of domestic supplier industries and services and regional development. Current and forthcoming policies are discussed in the following sections. First, however, some general issues concerning the developmental impact of FDI and their policy implications are briefly reviewed.

There is some concern in Hungary about the possible crowding-out effect by foreign-controlled enterprises on domestic firms. Inasmuch as the former have easier access to investible resources, modern equipment, know-how and up-to-date management practices from abroad, as well as access to international market and information systems, they enjoy clear advantages over domestic firms, especially SMIs. Moreover, acquisition of privatized enterprises provides them with additional benefits. While domestic- and CMEA-market-oriented local enterprises needed drastic adjustment to compete in Western markets with new products, foreign enterprises could, in most cases, rapidly apply their business practices and contacts for export production. Nevertheless, significant FDI inflows have spurred on domestic enterprises. The sharp increase in industrial productivity is a case in point. Development of the overall business climate has inspired domestic enterprises to catch up in the modernization process. However, even under these circumstances and even if growth in overall domestic income/demand recovers, there will be a need for policies to encourage domestic entrepreneurship and investment in the coming years. The government must, therefore, consider a number of issues.

First, investment promotion policies and incentives must be devised to ensure that, in their application, they do not discriminate against domestic enterprises.

Second, in carrying out privatization programmes, the government should ensure competition and potential market entry by applying appropriate complementary measures. There have been indications that tendencies towards concentration and barriers to entry can otherwise arise in the processes of privatization and FDI.[18]

Third, attention should be given to increasing foreign-owned firms' domestic sourcing. As stated in an official government document, FDI flows have resulted in a growing reliance on international supplier networks whereas Hungary still lacks 'home-grown suppliers capable of meeting high quality requirements'.[19] It has, for instance, been reported in the food industry – previously one of the strongest subsectors – that among fully foreign-owned companies the 'links with indigenous suppliers (as subcontractors) erodes to almost zero, while they paid increasingly to foreign suppliers and the dividend paid out increased on average by three times'.[20] This shows that some FDI projects have established 'cathedrals in the desert', with no linkage to other Hungarian industries for deliveries or subcontracts. International firms with export-oriented production are, however, operating in highly competitive global markets and, therefore, need to identify and use optimal sources of supplies in term of costs, quality and delivery time. These sources seem to be more easily accessible for MNCs internationally than on the Hungarian market. So far domestic industries do not seem able to cope with these requirements. Policies to attract and maintain FDI by MNCs need to be complemented by policies stimulating domestic investments, in general, and developing supplier industries in particular.

Fourth, as in many other developing countries and economies in transition, FDI tends to locate in or near urban centres where physical and institutional infrastructure is most advanced and service industries and other inputs are available, unless particular attention is given to this issue in policy incentives relating to FDI. Consequently, overreliance on FDI flows may aggravate regional development disparities. The government is further refining regional development policies to counteract these trends (see below).

Fifth, encouraging both foreign and domestic enterprises to establish or strengthen R&D in the country, which is currently declining, is considered crucial for Hungary's current and future manufacturing competitiveness. The government plans to provide special incentives to induce foreign investors to set up R&D capacity and attract investments for R&D–intensive industrial activities.

Supporting Corporate R&D and Innovation

Overall decline in R&D

When Hungary launched its reform programme, a rather substantial S&T base had been built up over decades and was internationally recognized in various fields. Industrial R&D was carried out both in manufacturing SOEs and in specialized research institutes linked with industry. Industrial R&D was thus backed up by a considerable number of first-rate scientists. However, commercialization of R&D results remained low by international standards. In spite of Hungary's significant R&D outlays, a considerable technological gap had developed by the start of the transformation process in relation to foreign industries competing in international markets and, later, in the Hungarian market.

With the collapse of the previous economic system and the advent of the transformation process, S&T capacity declined drastically. Whereas the share of R&D expenditure in GDP in 1988 amounted to 2.24 per cent, it had fallen to 0.99 per cent by 1993.[21] This decline meant a decrease by 54 per cent in real terms.[22] The overall number of researchers, scientists and engineers dropped by half. R&D expenditures by the business sector declined faster than state-financed R&D. Two-thirds of previous R&D capacity in the enterprise sector have been discontinued. A distinct impact of the decline in R&D capacity and outlays was a drop of 52 per cent in patent applications by Hungarian R&D institutes between 1989 and 1993.[23] If overall expenditures on R&D continue to decline at such a pace, established research laboratories and institutes are likely to lose even more of their human and other resources while future Hungarian S&T development will further deteriorate.

This downward trend is a direct consequence of the severe economic crisis and associated breakdown of markets for many industrial firms that occurred during the first few years of Hungarian transformation. It also cut traditional links between research institutes and industry. Many industrial enterprises were liquidated while others could not maintain their own R&D activities. Although enterprise restructuring entailed initial drastic changes in process and product technology, further technology upgrading was not pursued to any significant extent, at least not through domestic R&D expansion. In the first years, the privatized and restructured as well as newly established enterprises failed to respond in any substantial way to the new requirements for developing manufacturing competitiveness through technological innovation. Most domestic enterprises lacked the resources and, possibly, the motivation for continuing R&D or for building up new innovation capacities. Moreover, the break-up of large SOEs into smaller, privatized companies deprived many of these of the financing required for R&D. SMIs with common areas of technological interest could form research consortia or other joint programmes to rationalize R&D activities and share expenditures. So far, however, such consortia do not appear to have been established, probably due to uncertainties and lack of transparency in the initial phases of the ongoing restructuring process. These uncertainties reflect government policies, business prospects, competition and international technology developments. Government and international support to increase awareness and motivation for technological innovation among SMIs would be an important aspect of industrial development policy, which could pave the way for SMI clustering in this field. Process and product upgrading has so far been primarily undertaken through imports of new industrial technology and know-how. In the case of foreign-owned enterprises, R&D capacities in the parent company have been relied on rather than building up domestic capacities. Another reason for the decline in R&D is increased requirements for adherence to intellectual property rights. As a consequence, most previous R&D activities aimed at technological reproduction could no longer be pursued.

The state budget crisis had a major negative impact on S&T programmes. This meant a decline in backing for public sector research institutions as well as industrial enterprises through financial incentives and direct support. The current situation of S&T is, therefore, of great concern to the Hungarian government. In an official document, it is described as 'companies following passive adjustment strategies, a drastic reduction of expenditure on innovation and a weakening domestic knowledge base primarily in the area of industrial R&D'.[24]

R&D patterns

In 1993, 40.5 per cent of R&D was funded by Government and 53.1 per cent by the business sector. Currently, foreign-owned or foreign-controlled enterprises account for 41.3 per cent of total private R&D expenditure. In 1993, in-house enterprise R&D expenditure as percentage of turnover was 0.96 per cent in foreign firms and 0.31 per cent in domestic firms.[25] In addition, the former enjoy access to intercompany technology flows. Initially, significant technological upgrading in terms of products and processes was achieved through FDI but, with a few exceptions, further investment in innovation capacity was minimal. The process technology that foreign companies import is often less advanced than in Western European and other advanced industrial countries. Product development dominates R&D programmes. Basic research has the smallest share of R&D in all types of industrial enterprises. General Electric is an example of a foreign company that pursued and further expanded R&D in a former SOE with apparent success. Upon acquiring Tungsram, it turned it into a centre of research excellence, which is developing a range of new advanced products and processes to meet the highest international standards. In some other know-how-intensive industries, such as pharmaceuticals, innovation has been focused on adapting original technologies for use in generic or rediscovered products.

A review of the number of patents granted to foreign residents during 1989–93 shows that the pharmaceutical industry had the largest share, at 47 per cent and that this share has increased. The share of the engineering industry has declined, accounting on average for some 7 per cent during the period. In its 1993 policy statement the government emphasized support particularly to food products and agricultural machinery, treatment and disposal of nuclear waste, autoparts and information and communication technology.[26] An EU study listed pharmaceuticals, agriculture-related subjects and medical instruments as research fields where Hungary enjoys a competitive edge.[27]

Need for innovation policies

Hungary faces the dilemma of eroding R&D capacities while needing to develop competitive industrial structures. In the longer term, these structures must be based on skill and innovation rather than low-wage labour. This makes a solid R&D base indispensable. A working paper by the Hungarian Institute for World Economics emphasizes that the fact that Hungary is reliant on FDI for its industrial development does not imply that the country is restricted to a passive industrial development policy.[28] Rather, the technical and intellectual basis for industrialization in Hungary must be built up through deliberate government policies. This foundation must be capable of accepting, supporting and absorbing new technological development. It must also provide an environment and a scientific infrastructure attractive for foreign and domestic investment in technologically advanced industrial activities. So far, the paper concludes, Hungary has not 'laid the foundations of such a conscious state policy on S&T or an economic policy for allocating resources to them'. The OECD report referred to above states in this connection that 'like industrial policy, technology policy was passive at the beginning of the transition period'.[29]

Aware of the need for a comprehensive and consistent policy framework for R&D, the government has established an organizational structure for the formulation and implementation of an S&T policy as well as the concepts for its various elements. In 1993, the government prepared a concept paper, 'Innovation Policy of the Hungarian Government', in which clear emphasis was laid on systematic development of the country's ability to renew, acquire and transfer knowledge, production and utilization of R&D results.[30] The policy paper states that 'innovation policy and state orientation are required in market economies since market mechanisms themselves do not solve, even if they dominate, the R&D of new high-tech products, the desirable movement of innovation and, especially the rapid evolution from a certain transitional situation'. The task of the government is to transform these concepts and basic principles into a comprehensive, concrete programme and to ensure that financial and other resources are available to implement it.

The dilemma is that the government is committed to pursuing its stabilization policy and that, based on a precarious state budget, the Ministry of Finance cannot provide any substantial or stable allocation of resources for S&T development. Whereas at the beginning of the reform process enterprise

R&D expenditures were tax-deductible, such incentives were eliminated owing to the budget deficit.

Towards a new policy

In its statement on the industrial development policy concept, the Ministry of Industry and Trade listed a range of measures to support company R&D and innovation, including:

- support for implementation of technological investment projects;
- government R&D contracts (Public Procurement Act);
- support for participation in international R&D programmes;
- rules for charging R&D expenditure against tax;
- legal regulation (for example, the Technical Non-profit Act); and
- enforcement of environmental criteria.

Incentives were also listed concerning a system of development ventures:

- development of the network of entrepreneurial incubator houses;
- expansion of industrial and technological estates;
- reorganization of industrial R&D institutions for meeting the requirements of SMEs; and
- harmonization and development of information systems.

The encouragement of SMEs would be pursued by means of tax policy, support for quality assurance, establishment of quality centres, support for technological transfer, and development of institutional support mechanisms and supplier company networks.

The development of industrial standards is to be supported by education, training and retraining. Targeted allocation for economic development as well as EU financing through general programmes are expected to provide the required financial support. The Ministry also emphasizes the need to assist SMEs by establishing an information system on technical specifications of products and services and setting up an R&D service network primarily for SMEs. The Ministry is advocating that existing organizations be used to develop a business consulting network. This would deal with application for participation in international R&D programmes and search for foreign partners, marketing, training and the like.

After the first phase of transformation, up to 1993, the government created a modified institutional framework for dealing with overall policies in S&T

which remains rather complex and difficult to grasp. A main element of the system, the Science Policy College, reports to the Prime Minister. It acts as an advisory body on science policy, basic research, support to applied research and linkages between research and higher education. Another body is the National Committee for Technological Development, which reports to the Minister of Industry and Trade on promotion, support and coordination of innovation activities. The various sectoral ministries, in particular the Ministry of Education and Culture, are involved in the process of policy formulation on S&T.

The state provides support to R&D in the industrial sector through a range of mechanisms, such as subsidies and loans. There are special funds in support of basic research, renewal of higher education and applied research. The precise methods and criteria for allocation and the actual volumes of funds available are subject to considerable change.

Promoting technological development in Hungarian industry is not so much a problem of conceptual policy or of lack of an appropriate institutional framework but, rather, of severe constraints on the state budget. In this situation, further prioritization and narrowing the focus of the government's innovation policy may be needed. At the same time, increased reliance must be placed on the corporate sector's capacity for innovation. This could be fostered through tax incentives and procurement policies, as well as through special support and attention to investment promotion in technologically advanced fields of industry and in research and related services. Increasing the awareness of and information to the industrial sector on pertinent technological development issues would also be important in this context so as to mobilize the sector to respond to emerging challenges and opportunities. The existing and planned Hungarian industrial parks, together with the availability of well-trained and experienced scientists and research staff, should offer considerable scope for attracting FDI. In this way, not only can Hungary's significant research potential be realized but it can also be safeguarded against further migration abroad.

For SMIs, the Government will, no doubt, intensify its endeavours to increase information campaigns on new and emerging technologies and to promote establishment of clusters and joint innovation programmes. In this area, international cooperation through the United Nations system and the EU is under way and should be further expanded.

Another important task is to forge new linkages between industry and academic research, which have at best been sporadic. In the long run, Hungary cannot afford not to utilize fully such potential synergies. Universities should assume a more developmental role and become involved in issues of importance for industrial application.

To promote the application and commercialization of research, the government created the Zoltán Bay Foundation for Applied Research in 1992.[31] By 1995, it had established three specialized institutes – for biotechnology, logistics and production technology, and material sciences and engineering. Part of the funding for these institutes will come from contract work for industry. The overall decline in state budget resources for R&D has also led to the emergence of a number of commercial, profit-based research units and firms. In addition, two R&D associations have been established, the Novofer Innovation Company, aimed at diffusion of R&D results, and the Hungarian Innovators' Association, which assists R&D institutions in technology diffusion through a local network.

Support for technological development in industry is particularly important for environmental protection. An essential task for Hungarian industry is to adapt to the increasing requirements for cleaner technologies. The cost can be gauged by the huge investments in cleaner technologies by some of the large-scale, foreign-owned enterprises. New regulations on environmental protection came into force in May 1995.[32] They incorporate the principles of EU rules and stipulate, *inter alia,* unified licensing procedures for new investments and operating technologies, discharge limits, technological standards, charges to induce the phasing out of obsolete technologies and financial measures relating to the elimination of environmental problems.

Reinforcement of the Modernization Role of FDI

FDI has been and will continue for some time to be the key factor in the modernization and growth of Hungarian industry. Policy makers, therefore, give major emphasis to promoting FDI inflows and reinforcing their impact on the modernization of Hungarian industry, including, the introduction and continuous upgrading of new process and product technologies and know-how, the induction of new organizational structures in enterprises and the application of modern business and management practices. The general upgrading of industrial skills, both in technical and commercial areas, is another important dimension of the modernizing effect of FDI. It also has an impact on development and utilization of business information systems and creation of production linkages. Hungarian policy makers need to focus on the following issues: (i) enhancing the attraction of FDI projects that bring optimal technology and skill intensity, as well as associated modern business practices to production; (ii) inducing foreign enterprises to bring in and expand R&D; (iii) promoting formation of internal training systems within foreign-owned and domestic enterprises; and (iv) supporting the spread effect of foreign enterprises' modern systems throughout Hungarian industry.

In its conceptual paper on industrial policy, the government has specified measures to promote industrial modernization through FDI:

- establishing an attractive investment environment and strengthening the attractions of Hungarian locations;
- reinforcing preferences granted to infrastructure development for improvement of industrial sites;
- encouraging investments within the framework of the uniform investment promotion system;
- giving priority treatment to large-scale investors;
- developing domestic investment projects attractive to investors;
- vigorous economic diplomatic action to win over major investors;
- developing a domestic supplier system; and
- reducing taxes and contributions.[33]

To become an effective and consistent set of measures this list needs to be further elaborated and assessed. Also, FDI for production and R&D can be attracted through enhanced international awareness of the S&T capacity and resources available in Hungary. There are major prospects for utilizing potential linkages to science and research capacity. Current endeavours, such as the programme of industrial parks, could be further developed.

In investment promotion, privatization and negotiations with potential investors and preference for technology- and skill-intensive activities and for development of domestic technological and subcontracting linkages should be emphasized. Development of a domestic supplier systems is particularly pertinent as it constitutes a major requirement for spreading the benefits of modernization. Domestic SMEs can be encouraged to adopt modern industrial production systems through exposure to quality-conscious foreign enterprises with modern technology and know-how. In order to enhance the spread effect through inter-industry linkages, the government could foster industrial networks by increasing the transparency of the Hungarian production system and market through improved industrial information systems and programmes to develop industrial chambers and associations. Both government authorities and the business sector have taken initiatives in these fields but agree that further efforts are necessary. A further area for government incentives and support is development of crucial skills in technical and business administration for potential sub-suppliers within the SMI sector as well as raising awareness about new, relevant technologies for SMEs through existing institutes, foreign enterprises and international assistance.

Development of suppliers networks

SMIs' technological standards and competitiveness are low. Through sub-deliveries and specialized production by support industries, efficient production networks are the backbone of industrial growth, employment and competitiveness in industrial countries. In Hungary, such networks have yet to develop for the most part, after the disruption of industrial linkages within Hungary and with other CMEA member countries. Most enterprises that had previously functioned as supplier industries disappeared in the course of the initial stages of the reform process. Restructuring of industry and growth recovery have been spurred on primarily by FDI and have not led to establishment of new, modern production networks. The goal of the Hungarian policy makers is, therefore, first, to promote SMIs' upgrading in technology, skills, quality of production and modern business practices; second, to foster business information systems that provide easy and quick access to data on business opportunities in Hungary and abroad; and third, to encourage large-scale, mostly foreign-owned industrial enterprises to develop linkages with the SMI sector in Hungary and stimulate foreign sub-delivery industries to establish production facilities there. Entrepreneurship development requires foremost attention both in industry and in industry-related services. The government sees as its immediate tasks to: (i) review prevailing conditions of suppliers and potential users; (ii) assist institutions and businesses to capitalize on partner brokerage; (iii) develop and upgrade SMIs as suppliers; (iv) modernize production organization, including delivery scheduling, TQM and certification; (v) encourage foreign companies in Hungary to provide assistance to SMI suppliers; and (vi) promote greater reliance on foreign assistance for the development of contacts and networks.

To develop SMIs, the government recently launched a new set of policy support measures. They were conceived on the basis of a review of the prevailing EU policies to ensure full compatibility and an analysis of the main problems currently encountered by SMIs. The analysis confirmed the prevalence of a number of known problems.

First, SMIs report that they suffer from exceptionally high administrative costs arising from their need to comply with the complicated procedures of the tax system and changing, complex regulations and laws. Many SMIs are not fully conversant with all prevailing policy instruments and their application and possible effects. Second, because SMI management often lacks experience in various commercial functions, such as market research and marketing, it is not always able to grasp and utilize emerging opportunities. Third, high taxation, prevailing interest rates and lack of access to capital and/or lack of collateral for bank loans represent major problems leading to high bankruptcy rates among SMIs.

The new policies are aimed at alleviating some of these difficulties. Tax concessions have been introduced for new establishments, technology upgrading and general modernization. Two special credit programmes for SMEs have been established. In order to provide assistance to SMIs, the Hungarian Foundation for Enterprise Promotion was set up jointly by the government, major banks and business associations and has been supported by the EU and bilateral programmes of several countries. It aims at improving knowledge and skills, strengthening the financial capacity of existing SMEs, facilitating the establishment of new enterprises and contributing to developing a business culture. It has a local agency network, operating through offices in each of the 18 counties as well as in Budapest, which offers a financial programme for providing micro credits, reorganization loans and other loans and interest rebates. The Foundation has developed a system of making credits available on favourable terms and with great expediency. Banks appraise projects and, within eight days, a decision is reached by the relevant interministerial committee. The Foundation also provides basic services to the SMEs with the first ten hours free of charge and 50 per cent payable thereafter by the enterprise. It participates in regular meetings of the Enterprise Development Council, in which both government ministries and enterprises are represented.

Support also comes in the form of strengthening information systems on potential supplier industries. So far, SMIs do not seem to be fully aware of the need to take part in today's rapid technological developments. Whereas foreign enterprises have brought in advanced technology from abroad, domestic SMIs have not engaged in technological upgrading to any great extent. Since larger, foreign-owned firms tend to source their inputs from abroad, most Hungarian SMIs have not been challenged to deliver high-quality specialized items to precise time schedules. With a new information programme, which also includes the establishment of the Euro-Info Correspondence Centre, aimed at fostering SME interaction and business linkages with other enterprises, it is hoped that some of these problems can be gradually overcome.

While much attention is being given to SMI development, financial and other resources for investment and support programmes are meagre. Macro-economic imbalances and uncertainties about a stagnant domestic market lower SMIs'motivation to invest and upgrade. Any significant take-off of Hungarian SMIs and industry-related services is still awaited. Government procurement may play a role in fostering development of SME supplier industries. Currently, domestic firms are given a 10 per cent price preference, but this applies only to production with at least 50 per cent domestic content. This means that domestic content of 51 and 100 per cent is treated equally. Further differentiation may be called for to encourage local production. Moreover, many SMEs may not be fully aware of the procurement programmes nor able to respond in time. Those Hungarian suppliers under threat of bankruptcy or liquidation and those indebted to the state are not permitted to participate in the bidding. Consideration needs to be given to facilitating domestic enterprises' enhanced involvement in procurement and to increasing the impact on local production.

Export Incentives and Market Protection

These two broad areas of horizontal policies for industrial development form part of the overall trade regime of the country. They are also included among the industrial development policies contained in the government's policy document.

Exports

During the recent years of the transition process, exports have played a key role in industrial and economic growth. To a large extent, this is attributable to the strategies and performance of enterprises that have significant foreign ownership. From the outset, these companies were able to bring in modern, competitive technologies and business practices and to rely on well-established international connections for marketing and sourcing. They could successfully combine favourable local costs with international market know-how and opportunities. The issue faced by the government is how to maintain the trends through appropriate policy measures.

To this end Hungarian policy makers must promote:

- sustainable FDI flows, in particular to export-oriented industrial activities;
- increased export drive in currently operating foreign enterprises through innovation and other adjustments; and

- upgrading of Hungarian SMEs in terms of improved international competitiveness and export orientation.

Besides pursuing measures to promote a favourable investment climate, including attainment of macroeconomic equilibrium and SME development, various specific export support schemes, including those for financing, are being pursued. The government has drawn up a list of such measures which includes improvement of conditions for finance of export developments, better conditions of export financing; an exchange rate policy favouring exports; and improved company access to foreign markets through trade promotion and economic diplomacy. The appropriate institutional backing comes from the Eximbank; the MEHIB, covering risks of non-payment by the buyer; and the institution for export promotion, as well as commercial representation in a number of countries. Export credit arrangements and conditions are in conformity with the OECD.

Domestic industrial companies, especially SMIs, are constrained by insufficient knowledge of business contacts in key foreign markets. Within current resources, the government provides some assistance to enterprises for preparation of sale brochures and related publications in foreign languages as well as for participation in international fairs. Some eighty Hungarian trade offices in various countries offer free services in basic foreign market orientation. Financial support is also available for the certification under ISO 9000/9001.

However, these measures can at best only support otherwise already competitive industries. It is crucial, therefore, that these trade promotion measures be complemented by policies aimed at enterprise restructuring and, above all, stimulating domestic demand so as to enable local companies to become competitive internationally on the basis of a sizeable and growing home market.

Market protection

At the beginning of its reform process, Hungary introduced far-reaching import liberalization which, in many instances, went beyond other countries' import regulations. It then proved difficult to meet fierce international competition as some industries were not yet modernized. Moreover, policies were more protectionist in other countries as, for instance, the EU agricultural sector, causing market distortions and hampering the exports of economies in transition. In the recent years, Hungary has taken several *ad hoc* measures temporarily to safeguard specific industries. These included direct government intervention and support through crisis management as well as import protection measures. Industries favouring such intervention included iron and steel, fertilizers, truck tyres and PVC-based subsectors. Compliance with international trade conventions and harmonization with EU policies mean that import quotas and tariffs will have to be gradually abolished. Use of these protection measures will have been abandoned by 2001.

The import surcharge that Hungary introduced in early 1995 was to have been phased out by 1997. The plan was to reduce the surcharge gradually, by one percentage point each in July and October 1996 and two points each in January, April and July 1997. The crawling peg exchange system and anti-dumping code will be among the few policy instruments that will be used in future. Consumer protection regulations and procurement policies may have some additional relevance in this context. Application of consumer protection measures will undoubtedly be carefully monitored by EU so as to ensure non-discriminatory treatment of products from its countries.[34] The special procurement preferences currently applied must be abolished by 2004.

The high import content of Hungarian industrial production and exports constitutes an inherent feature of current industrial growth. In the long run, however, the problems of high import dependence and the current account deficit will have to solved. With increasing international competition and further liberalization of Hungarian imports, Hungarian industrial enterprises need to increase efforts to become competitive. To meet this challenge, the government must provide the required policy support for developing and upgrading domestic supplier industries. Eventually, these policies could have a favourable effect on the current sourcing pattern of larger enterprises, and also enable SMEs to penetrate foreign markets. Domestic demand stimulation through appropriate policies is, therefore, crucial.

Labour force

Labour policy is decisive for sustaining Hungary's manufacturing competitiveness. The issue has two dimensions. First, industrial skills cannot erode or become obsolete but must keep pace with international competition. If the effects of the reform process are to have continuity and spread among the industrial subsectors, particularly in the SMIs, major advances should be achieved in terms of technological, organizational and commercial capabilities. Relevant industrial skills must be developed to achieve these goals.

Second, in spite of current prudent wage policies, it is expected that wages will not remain low over time. Wage increases will need to be accompanied by corresponding productivity increases, requiring major skill upgrading.

Third, an active labour market policy is essential to combat severe and prolonged unemployment. Government policies will be needed to stimulate industrial growth, including development of industry-related services. Other essential measures include upgrading of training and retraining facilities and policies for entrepreneurship and regional development.

The government is trying to meet these challenges with a set of policies for improving labour cost competitiveness:[35]

- a wage policy that acts as an incentive to improve efficiency and productivity within the framework of a sound macroeconomic policy;
- reduction of other employment-related costs;
- development of a vocational training system; and
- modern management and organization methods and ergonomic procedures.

This set of policies needs to be viewed against past and current developments. In the past, individual industrial SOEs had their own internal training capacity and cooperated with public vocational training schools. With the collapse of the former economic system, privatization of the large SOEs and their break-up into smaller enterprises, training capacities gradually diminished. In several large-scale enterprises that have been privatized, and especially those in which foreign investments have been made, new internal training programmes have been developed, with no direct state assistance. FDI legislation, however, contains provisions for a subsidy for training employees in such areas as business, computer and language skills. Workers who are or are about to be unemployed can receive subsidized training. The subsidy includes supplementary earnings and reimbursement of various other costs. The regional labour force development centres of the Ministry of Labour are responsible for organizing the training. Other public institutions active in training include the Hungarian Foundation for Enterprise Promotion and the Hungarian Productivity Centre.[36]

The dramatic increase in productivity in recent years can be seen as a reflection of the first major leap forward in the initial restructuring following the deep economic crises. It was primarily due to rapid technological upgrading in those industries receiving FDI. Upgrading and restructuring also caused a significant decline in industrial employment, which contributed to the overall increase in productivity. To maintain the pace of increasing productivity in the coming years will be much more difficult, requiring considerable effort by policy makers. Skill intensity is still relatively low in the

Hungarian industrial structure and will need to be enhanced. It must also be expected that some of the prevailing skill shortages will grow and that other skill gaps will emerge.

Foreign investors, on the other hand, often state that they have little difficulty in recruiting competent Hungarian management and other staff for senior local positions. Ample industrial management talent exists in the country, but skill gaps still prevail in fields such as marketing, product and production and development, quality and productivity improvement systems and accounting and finance.[37] Priority areas for government training assistance in this connection include programmes for supervisors and instructors; retraining and transfer of employees into fields such as marketing, accounting and finance; and modern management techniques. Special training programmes, for instance, in JIT production systems, need to be set up to enable potential supplier industries to develop.

Although Hungary has a skilled labour force and a vast reservoir of skilled and motivated young people, the question is how the educational and training systems can cater for the need to develop skills further and, in particular, to fill the prevailing gaps in industrial skills.

The problem of adequate training facilities and resources still prevails and is particularly severe in the case of SMEs. They lack the financial and technical resources required for this purpose as well as the critical mass of staff to be able to undertake their own training or even to determine precise training needs. To remedy this problem, state authorities can assist in taking stock of skill requirements and in organizing specific training programmes. Financial support through tax concessions and other measures could also help. An important precondition for undertaking such programmes would be for SMEs to form efficient clusters or associations. Together with such associations, the Hungarian government could expand programmes of technical cooperation from bilateral and multilateral sources in the area of human resource development for industry. They could systematically apply the recent experiences of advanced industrial countries in creating efficient training and retraining systems.

Apart from the need to develop skill-generating capacities for the modernization of industry, the business community sees two other labour issues as hampering the performance of enterprises. One is the high level of social security contributions by companies that would have a deterrent impact on employment creation in the formal economy and encourage the informal economy. The government is aware of this problem and plans to take steps to reduce social security contributions. The other issue concerns the need to provide better incentives for workers. Reform of the wage structure and reduction of the high tax burden, including compulsory social payments, would stimulate greater motivation and productivity.

Regional development

Although not explicitly one of the eight horizontal policies described in the Hungarian Government's recent industrial development policy document, regional development and, in particular, regional industrial development is increasingly regarded as an essential dimension of all other industrial development policy areas. Discussions by the Hungarian government authorities with UNIDO in 1989 pointed to the possibility that reform and industrial restructuring could lead to a concentration of industry in Budapest and some other urban centres and, in turn, to greater regional disparities. Many large-scale industries and mining activities in outlying regions closed down in the course of reform, with little new productive activity attracted to those locations. Regional development disparities have increased in terms of industrial capacity, networks, employment, and investment flows, including FDI. A series of surveys of development potentials in different Hungarian regions was carried out and attempts are being made to initiate bottom–up developments. The government has initiated measures to stimulate regional development, including decentralization of support to SMEs and establishment of industrial parks in the regions. In its Act XXI of 1996, the government defined instruments and institutions in support of regional development. These cover non-repayable grants, repayable subsidies and interest subsidies on development loans. The Ministry for Environment and Regional Policy has control over the central fund, with half of the allocation disbursed through county development councils in a decentralized manner. Because funds for these purposes depend on the allocation from the state budget, they are subject to severe limitations.

So far, economic decline in some regions continues, owing to the disappearance of established production capacities, rerouting of transport or lack of foreign and domestic investment. Budapest and the western parts of Hungary have been the primary beneficiaries. These parts have relatively low unemployment, at around 7 per cent, whereas eastern and northern regions have been severely hit by the economic crises, with unemployment levels as high as 25 per cent. In this context, it should be noted that labour mobility has traditionally been rather low in Hungary, so incentives may be needed to stimulate an increase in labour mobility region-wise and sector-wise, supported by appropriate training and retraining schemes.

Promotion of regional development represents a major challenge for Hungarian policy makers. Entrepreneurship development and investment promotion in industry and infrastructure, as well as industry-related services, will constitute essential elements of such a policy package.

CONCLUSIONS AND OUTLOOK

Hungary has gone through the most difficult phases of reform in terms of establishing the basic policy and institutional framework for market- and private-sector-led economic development. Within a limited time, the political and administrative bodies have successfully formulated this framework and reached a point at which the parameters and functional responsibilities of the economic actors are defined in terms of the restructuring and recovery process. Privatization has proceeded apace and was to have been completed in 1997. Positive growth rates in overall and industrial production, attraction of FDI and growth and restructuring of exports are positive signs. Hungary has rapidly built up a cadre of competent industrial managers and business people able to foster manufacturing competitiveness. The country enjoys an excellent international reputation as a reliable business partner and continues to be regarded as a favourable location for investment in industrial production, largely for exports.

While the reform process has been successful, it has confronted major constraints. Far-reaching economic, financial, legal and institutional reforms had to be carried out at a time when the economy was undergoing a drastic decline in production and a prolonged crisis. During this period, the government changed twice. Moreover, changes in the international geopolitical situation and global economic parameters exposed Hungary to various challenges. Transformation was made harder by internal constraints as well as by external pressures and challenges. This meant that no steady, predictable economic and policy environment prevailed, which would have been a major asset for undertaking the transformation and the build-up of a new, competitive production and market system. As a result, significant problems arose and some policy measures later proved to be either too abrupt and drastic or too partial and short-term.

Shortcomings of past policies can thus be summarized as follows. First, Hungary has not yet been able to attain macroeconomic equilibrium in spite of the application of ambitious financial and trade policy and austerity measures. Current account deficit, fiscal deficit, inflation and unemployment still prevail. A second problem of past policy making was the frequent change of economic policies, which caused considerable uncertainty for the industrial sector. A third, related problem was over-expectation of the ability and readiness of domestic industrial enterprises to respond to new and changing macroeconomic policies and liberalized markets. The micro level could not react sufficiently and adjust adequately in time. A fourth major problem concerned the dilemma of striking the right balance in policy emphasis between short- and long-term development goals, in terms of measures for macroeconomic stabilization versus measures to enhance industrial restructuring and investment.

In retrospect, the reform process up to about 1992, could be characterized more as crisis management than long-term growth promotion. Short-term measures for macroeconomic stabilization were dominant whereas the long-term development issues confronting the industrial sector received less attention. Foreign trade and finance policies, rather than explicit industrial development policy, have been the primary influence on industry since 1989. Real conditions and specific constraints in industry and its subsectors do not seem to have been fully realized or taken into account by policy makers. A contributing factor may have been the lack of adequate information flows. The crisis period was characterized by capital destruction and drastic investment decline. Investment levels then picked up but remained low. Even in 1994, after recovery began, investment volumes only reached a level corresponding to that in 1974. As a result of years of central planning and the transformation process, Hungarian industry has lost pace in its development and has accumulated a huge backlog in terms of capacity, structure and performance in the international system.

While it was crucial for the success of the reform process to expose industry to foreign competition and investment from the outset and ensure that non-viable industrial enterprises were rapidly wound up, a period of grace might have been granted to some potentially competitive industries. Trade liberalization at the start of the reform process probably occurred too rapidly and, in many ways, went beyond actual trade policy practice in other countries, including many advanced industrial countries. The government, however, subsequently recognized the need to introduce some temporary market protection measures as well as a revision of the tax system in order to motivate and enable domestic industry to respond to the open market by restructuring and undertaking new investments.

The dilemma between attaining overall equilibrium and fostering long-term industrial growth still prevails. The issue is how to balance the effects of financial stabilization and the state budget, on the one hand, and construct a strong real economy by supporting modernization of industry, on the other. The latter entails providing support to enhanced restructuring through promotion of investments and technological upgrading so as to enable industry to strengthen competitiveness and achieve sustainable growth. After a lost half-century, manufacturing competitiveness and longer-term growth need to be given priority. This is the aim of the government's industrial development policy. In this context, some of the major current and emerging problems to be tackled include the structure of industry, regional development, development of SMIs and the organizational dimension of industrial development policy making.

NOTES

1. This observation is due to Professor A. Inotai of Budapest's Institute of World Economics.
2. See, for instance, Ministry of Industry and Trade (1995a).
3. See KOPINT-DATORG (1995).
4. See KOPINT-DATORG (1996).
5. Ministry of Industry and Trade (1995b). Trade by Hungarian free zones is not included.
6. OECD (1995a).
7. ECOSERVICE (1995).
8. As was recently reported, the excise tax of 80 per cent on spirits has given rise to an informal sector now accounting for some 30–40 per cent of total sales.
9. A number of statements outlining the country's policy approach to industrial development have recently been issued. They constitute the basis for this section. The statements clarify the challenges to and general policy solutions for manufacturing competitiveness and growth while ensuring compatibility with international regulations and, in particular, with EU policy principles.
10. See Török (1996).
11. Ibid.
12. The conditions are laid down in the Commission's 1995 White Paper 'Preparation of the Associated Countries of Central and Eastern Europe for Integration into the Internal Market of the Union'. It covers legislation and administrative and technical structures for implementation of internal market legislation and outlines possible areas of EU technical assistance in support of the efforts of the countries concerned. For detailed information on the compatibility of Hungarian industrial policies with EU principles, see Gatsios (1996), a report resulting from the Roundtable Discussion, Budapest, 2 November 1995, on which this subsection is based.
13. *Business Europa* (1996).
14. The Visegrad countries are the Czech Republic, Hungary, Poland and Slovakia,.
15. The Company Act (Act VI) provides the legal basis for the different forms of foreign companies' operations in Hungary and lists all applicable laws. Act XXIV, Investments by Foreigners, specifies the fields in which joint ventures may operate – manufacturing, services, retail or wholesale trade and, pending government approval, banking and

insurance and the various conditions and incentives applicable to foreign investments. According to the Act, foreign investment can take the form of a 100 per cent purchase of a Hungarian firm; purchase of a majority or minority interest in an existing Hungarian company; establishment of a joint venture with a Hungarian partner; or establishment of a company wholly owned by foreign interests. The policy package for foreign investment promotion includes the standard rules and incentives of most European countries, in line with EU practices.

16. This is in line with current practices of EU members, which spend an estimated 3-4 per cent. See Gatsios (1996).
17. Ibid.
18. See, for instance, Ferenc (1994).
19. Ministry of Industry and Trade (1996), p. 3.
20. Hamar (1995).
21. International Development Center of Japan (1996).
22. ECOSERVICE (1996).
23. OECD (1995b), p. 21.
24. Ministry of Industry and Trade (1996) p. 11.
25. OECD (1995b), p. 14, Table 1.7.
26. Ibid., p.36.
27. Gorzalek, et al. (1995).
28. Hungarian Institute for World Economics (1995), mimeo.
29. OECD (1995b), p. 39.
30. Government of Hungary (1993), 'Innovation policy of the Hungarian Government', mimeo.
31. OECD (1995b), p. 27.
32. *Newsletter Hungary* (1995).
33. See Törok (1996), p. 8.
34. See Gatsios (1996), p. 50.
35. Ministry of Industry and Trade, 1996, op cit, p.23.
36. *Investors' Handbook 1996,* page 12.
37. Results of a series of interviews on this subject are referred to in International Development Centre of Japan (1996), Ch. 7.

REFERENCES

Business Europa (1996), Interview in September/October.

ECOSERVICE (1995), *Survey on Actual Situation of Investment in Hungary by Western European Countries United States and Korea,* Budapest, p. 31.

ECOSERVICE (1996), *Survey on Interdependence of Former COMECON Countries,* ch. 5.1.

Ferenc, V. (1994), 'Foreign direct investment and competition', Working Paper no. 31, Institute for World Economics, Budapest April.

Gatsios, K. (1996) 'Industrial policy in the context of Hungary's preparation for integration in the EU', in *Hungarian Industrial Policy – New Perspectives,* Vienna, Austria: UNIDO.

Gorzalek, G. et al. (1995) *Eastern and Central Europe: Final Report,* Brussels, European Commission.

Hamar, J. (1995), 'Industrial policy, structure and efficiency in the Hungarian manufacturing industry', KOPINT–DATORG Discussion Papers no. 31, September, p. 31.
International Development Centre of Japan (1996), *Industrial Policies of Hungary Emphasizing Export Promotion,* March, pp. 76–84.
Investors' Handbook 1996 (1996), Hungary.
KOPINT–DATORG (1995), *Economic Trends in Eastern Europe,* **4** (3), Budapest.
KOPINT–DATORG (1996), *Economic Trends in Eastern Europe,* **5** (1), Budapest.
Ministry of Industry and Trade (1995a), *The Investment Brief – Hungary 1995.*
Ministry of Industry and Trade (1995b), *Hungary's Foreign Trade 1995.*
Ministry of Industry and Trade (1996), *Hungarian Industrial Policy.*
Newsletter Hungary (1995), Vol. 7, Nos. 5–6, October–December, Budapest.
Newsletter Hungary (1996), Vol. 8, No. 1, February, Budapest.
OECD (1995a), *Economic Surveys: Hungary 1995,* Paris: OECD.
OECD (1995b), *Review of Recent Developments in Science and Technology in Hungary,* Paris: OECD.
Török, A. (1996) 'Hungarian industrial policy from the point of view of Hungary's joining the European Union', in *Hungarian Industrial Policy – New Perspectives,* Vienna, Austria: UNIDO.

ANNEX 10A. RECENT CHANGES IN HUNGARY'S TAX CODE

In January 1995, new corporate tax rates were introduced. They were intended to encourage firms to reinvest profits. To this end, tax rates were split into two parts: an assessed tax of 18 per cent on reinvested profits, deductible through tax preferences, and a supplementary tax of 23 per cent on dividends actually paid. The supplementary personal income tax makes avoidance of double taxation possible. Special allowances exist for firms that create new employment opportunities or increase exports. To stimulate investments in enterprises, corporate tax relief can be granted on the basis of actual improved performance. Parts of interest payments on certain long-term loans may be allowable up to an interest rate of 30 per cent. Corporate travel and entertainment expenses are to a certain extent deductible.

As of January 1996, incentive policies for FDI were further expanded to include:[1]

- An investment tax preference corresponding to half of the 18 per cent tax is available in fiscal years following the putting into operation of an investment project launched after 31 December 1995 aimed at manufacturing and worth at least Ft 1 billion in which export sales increase by 25 per cent relative to the preceding year up to to at least Ft 600 million. The preference can take a maximum 70 per cent of the 18 per cent calculated tax.
- In priority areas, without a value limit, the preference is available in those years following the five years from the putting into operation of an investment aimed at manufacturing when sales from exports or receipts from agriculture increase by 1 or 5 per cent respectively, in cases of setting up commercial accommodation facilities in all five years irrespective of turn-

over. The preference may extend up to 100 per cent of the calculated tax. It also applies to entrepreneurial zones on the condition of a 1 per cent increase in exports. The amount of preference may be deducted from the calculated tax; hence the 70 per cent limit on tax preferences applies to the amount of the calculated tax reduced in this manner.

- For plant and machinery acquired after 1 January 1996, 30 per cent depreciation may be deducted. In entrepreneurial zones, the investment costs of machines can be written off in a single amount; those of buildings can be charged at a preferential 10 per cent linear annual depreciation rate.
- Companies registered in priority regions specified by the corporate tax law either as crisis-stricken regions where the rate of unemployment exceeds 15 per cent, or regions qualifying as entrepreneurial zones, may benefit from a tax preference corresponding to 6 per cent of the purchasing cost of the machines from the 18 per cent corporate tax in the years of procurement. If the machine is sold or relocated to regions not covered by the law within three years, the tax benefit must be repaid. In this case, a penalty also has to be paid for the delay in meeting tax obligations.
- Offshore companies registered in and having their headquarters in Hungary and held exclusively by non-residents enjoy an 85 per cent tax break applicable to both the 18 per cent corporate tax and 23 per cent supplementary tax on dividends. Offshore companies should be wholly foreign-owned and not engaged directly in any business in Hungary. They should be involved in providing commercial services exclusively between third countries and/or other services abroad.
- Local governments may grant local tax breaks for a certain period. Some of them automatically provide tax exemption for five years plus another five-year period of 50 per cent tax relief. The current local tax rate for companies amounts to 0.8 per cent.
- The targeted allocation facility was introduced to encourage investments, economic restructuring and trade. Businesses registered in Hungary may benefit from the repayable or non-repayable grants of the Allocation Fund. The amount of the funds may amount to as much as 33 per cent of the combined costs of investment in infrastructure and investments in production facilities to a maximum of Ft 200 million.
- The Regional Development Fund provides financial help for companies that create new jobs and hire the unemployed in regions where the rate of unemployment exceeds 15 per cent. Business organizations registered in Hungary are allowed to apply for support by submitting economically viable proposals. Applicants may be awarded a few hundred thousand forints per new job created. Fifty per cent of the resources of the Fund is allocated in a decentralized manner, based on the decisions of the regional development councils of the individual counties.

NOTE

1 Based on information supplied by the Ministry of Industry and Trade.

11. Less Developed Countries: The Case of the United Republic of Tanzania

INTRODUCTION

The United Republic of Tanzania had an estimated GDP per capita of some US$100 (at constant 1985 prices) in 1995, though household surveys show a value closer to US$200.[1] The socio-economic situation of the country is characterized by a large subsistence sector with agriculture, fishing and live-stock occupying a dominant position in rural production. Agriculture is the backbone of the economy. It contributes 50 per cent to GDP and employs some 85 per cent of the labour force. Traditional export crops – coffee, cotton, tea, sugar, cashew-nuts, tobacco and sisal – account for more than 60 per cent of foreign exchange earnings. Manufacturing accounts for 6.5 per cent of GDP.

In 1967, the government enacted the Arusha Declaration which set a significant landmark in the ensuing political and economic regime of the country as it adopted a philosophy of socialism and self-reliance. The government extended its control throughout the economy by nationalizing all the 'commanding heights', of the economy. From then until the mid-1980s, the public sector played a leading role in the economy, making notable strides towards improving social services.

From the late 1970s to the early 1980s, the country was buffeted by a wide array of external shocks, including quadrupling oil prices, severe drought, the break-up of the East African Community (EAC) and war with Uganda. These events resulted in a persistent economic crisis in the early 1980s. To try to reverse the situation, initial economic reforms were introduced, mainly in the form of economic stabilization policies. These consisted of the National Economic Survival Programme (NESP) from 1981 to 1982 and the Structural Adjustment Programme (SAP) from 1982 to 1983. The SAP was short-lived because resources for implementation could not be mobilized and it represented merely a list of good intentions and proposals to formulate plans. Gradual devaluation took place from 1981 to 1985, with a mild attempt to liberalize the economy (Valk, 1992). These programmes were ineffective due to their lack of policy consistency and sufficient assistance from donors. The failure of these initial efforts to stabilize the economy provided a basis for the later Economic Recovery Programme (ERP) from 1986 to 1989 and the Economic and Social Action Programme (ESAP or ERP II) in 1989–92. These programmes, however, gave no indication of how manufacturing should have achieved their targets.

Some results of economic reforms began to emerge by the late 1980s and early 1990s, with a significant reversal in decline of output, improvement in exports and investment growth, among other features (see Table 11.1). Fiscal and monetary policies succeeded in checking inflation, trade and market liberalization contributed to the increased supply of wage goods in the economy, and availability of foreign exchange has improved since 1986 with introduction of more import-funding schemes and establishment of exchange bureaux.

Table 11.1 United Republic of Tanzania: selected indicators of economic recovery programme achievements (percentages)

Indicator	Pre-crisis period 1970–80	Crisis period 1981–85	Reform period 1986–91
Average annual real GDP	4.6	0.1	4.0
Average annual export	0.1	−10.4	5.6
Investment as percentage of GDP	20.1	14.3	31.6
Average annual inflation rate	14.0	31.0	25.7
Fiscal deficit as percentage of GDP	12.1	9.4	7.0
Agricultural producer prices as percentage of international prices	64.5	72.5	59.0
Average annual depreciation of real exchange rate	0.2	16.1	–24.3
Gross domestic savings as percentage of GDP official incl. unofficial exports	–	10.4 10.7	1.0 13.3
Manufacturing rate	–	–4.7	5

Sources: World Bank data, IMF and Bank of United Republic of Tanzania (various reports).

Nevertheless, the manufacturing sector did not really recover, despite a reversal in the former negative growth rate, as envisaged by policy reforms. The extent of technology and skill upgrading in industry remained limited. The ability of domestic firms to withstand competitive pressure from imports was eroded by the low level of competitiveness of most subsectors and lack of fiscal policy measures to provide room for a learning stage. As a result, the response of firms to the import liberalization policy was mixed, with some collapsing and others striving to attain higher levels of manufacturing competitiveness through various survival strategies.

This chapter examines the interactions between industrial development policies and other policies, and provides an account of how they have been instrumental in enhancing manufacturing competitiveness in the United Republic of Tanzania. The following section focuses on the tenets of the economic policy regime. Next is a discussion on manufacturing competitiveness policies and their interface with other policies, followed by a review of the industrial development policy agenda at work. The final section summarizes key findings. Policy experience and performance are considered at the firm, subsector and industry-wide levels.

TENETS OF THE ECONOMIC POLICY REGIME

Past Policy Regime

The past economic policy regime was disproportionately restrictive and interventionist, with little role for market forces to play in resource allocation. Prices were generally controlled and the market was mainly monopolistic.

Fiscal policy and management were characterized by persistently high deficits financed by substantial domestic bank borrowing. There was inadequate control of expenditures, chronic under-funding, and too many public investment projects. The planning system did not ensure efficient and prudent allocation of budgetary resources and the bulk of donor funds were not accounted for in the budget. Increased taxes on manufacturing firms led to cost escalation that rendered them less price-competitive.[2]

The exchange rate regime was characterized by a fixed rate that overvalued the shilling as well as by a system of foreign exchange allocation and regulation for imports. The black market premium for dollars reached 80 per cent in 1985. All foreign exchange was allocated administratively. Imports were regulated both in terms of the type of goods and quantity, mainly through NTRs. The exchange rate policy had a considerable negative impact on the competitiveness of the manufacturing and export sectors. Administration of foreign exchange meant that there was little access by manufacturers to the much-needed production inputs, particularly in those subsectors where inputs were mainly imported (80 per cent for chemicals).

The international trade policy reflected a highly restrictive system of state involvement in exports and imports of all goods. External trading activities were controlled by the State Trading Corporation (STC) and marketing boards, among others. Import duties ranged from 0 to 200 per cent, with additional sales taxes of as much as 300 per cent. Tariff rates were prohibitive, ranging from 0.5 to 500 per cent. Highly protected industries included beverages and tobacco, tanneries and leather, rubber, glass and wood. The highest tariff rate was for beverages and tobacco, reaching 532.60 per cent in 1984, with the lowest for chemicals and fertilizers.

In the case of internal trade, the government created a number of SOEs to undertake trading activities domestically, such as the regional trading companies (RTCs). Goods were restricted from crossing borders, regions and even districts within the country. Failure by traders to trade freely within and outside the country limited the product market and exacerbated inefficiencies resulting from excessive supply in some areas and shortages in others. Product and inputs processes were controlled through the Price Commission. More than 400 goods were subject to price controls in the early 1980s, and wholesale trade in more than 50 major commodities was restricted to SOEs. In agriculture, producer prices for traditional crops were fixed by the government, at only some 65 per cent of world prices on average. Marketing of agricultural produce was done through a single government channel.

The banking system was dominated by state banks which were highly monopolized, inefficient, and largely insolvent. Much bank credit was directed to the public sector and cooperative unions, despite repayment problems. A multiplicity of interest rates was set. Credit availability was not a major issue since public investments enjoyed lax budget constraints. The Bank of Tanzania had little control over monetary expansion, and commercial banks enjoyed almost unlimited access to Bank of Tanzania refinancing. Credit growth was excessive, fuelling inflation rates of more than 50 per cent from 1981 to 1985.

The civil service was considerably overstaffed in the pre-reform period. Wages were low and unrealistic. Labour productivity in manufacturing increased in the early 1970s but declined from 1981 onwards, staying below the 1970s levels since then. By 1986, the real minimum wage was less than a third of its 1970 level. Investment was characterized by the dormant role of government investment and low level of investment productivity.

Current Economic Policy Regime

The current economic policy regime stems from the economic reform and market liberalization policies adopted since the mid-1980s. Development policy during this period was dominated by responses to emerging resource gaps via stabilization measures, macroeconomic policy reforms in trade, the exchange regime, and the financial sector and related institutional structures.

Central to the overall policy regime is the broad thrust of macroeconomic objectives geared to reducing internal and external imbalances so as to promote sustained economic growth. The overall macroeconomic objectives for 1996/97–1998/99 aim to accelerate real economic growth to 5 per cent annually in 1996/97, rising to 6 per cent in 1997/98–1998/99; to reduce the average rate of inflation to 15 per cent in 1996/97, 7.5 per cent in 1997/98 and 5 per cent in 1998/99; increase central government savings to 1.1 per cent of GDP in 1996/97, 1.5 per cent in 1997/98 and 2.5 per cent in 1998/99 with an equivalent reduction in outstanding credit to the government; and to reduce external current account deficits, excluding grants, to 13.3 per cent of GDP by 1998/99, compared with 20.6 per cent in 1994/95 to reduce dependence on foreign assistance.

To achieve these aims, a number of measures have been instituted. The exchange rate policy regime was liberalized. The official exchange rate was depreciated by more than 75 per cent in real effective terms from 1987 to 1992, reducing the premium to 20 per cent at the beginning of 1994. Tanzanians were allowed to hold foreign currency accounts. The degree of administrative allocation of foreign exchange was reduced with the introduction of the open general licence and foreign exchange bureaux. These policy changes are envisaged to enhance export competitiveness and attract FDI. The premium in the parallel market was reduced from a peak of 80 per cent in 1985 to some 50 per cent in 1991. A new foreign exchange act was adopted in early 1992 providing a legal basis for the foreign exchange bureaux introduced in April 1992 as well as a regulatory framework within which the Bank of Tanzania operates. In 1994, the central bank introduced the interbank foreign exchange market in order to achieve a market-determined exchange rate. This significantly reduced distortions in the foreign exchange market.

Financial reforms have entailed restructuring the state-owned banking sector to make it operate commercially, promoting competitive banking and encouraging private banks. Restructuring of the central bank is being accelerated to ensure market-related mechanisms for monetary management. Entry by new private banks is being encouraged. The balance sheets of the state-run banks are being restructured, including removal of the worst-performing loans to a recovery trust. Banks have greater managerial autonomy and the right to set their own interest rates, subject to a minimum deposit rate set above that of inflation, and a maximum lending rate. These reforms were introduced in 1991. There are indications that, as a result, banks are making more prudent decisions, are under less pressure to lend and are increasing credit to the private sector.

On the fiscal policy front, central government finance improved from a deficit of 4 per cent of GDP in the fiscal year 1988 to a surplus of 1.5 per cent in 1992 while substantially reducing reliance on domestic financing of the deficit. Monitoring of revenue and expenditure has aided preparation of a three-year rolling plan to take into account availability of resources and intersectoral priorities. At the same time, there is increased coverage of the budget by donor funding. Strict measures to increase revenue and reduce growth of both current and development expenditures have been instituted, with establishment of the Tanzania Revenue Authority (TRA) and other such bodies. The objective is to eliminate domestic bank financing from the budget deficit.

In terms of monetary policy, action has been taken to stem the essentially automatic access to central bank credit for the commercial banks. The central bank now exercises a greater degree of independence; its role has been streamlined from multiple responsibilities to that of ensuring price stability. The principal approaches to reducing inflation are now coordinated with fiscal policy to ensure that the country's broad economic objectives are achieved.

As for interest rate policy, the current broad objective is to achieve a market-determined interest rate with Treasury Bill market rates constituting the benchmark for the Bank of Tanzania's discount rates. On this basis, interest rates on bank deposits will be pegged. The Bank is expected to use open market operations as a key policy instrument for liquidity management, and to enhance the institutional framework to ensure integrated, market-determined structures of interest rates. High interest rates have made the very high cost of capital borrowing necessary to increase manufacturing competitiveness.

Along with these macroeconomic reforms are the microeconomic and sector policies. The domestic market has been considerably deregulated in tandem with successive measures to liberalize imports further. The early liberalization of food grain sales was essential to demonstrate that private marketing could work as well as to provide quick, visible benefits from reform. However, liberalization of the marketing of traditional agricultural exports is not yet comprehensive, partly because of the political nature of the cooperative unions. For export crops, the government has taken initial steps during the past two years towards allowing markets to set prices and opening export marketing to competition.

Reforms in external trade include import liberalization. Tariffs have been reduced significantly as have QRs on imports. Overall, the import regime has been very liberal and market-oriented. In view of this, the external sector policies under the Economic Recovery Programme (ERP) have focused on maintaining external competitiveness to encourage strong performance in traded goods. Development of the interbank foreign exchange market will promote efficiency in the new market-oriented economy.

As regards investment, the current policy regime is centred on measures to promote and attract private investors through prudent macroeconomic management, favourable and adequate investment packages and an environment conducive to private investment promotion. Opportunities for doing business in the United Republic of Tanzania have been considerably widened by the National Investment (Promotion and Protection) Act No. 10 of 1990 and establishment of the Investment Promotion Centre (IPC)[3].

Changes in the economic policy regime have also been reflected in, and induced by, specific sectoral policy reforms. In the agriculture sector, most reforms have been focused on the marketing of agricultural produce and deregulation of supply inputs to allow for price efficiency. While there has been a significant change in the marketing of food crops and related inputs, little has been liberalized in export crops and only on a crop-by-crop basis. Agricultural liberalization meant that industry had to compete with exports for procurement of agricultural raw materials. In some cases, prices went up with devaluation.

For the manufacturing sector, more detailed policies during ERP specified priorities of the enterprises to contribute to at least one of the following objectives: (i) to increase the availability of consumer goods whose scarcity acted as a disincentive for productive activities (soap, textiles, garments, shoes, food and beverages); (ii) to increase the supply of intermediate inputs and raw materials in support of agricultural production, transportation or manufacture of key inputs (light engineering and metal and steel); (iii) to generate net export earnings (agriculture, agro-processing, handcrafts, tobacco and cement); and (iv) to generate additional public sector revenue (beer, soft drinks and cigarettes). In addition, the industrial rehabilitation programme was aimed at carrying out comprehensive repairs and replacement of equipment to restore production capacity. During ESAP, particular importance was given to rehabilitation of physical infrastructure, in particular transport and communications. In addition, contrary to ERP I, more emphasis was put on SMEs and less on public-revenue-generating industries.

The policy environment has encouraged entry of industrial firms and expansion of efficient firms while discouraging inefficient producers. According to the ESRF survey of divested firms, (ESRF, 1996) former manufacturing SOEs met the set productivity and competitiveness targets. The most striking of these is the Tanzania Breweries Limited, in which production levels have increased by more than 200 per cent following its divestiture in 1993 (see Box 11.2 on p. 354).

Transition from the Past to the Current Economic Policy Regime: Extent, Thrust, Sequence and Pace of the Reform

Table 11.2 summarizes information on the extent, pace, thrust and sequence of the reforms under way. As depicted in the table, some of the reforms carried out in the United Republic of Tanzania have been comprehensive and others less comprehensive. In the external sector, for instance, import and trade liberalization policies were implemented in a much more comprehensive and committed manner than those for export promotion, agricultural market deregulation and institutional reforms. Other reforms that have been carried out comprehensively include exchange rate policy and management, price reforms and the internal trade regime, but much still remains to be done in these areas.

Sequence has had a significant bearing on the results of the reform programmes. For example, the United Republic of Tanzania began with exchange rate liberalization before export promotion procedures were in place. Privatization has been fuelled at the expense of preparing potential indigenous investors, resulting in most of the privatized companies being bought by foreigners.

Rapid reforms took place through import liberalization and market deregulation, but the removal of exchange controls took longer. Removal of price controls took place quickly, unlike financial sector and social sector reforms. Privatization has been rather slow.

Table 11.2 Grading of economic reforms in the United Republic of Tanzania

Reform	Extent	Pace	Thrust	Sequence [a]
Macroeconomic reforms				
Fiscal balances and management	Moderately comprehensive	Slow	Most committed	3
Monetary policy	Moderate	Moderate	Moderate	5
Exchange rate policy	Comprehensive	Moderate	Less committed	3
Financial sector policy	Moderate	Slow	Less committed	5
Microeconomic reforms				
Market deregulation	Less comprehensive	Slow	Less committed	1
Price reforms	Comprehensive	Fast	Most committed	4
Import liberalization	Comprehensive	Fast	Most committed	1
Export promotion policies	Less comprehensive	Slow	Most committed	5
Civil service reform	Less comprehensive	Slow	Moderately committed	2
Public enterprise reform	Less comprehensive	Slow	Least committed	5
Social sector policies	Less comprehensive	Slow	Least committed	1[b]
Industrial sector reforms	Less comprehensive	Moderate	Moderately committed	3

Notes: [a]Sequencing is expressed here in terms of the year in which the reform was started. In this case, 1 represents the earliest year (mid-1980s) and 5 the latest year (early 1990s). [b]Reform was initiated early but implemented only in recent years.

Source: Author's assessment.

Market deregulation, import liberalization and civil service reforms were instituted at the outset. Reforms in monetary policy, the financial sector and export promotion came later. The emphasis in the SAP has mainly been on correct pricing and liberalization of trade and imports. However, manufacturing competitiveness requires interventions for capability building in order to spur on the rest of the economy and provide a proper launching pad for the emerging private sector.

The evaluation of the reform process in the United Republic of Tanzania points to several conclusions. First, the process is still ongoing, so the outcome cannot be predicted. Second, political and other not necessarily economic factors play a crucial role in the transition. This is the period when the stakeholders, including government, businessmen, peasants, farmers and civil servants, are taking stock of what has happened to assess gains and losses. The support for and credibility of reforms depends on stakeholders' views. They will decide whether they will continue to support them.

Summary

The past economic regime was characterized by restrictions and government control coupled with policies that had a negative impact on industrial efficiency and productivity, resulting in lower manufacturing competitiveness. This provided the impetus for reform towards a more liberalized and market-oriented policy environment. With reforms still under way, the pace, extent and thrust of the transition differs across sectors and variables. The relationship between industrial development policy and macro- as well as microeconomic policies has a significant bearing on the development and sustainability of manufacturing competitiveness.

MANUFACTURING COMPETITIVENESS: THE CURRENT POLICY AGENDA

Performance

Post-independence industrialization in the United Republic of Tanzania took off from the initial stage of import substitution, coupled with a rapid growth of the economy. Manufacturing's contribution to GDP raised from 4 per cent in 1966 to some 12 per cent in 1977. A period of deindustrialization came during 1980–84, when the economy recorded a real GDP growth of 0.8 per cent annually and manufacturing declined at an annual average rate of 5 per cent. The growth of the industrial sector rose from an annual average of –4.7 per cent between 1980 and 1985 to some 5 per cent annually between 1986 and 1990 and declined to about 2 per cent between 1991 and 1995.

While the foreign resource inflow that accompanied the economic reforms of mid-1986 led to recovery of industrial output in the latter half of the 1980s, this recovery could not be sustained into the 1990s largely because the initial sources of this growth momentum were based on better utilization of existing capacities rather than improved manufacturing competitiveness (Wangwe, 1995a). Growth did not translate into significant industrial restructuring and capability acquisition. Most of the growth came in a spurt, in 1991–92, with a substantial slowdown in subsequent years. With increased import competition, the momentum could not be sustained. A similar deceleration in growth occurred in other adjusting countries in sub-Saharan Africa (See Annex 11.A).

During the 1980s and 1990s, the structure of manufacturing output remained unchanged, with food, beverages, tobacco, textiles and leather remaining the dominating subsectors. Their contribution to MVA in 1991 stood at some 48 per cent, compared to the chemicals subsector, at 24 per cent, metals and engineering, at 13 per cent, wood and allied products, at 9 per cent, and non-metal subsectors, at 6 per cent. During 1980–94, few industries, except for tobacco, chemicals and plastics, expanded successfully while many others, such as textiles and garments, continued to suffer due to production constraints that caused nearly all firms to perform below their installed capacities. Many SMIs continued to lack adequate working capital.

The ownership structure of industry changed significantly. Private industrial firms expanded while public sector firms contracted. More than two-thirds of private firms increased production, less than half of SOEs managed to do so and the remainder experienced absolute decline. Economic efficiency, ownership and export orientation appear to be the major determinants of firms' supply response to policy reforms (Mans, 1994).

Data for 1977–91 on net exits and entries in Tanzanian manufacturing show that wood, furniture, transport equipment and food were the manufacturing activities most affected, especially in 1977/78, 1981/82 and 1990/91. The number of market entries dropped from 262 during 1974–80 to 214 during 1980–84. The number increased slightly, to 279, during 1984–93. In the early 1990s, the manufacturing sector experienced net exits, apparently due to the reforms in the economy that included shutting down inefficient firms, mostly SOEs, and to others dying off as a result of exposure to competition.[4] Cross-sectional data suggest that entries and exits occurred especially among SMIs (Regional Private Enterprise Development Programme, 1995) .

Semboja and Lecomte's study (1966) reveals three important findings. First, weak profitability, uncertainty about government industrial development and trade policies and fierce competition have been the most significant reasons for exit by Tanzanian firms. Other causes include high production costs, management disagreements, changing policies, inappropriate industrial location and poor market strategies, and lack of reliable supplies of power, water, raw materials and appropriate skills.

Second, the exit process lacks a legal and institutional framework, except for the winding up of non-performing firms which, despite its long existence, has not been used as a tool for reallocating of resources for more efficient uses. Only a few cases occurred in the period before the establishment of the Loans Advances and Realization Trust (LART) and the Parastatal Sector Reform Commission (PSRC) in 1991 and 1992 respectively. The majority of firms are not sufficiently informed about the legal aspects of exit procedures, with the length and costs of court procedures being the main obstacles.

Third, although the current transitional legal environment in the United Republic of Tanzania does provide forums for exit, it needs to be improved to allow for effective reallocation of resources and for current initiatives to be sustained, even if LART and PSRC were non-existent.

Many industries seem to have been too immature to withstand the severe competitive pressures brought with import liberalization. Rapid deindustrialization in textiles and garments, for instance, has taken place due to cheap imports that do not offer fair competition with domestic products. While tariffs on imports have been in place, weaknesses in tax administration have made evasion pervasive. Moreover, high production costs have made it hard for local industries to compete against cheap imports coming from countries with industries that enjoy significant economies of scale. In general, the performance of the sector has not been very impressive. Many SMIs have had limited capacity to invest in technology and modernization of their ageing plant and machinery, partly because of their weakened financial position.

The share of the private sector in manufacturing investment increased from 37 per cent in 1970 to 46.4 per cent in 1980, reaching a peak of 66.2 per cent in 1993. The share of investment allocated to other equipment and machinery was relatively high, at some 40 per cent in the 1990s. Recent trends suggest that total gross fixed capital formation has increased slightly, but the share of manufacturing in it has remained almost the same, at 22.2 per cent, for the last five years. Part of the reason for the relative inability to stimulate significant new investment lies in the fact that, in spite of reforms, the list of constraints impeding investment in manufacturing remains long. These constraints include ambiguity and contradictions in prevailing reforms, lack of adequate physical and communication infrastructure, low level of technological skills and bureaucratic procedures.

The effects of reform on labour productivity have been mixed (Mjema and Shitundu, 1995). Value-added per employee in manufacturing went up from T Sh 18 200 per employee to T Sh 20 900 in 1989 before falling in 1990 to T Sh 19 500 and again recovering to T sh 21 300 in 1991. These levels are lower than those foreseen in the reforms.

Total industrial employment shows that industry is an important employer, accounting for nearly 18 per cent of total wage employment and the largest single source of urban employment in the 1990s. During the period 1980–91, employment in the industrial sector ranged between a minimum of 94 210 in 1985 and a maximum of some 123 000 people in 1991.[5] But this is a rather small proportion compared to the target of 400 000 jobs by 1995, envisaged in the industrial plan for 1975–95. The manufacturing employment situation was much worse during 1985–86, when employment declined at an average rate of 4.5 per cent annually. However, significant employment growth was recorded during 1986–90, when employment rose at an average of 6.4 per cent annually.

The main employing subsectors in manufacturing are food, beverages, tobacco and textiles. During 1980–91, these subsectors accounted for more than 60 per cent of total employment in industry, while employment in the leather and leather products subsector ranged between 4.1 per cent and 5.8 per cent and in the wood, paper and allied products subsector fluctuated between 9.0 per cent and 9.8 per cent. During the 1980s and 1990s, SOEs accounted for an average of some 67.5 per cent of the total industrial employment.

The performance of Tanzanian manufactured exports is loosely associated with the performance and growth of the manufacturing sector as a whole (Valk, 1992). The share of manufactured exports to total exports stagnated at some 14–15 per cent during 1970–80, declined to 13.1 per cent during 1981–85 and started rising after the mid-1980s, averaging 22.0 per cent during 1986–90 (Ndulu and Semboja, 1992). However, this share decreased from 26 per cent in 1990 to some 14 per cent in 1992, due to lack of competitiveness and investment in export capabilities. Nevertheless, manufactured exports show a potential for boosting export earnings in the future, as they form a significant share of total non-traditional exports in the United Republic of Tanzania (Mjema and Shitundu, 1995). Anti-export biases and distortions should, therefore, be eliminated while streamlining export procedures and adopting an export trade policy that promotes manufactured exports.

Following the introduction of economic recovery policies, capacity utilization improved slightly, from less than 30 per cent in the early 1980s to some 50 per cent in 1994. The average level of capacity utilization in industry ranged between 37.1 per cent and 49.8 per cent during 1983–92. There is also evidence that the efficiency of the industrial sector has improved. In the 1990s, power shortages and demand constraints hindered industrial development, manufacturing competitiveness, investment opportunities and production capacity. Deficiency in demand caused by competing imports, rather than supply bottlenecks, was the major constraint. The adverse impact of import liberalization policies on manufacturing competitiveness was felt especially in garment and textile firms (Semboja and Kweka, 1996).

Interface between Industrial Development Policy and other Policies

The interface between industrial development and other policies is critical in the context of the reform process. This is now examined at the firm, subsector-specific and industry-wide levels.

Firm-centred policies

Firm-centred policies include those directed towards productivity and quality, design, training and skills acquisition, incentives to R&D and investment in plant and equipment and development of SMIs and micro enterprises.

Quality and productivity Product quality makes firms pass or fail the test of markets and consumers. There are two types of quality standards – mandatory and voluntary. The former relates mostly to products such as food and medicines which are subjected to embargoes. The latter relates to the efforts of producers to upgrade standards to match current tastes. Firm-level policies for manufacturing competitiveness focus on the latter.

To improve competitiveness of industrial products in domestic and export markets, Tanzania's industrial development policy envisages that the government will strive to strengthen the implementation of national standards and quality assurance, including weights and measures, through legal provisions, adequate test facilities, equipment and training, formulation of new standards, accreditation of qualified assurance units in specialized areas and development of packaging technology. Firms are obliged to meet the requirements of the Tanzania Bureau of Standards, as established by the Act of Parliament No. 3 of 1975, to promote standardization and establish a national standards institute.

However, the long period of protection of the manufacturing industry in the United Republic of Tanzania, cost plus pricing and operation in a seller's market have not been conducive to encouraging product quality. The work of the Tanzanian Bureau of Standards in promoting quality awareness, assurance and standardization has been an uphill task.

To increase productivity, the United Republic of Tanzania instituted the national policy on productivity, incomes and prices by an Act of Parliament of 1981. Low industrial productivity has been attributed to shortages of skilled manpower, inappropriate skills, insufficiencies in training, poor industrial motivation, inadequate infrastructural services, deficient capital and inappropriate technology. The current industrial development policy is aimed at ameliorating these deficiencies so as better to utilize manufacturing potential. The policy requires firms to set production targets, which form the basis for increased manufacturing productivity.[6]

Evidence from the engineering and garment subsectors shows that engineering firms' productivity, defined as sales per employee, improved following liberalization. Negative real growth rates of 12 per cent between 1984 and 1989 were followed by positive real growth rates of 2.6 per cent between 1989 and 1994. Data on employment indicate a general contraction of engineering firms, with a median average growth rate in employment of –11 per cent. The average number of employees dropped from 103 in 1989 to 75 in 1994. Some 65 per cent of firms reduced their workforce, 25 per cent increased it, and the rest stayed constant. Heightened import competition appears to be associated with falling average firm size in this industry.

The performance of sampled garment firms was very poor. In aggregate terms, sales growth declined by 6 per cent annually in real terms during 1989–94, in contrast to an annual growth rate of 12 per cent during 1984–89. Export affiliates experienced falling sales in this period. Capacity utilization declined sharply, with average levels falling from 60 per cent in 1989 to 30 per cent in 1994. More than 90 per cent of firms experienced a decline in capacity utilization rates during that period.

While there has been a general decline in productivity and quality standards, some firms have achieved higher levels of productivity and quality. In the engineering sector, for instance, firms producing construction-related products, such as steel roofing and galvanized sheets, have had significantly higher levels of productivity than other firms owing to the fact that they use distinctly different types of continuous process technology. Contrary to expectations, equipment upgrading has not been related to higher productivity, probably because most of the firms that invested in sophisticated machinery and equipment failed to master the efficient use of these technologies. Training in the operation of new machinery was also generally limited.

Human resource development Tanzania's active labour force accounts for 38 per cent of a population of 28 million people. Only between 30 and 40 per cent of the labour force is actively employed throughout the year leaving the bulk of the labour force underemployed. Increased utilization of the industrial labour force would increase per capita income and enhance internal market demand.

Manufacturing competitiveness policy is intended to emphasize technical training, investment in technical education through establishment of Vocational Education and Training in Tanzania (VETA) and National Vocational Training Centres (NVTCs), promotion of light engineering industries and practical training in the curriculum. Technical skills and vocational training are envisaged to fill the gap in technical skills in manufacturing and develop technological capability for increasing productivity and manufacturing competitiveness.

At firm level, industrial activities aimed at HRD for manufacturing competitiveness include those that support development of indigenous entrepreneurship, such as SMI and informal sector activities as well as metalworking and light engineering (Government of United Republic of Tanzania, 1996). Several kinds of skill development are also relevant to manufacturing competitiveness in the United Republic of Tanzania. One that needs immediate attention is training in specific industrial skills that can give a dynamic edge to industrial growth in terms of competing with imports and entering the export market. Activities such as garment-making and design, textiles, woodworking, food processing, metalworking and other light consumer goods need top priority for specialized training. Another key area that needs policy intervention is fostering in-firm training.

The national employment policy calls for wider access to training and skill upgrading for increased productivity by formal and informal workers. The main objective of the policy is to institutionalize employment promotion through added support to the flourishing informal sector micro enterprises.

However, the major policy gaps and constraints in HRD policy include lack of guidelines on policy implementation against which performance criteria can be set and stakeholders coordinated to achieve the firm-level, subsector, industry-wide and national objectives.

Analysis of light engineering and garment firms shows that training of entrepreneurs is directly related to technological performance. The importance of entrepreneurship is not surprising given the centralized nature of decision making in most firms. Local training institutions however, do little to promote technological dynamism. This can be interpreted, in part, as reflecting the poor quality of training at domestic technical institutions. It also reflects a certain degree of endogeneity relating to training and technological activity. However, domestic training institutions have lacked practical training for their students. This problem has been more pronounced in the years following reform, with emerging private firms not interested in offering practical training, for example, to engineering students from university. In addition, private firms are reluctant to recruit qualified workers for fear of having to pay high wages. For instance, an entrepreneur is likely to employ a technician in place of a fully qualified engineer. As a result, firms suffer from lack of vision in their technological and quality upgrading and attach little or no importance to investment in R&D and training. Firms that send their employees abroad for training and those that have in-house training centres are likely to be more technologically dynamic.

Investment Investment helps increase productivity by raising the level of capital per worker and hastening the adoption of new technologies. Investment policy is supposed to create a stable package to attract competitive investors. Before reform, the government did most of the manufacturing investment through SOEs; private investment was not forthcoming. This resulted in inefficient investments with negative incremental capital – output ration (ICOR) in industry. After reform, the increasing role of private investment in the economy helped usher in a new investment policy together with establishment of the Investment Promotion Centre (IPC) and enactment of the Investment Promotion and Protection Act No. 10 of 1990, which also established the Centre. Since its creation, IPC has approved 763 projects worth US$1.9 billion, with an employment potential for some 120 800 persons. Out of these projects, more than 320 came from local investors and some 120 from foreign investors, the remaining comprising joint ventures. However, few approved projects have actually begun operations.

Improvement of the environment for private sector activities and promotion of private investment remains a key focus of the government's development programme, to be achieved by means of conducive macroeconomic and sectoral policies.

Entrepreneurship and SMIs Lack of entrepreneurship development is one of the key constraints on productivity and manufacturing competitiveness in the United Republic of Tanzania. Industrial development policy gives priority to measures for promoting local entrepreneurship through establishment of SMIs. The informal sector, which is the immediate and potential source of entrepreneurs in the United Republic of Tanzania, is being encouraged and assisted to become formal. This issue is addressed in the proposed national policy for development of the informal sector and micro enterprises.

Networking, linkages and subcontracting Efforts have been made to strengthen interfirm linkages and networking to boost manufacturing competitiveness. Few firms, however, have pursued such measures. Indeed, linkages hardly exist in the United Republic of Tanzania. Contracting and subcontracting culture is underdeveloped. Economic and Social Research Foundation surveys of industrial performance (for example ESRF, 1996) have, however, shown that some types of interfirm linkages such as financial and business support linkages do operate in the Tanzanian manufacturing sector. These have been utilized mainly on an *ad hoc* basis. Divestiture programmes have made it possible for some local firms to gain access to and link up with foreign firms in the procurement of technical expertise, machinery, equipment and product technology as well as for entering new markets. This has contributed significantly to improving firms' technological capability and competitiveness.

Subcontracting activities among engineering and clothing firms, for instance, is limited, reflecting both the basic level of production and lack of firms capable of undertaking subcontracting work. While cooperation with sister firms did promote technology transfer in early years, these relationships were largely dormant at the time of survey. Further, most of these firms were responding to trade liberalization by retreating into non-tradable activities, such as basic repair work which generated few positive spin-offs in terms of skills and information transfer.

Micro enterprises Policies towards SMIs and micro enterprises have high priority in the United Republic of Tanzania because of their potential for income and employment generation, promotion of entrepreneurship, and local technological capability building for manufacturing competitiveness. One of the most important and difficult challenges for policy makers in the United Republic of Tanzania is the technological upgrading of the myriad of SMIs and micro enterprises that form the backbone of industry and provide the bulk of employment. This sector is the seed-bed of modern industrial entrepreneurship, with the potential to become the catalyst for growth of new manufactured exports. Traditionally associated with informal sector activities, micro enterprises consist mainly of small-scale businesses, workshops and craftsmanship, food vendors, metalworking and small-scale agriculture and horticultural activities.

The SMI and micro enterprise sector has grown very quickly, providing employment and income to more people while becoming a means for technology dissemination and capability building. However, it faces basic handicaps such as lack of access to sufficient credit, regulatory constraints, technological impairment, inexperience in marketing, insufficient basic utilities and poor managerial abilities.

Technology development The United Republic of Tanzania has drafted S&T policy to meet the new prerequisites for sustained manufacturing competitiveness. This includes: (i) completion of a master plan and consolidation of existing S&T institutions by providing adequate support, expertise, infrastructural facilities and motivation for retention of technical experts; (ii) reviewing R&D institutions to rationalize and synchronize them in line with changing reform policies, and (iii) carrying out regular consultations with the enterprise sector to select areas for collaboration and management of industrial support and R&D organizations.

In general, the United Republic of Tanzania has fared well in setting up scientific research and technology development institutions, which have acted as the basic technology parks and innovation centres of the country. These institutions include the Small-Scale Industries Development Organization (SIDO, started in 1973), the Tanzania Bureau Standards (TBS, 1975), the Tanzania Industrial Studies and Consulting Organization (TISCO, 1976), the Tanzania Industrial R&D Organization (TIRDO, 1979), the Institute of Production Innovation (IPI, 1974), the High Precision Technology Centre (HPTC, 1980), the Centre for Agricultural Mechanization and Rural Technology (CAMARTEC, 1981) and the Tanzania Engineering and Manufacturing Design Organization (TEMDO, 1983). The aim of these establishments is to offer technological advice and innovation to the manufacturing sector to promote sustainable and ensure competitiveness.

With manufacturing still at an early stage, little or no enterprise R&D is carried out. Links between industrial R & D institutions are weak, and where they do exist, they are usually *ad hoc* in nature and often driven by necessity and dictated by prevailing circumstances. The link between technology parks and manufacturing firms is also weak.

With no formal R&D in most firms, there are few instances of major improvements in process technology or introduction of new processes based on local initiatives. The lack of local research and design capability is one factor keeping African producers at the bottom of the quality chain or, in complex product segments, forcing them to exit in reaction to rapid trade liberalization.

This weakness is mainly due to the failure to commercialize many R&D results and tackle the major technological problems commonly facing production activities. It is yet a further indication and cause of weak technological capabilities. The failure by R&D and technological support organizations to commercialize their results also stems from the fact that technology entrepreneurs have been missing in the United Republic of Tanzania. Proven research results have been attained by these institutions but have failed to be applied on a mass scale.

Subcontracting is not widespread, and firms tend to rely on imports or in-house production of components. Many industrial firms' lack of significant forward and backward linkages within the economy is symptomatic of the inability of local firms to locate customers and suppliers (Bagachwa, 1993). With the advent of economic reforms and the mushrooming of the private sector in productive activities, most innovation and R&D activities are carried out in cooperation with foreign parent or supplier companies.

Tanzanian firms differ a great deal in their ability and culture to finance innovation, with firm size and financial strength the determining factor. At national level, the problem of underfunding of S&T activities has had an impact. It had been proposed that S&T expenditure in GDP be raised from the less than 0.5 per cent in 1984 to more than 3 per cent by the year 2000 (Government of Tanzania, 1985). No firm evidence shows that this share has changed significantly since 1984 (Wangwe, 1994). This suggests that initiatives such as those taken by the Commission for Science and Technology (COSTECH) in 1988/89 to mobilize non-governmental sources to meet the more demanding S&T activities in the country should go hand in hand with measures to oblige the direct beneficiaries to finance technology development. Expenditure and utilization of the incomes of R&D institutions should be monitored and oriented in this direction.

Lack of adequate financial resources has affected the extent of technological upgrading in firms. In the engineering subsector, for instance, there has been some upgrading of production technology following liberalization, but this has been fairly limited and confined to a small group of firms. In terms of recent equipment upgrading, firms sampled fell into three basic categories. First, a small minority of comparatively advanced firms, consisting of some 11 per cent of the sample, upgraded technology by investing in fairly sophisticated machinery, such as numerically controlled (NC) and computer numerically controlled (CNC) machine tools and computer-aided design

(CAD). For these firms, import liberalization had a positive effect on technological activity. Although they were diverse, firms in this group had certain features in common. They all upgraded technology as part of a longer-term strategy to improve competitiveness. In most cases such a strategy was adopted as a response to both increased import competition and greater availability of imported capital equipment. Access to foreign expertise was important in facilitating technological upgrading in all cases. In the case of foreign firms, the parent company played a key role in the selection and installation of the new technology.

The second group of firms, consisting of some 35 per cent of the sample, undertook some replacement investment that did not involve moving to a markedly more sophisticated level of technology. They merely invested in simple, general purpose machinery. Much of the equipment purchased since liberalization was new, in contrast to the high concentration of second-hand machinery purchased in the earlier import-constrained environment. Easier access to imported capital goods prompted these firms to replace obsolete plant and equipment.

The third group, consisting of more than 50 per cent of the engineering firms sampled, was relatively stagnant in terms of technology. These firms introduced few changes to their production technology in the wake of liberalization, most of them being repair shops and service centres for small, regional markets.

The impact of trade liberalization on technological dynamism is hard to predict. Opening up might stimulate technological change, with import competition spurring on innovative activities. However, the types of technological activity undertaken in the engineering and garment subsectors vary, and results depend on the nature of competitive pressures exerted behind protective barriers. Import substitution produces less dynamism than export orientation with more selective policies (Lall, 1992). Table 11.3 presents a summary of the types of activities undertaken by the sample firms.

Upgrading of plant and equipment, process engineering and product quality in the post-liberalization period has been limited. Only a minority of engineering firms responded to policy reforms by upgrading technology, but their efforts were often below the levels of competence and comprehensiveness needed to sustain competitiveness in a liberal trading environment. In the majority of cases, trade liberalization has done little to overcome the technological stagnation that existed before liberalization. In general, there was even a deterioration in technological competence since the introduction of trade reforms, particularly where initial levels of competence were low.

Table 11.3 United Republic of Tanzania: technological activity of sample firms

Type of activity	Firms undertaking the activity (as percentage of total)	
	Engineering	Garment
Plant and equipment		
Equipment upgrading	35.0	13.0
Introducing CAD	6.5	6.6
Introducing CNC	11.0	13.0
Organization		
Quality control	10.0	6.6
In-house repair shop	60.0	40.0
Inventory control	20.0	13.0
Product technology		
Formal design	15.0	–
In-house R&D	4.0	–
Introducing new products	55.00	–

Source: Semboja and Lecomte (1996).

Some 30 per cent of firms provided some form of systematic training other than routine on-line training, to their workforce. In most cases, this involved short training programmes at domestic training institutions. Some 10 per cent of engineering firms sent a few employees abroad for training. Mainly focused on importing new and advanced technology, this sort of training was often conducted by foreign experts and equipment suppliers. Only 15 per cent of firms in the engineering sample increased the numbers of graduate engineers employed after liberalization, and these were mainly firms that substantially upgraded their equipment. Additional engineers were employed both to make the technology operational and to improve product design and quality. However, the intensity of formal engineering skills in most of the sample firms remained unchanged in the post-liberalization period.

The majority of firms, however, undertook little training of any type and seemed unaware of their skill deficiencies. Apart from local training centres, the only technology institute with which firms had contact was the TBS, which 35 per cent of firms used to test materials and product standards involving technology transfer. However, these were largely one-off contacts usually related to design problems at the early stages of product development and were not maintained for longer-term product improvement. Most firms considered that technology institutions provided poor services or were irrelevant to their requirements.

In the clothing industry skill levels are low. Only one exporting firm employed a production manager with formal qualifications in clothing technology. None of the firms had provided external training, conducted by its parent company, in recent years. The contrast between this export-oriented company and others highlights the technological gaps that exist in most Tanzanian garment firms.

The engineering industry has faced gradual import competition, while the garment industry has been exposed rapidly and rather drastically. The extent of technology and skill upgrading in the engineering industry since liberalization has been limited. A small proportion of firms have adopted fairly advanced technology, responding to availability of imported equipment rather than to meet direct import competition and upgrade skills. The remainder have been largely stagnant in terms of technology and skill development after liberalization, with some regressing to lower levels of technology. In the clothing industry the situation is even bleaker, with little improvement in technology or skill levels in almost all firms. The poor performance appears to be a result partly of the inability of firms to compete with imports of second-hand items, in the face of which most firms have moved out of cloth and garment manufacturing into trade.

The picture that emerges is that the initial levels of technological capability were low and reactions to opening up have, on the whole, been passive or negative.[7]

Subsector-specific policies

Subsector-specific policies concern trade, restructuring, targeted capacity creation, regional focus and government support for export promotion (see Chapter 4).

Trade policy and performance Since the early 1970s, Tanzania's trade policy has gone through three phases. The first one, between 1970 and 1984, was typified by numerous QRs, culminating in severe controls between 1980 and 1985. An open general licence (OGL) for imports was introduced in the early 1970s but was suspended in 1980. An import substitution basic industrial strategy (BIS) was launched in 1975 to promote the domestic manufacturing base.

The second phase, between 1985 and 1988, was characterized by partial trade liberalization (Ndulu and Semboja, 1992). After 1984, the exchange rate was devalued and imports of selected consumer, intermediate and capital goods were permitted.

During the third phase, between 1988 and the 1990s, import restrictions were dismantled and tariffs reduced, rationalized and harmonized. In 1980, for example, there were 18 main tariffs ranging from 0 to 200 per cent. In 1992, these were reduced to five categories ranging from 0 to 40 per cent (Ndulu and Semboja, 1992).[8]

The effective rate of protection declined after 1986 and, by 1993, had gone down by more than half in eight of the ten industrial sectors surveyed. the United Republic of Tanzania had one of the highest levels of effective protection on domestic manufacturing with tariff rates ranging from 0.5 to 500 per cent. Beverages and tobacco, tanneries and leather, rubber, glass and wood, among others, were highly protected. Table 11.4 shows that the highest level of protection was in beverages and tobacco, peaking in 1984 at 532.60 per cent. The lowest level of protection on the other hand, was in chemicals and fertilizers, at 0.50 per cent in 1966 and –2 per cent (that is, a negative tariff) in 1989. In 1993, the lowest level of protection was in rubber, glass, wood and paper, while that in textiles and apparel was the highest, followed by beverages and tobacco. The table also lists industries that had been facing moderate protection throughout the period under consideration, including agriculture, machinery and transport, rubber, glass, wood and paper. Generally, the overprotected industries were those that were economically inefficient and less competitive. Liberalization of external trade, undertaken as part of the economic recovery programme of 1986, has changed the quantitative restriction on tariff imposition to facilitate revenue collection.

Estimates of import-demand functions show that, while the tightening of import and exchange rate controls between 1980 and 1985 had resulted in a contraction of real imports at an average annual rate of 18 per cent, the relaxation of these measures between 1986 and 1993 caused real imports to rise at an average rate of 9.5 per cent (Ndulu et al., 1995). Concurrently, export performance also improved. As a percentage of GDP, real exports at 1987 prices increased from 12.3 per cent in 1986 to 15 per cent in 1992. The rate of exports reversed its negative trend during 1980–86 to 9 per cent annually during 1987–92.

Restructuring of SOEs and privatization Reform of the SOE sector is aimed at improving operational efficiency of enterprises, reducing the fiscal burden

Table 11.4 *Prevailing rates of effective protection in the United Republic of Tanzania*

	1966	1984	1986	1989	1993
Beverages and tobacco	391.60	532.60	83.80	63.70	35.00
Textiles and apparel	263.00	240.00	55.40	38.10	39.19
Food products	184.00	335.00	65.10	36.10	24.67
Tanneries and leather	126.50	230.00	41.30	40.10	2.48
Plastics and pharmaceuticals	105.30	252.00	45.40	22.70	2.64
Iron, steel and metal products	93.00	257.60	28.10	19.20	14.47
Agriculture	1.00	22.40	24.00	31.70	35.00
Machinery and trans. equip.	82.30	129.00	25.00	17.60	8.00
Rubber, glass, wood and paper	23.00	256.00	27.90	9.40	2.85
Chemicals and fertilizers	0.50	2.60	1.60	–2.00	7.38

Sources: Semboja and Lecomte (1996).

and promoting industrial development participation by nationals in business ownership and management. Privatization became central to reversing manufacturing decline and boosting economic growth. The process has stimulated investment and productivity in manufacturing and more quality and productivity conscious management styles (see Boxes 11.1 and 11.2). In the process, a number of SOEs have either been commercialized, privatized, sold or closed. The Parastatal Sector Reform Commission (PSRC) and Loans Advances and Realization Trust (LART) are in charge of overseeing the transition.

Preliminary studies on the impact of privatization indicate that enterprises successfully divested through joint ventures have improved dramatically in terms of increased productivity and profitability.[9] These successes were coupled with rehabilitation measures, improvement in technological capabilities and a favourable financial capital structure (see Box 11.2). However, Tanzania's manufacturing sector is still in transition in the context of the economy-wide reforms. Limited short-term achievements have yet to be translated into longer-term manufacturing competitiveness. This indicates that there are other critical constraints to manufacturing competitiveness in the United Republic of Tanzania that cannot necessarily be solved by privatization alone. Issues such as adequate skills, entrepreneurship, technology, fiscal and monetary policy, competition and infrastructure still constitute a deterrent to increasing manufacturing competitiveness. For this purpose, an adequate mix of macro and micro policies is needed.

Box 11.1 Scope and status of SOE restructuring

The divestiture status as at 1 January 1995 showed that the total number of SOEs scheduled for divestiture was 317, of which action has been taken so far on 46, with 20 transferred to LART for liquidation. Of the remaining 305 companies the route for divestiture of 242 is clear and the strategy agreed. At the end of 1996 127 companies were ready for sale, for which 106 had received bids, 80 were under negotiation, 75 had a memorandum of understanding (MOU) signed and 60 had their sale agreements already signed. By that date, only 141, or 38 per cent of the original number of SOEs were expected to be divested, including some of the significant firms such as utility companies. Performance agreements currently exist for two firms, the Tanzania Harbours Authority (THA) and the National Urban Water Authority (NUWA). A ban on lending to non-credit-worthy SOEs by the National Bank of Commerce (NBC) is in place. The government also plans to divest itself of major utility companies whose activities have a marked effect on the rest of the economy. They include the Tanzania Postal Corporation (TPC), the Tanzania Electrical Supply Company (TANESCO), telecommunication company (TTCL), NUWA, THA, the Air Tanzania Corporation (ATC), the Tanzania Railways Corporation (TRC) and the National Shipping Agencies Corporation (NASACO).

Though it is still too early to pass definite judgement of the impact of the divestiture, preliminary assessment shows that it has become a new force for revival of manufacturing competitiveness in Tanzania. Current performance at Tanzania Breweries Limited (TBL) (see Box 11.2), Tanzania Electrical Goods Manufacturing Company (TANELEC), Morogoro Tanneries, Mwanza Tanneries, Moshi Tanneries, Morogoro Shoe Company, Bora Shoe Company and Williamson Diamonds shows positive results in terms of investment in modernization and technological capability, productivity, marketing, workers' motivation and profitability. Forward and backward linkages have been significantly reinforced, as increased productivity has triggered increased demand for domestic inputs. As a result, firms have made concerted efforts to increase product quality through enhanced training and skill and capability acquisition. The competitive environment has promoted efficiency and competitiveness of local industry. Elimination of subsidies has been replaced by increased government revenue from divested companies in terms of sales and other taxes. Where the government is also a shareholder, as in the case of TBL, it has benefited from dividends.

Box 11.2 Impact of divestiture on firms' performance: Tanzania Breweries Limited

The successful joint venture, in 1993, and divestiture process of Tanzania Breweries Limited (TBL) was followed by dramatic changes and improvement in the firm's performance. The result was that production and quality of beer improved, as did sales. Cash flow operations improved from a minus of T Sh 739.0 million in 1993 to a plus of T Sh 1.6 billion in 1994, rising to T Sh 8.1 billion in 1995. Although negative in the first year of operation, TBL made a profit of T Sh 11.3 billion in 1995, after reporting losses for a number of years in the past.

Regardless of the emerging ownership structure, divestiture has widened manufacturing firms' access to finance and FDI. This has direct implications for firms' acquisition of frontier production technology and, thus, productivity and competitiveness. TBL is now approximately 60 per cent privately owned. As well as being both higher in quality and lower in price, it is now introducing new brands to compete in the international and domestic beer markets. Capacity utilization has increased from less than 20 per cent before divestiture to more than 65 per cent following divestiture. This represents an increase of nearly 225 per cent between 1993 and 1995. For June 1996, this increase is expected to reach 400 per cent. Installed capacity has increased by more than 23 per cent.

TBL has already captured more than 50 per cent of the domestic market. With a favourable macroeconomic environment, legal framework and business climate, the firm expects to displace imports. Dramatic improvements in production technology at TBL have stabilized the performance of the company. This trend began with construction of the Mwanza brewery. In process engineering, there has been significant improvement in quality management using international standards such as ISO 9000. The aim, which is also the major success of TBL, is to improve the quality of the Safari brand beer. As a result, quality increased from 1.5 to 5.1 from 1993 to 1995, according to the international quality rating system.

Other major improvements include changing processes to use local raw materials and components, energy saving and down-scaling. For example, in energy saving, TBL used 24 litres of fuel per 100 litres of beer in the pre-divestiture period. Now it uses seven litres of fuel for

100 litres, surpassing the international standard which is 8 : 100. This has placed the company in the technological forefront of energy saving. In the case of water usage, the firm used 48 litres of water per one litre of beer before divestiture. Now usage is close to the international standard of 10 litres of water per one litre of beer. Electricity usage has been reduced by more than 50 per cent of the amount in the pre-divestiture period. TBL consumes only 8 kWh per litre now compared with 20 kWh per litre before divesture. Fuel, water and electricity consumption were reduced by some 6 per cent, 37 per cent, and 76 per cent respectively between 1993 and 1995.

Box 11.1 shows that privatization has not been as fast and smooth as envisaged. The process encountered several problems, including slow investment response by prospective private investors due, among other things, to the poor condition of SOEs, inadequate resources and capacity of government machinery to expedite the process and concern among potential stakeholders about the legitimacy of the privatization.

With privatization, the emerging manufacturing sector should be better able to enhance its competitiveness. Further associated progress is currently being made in civil service reform, rationalization of ministries, and there has been substantial reduction in the regional administrations and further retrenchment to redirect resources to the priority sectors.

Regional focus The distribution of industrial subsectors by region shows that manufacturing activities have tended to concentrate in only a few areas. Data for 1990–95 show that the largest percentage of the country's manufacturing activities are found in Dar es Salaam (32.6 per cent), Arusha (10.3 per cent), Kilimanjaro (8.4 per cent) Mwanza (7.47 per cent) and Tanga (7.2 per cent). Other regions, such as Rukwa, Lindi, Cast and Mtwara, have only one or two industrial facilities.

A 1995 Regional Private Enterprise Development Programme (RPED) study revealed a regional variation not only in distribution of industrial activities but also in the regional dynamics of industrial activities in the United Republic of Tanzania. For instance, the study analysed the locational breakdown of competition from imports and domestic suppliers. It was found that Mwanza region appears to be affected by imports more than any other area. Not only is the proportion of firms that report no competition from imports the lowest in this area, but the proportion of firms that report having more than six to ten import competitors is also the highest. No firm in Iringa region reported facing competition from imports. This distribution has been dictated by the nature of industrial activities in specific areas. For instance, Iringa is characterized mostly by wood-processing firms, which are much less subject to competition from imports than any other industries, unlike Mwanza, Dar es Salaam and Arusha, whose industries, such as textiles, garments and leather products, are much more susceptible to import competition.

Regional cooperation The future of industrial development in the United Republic of Tanzania is likely to be influenced by, among other things, progress in regional integration (Wangwe, 1995). The United Republic of Tanzania is a member of various international and regional organizations including the Organization of African Unity (OAU), COMESA, the Southern Africa Development Community (SADC) and the East African Community (EAC). In addition, the United Republic of Tanzania pursues bilateral cooperation with other countries.

Regional cooperation opens opportunities for investors from the region to invest in manufacturing based on relative comparative advantages within the region. It also widens market potential in the region. To take advantage of the former, the government has tried, in its new investment policy, to encourage a conducive environment for promotion of competitive investment in other COMESA countries. COMESA is trying to promote cooperation in order to increase and create new industrial capacities that will boost manufacturing competitiveness. As for the latter, the regional integration initiatives have focused on widening the factor and product market. The multinational industrial enterprise (MIE) approach has been adopted to promote cross-border investment and trade. With the potential to break into the region, this will mean increased market for Tanzania's industries. Such industries include the Songo Songo gas project, Mufindi Southern Paper Mill, wood and clove production and certain lines of textiles and garments.

Rationalization of relevant institutions, efficiency of transport infrastructure, intraregional trade promotion and harmonization of existing macroeconomic policies are some of the prerequisites for achieving manufacturing competitiveness from the regional perspective.

Exports Tanzanian manufacturing exports in the 1970s experienced an impressive recovery due to the emphasis, at that time, on industrialization through import substitution. During the severe economic crisis of the early 1980s, export performance was dismal, with manufacturing exports falling drastically to less than 10 per cent of total export value. They picked up slightly between 1987 and 1991. The rise in manufacturing exports in the early 1990s resulted from an improved environment for export activity due to better primary production, stronger incentives for exports and easier access to imported inputs and equipment. These, rather than improved efficiency and resource reallocation in response to import liberalization, represented the first set of benefits of trade policy reform. As a result, after 1991, the recovery of exports of manufacturers ran out of steam, presumably because of lack of competitiveness.

The share of manufactures in total exports increased from 13 per cent during 1980–85 to 21 per cent in 1986–91. In 1995, this share reached 27.51 per cent. This coincided with a growing degree of openness in the economy, from 33.7 per cent in 1980 to 39.8 per cent in 1995 (see Table 11.5). Though the United Republic of Tanzania experienced a significantly greater improvement in manufactured exports compared with countries such as Zimbabwe and Kenya, the values involved in this improvement are relatively very small. Most of the growth came from processed local natural resources and from established firms, rather than from new manufacturing activities and new entrants.

Table 11.5 United Republic of Tanzania: basic economic and industrial statistics

	Value for selected years				Average annual growth rates		
	1970	1980	1990	1995	1970–80	1980–90	1990–95
GDP (US$ million)	1443	2065	2590	3094	3.65	2.29	3.62
GDP per capita (US$)	105.4	111.2	101.2	104.2	0.54	–0.94	0.60
MVA (US$ million)	76	108	94	115	3.55	–1.37	4.24
ULC (%)	12.75	9.36	5.48	6.83	–3.04	–5.21	4.49
Exports (US$ million)	236	528	415	519			
Manufact. exports (US$ million)	102	265	116	143			
Manufact. exports/total exports (%)	43.07	50.30	28.02	27.51			
Exports/GDP (%)	17.39	10.27	16.03	19.92			
Exports + manufact./ GDP (%)	37.2	33.7	32.1	39.8	–1.00	–0.49	5.58
Investment (US$ million)	263	1053	915	1079			
Invest/GDP (%)	19.36	20.49	35.33	45.45			

Source: UNIDO data base.

Growth in manufacturing exports, however, did not denote significant upgrading or diversification. Manufacturing activities whose exports increased most were paper and paper products, sisal fabrics, food products, leather and leather products, machinery, and transport equipment. In textiles, there was a downgrading of export quality. Table 11.6 reveals that the export/output ratio of some selected export sectors increased with the adoption of liberalization policies. The increase, however, was not sustainable in the early 1990s. While the established older firms were able to respond to improved incentives for exporting in the short term, the increase could not be sustained due to lack of weak and longer-term investment in export capabilities.

Table 11.6 Export/output ratio of selected export sectors in the United Republic of Tanzania

Sector	1980	1985	1986	1987	1988	1989	1990
Food	8.0	4.0	4.4	2.7	8.8	22.8	13.4
Tobacco	51.0	44.0	43.2	54.6	38.1	45.4	49.7
Textiles and garments	14.9	5.5	7.1	13.1	17.4	21.5	29.9
Wood and wood products	1.9	0.9	2.3	3.0	4.7	23.5	17.2
Paper and paper products	0.6	1.9	10.7	54.3	49.2	23.8	38.1
Industrial chemicals and petroleum products	45.8	27.0	8.0	14.4	21.2	33.7	25.9
Pottery, china, glass and non-metallic products	14.2	38.7	17.0	13.1	38.1	37.4	42.4
Iron, steel, non-ferrous metals and fabricated metal products	3.6	1.4	2.1	3.4	4.7	2.2	4.7
Machinery, including electrical and supplies	5.8	8.3	7.1	15.1	17.1	32.0	29.8
Transport and equipment	0.2	0.2	0.07	1.0	2.2	4.1	9.6
Total	18.2	10.5	8.1	11.9	18.0	23.5	25.9

Source: Government of Tanzania, Bureau of Statistics.

Import liberalization, therefore, seems not to have sparked off a process of sustained industrial growth. Many firms exposed to direct import competition are dying out. Where there is a more positive response, it is based on capabilities built up during periods of import substitution. It is not clear, however, that these capabilities will continue to grow once existing comparative advantages have been fully exploited.

Industries that invested in export capability were able to sustain their export competitiveness over relatively longer periods (Wangwe, 1995). Examples are Northen Electrical Manufacturers Limited (NEM), established in 1979, Themi Farm Implements (1981) and Matsushita Electric Company Limited (1967), among others. NEM experienced a consistent growth in exports by some 2.7 times between 1986 and 1991, rising from 14.3 per cent of total sales in 1986 to 58.2 per cent in 1991 (Bagachwa and Mbelle, 1995). While the productivity of Themi Farm Implements was adversely affected by liberalization policies, that of Afro Cooling was sustained over a relatively longer term but, in the early 1990s, lost impetus. The firm's major technological improvement has been standardization of the design for radiator tubes and structures. The decline in exports in Matsushita partly reflects a diversion of exports to the domestic market, where demand is greater. However, the performance of Matsushita has been generally satisfactory.

Given favourable subsector policies, the United Republic of Tanzania stands a chance to develop manufacturing competitiveness in some subsectors. These may include, *inter alia,* metal and light engineering products, glassware, paint, cement industries, electrical engineering, automatized engineering and other associated industries. However, the government has not accorded sufficient priorities to these industries. For instance, General Tyre Industry, which is the largest manufacturer of car tyres in East Africa, has been facing problems that the government could help to solve. The industry is burdened by high production costs as a result of high taxes. These Tanzanian costs constitute a burden rather than any assistance in enhancing manufacturing competitiveness.

Industrywide development policies Industry-wide policies encompass three basic areas: macroeconomic balances and public finance; physical and social infrastructure, and the regulatory and business environment, all of which are aimed at reducing the weight of country costs in total manufacturing costs (see Chapter 4).

Macroeconomic balances Low inflation rates, proper allocation of credit through realistic interest rates, controlled money supply, efficient and conducive tax structures, prudent expenditure mix and management and efficient exchange rate system are some of the variables crucial to manufacturing competitiveness. On the fiscal policy front, the government's policy objective of increasing tax revenue has resulted in higher taxes for some manufacturing products, in particular, beverages and tobacco, than for others. Because the increased taxes have come mainly from the sales tax, the increased prices of finished goods have reduced competitiveness. Garments, leather and textiles have become vulnerable to the competitive environment due to their high prices in relation to cheaper imported products, leading to their demise. Cuts in government expenditure have led to cuts in incentives for training, R&D and in support for micro enterprises. In general, reform in the fiscal sector has not, at least initially, favoured competitiveness of domestic industries.

To achieve a market-determined exchange rate, the interbank foreign market was introduced whereby the central bank, commercial banks and other dealers participate in buying and selling foreign exchange on a daily basis. Following these measures, exports have increased, especially the non-traditional exports. They have, however, resulted in greater exchange rate volatility and uncertainty among certain producers. Importers and exporters are not affected equally with the misfortune of one group being to the benefit of the other and vice versa. Producers whose inputs have a high import content, such as chemical industries, experience double effects. In such circumstances, although the exchange rate policy has enhanced competitiveness of exports, it is also endangering their production.

Financial and monetary policy in the United Republic of Tanzania has undergone extensive reform. There is still a lack of adequate institutions specializing in long-term finance to assist in industrial development. High risks have deterred investors from investing enough in manufacturing upgrading. Instead, most bank credit has gone to trading activities, following the profitable effects of import and trade liberalization. This has reduced manufacturing financing substantially, affecting investment plans and access to modern technology.

Higher interest normally leads to higher capital costs and vice versa (see Chapter 5). The United Republic of Tanzania has one of the highest lending rates in East and Southern Africa, some 40 per cent in 1995, compared with 21 per cent in Zimbabwe and 14 per cent in Botswana. The rate was 29.63 per cent in 1988, increasing to 31 per cent between 1990 and 1993 and to 39 per cent in 1994. This points to lower competitiveness in terms of capital costs. Associated with this are high capital depreciation costs that make servicing loans difficult. Inflation rates have not dropped as fast as anticipated and the resulting exchange rate appreciation has made imported inputs expensive, contributing to reduced manufacturing competitiveness.

As a result of price reforms, the relative price of products and factors of production is essentially determined by market forces, which can be expected to lead to market-based allocation of resources. However, the reforms have contributed to increased prices of inputs and, thus outputs, relative to the pre-reform period.

On the other hand, real wages have not been increasing at the same pace, as has been the case in other countries. The minimum monthly wage in the United Republic of Tanzania was US$10.55 in 1993 compared with US$24.96 in Kenya, US$44.85 in Mauritius and US$273 in South Africa in the same year. Gross hourly earnings are less than US$1, which is among the lowest in the world. Although the United Republic of Tanzania enjoys a comparative advantage in labour costs, it may not guarantee labour productivity and competitiveness, judging from the theory of marginal productivity. Only some reformed industrial firms as well as newly established private firms have managed to keep unit labour costs under control through important productivity improvements.

Underlying the general macroeconomic picture, the experience of individual firms and sectors reveals a different story. Relatively import-intensive industrial activities, for example, have more problems emanating from import competition and exchange rate and tariff constraints. Those that are utility-intensive have more problems associated with domestic power tariffs. Electricity costs at a paper mill account for 40 per cent of the firm's total cost of production.

Competition and de-regulation in factor and product markets The issue of competition in pre-reform the United Republic of Tanzania was almost non-existent. Lack of competition encouraged inefficiencies in the seller's market, exemplified by low-quality products. Many industries were monopolistic, most of them being SOEs. Reforms have exposed manufacturing firms to both internal and external competition, bringing with them a reduction in effective protection (see Table 11.4 on p. 352). Competition from imports has been most intense in the textiles and garments and food sectors. Statistical data show that 63 per cent of textile firms and 54 per cent of food processing firms faced import competition compared with 33 per cent in the metal industry and 14 per cent in the wood industry. Competition from imports appeared to relate inversely to the size of firms, with bigger ones experiencing more competition than smaller ones. This is, however, a different case with competition from domestic firms. The proportion of firms with a competitive domestic market was 61 per cent for micro, 59 per cent for small, 42 per cent for medium, and 25 per cent for large firms.

Many private firms are dealing in categories of consumer goods where a more competitive domestic market structure exists (Semboja and Lecomte, 1996). With access to foreign exchange, consumer goods are easier and cheaper to import. The trade and import liberalization policies of the mid-1980s have thrust the manufacturing sector unprepared into a competitive environment, with mixed results. While some firms have responded defensively, others have responded offensively. Defensive responses have manifested themselves in the form of radical measures, such as a move into non-tradables and reductions in the workforce. A case in point is the garment industry, which is moving into such activities as repair work.

Offensive responses, on the other hand, involve sector-specific measures to meet the challenges inherent in the liberalization process. In this regard, some firms responded to import liberalization by upgrading technology, introducing new products, improving product quality and lowering prices. Other responses included searching for potential foreign markets, boosting exports, attracting FDI to increase production, adopting new technologies, improving the quality of products and reducing production costs through redundancies, leading to further falls in the rate of capacity utilization.

In the current to short-term industrial situation, measures to protect domestic industries from unfair competition, dumping practices and the like, that could suffocate infant industries, are justified. Applied on selective basis, they could include fiscal, tax compliance, anti-dumping and countervailing measures. While using selective protection, efforts should be made to improve the quality of supportive infrastructure and put in place institutions that can create an enabling environment for infant industries.

Utility costs Relative utility costs given an indication of manufacturing competitiveness. The average price of electricity used in production in the United Republic of Tanzania is US$0.11 per Wh, which is higher compared with other neighbouring countries. The United Republic of Tanzania has the lowest cost for industrial fuel in East Africa, at about US$0.35 per litre, giving domestic users a potential competitive advantage. The United Republic of Tanzania also enjoys competitive advantage in water with the price for use in industrial production averaging US$0.104 per liter (Wangwe et al., 1996).

Physical infrastructure The role of infrastructure in implementing industrial development policy and developing manufacturing competitiveness cannot be overemphasized. Availability and reliability of supportive infrastructure is a prerequisite for industrial development. The available infrastructural development in the United Republic of Tanzania is not adequate to ensure manufacturing competitiveness. In the current policy agenda, the government is committed to expansion, improvement and increase in the provision of power, water, communication facilities, transport and road networks. It will give priority to rehabilitation of existing infrastructure during the first phase of the Integrated Roads Programme (IRP I) while further development will be undertaken in subsequent phases. The government will also use fiscal measures to compensate industrial investors who bear infrastructural diseconomies. Priority will be given to areas that have demonstrably valuable resource endowments but cannot be developed because of inaccessibility. Telecommunication facilities will be consolidated and expanded to increase efficiency. Further privatization of major SOEs such as those in railways, air services and harbours are scheduled and, once completed, these services are expected to work more efficiently.

Social infrastructure One of the critical factors for sustained industrialization is the creativity and productivity of entrepreneurs, managers and workers. The industrial sector in the United Republic of Tanzania is characterized by the poor quality of its labour force, inadequate technical and management skills, lack of an entrepreneurial cadre and a low level of industrial culture. This is detrimental to manufacturing competitiveness. According to the country's industrial development agenda, greater importance will be given to training workers at all levels by all employers. Substantial investment in education measures, such as reorienting training towards basic science, could help in this direction. Other government policies deal with education, health, housing and the like but, except for education, they are not linked with the current industrial development policy agenda. Indirectly, though, the industrial development policy is expected to lead to higher economic growth.

Summary Though the distinction between firm-level, sub-sector specific and industry-wide policy performance has not been very sharp, there is an indication that some efforts have been made to improve the role of particular policy levels in fostering manufacturing competitiveness. Nevertheless, reliance on macroeconomic policies to address firm-level performance may not work if the assumed trickle-down effect is missing. Moreover, there are significant contradictions at the macroeconomic level because of subsectoral non-neutrality. Efforts by the government are far from satisfactory, with a great need to improve the effectiveness of reforms. Despite efforts to achieve a high literacy level, for instance, Tanzania's quality of education has been declining during the reform period. The picture that emerges of technological responses to liberalization in the United Republic of Tanzania is not encouraging. The initial levels of capability have been low and reactions to the opening up of the economy have, on the whole, been passive or negative. The main response has been to move out of manufacturing into trading. Weak technological capabilities and a low level of entrepreneurial dynamism account to a large extent for the poor market performance of the majority of firms.

THE INDUSTRIAL DEVELOPMENT POLICY AGENDA AT WORK

The Implementation Timetable

Tanzania's current industrial development policy is planned for 25 years, with priority activities identified for different phases within the policy period. The immediate priority activity for the industrial sector under phase I is 'rehabilitation, revival and consolidation of existing structure' through the restructuring programme. During the first five years of the strategy, 1995 to 2000, the economy is expected to focus on this priority, combined with expansion of existing industrial capacity as privatization proceeds. In the second phase, 2000 to 2010, priority will shift to new capacities in areas where the United Republic of Tanzania has clear potential comparative advantages with a view to developing these through training This is the period when emphasis on manufacturing for exports and developing the requisite competence is most necessary. Phase III, 2010 to 2020, should focus on using the earnings and capabilities developed during the first 15 years to enter into intermediate and capital goods industries. This move is necessary to consolidate industrial structures established during the first 15 years.

Factors for Effectiveness of Policy Implementation

Industrialization in the United Republic of Tanzania faces the twin challenges of overcoming major constraints and optimizing available and potential opportunities.

Institutional and resource constraints

Industrialization and competitiveness have been adversely affected by the limited development of economic infrastructure, especially transportation, telecommunications, energy and water, which are inadequate to support manufacturing competitiveness. Hydro- and thermo-electricity are the main sources of industrial power. Production and distribution of water and electricity is a government monopoly through SOEs. The existing power tariff structure causes inefficient utilization of electricity and increases industrial production costs, thereby reducing competitiveness. The cost of electricity in the United Republic of Tanzania is the highest in East and Southern Africa.

Inadequate industrial finance represents yet another constraint on industrial development in the United Republic of Tanzania. The low level of domestic savings, resulting from the generally low level of income per capita, restricts mobilization of domestic investment to support financing of industrial development. Those financial and social security institutions that exist accord low priority to industrial projects because of their generally long gestation periods. Interest rates for loanable funds do not distinguish between short-term commercial projects and long-term industrial projects. In general, there is a lack of affordable working capital for industries, interest rates are high, and credit restrictions, as a means of combating inflation, have resulted in a liquidity constraint. Financial sector reforms are still incomplete and development finance institutions, in particular, are in a weak position. The provision of development finance has yet to regain the dynamism it had in the 1970s.

Legacies from previous regimes

The previous regime bequeathed a legacy of rigidities in the economy. SOEs were among its creations and their restructuring has been slow. Likewise, the past regime fostered inefficiencies mirrored in attitudes towards efficiency and competitiveness. The inherited labour force cannot be changed overnight to cope with the requirements of the new regime. Established institutions were created to cater for the past regime, so no swift transformation can be expected.

Learning by doing

The lack of broad-based local entrepreneurship remains a stumbling block to sustained industrial development. The Arusha Declaration discouraged private sector initiatives and development. In the new approach, in which the private sector is given the leading role, the challenge is how to create local entrepreneurs from a dominantly poor, ill-educated population. The population can, however, be encouraged to 'learn by doing' in the industrial process. This approach is encouraged in the new industrial development policy agenda. Private firms provide some in-house training. But the policy of learning by doing can be undermined by other motives, such as quick profit making. Private firms may minimize the time allocated to learning by its workers, especially where workers' loyalty to firms is not guaranteed and their mobility between firms is high. There is need for state intervention in promoting training through incentives and institutional arrangements.

Administrative capacity and availability of managerial cadres

The United Republic of Tanzania lacks experienced managerial and technical capacity. Commercial efficiency in domestic industrial firms is relatively poor due to limitation in capacity and competence at managerial and technical levels. Trade liberalization has exposed the inefficiency of many activities. Bureaucracy is also inefficient and slow to gear itself to administering operations in a competitive market environment.

Resistance to change

In the United Republic of Tanzania, the former economic system benefited some economic agents, so that they are as inclined to resist change as is the country's inefficient bureaucracy. Existing decision-making procedures and law enforcement institutions are fragmented, causing a chain of inefficient bureaucracy. This bureaucracy benefits in slowing down processes because red tape calls for rent-seeking activities, which are advantageous to those working within these bureaucracies. Other economic agents also gain by resisting change. Some industrialists can only survive in the absence of competition, while some importers benefit from not paying duties. Transparent policies cut their profits or push them out of business.[10]

The civil service reforms which seek to trim the government and enhance efficiency are yet to bear fruit because of job losses. Similar fears have been expressed about SOE reforms. Such apprehensions exist because the main reform tools – including those of ownership change and support for the private sector – represent a substantial change from those used for the first 30 years of corporate sector development. The fears are that jobs may be lost, some national interests may not be protected, foreign control may re-emerge, and ownership may be concentrated in the hands of minorities.

Monitoring Progress: Evaluation Yardsticks and Time-frame of the Current Policy Cycle

The implementation of the current policy falls into four phases: (i) setting up the legal framework and national coordinating body, organizing and staffing the nucleus for technical support and management groups; and identifying industrial subsystems and enterprises together with the relevant support service organizations; (ii) establishing baseline data and information from which the new approach can take off; (iii) the consultative phase, and (iv) focusing on implementation, monitoring, feedback and review of strategies, plans and programmes, the process of which is ongoing.

SUMMARY OF KEY FINDINGS

This chapter has explored the relationships between various policies for manufacturing competitiveness. The main findings, including recommendations for future policy directions, are summarized below.

1. The current economic policy regime results from economic reforms and market liberalization policies applied since the mid-1980s and is essentially market-oriented and reform-based. Tanzania's economic crisis was a product of unfavourable domestic policies, external shocks and disasters. Underlying the reforms were measures intended to overcome weaknesses in the economy and respond to global changes.
2. Manufacturing competitiveness performance has shown some success. Average annual growth rates of MVA improved after 1986, but recovery could not be sustained through the period 1990–95. Capacity utilization levels have increased in response to foreign resource inflows, although some industries have collapsed. Levels of protection have been drastically lowered. The manufacturing sector has been exposed to stiff competition following import liberalization policies. Labour productivity – one of the indicators of competitiveness – has declined, especially after the reforms (Table 11.7).
3. The new policy regime presupposes a greater degree of liberalism and marketization. National and sectoral policies have been proposed to cope with the resulting economic changes. To enhance manufacturing competitiveness, the new industrial development policy has been designed to be consistent with other national and sectoral policies. But a

Table 11.7 United Republic of Tanzania: wages, salaries, employment and labour productivity in manufacturing, 1970–95

	Absolute values			Index 1970=100		
Years	Wages (US$ million)	Employment in manufacturing (million persons)	Labour productivity (US$)	Wages (US$ million)	Employment in manufacturing (million persons)	Labour productivity (US$)
1970	36.37	0.048	1773.07	100.00	100.00	100.00
1971	38.73	0.053	1730.22	106.50	110.00	97.58
1972	44.36	0.062	1813.21	121.96	127.61	102.26
1973	47.82	0.063	2024.50	131.47	130.15	114.18
1974	51.40	0.069	1735.35	141.31	143.75	97.87
1975	50.97	0.076	1540.11	140.14	157.32	86.86
1976	55.51	0.082	1585.17	152.62	170.40	89.40
1977	52.86	0.090	1374.28	145.33	185.24	77.50
1978	50.49	0.096	1598.23	138.83	197.99	89.63
1979	54.88	0.097	1898.46	150.89	199.90	107.07
1980	54.14	0.100	1634.09	148.86	207.47	92.16
1981	49.74	0.104	1399.76	136.77	214.32	78.94
1982	43.94	0.001	1319.58	120.82	206.81	74.42
1983	40.95	0.103	1147.12	112.60	212.66	64.69
1984	38.82	0.097	1174.62	106.73	201.21	66.24
1985	34.39	0.093	1047.07	94.56	192.51	59.05
1986	31.09	0.109	910.99	85.30	225.20	51.37
1987	27.70	0.111	915.62	76.17	229.23	51.64
1988	24.77	0.113	876.68	68.12	233.24	49.44
1989	26.33	0.119	851.91	72.40	244.77	48.04
1990	25.11	0.124	791.84	69.05	255.67	44.65
1991	26.94	0.130	778.53	74.06	267.84	43.90
1992	27.30	0.135	695.69	75.07	279.37	39.23
1993	28.19	0.142	666.04	77.51	293.39	37.56
1994	30.20	0.148	674.12	83.05	305.89	38.02
1995	32.14	0.156	674.00	88.36	320.52	38.01

Source: UNIDO database.

major missing link has been in development of supportive infrastructural facilities and the institutional support system to enable manufacturing firms to respond to the demands of competition.

4. The new policy regime has advocated reforms but still hinges on an older bureaucratic cadre, characterized by a former economic regime that conflicts with the current one. To implement the new industrial development policy objectives without a change in attitude represents a formidable challenge.
5. Industrial development policy is being pursued against the background of a poor infrastructure. Physical, economic and social infrastructure constraints are one of the critical bottlenecks in trying to boost manufacturing efficiency and productivity.
6. Tanzania's economy is still based primarily on agriculture. Measures to increase productivity and efficiency in the sector could have a significant bearing on manufacturing competitiveness.
7. Manufacturing competitiveness can be built based on local resources, but this presupposes technological capability building. This can only be achieved if the environment supports investment in technology. Specific measures to support firm-level responses in this regard have not been put in place.
8. Firm-level technological capabilities for manufacturing competitiveness depend to a great extent on national technological capabilities. R&D institutions, industrial and technological support establishments and productivity centres need to be integrated into national industrial development policy for manufacturing competitiveness. Firm-level efforts alone may not be sufficient to ensure the longer-term sustainability of manufacturing competitiveness. Government intervention is required to commit more resources to establish and maintain the requisite level of national technological infrastructure. Access to the international policy experience as well as help in extending technical and technological support to create a supportive infrastructure for manufacturing competitiveness should be provided through specialized technical assistance.

NOTES

1. The figure may be higher given the extent of unrecorded informal sector activities in the country, whose output is estimated to be 30 per cent of official GDP. See Government of United Republic of Tanzania (1996) and World Bank (1996).

2. For instance, the beverage subsector was targeted for earning revenue for the government. As a result, such industries were subject to high sales tax rates, lowering their price competitiveness.
3. The Act was amended and investment policy revised in 1992 and again in 1994. The new investment policy has recently been finalized.
4. See Semboja and Lecomte (1996). Net entry or exit is defined as the difference in number of establishments between two successive years. It is net entry when the number is positive and exit when is negative.
5. USAID – CTI (1994).
6. The National Institute of Productivity (NIP) was made responsible for assisting the firms in target setting. The Institute gives courses on productivity analysis, promotion and development, which are also offered through research and consultancy services to both public and private clients. However, in the current policy reform environment, enterprises that are supposed to meet the costs of training are facing a liquidity squeeze. In addition, the courses on offer may not be tailored to meet the current challenges.
7. Patents, trade marks and licences play a role in technology development. Such development depends on existing policies, patents law and industrial property rights. In Tanzania, the patent law was formulated in 1930, which does not give much incentive for locals to develop new industrial innovations and hence impairs the ability to facilitate competitiveness in production. A new patent law was passed by Parliament as Act 1 of 1987, which is expected to motivate scientists and technologists to develop industrial technologies. However, patent activities are relatively few and underdeveloped in Tanzania, with the inability of the patent holders to apply the results.
8. Beverages and tobacco had the highest level of protection before the liberalization period, to be replaced by food products in the early 1990s. While chemicals and fertilizers were the least protected before the 1990s, tanneries and leather emerged as least protected in the early 1990s.
9. See, for instance, ESRF (1996).
10. Resistance has been reported in the ranks of the ruling party, as well as among SEOs and government officials, to privatizing major utilities and several other state-owned organizations (*Financial Times*, 13–16 November 1996).

REFERENCES

ADB (1995), *African Development Report 1995*, Abidjan.

Bagachwa, M.S.D. (1993), 'An agenda for sustainable of non traditional exports in Tanzania', *TET*, **5**, (3 and 4).

Bagachwa, M.S.D and A.V.Y. Mbelle (1995), 'Tanzania: export manufacturing', in S.M. Wangwe (ed.), *Exporting Africa: Technology, Trade and Industrialization in Sub-Saharan Africa*, London: Routledge.

ESRF (1996), 'The impact of divestiture and privatization process on industrial performance: the case of six divested companies', a report submitted to PSRC, Dar es Salaam.

Government of Tanzania (1985), The National Science and Technology for Tanzania, Ministry of Planning and Economic Affairs, Dar es Salaam.

Government of Tanzania (1996), *Sustainable Industrial Development Policy* (Industrial development, 1996–2020), draft, vol. I and II, Dar es Salaam.

Lall, S. (1992), 'Technological capabilities and industrialization', *World Development,* **20,** 165–186.

Mans, D. (1994), 'The United Republic of Tanzania: resolute action' in Husain Ishrat and Faruqee Rashis (eds), *Adjustment in Africa: Lessons from Country Case Studies,* Washington.

Mjema, G. and Shitundu (1995), 'Performance of industrial trade during the economic recovery programme: some reflections on future prospects', Paper presented at the Workshop on SAPs in Tanzania: 'Success, Failures and New Perspective', ERB, 2–4 August, 1995.

Ndulu, B.J. and J.J. Semboja (1992), *The Development of Manufacturing for Export in Tanzania,* Dar es Salaam: Department of Economics, University of Dar es Salaam.

Ndulu, B.J., J.J. Semboja and A.V.Y. Mbelle (1995), *The Impact of Import Liberalization on Manufacturing Industry in Tanzania,* Dar es Salaam.

RPED (1995), *Dynamics of Enterprise Development in Tanzania, Final Report on Round II Survey data,* Helsinki School of Economics.

Semboja, H. and J. Kweka (1996), 'Import liberalization, industrialization and technological capability in sub-Saharan Africa: the case of the garment industry in Tanzania', ESRF Research Paper, Dar es Salaam.

Semboja, H. and H.B. Lecomte (1996), 'Exit procedures and economic transformation: the case of Tanzania', ESRF Discussion Paper Series no. 010, Dar es Salaam.

UNCTAD (1995), *Trade and Development Report,* Geneva: UNCTAD.

UNIDO (1993), *African Industry in Figures,* Vienna: UNIDO.

USAID–CTI (1994), *Industrial Policy Proposal,* report based on Joint USAID and CTI Programme, Dar es Salaam.

Valk, P. (1992), *A General Framework for Evaluating the Performance of Textile Enterprises in LDCs, With an Application to Tanzania,* The Hague: Institute of Social Studies,

Wangwe, S.M. (1994), 'Technology development in Tanzania: some challenges for the 21st century', in L.A. Msambichaka, H.P.B Moshi, and F.P. Mtatifikolo (1994), (eds), *Development Challenges and Strategies for Tanzania: An Agenda for the 21st Century,* Dar es Salaam: Economic Research Bureau, Department of Economics, University of Dar es Salaam.

Wangwe, S.M. (1995a), *Exporting Africa: Technology, Trade and Industrialization in Sub-Saharan Africa,* Routledge.

Wangwe, S.M. (1995), 'Economic integration in Southern Africa: towards cost and benefit analysis in Tanzania', ESRF discussion paper series no. 002.

Wangwe, S.M., H. Semboja and G. Kahyarara (1996), 'Regional Industrial Location Strategy: Tanzania Study', final report to the Development Bank of Southern Africa (DBSA), South Africa, through ESRF, Dar es Salaam.

World Bank (1996), *The United Republic of Tanzania: Challenges of Reforms: Growth Incomes and Welfare,* vol. 1, main report, Washington, DC: World Bank.

ANNEX 11A. SUCCESS AND FAILURE OF POLICY REFORM PROGRAMMES IN LDCs

Commonalities and Differences

LDCs are low-income countries that suffer from long-term handicaps to growth, low levels of technology and HRD and severe structural weaknesses. Currently they comprise 48 countries located in African, Asian and Pacific Islands and the Caribbean.[1] Variations in resource endowments, levels of economic and infrastructure development and the socio-political conditions strongly affect the extent of success of economic reform policy. Differences in policy thrust and effectiveness are related to specific initial conditions before the adoption of reforms.

LDCs share low levels of per capita income and widespread levels of poverty. These conditions make equity unachievable. There are, however, significant regional differences. The majority of the LDCs are in Africa (33 countries) and have lower per capita income than Asian LDCs. Afghanistan, Ethiopia and Sierra Leone have per capita income below US$100, whereas Cape Verde and Vanuatu had an income per capita of more than US$1000 in 1995. Trends in real GDP per capita growth rate also exhibit remarkable differences among regions (see Table 11A.1).

Table 11A.1 Regional breakdown of the trends in economic growth in LDCs

	African LDCs		Asian LDCs		Pacific Islands LDCs		All LDCs	
	1980–90	1990–95	1980–90	1990–95	1980–90	1990–95	1980–90	1990–95
Real GDP	1.89	0.19	2.72	5.34	0.07	–4.31	2.22	2.59
Real GDP per capita	–1.01	–2.54	0.67	2.59	–1.93	–6.33	–0.31	–0.14

Source: UNIDO database.

The Pacific Islands have experienced a rather dismal growth, followed by African LDCs. While Asian LDCs continue to show signs of steady increase in their level of socio-economic development, other regions within the LDCs show signs of persistent decline. Variations also exist within regions. For instance, between 1980 and 1995, per capita income of some countries improved (for example Bangladesh from US$161 to US$220 and Bhutan, from

US$$115 to US$226), while others declined (for example Ethiopia, from US$75 to US$68 and Malawi, from US$265 to US$190).

In population LDCs range from very small (Tuvalu and other island LDCs), with less than one million inhabitants, to very big countries such as Bangladesh, with 120.4 million people. The remote and scattered island economies are small and highly susceptible to climatic conditions. They remain unable to manage nature. Climatic disruptions such as cyclones, droughts and floods are common in LDCs and are cited as one of contributors to low economic growth. Population growth among LDCs averages 2.6 per cent against 0.7 per cent for advanced industrial countries. These high rates of population growth are attributable to a combination of poverty and low level of education, health services and income-earning opportunities.

LDCs vary significantly in resource endowments. Two major categories can be identified: countries that are rich in minerals and countries with agricultural potential (see Table 11A.2).

Table 11A.2 Resource endowment in selected LDCs

Mineral resource		Agriculture resource (cash and food crops)-based countries			
Countries	(% of total)	Cash-crops-based	(% of total)	Food-crops-based	(% of total)
Democratic Republic of the Congo	55.9	Benin	75.6	Burundi	90.2
Guinea	78.7	Equatorial Guinea	60.1	Cape Verde	80.6
Mauritania	49.5	Mali	68	Guinea-Bissau	92.3
Niger	67.9	Sudan	56.3	Sao Tome and Principe	92.3
Sierra Leone	41.1	United Republic of Tanzania	50	Uganda	90.4
Zambia	87.2			Vanuatu	79.7

Source: World Bank (1995).

Some countries are endowed with good farming lands and hence depend on agriculture for their export earnings; others depend entirely on mineral exports. In view of this, changes in terms of trade and in world market trends have a differentiated impact on LDCs. Very few LDCs have manufacturing capability for raw material processing to be cushioned in face of such changes.[2] Heavy dependence on a particular item as source of export earnings implies inadequate level of export diversification, which undermines the modest development efforts under way.

LDCs are also endowed with abundant energy resources. Africa possesses 6.2 per cent of proven world reserves of oil, 6.9 per cent of natural gas and 6 per cent of coal. Also, there is considerable hydroelectric power potential, unexploited for the most part. Most LDCs have low levels of energy consumption and these are declining in per capita terms. Biomass, especially fuel wood, is the most important source of domestic energy in the region. High operating costs, low capacity utilization and generally inefficient operations in most manufacturing facilities owe much to the failure to utilize the energy potential in the region.

LDCs can be regarded as open economies, particularly following recent reforms in the external sector. For many LDCs increasing openness has led to persistent balance of payments deficits and high exposure to external shocks, in face of a very limited ability to cope with them.

LDCs have not fared well in terms of human and social development. Their life expectancy at birth, educational attainment and income are the lowest in the world on average. There are, however, significant variations. For instance, while in 1993 Afghanistan, Burkina Faso, Mali, Nepal, Niger, Nepal and Sierra Leone recorded an adult literacy rate of below 30 per cent, the Democratic Republic of the Congo, Equatorial Guinea, Myanmar and Zambia had reached over 75 per cent. Similarity, the average gross enrolment ratio of first-, second- and third-level education in Niger was 15 per cent, while Nepal recorded 57 per cent. Generally, LDCs are also identified with low life expectancy at birth, with an average of 50 years in 1993.

The regional distribution of transport and communication infrastructure is also highly uneven with low level of service in rural areas where most of the population live (over 80 per cent in most LDCs). In addition, in many of the LDCs the physical infrastructure has deteriorated due to poor maintenance and outdated equipment. This problem is most acute in landlocked LDCs. Africa as a whole, with a population of nearly 700 million and a land area of 30 million km^2, has 1.6 telephones per 100 people, 2.2 million km of all-weather roads and 73 000 km of railways. Needs for telecommunication equipment and spare parts are met almost entirely through imports. These generally take place on a non-selective, package-deal basis, leaving little room for adaptation to local needs through domestic enterprises and know-how. Thus investment in telecommunications does not have the multiplier effects (via research, development and engineering (R&DE), local manufacturing, services and employment) as is the case in other regions of the world.

The global spread of the information revolution is for the most part still to reach LDCs, especially in Africa. Despite rapid investments in this sector, no more than 15 African countries had full access to the Internet in 1994 and some remain without electronic connectivity at all. In 1994, the average 'teledensity' (number of main lines per 100 inhabitants) was only 1.6 as compared with 45 in Europe. The average teledensity outside large cities in Africa was only 1.2 (*World Telecommunication Development Report,* 1995). These figures are much lower in sub-Saharan Africa. Africa has only 2 per cent of the world's telephone lines, most of them in a few large cities. Levels of indebtedness remain very high among LDCs, which is a major hindrance to their development efforts. The stock of outstanding debt equals or exceeds GDP in almost half of them; they still confront heavy external debt-servicing obligations, while their debt-servicing capacity weakens over time. In terms of absolute size, the largest LDC debtors are Bangladesh and Sudan, each with over US$10 billion of external debt in 1992, followed by Afghanistan, the Democratic Republic of Congo, Ethiopia, Myanmar, the United Republic of Tanzania, Yemen, and Zambia, with outstanding external debt in the range of US$5 billion–10 billion.

Three groups of LDCs can be identified in terms of manufacturing performance in the 1990s. First are countries with positive per capita MVA growth. Performance varied greatly within this group, which comprises 15 countries. Bangladesh, Bhutan, Cape Verde, Lao People's Democratic Republic, Lesotho and Maldives enjoy high MVA while others, such as Comoros and Mali barely keep pace with population growth. In the Lao People's Democratic Republic, Bangladesh and Mali, MVA growth has picked up great momentum in recently after years of depressed performance. Second is the group of eight LDCs with slow MVA growth. Among these, Guinea and the Solomon Islands experienced deceleration in MVA in recent years, while Mozambique, Sao Tome and Principe, Sudan and United Republic of Tanzania were able to improve their performance in the 1990s. Finally the third group (23 LDCs) experienced negative MVA growth on average since the mid-1980s. Rwanda and the Democratic Republic of Congo experienced the most severe losses (declines of 19.0 and 12.6 per cent, respectively, during 1990–95. The collapse of manufacturing in this group of countries is a major source of concern. Table 11A.3 gives a more detailed picture of trends in MVA rate in specific LDCs (see also Table 11A.1).

Closely related to LDCs' low manufacturing base is the issue of technology. Many LDCs lag substantially behind in their domestic technological learning processes. This owes in part to low expenditures in skill building and insufficient technology transfer. Overall, investment in technology is very low and has been declining. Africa spent 0.33 per cent of its GDP on technological development in 1970, falling to 0.29 per cent in 1990.

Table 11A.3 The manufacturing sector: annual average growth rates and shares in GDP

	Share in GDP		Annual average growth rates		
Country	1980	1995	1970–1980	1980–1990	1990–1995
Afghanistan	21.68	18.59	2.43	–3.13	2.38
Bangladesh	10.00	10.79	6.92	2.78	8.90
Benin	9.55	7.39	0.44	1.26	2.82
Bhutan	3.82	10.95	10.60	15.39	12.37
Botswana	4.62	4.91	9.64	9.17	6.98
Burkina Faso	13.76	12.45	4.02	0.90	2.62
Burundi	9.91	21.68	6.47	9.59	2.31
Cambodia	2.34	5.85	6.38	7.20	6.50
Cape Verde	5.59	9.66	1.71	6.26	15.42
Central African Republic	5.74	6.50	–1.95	3.11	0.40
Chad	17.33	13.36	2.92	3.37	–0.43
Comoros	4.08	5.50	–2.45	2.94	7.65
Democratic Republic of the Congo	12.61	9.14	–0.91	0.60	–9.76
Djibouti	4.31	4.35	5.79	1.01	2.11
Equatorial Guinea	1.46	1.32	–11.27	1.75	6.99
Ethiopia	9.24	9.81	3.87	3.34	–0.28
Gambia	5.15	5.66	6.27	4.38	2.81
Guinea	2.65	3.77	2.73	5.09	5.21
Guinea Bissau	14.88	5.76	1.31	–4.00	–0.16
Haiti	21.24	10.94	8.35	–1.91	–15.32
Kiribati	1.94	1.89	–1.49	0.38	2.37
Lao People's Democratic Republic	4.49	4.96	0.96	4.99	8.65
Lesotho	5.17	14.84	9.69	12.35	9.78
Liberia	6.20	9.42	5.12	0.41	2.36
Madagascar	15.34	12.71	1.85	–1.65	1.19
Malawi	13.42	15.73	9.42	3.66	1.12
Maldives	6.10	10.27	20.36	13.87	12.11

Mali	4.91	9.21	3.95	8.62	6.81
Mauritania	7.45	13.31	3.31	6.45	7.44
Mozambique	39.94	24.67	–0.64	–5.31	4.37
Myanmar	8.19	7.66	3.45	0.74	6.31
Nepal	4.11	5.98	3.03	7.32	7.05
Niger	3.25	6.70	–2.22	6.51	0.76
Rwanda	14.12	10.45	6.10	1.63	–16.90
Samoa	8.38	7.75	3.09	–1.03	–1.17
Sao Tome and Principe	6.43	5.54	0.00	–3.67	4.30
Sierra Leone	13.91	6.44	2.93	–4.31	–6.65
Solomon Islands	2.37	2.91	6.57	4.90	5.58
Somalia	4.18	3.76	3.62	0.48	1.27
Sudan	8.75	9.27	2.43	–0.07	3.99
United Republic of Tanzania	5.21	3.73	3.55	–1.37	4.24
Togo	11.95	6.90	–0.20	–0.39	–6.38
Tuvalu	–	–	–	–	–
Uganda	3.57	5.89	–9.87	6.75	8.98
Vanuatu	2.64	7.80	5.63	13.71	9.14
Yemen	9.26	10.19	12.19	6.82	5.75
Zambia	17.09	27.05	1.47	4.12	2.22
All LDCs	9.88	9.47	2.89	1.78	3.18

Source: UNIDO database.

Manufacturing performance in LDCs shows a wide range of variation by sector and, on the whole, has weakened in recent years. Some LDCs have recorded declines in output due to lack of competitiveness and inability to respond to price and non-price signals. While some two-thirds of LDCs maintained a positive growth of manufacturing value added (MVA) in the 1980s and in the 1990s, most LDCs experienced stagnation and even declines in manufacturing output. In addition to legacies from past policies and strategies, and the impact of reform and adjustment, manufacturing activities were constrained by low investment, low level of technology and import compression.

Two consumer-oriented subsectors, food processing and textiles and clothing, dominate LDCs' manufacturing. They command two-thirds of MVA. Food processing alone accounts for nearly half of total LDCs' MVA. In Burkina Faso, Burundi, Central African Republic, Sudan and Yemen, this subsector alone accounts for 60 per cent of their respective MVA, while in the Democratic Republic of the Congo, Ethiopia, Gambia, Togo and Zambia it is over 40 per cent. Textiles (including garments and leather) is close to final demand, with few backward and forward linkages with other sectors. The relative importance of this subsector also varies. In Bangladesh, Madagascar and Mali, for instance, textiles represents the largest manufacturing activity, while for Ethiopia and the United Republic of Tanzania it accounts for almost 20 per cent of total MVA compared to its small contribution in the Central African Republic (2.1 per cent) and Yemen (4 per cent). Another subsector of considerable importance in LDCs is chemicals, which accounts for around 20 per cent, followed by metal and nonmetal products (especially in Ethiopia and Yemen). In five LDCs (Democratic Republic of the Congo, Mali, Sudan, United Republic of Tanzania, and Yemen) machinery and equipment contribute with at least 8 per cent to their respective MVA.

Thus overall, the subsectoral distribution of MVA points towards concentration of manufacturing in a few activities that are close to final demand. LDCs have made only limited progress towards diversifying their manufacturing base. The countries with most highly skewed manufacturing sectors are Burundi, Guinea, Lesotho, Mauritania and Sierra Leone (UNIDO, 1993). On the other hand, few other countries (for example Bangladesh, Haiti, Malawi, Uganda and United Republic of Tanzania) made some strides to diversify their manufacturing base. Some countries, such as Burundi and Lesotho, experienced strong MVA regardless of lack of diversification in their economies. More often than not subsectors are integrated by just a handful of firms.[3] Subsectors such as garment making and design, woodworking, food processing and metalworking are considered to have the potential to dynamize industrial growth (ADB, 1996).

Policy Consistency

Manufacturing performance has also been affected by lack of consistency between different policies; details are given below.

Exchange rate reform

Adjusting countries are grouped into two categories: those with fixed exchange rate regime and those with flexible exchange rates. Countries with flexible exchange rates devalued in order to curb worsening terms of trade and large premiums between the official and parallel markets. The outcome of this approach was strongly affected by the fact that in most LDCs output response is driven by economic rigidity, structural impediments and non-price barriers rather than price incentives. Nominal devaluations did not easily lead to a real depreciation of the currency, partly because of its inflationary impact.[4]

Significant price incentives worked successfully in Zambia owing to the absence of serious structural problems. Price incentives are a valuable tool for fostering exports in economies with relatively well-diversified economic bases and infrastructure, while in countries with deep-seated structural problems such policy instruments are ineffective and may even be destabilizing.

Elimination of administrative controls is a significant feature of reforms in most LDCs. However, in LDCs with ill-developed or absent markets, expected gains in efficiency have proved elusive. In Zambia, for example, the shift from administrative controls to an auction system for allocation of foreign exchange led to the pre-emption of almost all forex markets by MNCs, while smaller enterprises and the agricultural and social sectors received only marginal allocations. Thus undifferentiated market solutions did not offer a satisfactory alternative. Uganda, instead, successfully adopted a two-tier system, while the United Republic of Tanzania adopted a managed floating system.

Monetary policy reforms

Credit restructuring and positive real interest rates characterize the current monetary regime in most LDCs despite their adverse effects on indigenous entrepreneurship and SMIs in face of low degrees of monetization, poor infrastructure and widespread informal financing. These features offset the impact of private savings and investment on interest rate policies. Growth in deposits was discouraged in countries such as Gambia, Malawi, Nepal and Samoa owing to lack of viable investment projects and credit-worthy borrowers. Crowding out of private investment and deindustrialization have been reported in Ghana, the United Republic of Tanzania and Zambia. In Burkina Faso, Sierra Leone and United Republic of Tanzania the loss of credit facilities was associated with dismantling of crop-marketing SOEs.

Trade liberalization

LDCs' experience does not reveal a clear and systematic association between trade liberalization and currency devaluation. A number of countries that undertook substantial liberalization and devaluation experienced a fall in industrial output. Various Asian LDCs obtained positive results from selective rather than generalized trade liberalization.

Three categories of LDCs can be distinguished in terms of the impact of liberalization on manufacturing according to whether they undertook extensive liberalization (high liberalizers) or weak liberalization (low liberalizers) and those in between (medium liberalizers). Countries which liberalized least extensively appear to have been the worst performers in terms of MVA share in GDP (it declined by 0.3 per cent between 1980 and 1995). Among African LDCs this category includes the Democratic Republic of the Congo, Djibouti, Ethiopia, Madagascar, Mali, Mauritania, Niger, Rwanda, Sierra Leone, Somalia, Sudan, Togo, Uganda and Zambia. Both high and medium liberalizers were able to increase their MVA share in GDP over the 1980s, although some medium liberalizers (Burundi, Central African Republic and Lesotho) fared better by registering an MVA growth rate of 6.3 per cent while the high liberalizers (Benin, Burkina Faso, Chad, Gambia, Guinea and Malawi) recorded a growth rate of 2.4 per cent. However, the performance of the group of medium liberalizers varied significantly between countries.[5]

Privatization and public sector restructuring

Although privatization has an important place on the current policy agenda of most LDCs, the extent of its implementation differs depending on the extent of public sector dominance and strength of the reforms. LDCs have implemented this policy through a combination of three types of measures: outright privatization, association with the private sector and enterprise reform.

Some LDCs started privatization some years before the adoption of SAPs. For instance, Bangladesh carried out privatization in 1975, Nepal in 1970 and Uganda in 1982. In the context of adjustment, Togo began its privatization process in 1990 and Lao People's Democratic Republic in 1985. In Zambia and the United Republic of Tanzania (1992), this was done through policy statements and establishment of executing agencies (for example the Parastatal Sector Reform Commission in the United Republic of Tanzania).

The extent and speed of privatization differed markedly among the LDCs. While most countries divested between 0 and 10 per cent of their assets (for example Gambia, Kenya, Malawi, Sierra Leone, Uganda, United Republic of Tanzania, Zambia and Zimbabwe), Ghana divested about 25 per cent and Nigeria went as far as 51 per cent. The number of SOEs also differed widely across countries, some with less than 50 and others as many as 400. Only a few countries had their utilities sector commercialized (for example Ghana, Kenya, Nigeria and Zimbabwe).

In spite of the policy statements in many LDCs, little has been achieved in terms of results, largely because of lack of momentum. In 1993, Bangladesh envisaged privatizing 32 industrial units but, at the end of 1994, only three had done so. Between 1992 and 1994 the Tanzanian government succeeded in privatizing only 24 out of 400 SOEs. Such a slow pace may be attributable to factors such as government uncertainty about the credibility of privatization, institutional inadequacies and bureaucratic delays, dearth of local entrepreneurship, lack of financial resources and poor financial state of the SOEs offered for privatization. In the end, the success of privatization programmes will have to be judged not merely by the number of enterprises privatized, but against such considerations as output and efficiency gains, skill development, improvement in technological and managerial capabilities and contribution to domestic saving and investment.

Privatization may be a necessary but not sufficient condition for manufacturing efficiency. In Africa progress has been rather uneven. Five countries account for two-thirds of divestiture (Ghana, Guinea, Mozambique, Nigeria and Senegal). Only a handful of countries have divested more than 40 per cent of their enterprises, and half the countries have been very slow to privatize (see Table 11A.4).

Table 11A.4 Divestiture of SOEs among African LDCs, 1986–92

Percentage of enterprises divested	Number of Enterprises before Divestiture			
	0–50	51–100	101–200	More than 200
0–10	Gambia Mauritania Rwanda Sierra Leone Zimbabwe	Burkina Faso Congo Uganda Zambia	Cameroon Côte d'Ivoire Malawi	Kenya United Republic of Tanzania
11–25	Chad	Burundi Central African Republic	Madagascar	Ghana Mozambique
26–40	Niger	–	Guinea Nigeria	–
41–60	Guinea-Bissau	Benin Mali Senegal Togo	–	

Source: World Bank, 1994.

The process of privatization often involves shifts in the balance of power between various groups of society, which makes implementation far from smooth (for a Latin American view of this, see Annex 9C). This is aggravated by the fact that privatization is often carried out in response to conditionalities agreed with financial partners.

Civil service reform

Until recently, the World Bank's civil service reform consisted of two packages in all countries–retrenchment of civil servants and reduction in the wage bill. Most LDCs have reduced their wage bill, but the number and extent of retrenchments still varies across countries and data are rather sketchy. Civil service reform in many countries has been associated more with retrenchments than with shifts in core government functions or in organization and efficiency of the civil service. These remain key challenges in many LDCs.

Financial sector and monetary reforms

The main purpose of financial sector reforms in LDCs has been to enhance efficiency by moving towards a market-oriented financial system and removing administrative controls. Rises in capital costs were supposed to correct earlier inefficiencies by justifying only investment projects with high enough returns and by removing the earlier bias in favour of capital intensive technology. Higher interest rates were expected to increase saving by the public and, in turn, to use it for lending to productive investment. Implementation has taken place in four major ways: liberalization and rationalization of interest rates, restructuring of state-owned banks, privatization and liquidation. Different mixes were adopted according to country (see Table 11A.5).

These measures do not appear to have had a positive impact on manufacturing investment. Industrial financing in LDCs used to come from specialized financial institutions, mainly state-owned national development banks and commercial banks. With the emergence of private commercial banks, industrial financing has declined to a larger extent. The private commercial banks favour short-term financing to activities with quick returns, and these are mainly in trade. The other source of finance for investments in SOEs used to be external assistance in the form of concessional loans and sometimes grants. This source has dwindled as aversion to long-term tying of funds and high-risk ventures such as manufacturing investments has grown. Donors currently place low priority on manufacturing in their aid programmes.

Table 11A.5 Financial sector reforms undertaken in LDCs during the adjustment period

Liberalization and/or rationalization of interest rates	Restructuring of banks	Privatization of banks	Liquidation of banks
Benin	Côte d'Ivoire	Côte d'Ivoire	Benin
Burundi	Guinea	Guinea-Bissau	Côte d'Ivoire
Democratic Republic of the Congo	Madagascar	Madagascar	Guinea
Côte d'Ivoire	Mali	Mauritania	Niger
Gambia	Mauritania	Senegal	Rwanda
Madagascar	Rwanda		Senegal
Malawi	Senegal		
Mauritania	United Republic of Tanzania		
Mozambique	Uganda		
United Republic of Tanzania			
Rwanda			

Source: World Bank (1994).

Rationalization and liberalization of interest have been fairly successful, however, in easing financial repression in most LDCs. Interest rates were fully liberalized in Burundi, Gambia, Ghana, Kenya, Madagascar, Malawi, Mauritania and Zambia. The central banks in the CFA franc zone raised interest rates and eliminated preferential rates to maintain competitiveness with France. Reforms have not succeeded, however, in reducing financial repression in countries with highly negative interest rates.

Fiscal reforms

Fiscal reforms pursue the objective of removing budget deficits by putting in place an efficient tax system that can ensure a predictable and adequate level of public revenue with minimum administrative cost and distortions. While in many LDCs fiscal adjustment brought about higher levels of tax revenue, in many other LDCs it led to expenditure compression, particularly development expenditure. The vulnerability of social expenditures to cuts has been an issue of particular concern to LDCs, given the very low sums allocated to the social sector. This problem is being addressed in some countries (Bangladesh, Gambia and United Republic of Tanzania). In LDCs unable to mobilize greater revenue, improvements in budget balance were mainly achieved through the compression of expenditures, sometimes dramatically as in Sierra Leone where they fell by 6 per cent and in the United Republic of Tanzania where they fell by 14 per cent in 1985–90 from their 1980–85 levels.

The strategy of fiscal adjustment through compression of public expenditures must be assessed in the light of particular socio-economic characteristics of LDCs, namely, widespread prevalence of market failures, skewed income distribution and poverty.

Impact of Policy Reform

A distinction can be drawn between adjusting and non-adjusting LDCs and according to whether there was improvement or deterioration (see Table 11A.6). (See Box 11A.1 for the case of Ghana.) Non-adjusting countries are divided into the North African group and the low-income non-adjusters. None of the groups exhibits significant differences in manufacturing growth rates, which derived no special effects from adjustment. Differences in growth rates were caused by other factors such as initial conditions before adoption of the economic reforms, and resource endowment. Manufacturing is better off in countries with policy improvements. Countries with policy deterioration performed significantly worse in 1990–93 than countries with improvements and non-adjusters.

Industrial Development and Manufacturing Competitiveness Policy

Human resource development

HRD has not been addressed appropriately in LDCs so far. SAPs do not seem to address skill shortages, despite the fact that many subsectors might become competitive with improved human resources. The design of SAPs should therefore include education and training as an integral part of the restructuring process.

Firm-led training and investment in training are important factors in LDCs' export competitiveness. Many successful exporting firms have carried out training programmes, but appropriate local training institutions for specific skills are limited. HRD is instrumental in enhancing competitiveness at the level of firms and subsectors. It is in this area that government should pledge to take a lead, since industrial demands for upgraded educational levels will have to be met by further investments in education.

Table 11A.6 African Development Bank classification of countries by policy on structural adjustment

Adjusting countries		Non-adjusting countries	
Improvements in policy	Deterioration in policy	North Africa	Low-income Africa
Burkina Faso	Benin	Algeria	Angola
Burundi	Cameroon	Egypt	Botswana
Gambia	CAR	Libya	Cape Verde
Ghana	Chad	Morocco	Comoro
Kenya	Congo	Tunisia	Djibouti
Madagascar	Cote d'Ivoire		
North Africa	Low-Income Africa		
Algeria	Angola		
Egypt	Botswana		
Libya	Cape Verde		
Morocco	Comoro		
Tunisia	Djibouti		

Table 11A.6a Mean GDP growth rates by group

	1980–93		1990–93	
Countries	Weighted	Simple	Weighted	Simple
Policy improvements	2.65	2.88	3.38	2.35
Deterioration in policy	1.27	2.63	0.55	2.01
North Africa	2.11	2.63	1.04	1.62
Low-income non-adjusting	2.0	2.82	0.24	1.52

Table 11A.6b Mean annual real growth rates of manufacturing value-added

	1980–93		1990–93	
Countries	Weighted	Simple	Weighted	Simple
Policy improvements	2.70	3.59	4.41	3.09
Deterioration in policy	1.64	1.91	–1.67	–3.35
North Africa	3.75	2.2	0.33	1.43
Low-income non-adjusting	2.12	3.17	0.05	1.87

Source: ADB (1995).

Box 11A.1 Ghana: an example of an adjusting country in Africa with policy improvement

Ghana is acknowledged in Africa as the country with the longest record of consistent adjustment in terms of liberalization of the economy and increased reliance on market forces. It has undertaken massive devaluations, from 2.75 cedis to the dollar in 1982 to 920 cedis to the dollar in 1994; removed NTRs; lowered tariffs to a relatively uniform 10–25 per cent range; reduced corporate taxes to 35 per cent and capital gains tax to 5 per cent; removed price controls and subsidies; abolished credit ceilings and guidelines; privatized SOEs; revised its investment code; priorized exports and investment in infrastructure. The private sector was to be the prime mover of the economy; the balance of payments deterioration was to be reversed and public sector management improved. The widespread reforms have had important implications for the manufacturing sector in terms of output, employment, productivity, technology, efficiency, investment, international competitiveness and linkages. The response of the manufacturing sector was initially fairly good, with value-added in manufacturing rising rapidly in 1983, when imported inputs were made available to incumbents that were suffering from substantial excess capacity. The rate of growth was 12.9 per cent in 1984, 24.3 per cent in 1985, 11.0 per cent in 1986 and 10 per cent in 1987. As liberalization spread to imports and excess capacity was used up, however, exposure to world competition led to a steady deceleration of industrial growth. The rate of growth of MVA fell 5.1 per cent in 1989, 1.1 per cent in 1990, 2.6 per cent in 1991 and 1.1 per cent in 1992. Employment in manufacturing fell from a peak of 78 700 in 1987 to 28 000 in 1993. There was a small rise in the number of SMIs, but in low-productivity activities aimed at local markets. FDI did not respond well to the adjustment and most of it is concentrated in primary activities. Domestic private investment has not picked up sufficiently to dynamize the manufacturing sector. As far as exports of manufactures are concerned, the expectation was that they would grow and diversify rapidly under the new incentive regime. But they grew very little, mainly in wood and aluminum products, long-established sectors with firms established in export markets. Large sections of manufacturing have been devastated by import competition, while those that remain and new entrants are in activities with natural protection from imports. Low-technology 'entry-level' manufacturing activities, such as garments and footwear, where Ghana had chances to develop a competitive edge, have been unable to survive the import threat. Cheap labour has not emerged as a source of comparative advantage to Ghanaian industry because the ability to compete internationally in low-technology labour-intensive industries requires a level of productivity and managerial and technical skills that Ghana lacks at present.

Technology development

Lack of technology development is one of the main factors constraining dynamic industrial development and progress in manufacturing competitiveness in the LDCs. Apart from skill development, the development of science, technology and engineering (ST&E) infrastructure and the provision of technical extension services to industry enhances technological capability. Requirements of quality control have changed significantly for LDCs and international trade in manufactured products increasingly requires stringent standards of quality management.[6] A concerted effort by governments is needed to strengthen standards, to provide support to firms to obtain quality certification and give incentives to firms to invest in this process. Not much of this is observed in most LDCs, and SAP packages make no explicit provision in this area.

Most existing technical extension services are largely ineffective in assisting firms to sharpen their competitive edge. LDCs' manufacturing firms do little or no in-house RD&E because of limited skills and resources, that is, heavy constraints on the supply side; there is also limited interaction between the industrial sector and the technological infrastructure to provide technical support for RD&E efforts. RD&E and technological support institutions are fragmented, poorly funded, ill-equipped and have unmotivated staff.

Thus they do not aggressively assist firms to attain competitiveness. The challenge is to restructure and revamp these institutions to enable them to support manufacturing firms in enhancing competitiveness.

Entrepreneurship and SMIs

There is an economic rationale for measures to promote SMI in LDCs. Measures need to be taken to attract informal sector activities to the formal sector in order to strengthen the linkages between the two.[7] This points further to the fact that paucity of entrepreneurial, managerial and technical skills is a major endowment-related constraint for LDC manufacturing competitiveness. The challenge is how various stakeholders can appropriately intervene in the skill market to promote broad-based entrepreneurial (medium-level) cadres. As part of the supply-side measures, existing training centres/institutions may be rationalized, modernized and decentralized towards better meeting client requirements (including rural-based enterprises) and attaining higher quality and efficiency. To enhance manufacturing competitiveness, skill development measures need to be an integral part of the policy package.

LDCs are characterized by weak subsector linkages largely because of the paucity of locally produced intermediate goods. Except for a small number of subcontracting arrangements (for example knitting and shoe manufacturing firms in Lesotho and the garment industry in Bangladesh), forward and backward linkages are limited. Nevertheless, linkages between manufacturing and other sectors (for example agriculture, mining, utilities, construction and trade and services, and transport) seem to be relatively more developed. However, there has been little policy effort to encourage the development of sectoral linkages and firm networks.

Special regimes

Regional cooperation The need for regional cooperation among and within the LDCs cannot be overemphasized, particularly because of their small internal markets. A major reassessment of the viability of small-scale import substitution is underway as is an approach towards regional cooperation and regional trade as a strategy for tapping economies of scale and attaining international competitiveness. Regional cooperation helps to promote intraregional trade through removal of tariff and NTBs to trade and establishment of basic and support transport and communication services infrastructure. The benefits accruing from regional cooperation in setting up support systems for technology and training would greatly relieve the pressure on individual governments and allow diffusion of knowledge and technical experience. Thus economies of scale will be realizable and competitiveness of the manufacturing sector improved within the locality, the region and beyond. However, there is of lack of information on potential networks in the region.

The SADC (Southern African Development Community), for instance, follows a development approach in its areas of cooperation.[8] The SADC can be said to have been successful in mobilizing external financing resources for its projects and programmes. It has also recorded reasonable success in agriculture research, energy, transport and communication. It has not been very successful, however, in mobilizing resources from within the region, which raises the question of the sustainability of the envisaged long-term programmes. A big sensitization programme to attract businessmen and women and industrialists of the region to invest in Southern African countries is under way. South African industrialists are expected to inject more viable investments into the region following the recent entry of South Africa to the SADC.

Trade should be accompanied by investment flows, which should be encouraged by the creation of guarantee mechanisms for cross-border investments. Appropriate investment mechanisms should be put in place, incorporating some elements of a regional policy designed to influence, through incentives, the allocation and location of investment even at the cost of some loss from the full benefits of integration.

Within the broader context of forging interfirm linkages and cooperation arrangements, special attention needs to be paid to promoting investments not only by AIC-based transnational corporations (TNCs) but also among countries in the region and with other developing countries. There is evidence that TNCs from developing countries can share their capabilities with other developing countries in ways not yet effectively utilized.

Adaptations made by developing-country firms with respect to characteristics of raw materials (type, quality and input mix), scale, product quality, product mix, simplicity and factor intensity allow them to produce lower-technology, lower-cost products, which are easier to sell in world markets. Such firms have a higher propensity to form joint ventures with local firms, use more local human resources and raw materials and often transfer down-scaled technologies. Developing-country TNCs often set up overseas enterprises using machinery imported from the advanced industrial countries which required adaptation to local conditions. Developing-country TNCs tend to be skilled in specific technology adaptations and may be in a position to transfer those skills. Such firms also have the ability to design smaller size plants for small market segments. Through these various forms of learning, adapting and modifying imported technologies, developing-country TNCs acquire unique technological capabilities that they can transfer to LDCs.

Various obstacles, however, such as lack of information, inadequate institutional framework and economic and legal barriers inhibit further

South–South technological cooperation. A shift in trade policy in the direction of improved South–South trading infrastructure is needed, along with liberalization of intra-South–South trade restrictions, forging organizational ties to enhance the exploitation of economies of specialization and creating an effective and innovative capacity for more efficient and appropriate processes and products.

Promotion of South–South interfirm linkages and cooperation arrangements should be viewed as complementary to the kinds of benefits which can be obtained from interfirm networks and cooperation arrangements with TNCs from the North and not necessarily as substitutes. The Abuja Declaration on the establishment of the African Economic Community is an encouraging step. Its implementation, however, should involve taking preliminary steps towards establishing the institutional framework to spearhead the development of these kinds of interfirm linkages and cooperation arrangements not only within Africa but between Africa and other regions.

Regional cooperation needs to take on board the experience gained in the past and current shifts in market and technological conditions. At the national level, the policy shifts towards market- and private-sector-driven development need to be reflected in regional cooperation arrangements. At the international level, the globalization process and its formalization through the establishment of the WTO has important implications on designs of regional cooperation.

These developments imply that regional cooperation arrangements need to: (i) proceed on a multi-speed basis with several local points; (ii) be based on the market and engage in public intervention in policy formulation with a view to creating a regional policy environment that will facilitate market-based integration; (iii) allow greater room for private sector involvement consistent with the shift towards private-sector-led development at national level; (iv) permit systematic regional policy coordination to minimize inter-state conflicting policy reforms and harmonize various national policies; (v) cope with the WTO provisions for reduced trade barriers and make regional integration arrangements more open and outward-looking; and (vi) invoke cooperation in production and delivery of services, and promote joint investments and collaboration in technology development efforts with a view to enhancing international competitiveness.

Quality standards Unfolding competition intensified by trade liberalization implies that regional markets can be retained basically on grounds of international competitiveness. Quality is an important element of competitiveness which deserves greater attention in the emerging competitive environment. Opportunities in the regional markets have been tapped on the basis of product quality and appropriateness to the specific conditions in the region. For instance, Zimbabwean firms exporting agricultural machinery had developed products which suited the soils and climatic conditions in the region. Their competitiveness in this case is attributed to many years of continuous investment in searching and learning through their R&D activities. The quality of products that underline firms' competitiveness resulted from initiatives to copy from imports in the initial years and were largely demand-driven. Quality control is a key aspect of S&T infrastructure whose requirements have changed to become more stringent, particularly in the case of manufactured products. The whole of low-income Africa, for instance, has fewer than ten ISO 9000 certificates, while Singapore alone has over 550. The promotion of ISO 9000 quality assurance standards is becoming a major objective of standard bodies in many LDCs, but achievements so far are uneven.

Specialization, competition and economies of scale The degree of specialization at firm level is usually a function of the size and stability of the targeted markets and the supply conditions. A study of 55 exporting firms in Africa found that firms which targeted the export market from the outset tended to be more specialized than those that were primarily catering for the domestic market (Wangwe, 1995a). The study identified the lack of specialization in manufacturing industry of LDC's as one factor which inhibited attainment of international competitiveness. Specialization has a necessary implication for product quality and, hence, competitiveness. The challenge is how these observations can be translated into reality by appropriately utilizing opportunities for specialization and tapping economies of scale through regional cooperation arrangements.

Exports The purchasing power of LDCs, exports and their share in world exports has been declining. This dismal performance implies that reforms in many LDCs have not succeeded in augmenting the competitive supply of the manufacturing sector's tradable goods. The need for export diversification to expand the share of manufactured exports is being emphasized, along with the acknowledgement of the little progress attained so far in establishing viable non-traditional export industries.

The benefits accruing from reform policies, notably exchange rate devaluation and trade policy reforms, have been confined largely to primary products producers (traditional exports). Policy measures during reforms have given little attention to export diversification. Complementary policy measures to address critical supply constraints on the growth of non-traditional exports have not been given adequate attention in the formulation of policy reform programmes.

Factors Affecting the Effectiveness of Policy Implementation

Institutional constraints

Institutions in LDCs must be transformed to be able to assume new roles and face new challenges. A reformed legal framework is needed that can provide investors (domestic and foreign) with an economic and political environment that is stable, predictable and legally enforceable. Since, following economic reforms, government objectives and modalities have changed, implementing institutions need to adapt to the new policy environment. Government bureaucracy has to be changed as do corporate structures that allow companies to meet the challenge of competitive market conditions. Good governance and political stability are instrumental in stimulating investment and production.[9]

Impediments from previous regimes

Many LDCs' problems are deeply embedded in their economic and political structures and attitudes carried over from previous regimes. These were characterized by bureaucracies that hindered the efficient utilization of resources. Institutional reforms cannot be complete without inculcating a new kind of thinking and way of doing things commensurate with the new socioeconomic and political conditions. The behavioural codes of stakeholders must change to fit into the new environment.

Learning by doing in policy reform

Learning by doing in policy making will facilitate a better prioritization of needs and, in the case of industrial development policy, enhance skills and local entrepreneurship in a sustainable way. Many firms in LDCs lack the knowledge, time and resources to identify their technological needs. They often seek assistance to resolve key issues underlying their development. There is little effort to learn systematically from past experiences and from the experience of other countries. This applies to policy making.

Administrative capacity and managerial cadres

The lack of skilled administrative and managerial cadres to implement policy changes effectively is, in the reform of many LDCs, one of the key adverse factors. Skill shortages, including managerial and entrepreneurial deficiencies, are manifested in the lack of adequate response to new investment and trade opportunities. Private sector managers need to be equipped with knowledge and expertise to manage in a new market and technology environment where flexibility and adaptation to new situations are more important now than in the past.

Resistance to change by economic agents

The importance of governance in the context of policies, strategies and instruments of the manufacturing sector arises from a number of considerations. First, the discretionary use of promotional instruments may give rise to rent-seeking behaviour. Second, there is a need to change the thrust of government intervention from regulation to promotion. Third, administrative efficiency, accountability, participation and transparency are of critical importance for the success of policy implementation. The long history of protection and dictatorial regimes, combined with rent-seeking behaviour, is associated with sectors in society which strive to safeguard their interests.

Exogenous constraints

LDCs depend mainly on primary commodities, for which there are generally declining market prospects. Structural impediments increase the exposure of these economies to external shocks and limit their capacity to adjust. The lack of well-developed irrigation systems means that agriculture, the mainstay of LDC economies, is mostly rain-fed and therefore highly vulnerable to variations in weather conditions. In addition, monoculture renders them susceptible to terms of trade shocks transmitted by the world economy.

A major concern for LDCs regarding the outcome of the Uruguay Round is that they will suffer erosion of preferential margins on most of their important exports to major markets, implying a loss in export market shares. Debt also poses a big problem in LDCs since almost no resources are available to invest in appropriate technologies and RD&E activities.

Globalization and information technology

Increasing globalization and intensified competition in world markets is associated not only with liberalization of trade policies but also with major advances in communication, transportation and storage technologies. The organization of production and marketing is now focused on the management of logistics to achieve cost savings in inventory and working capital, and to allow for swift responses to changing consumer demands. The gap between

LDCs and advanced industrial countries in this sphere is already substantial and will broaden as long as LDC investment does not address the problem. Africa, where most of the LDCs are situated, has startlingly low figures of expenditure in computers: in 1988 such spending averaged 0.34 per cent of GDP, compared with 1.4 per cent in Italy and 2.5 per cent in the United States. One reason for this is lack of qualified personnel to man and maintain computer equipment. Firms are reluctant to invest in such a technology if they do not have a reasonable assurance that the equipment can contribute to labour productivity and can be reasonably easily maintained.

Changing approaches to policy formulation

The environment of policy making is undergoing continuous and rapid changes that raise the need to review how individuals and institutions carry out their activities and businesses in a continuous manner. Mechanisms must be devised and capacity built to cope with an increasingly dynamic environment.

There is a demand for more informed, participatory and focused policy making. The domain of economic management has expanded to encompass demands for continued macroeconomic stability, to foster supply response and to enhance efficiency of resource use in a systematic manner. Economic and political liberalization have generated high demands for changes in the way of doing business. Policy making is influenced by five recent developments: (i) transition from controlled and interventionist to more open and market-oriented economies; (ii) passage from closed political regimes run through patron–client networks to more open and liberalized political systems allowing for a more explicit articulation of interests of various groups in society; (iii) change in donor attitude towards promoting recipient's ownership of policies and development strategies to enhance aid effectiveness, broad-based accountability and transparency of policy action; (iv) considerable influence of the media in bringing policy issues into the public domain and enhancing public scrutiny of policy performance, and (v) intensified challenges from changing world market conditions and rapid technological progress.

Democratization and political liberalization are signs of current political changes. There is greater freedom for various groups in society to articulate their positions on diverse issues and hence have an impact on policy making. This has been accentuated by a significant increase in freedom of the press and the media's involvement in bringing policy issues into the public domain thus enhancing public awareness and facilitating greater public scrutiny of policy performance. Policy mistakes are becoming more risky and costly under this increased scrutiny. In this new socio-political environment, policy making is no longer the monopoly of the government. Greater attention is being paid to devising the most appropriate ways for all actors to have an opportunity to present their views on policy proposals and have them incorporated in the policy-making process (see Chapter 10 for the case of Hungary).

An Agenda of Policy Priorities for Industrial Development and Manufacturing Competitiveness

Fostering industrial development and manufacturing competitiveness requires convergent policies to enhance resource mobility by removing distortions stemming from market- and policy-induced failures. Such distortions introduce rigidities and raise the cost of entry into manufacturing activities. One way to reduce entry costs and ensure efficiency in the private sector is to create an enabling environment through a combination of appropriate incentives and competition measures such as better access to credit by SMIs. National initiatives need to be taken to facilitate development and sustenance of the capital and financial markets and upgrade capabilities with competitive potential.

Regional integration is emerging as a viable way to upgrade skills and gain competitiveness through economies of scale in manufacturing. Intraregional trade needs to be promoted through removal of trade barriers, improvements in infrastructure, particularly transportation and communications, and greater opportunities to share knowledge and experience. For instance, some of the S&T training and information infrastructure can be viably extended and accessed on regional bases. Domestic industrial development policy should give priority to regional cooperation as a means to develop manufacturing competitiveness.

SMIs are another important policy priority. Macroeconomic policies have not dealt adequately with the incentive framework for SMIs, with focus on rural areas. Supportive supply-side policies have not been given adequate attention.

Skill building is indispensable to developing technological capabilities and is an integral part of industrial development policy. As such, it should take into account new and emerging technologies, product quality requirements, environmental considerations and demand orientation. These issues are conspicuously absent in much policy discussion in LDCs. In particular, they have not been part of discussions on economic policy reforms. Yet existing manufacturing industries can only become competitive if human resources are improved (ADB, 1995). The design of economic policy reforms should therefore include education and training for capability development as a policy priority. Firm-led training should be an important measure of technological capability enhancement.

Industrial development and sustainable manufacturing competitiveness policies need to address structural constraints such as serious infrastructure deficiencies, with a focus on improving existing physical infrastructure and realizing network economies through enhanced backward and forward industrial linkages and emphasis on measures to resolve transportation and telecommunication bottlenecks.

Development of the S&T infrastructure and provision of technical extension services to industry especially SMIs are also key to enhancing technology development. Acute shortages of experienced trainers of staff and management of industrial training systems is the first bottleneck that governments should address in the context of economic reforms in African LDCs (ADB, 1995). The need to promote investments in technology improvement must also be emphasized, along with mechanisms to facilitate technology diffusion.

In conclusion, industry-level policies have been put in place in many reforming LDCs and notable improvements have been made. Such is not the case with subsector-specific policies and firm-level policies. In particular, policy has failed to stimulate investment in technology (hardware, training, organization). Greater emphasis must be placed on policies to stimulate firm- and subsector-level responses and investments in skills and technology capability building.

NOTES

1. The list includes: Afghanistan, Angola, Bangladesh, Benin, Bhutan, Burkina Faso, Burundi, Cambodia, Cape Verde, Central African Republic, Chad, Comoros, Democratic Republic of the Congo, Djibouti, Equatorial Guinea, Eritrea, Ethiopia, Gambia, Guinea, Guinea–Bissau, Haiti, Kiribati, Laos, Lesotho, Liberia, Madagascar, Malawi, Maldives, Mali, Mauritania, Mozambique, Myanmar, Nepal, Niger, Rwanda, Samoa, Sao Tome and Principe, Sierra Leone, Solomon Islands, Somalia, Sudan, Togo, Tuvalu, Uganda, United Republic of Tanzania, Vanuatu, Yemen and Zambia.
2. Despite their huge potential in mineral resources, the LDCs have not had a satisfactory performance. Mineral development has been inhibited by some structural constraints such as the shortage of foreign exchange to purchase equipment and spare parts for ageing machinery, and a low level of investment. For instance, only a small quantity of the

bauxite produced in Africa is refined to aluminium in Guinea. Surprisingly, the aluminium industry is disjointed and uncoordinated in that country. No country in Africa has vertically integrated aluminium industries – combined capacity for bauxite mining, aluminium refining, aluminium production and metal fabrication is seriously lacking.

3. Such a situation makes the entry or exit of one enterprise highly significant for the sector. The closure of a single textile factory in Central African Republic led to the virtual disappearance of this subsector, which contributed more than 30 per cent to MVA in the early 1980s (UNCTAD, 1995).
4. In a number of LDCs it did work. Real effective exchange rates went up in at least four countries (Cape Verde, the Central African Republic, Rwanda, and Sudan) out of 22 countries examined during 1980–90. There is no clear relationship between real effective exchange rate and export growth, nor a clear association between movements in real exchange rate and MVA growth rate. Countries with mild real depreciation registered better MVA/GDP growth than those with massive real devaluation (UNCTAD, 1995).
5. Most adjusting countries have better results than non–adjusting countries. Within the former group, countries with improved policies performed better during 1990–95 than those with deteriorating policies. On the other hand, growth rates have deteriorated in all countries in the first half of the 1990s, suggesting that the achievements of the 1980–90 period were mainly a reflection of increased utilization of existing capacities rather than enhancement of technological capability to attain and sustain competitiveness. Differences in performance may be attributable to the manner in which reforms have been implemented and the initial conditions facing particular countries.
6. A coherent policy to promote ISO 9000, increasingly important to reach export markets, requires expensive training.
7. Such measures include, on the demand side, encouraging a subcontracting culture and sales promotion and techniques and, on the supply side, measures such as targeting fiscal and financial instruments to promote SMI (access to credit for SMI, tax holidays for new enterprises, simplified tax collection procedures and so on); infrastructure and other support services (technological upgrading, RD&E support); and entrepreneurial and vocational training facilities.
8. The areas of cooperation are, mainly: food security to achieve sustainable food production, infrastructure and services such as railways, roads, civil aviation and ports; industry and trade for greater movement of goods and services by removal of trade barriers; and HRD through measures to support science and technology. Others include: natural resource and environment; energy; social welfare; and diplomacy by advocating peace and harmony in the region.
9. Legal reforms in LDCs constitute another important underpinning for the envisaged improvement in economic performance, especially in inducing investors and entrepreneurs. Without some realistic expectation that the legal system is sufficiently insulated from the locus of political authority, investors will consider the risk of legal conflict exceptionally high.

12. ASEAN and MERCOSUR[1]

INTRODUCTION

Important new departures are taking place in subregional, regional and interregional integration processes in the developing world. State-driven trade integration processes are being superseded by enterprise-led investment, technology diffusion and networking processes as prime movers in the accommodation to new trends in the world economy. Key among these trends are the withdrawal of the state as manager and entrepreneur, the renewed leading role of the innovative enterprise, major technological breakthroughs, the increasing narrowness of domestic markets and the globalization of FDI decisions.

Gains in competitiveness through better allocation of resources, economies of scale and specialization, and technological learning and efficiency increases in ever more competitive markets are the key to the success of regional trade arrangements (RTAs). Static comparative analyses of the trade diversion versus trade creation variety fail to factor in these highly dynamic processes driven by the mobilization of entrepreneurial resources. This chapter examines the experience of the two most vibrant cases of South–South RTA, that is, ASEAN and MERCOSUR in the context of the new challenges brought about by the emerging WTO order.

OLD AND NEW TRENDS IN BUSINESS-DRIVEN ECONOMIC INTEGRATION

The development of intra-developing countries integration and cooperation at the subregional, regional and even interregional levels is being increasingly enterprise-led. This is shown, first, by the expansion of intraregional trade, which has not only increased significantly in value but also in the number of participating enterprises.

Table 12.1 contains figures on trade patterns in ASEAN and MERCOSUR. It also contains a comparison with those for the EU and the

North American Free Trade Agreement (NAFTA). These four blocs, the world's largest, accounted in conjunction for 70 per cent of total world trade in 1994.

Table 12.1 Total and intraregional merchandise trade by trade bloc, 1988, 1990 and 1994

	Trade value (billion US$)			Percentage shares in total merchandise trade			Average annual growth rate	
	1988	1990	1994	1988	1990	1994	1988–90	1990–94
MERCOSUR								
Total	67.6	75.7	124.0	100.00	100.00	100.00	5.82	13.13
Intraregional	5.8	8.4	21.4	8.58	11.10	17.26	20.34	26.34
Rest of the world	61.8	67.3	102.6	91.42	88.90	82.74	4.36	11.12
ASEAN								
Total	206.1	303.4	529.1	100.00	100.00	100.00	21.33	14.92
Intraregional	35.8	52.4	116.2	17.37	17.27	21.96	20.98	22.03
Rest of the world	170.3	251.0	412.9	82.63	82.73	78.04	21.40	13.25
NAFTA								
Total	1050.5	1222.6	1665.0	100.00	100.00	100.00	7.88	8.03
Intraregional	396.4	4799.2	709.4	37.73	39.20	42.61	9.95	10.30
Rest of the world	654.1	743.4	955.6	62.27	60.80	57.39	6.61	6.48
EU								
Total	2135.8	2783.4	3318.0	100.00	100.00	100.00	14.16	4.49
Intraregional	1253.0	1641.2	2144.0	58.67	58.96	64.62	14.45	6.91
Rest of the world	882.8	1142.2	1174.0	41.33	41.04	35.38	13.75	0.69

Sources: UNIDO database based on WTO (UN); *Industrial Statistics Yearbook*, UCLA (various years); UNCTAD, *Commodity Yearbook*, 1994; UN, *Industrial Trade Statistics Yearbook*, 1994; and UCLA, *Statistical Abstract of Latin America*, 1995.

ASEAN and MERCOSUR, although smaller, are much more dynamic players in the world trade arena than either the EU or NAFTA. Over 1990–

94 ASEAN's and MERCOSUR's total trade has been growing over three times as fast as the world average, around three times as fast as the EU's and some 175 per cent as fast as NAFTA's. Second, ASEAN and MERCOSUR are much more open trade blocs than either NAFTA or the EU. The rates of self-sufficiency of the latter are 65 per cent and 43 per cent, respectively, while those for ASEAN and MERCOSUR are just 22 per cent and 17 per cent, respectively. Finally, although intra-bloc trade has been expanding in all the four blocs more rapidly than extra-bloc trade, the latter has been growing at a much faster rate in ASEAN and MERCOSUR than in the others. This means that ASEAN and MERCOSUR, in addition to endorsing the principle of 'open regionalism', are its leading practitioners. The principle that expansion of intra-bloc trade ought not take place at the expense of trade with the rest of the world enjoys full vigour in these two South–South RTAs (SSRTAs).

The trend towards enterprise-driven South–South integration processes is also reflected in investment flows. Enterprises from first-generation newly industrializing economies (that is, Hong Kong Special Administrative Region, Taiwan Province of China, the Republic of Korea, and Singapore, which is also an ASEAN member) are becoming more important investors in the ASEAN countries than Japanese enterprises. Cross-investments in MERCOSUR are also registering unprecedented levels. For example, Chile, associated with MERCOSUR through a free trade agreement (FTA), has invested over US$6 billion since 1991 in Argentina alone.

Business diplomacy, as a complement of government diplomacy, is a third dimension of the same phenomenon. It operates through the impact that systematic actions by businessmen and their organizations have on policies and instruments of economic integration. The role played by the ASEAN Chambers of Commerce and Industry is a good example (see below).

Business-led economic integration is not just accepted by governments, they actually seek it. It has become a key factor in the SSRTAs of the 1990s. This new breed of RTAs, epitomized by ASEAN and MERCOSUR, seeks to release business energies in the context of policies designed to stimulate the opening up of internal markets across the board, foster structural change and enhance the entrepreneurial ability to compete in regional and global markets. They do so by coupling the removal of domestic barriers to the mobility of resources with the phasing out of restrictions on the flow of goods and services across borders and the enactment of regulatory frameworks that ensure evenness of opportunity in business competition.

SSRTAs concluded recently around the world are specifically aimed at enabling and indeed promoting the growing internationalization of local enterprises by inserting them in domestic, subregional, regional, interregional and global production and marketing networks through various forms of strategic alliances with enterprises at home and in associated countries as well as with global players based in advanced industrial countries and in other developing regions (Box 12.1 gives an example of the last). These steps are premised on the tenet that, given the necessary enabling environment, open markets prompt enterprises to achieve international competitiveness by enlarging their scale of operation, focusing on a narrower range of product lines and adopting best international practices.

Box 12.1 Doing business across regions: the case of IMPSA

Industrias Metalúrgicas Pescarmona Sociedad Anónima-(IMPSA) is one of the leading heavy engineering Argentine firms with headquarters in the province of Mendoza, where it was established 90 years ago. With the sluggish and sometimes negative growth of the 1980s, IMPSA had little choice but to try its luck in foreign markets. It did so, and with a great deal of success that owes much to a truly thorough mastery of technological best practices accessed through a wide range of licensed agreements with advanced-country-based technology suppliers and an emphasis on skill building and management proficiency. Initially, it started doing business in South and Central America, and later its presence began to make itself felt elsewhere, particularly in Asia. This note provides some examples of IMPSA's recent activities during this last chapter of its success story as a global competitor now associated with ASEAN partners.

IMPSA Asia was established in 1986 to service Asian regional markets. Its Malaysian operations started in 1988 when Kuala Lumpur was chosen as the regional base. The company started training local engineers and manufacturing container cranes in Lumut for domestic use and for export to Saudi Arabia, China and the United States. It won its first contract in Malaysia in 1990 to manufacture a container crane for the Kuantan Port Authority, with 40 per cent local content. In 1992 it was awarded two more contracts by the Johor Port Authority and Klang

(continued)

Box 12.1 continued

Port Authority. Each of the two ports was supplied with a Malaysian-made Post-Panamax container crane, both cranes being shipped fully erected from Lumut, the first time this was ever done in Malaysia. To date, IMPSA has supplied a total of 22 port cranes throughout Malaysia to Kuantan Port, Johor Port, Klang Port Management, Klang Multi Terminal and Klang Container Terminal. Besides manufacturing and selling port cranes and equipment, IMPSA also manufactures hydro-power equipment. Last August the company signed a memorandum of understanding with Ekran Bhd for the supply of high-tech equipment to be manufactured in Malaysia for the Bakun hydroelectric dam project. Total orders for this project are expected to amount to US$5.5 billion.

IMPSA's headquarters were recently visited by the Indonesian Minister of Industry and Trade, Mr Tunku Ariwibowo, accompanied by the President of the Indonesian and ASEAN Chambers of Industry and Commerce, Mr Aburizal Bakrie. Mr Ariwibowo invited IMPSA to cooperate with Indonesian firms to develop the capital goods industry in Indonesia. Mr Bakrie stated that Argentine capital goods firms can contribute to the development of this industry not just in Indonesia, but also in the other ASEAN member countries searching for partners in this subsector. This strategy was supported by the meeting of ASEAN economic ministers in Jakarta in September, 1996.

An important indication of IMPSA's entrepreneurial drive was its rivalry in the Philippines with four consortia of local and foreign companies to upgrade and expand the National Power Corporation (Napocor) 350 MW Caliraya–Botocan–Kalayaan (CBK) hydro plant in Laguna. The four groups are led by: (i) Lopez-owned First Private Power Corporation (FPPC) in association with Sulzer Hydro of Switzerland, Siemens AG and Australia-based Snowy Mountain Engineering (ii) California Energy International with Swedish–Swiss ABB Sadelmi and Hydro Resources of the United States; (iii) AsiaPower Developments Ltd, which comprises Mitsui and Hitachi Corporation of Japan along with Siemens AG and Maxitron; and (iv) the Alcantara-owned Alsons Power Holding Corporation in tandem with Tomen Corporation of Singapore (which also includes Ansaldo Energia of Italy, Japan-based Electric Power Development Corporation and Kvaerner Bovin of Norway). These groups are expected to challenge the P 1.18

per kWh unsolicited price offer of IMPSA Asia Ltd. IMPSA plans to build two more power plants in Kalayaan with a combined capacity of 300 MW under a build–rehabilitate–operate–transfer scheme with a 25-year cooperation period. The competing consortia had until 25 November 1996 to submit their comparative technical and financial proposals. IMPSA, as unsolicited project proponent, had the right to match the lowest offer within 30 days after the offers are opened. The winning contractor was expected to be Napocor's strategic partner for the power plant once its assets were privatized.

Through joint financing from Argentina, Malaysia, Colombia and Canada, IMPSA also competed in an international tender to supply 14 turbine-generator units for China's massive Three Gorges project. The deadline was 18 December 1996. China was seeking wide international cooperation for the design and manufacture of these huge hydro-generating sets. In this case IMPSA linked up with Westinghouse and Turboatorn. The 14 units will each have a capacity of 700 MW. The combined capacity of 9.800 MW represents more than half the planned 18.200 MW total for the whole project. The contract value could amount to US$1-2 billion. The project has already awarded contracts worth US$1.4 billion.

Malaysian Transport Minister, Mr Datuk Seri, recently dismissed reports of the existence of a government directive that port operators must buy their cranes from IMPSA (M) Sdn Bhd, the Argentine–Malaysian joint venture engaged in gantry cranes manufacturing. IMPSA holds a 40 per cent stake, with the remainder in the hands of various Malaysian partners: Hicom Holdings Bhd (25 per cent), Permodalan Nasional Bhd (10 per cent), Kumpulan Pinang Holdings Bhd (15 per cent) and Emir Equity Sdn Bhd (10 per cent). IMPSA's products are reported often to be chosen by local ports because they are more competitive, with a local content of 70 per cent. Another of IMPSA's strong points is that it fully complies with the stated government policy of effectively transferring technology to local enterprises. IMPSA (M) Sdn Bhd plans to set up a plant which will manufacture, design, and research and develop high-tech capital goods. The company will also market and provide after-sales services to customers.

Source: Company information and Reuters.

Unlike the loose and geographically broad agreements of the past, such as the Latin American Free Trade Agreement (LAFTA) and the Latin American Investment Area (LAIA), the SSRTAs of the 1990s build upon a thinner base in the countries involved. They conform to what, for locational reasons, are called 'natural regions', that is, regions where it is reasonable to expect rapid results from the dismantling of barriers which hinder or prevent reciprocal access of goods and services thanks to lower transaction costs and efficiencies ensuing from physical proximity, and intense mutual trade and investment flows fuelled by readily accessible transport and distribution networks.[2] For enterprises that lack prior international experience, especially SMIs, these regions often serve as a competitive learning and testing ground before becoming exposed to more demanding and distant markets.

The integration agreements of the 1990s are open to world markets and abide by the multilateral rules of the WTO. They are outward-looking because the economies of the participating countries are outward-looking and rest on the premise that openness to international competition in goods and services, given the right framework conditions, is one of the most powerful tools of trade policy and spurs of structural change. In this sense, SSRTAs result from the profound changes in outlook which drive domestic economic policies across regions. Boundaries which once drew domestic and foreign enterprises and capital apart are now melting.

Indeed, one of the prime goals of SSRTAs is to attract investment, particularly that of global competitors, which can contribute with their mastery of technological and management best practices and ability to operate in all markets. Against the dynamic background of major economic policy reform programmes, the key parameter is not necessarily the size of the enterprise or its ownership structure, but its drive and ability to go international and to operate on a regional and global scale.

Economic integration policies are specifically aimed at upgrading enterprises' scale and scope of production and marketing and allowing a freer flow of goods, capital and services within the RTA. Regionalization of productive activity, understood as a springboard for globalization, is one of the key economic rationales underlying current South–South integration processes.

Current economic integration strategy among developing countries rests on two fundamentals: first, consistently competitive domestic environments predicated upon sound macroeconomic premises and active policies congruous with such premises, especially in the areas of skill building, technological innovation, institutional development and social cohesion; and second, an external network of subregional, regional and global covenants conducive to business competition on a level playing field. The latter, in turn, interacts closely with the web of extant intra- and interfirm cross-border production and trading networks. Developing countries' economic progress and their ensuing ability to compete in world markets relies ever more on the new standards of public/private synergy that evolve along these lines.

Private sector participation in economic cooperation and integration has been a subject of particular attention in Latin America and the Caribbean ever since the process of integration began in 1960 with the creation of LAFTA and the Central American Common Market. Since then, businessmen have repeatedly called for greater involvement in national and multinational decisions on regional trade and integration and for financial and technical support to allow them to operate more easily in the enlarged markets. They contended that governments ought to confine themselves to abolishing domestic obstacles to foreign trade, develop the infrastructure and facilitate negotiating forums in which they could act on their mütual understandings and even agree on opening up markets to be later formalized by their respective governments. This perspective is analogous to that found in ASEAN.

Critics were sceptical about these proposals, since instances where the business sector, including subsidiaries of MNCs, leaned towards stifling foreign competition and protecting local markets rather than towards liberalizing them were not at all rare. Such critics believed that, except when led by governments, the results of international trade negotiations would be more limited and less effective in prompting competition and efficiency gains. Indeed, this perception was justified by businessmen who, while adhering to free markets in principle, favoured protectionism in practice, and undermined the legitimacy of much of what they advocated.

In the 1990s, however, the role of the private enterprise sector in international and regional economic relations was strengthened by an evolving consensus between governments and businessmen whereby such a role is now perceived as the key to bridging the gap between what is planned and agreed between governments and what transpires in actual trade and, particularly, investment decisions. This consensus is the result of pro-democratic changes in political systems and economic reform policies geared towards greater market openness and the removal of barriers to competition. Once again, and with due regard to regional specificities, a remarkable degree of interregional convergence is in this respect illustrated by the MERCOSUR and ASEAN experiences.[3]

THE ROLE OF BUSINESS IN SUBREGIONAL AND REGIONAL ECONOMIC INTEGRATION

MERCOSUR

The origin of MERCOSUR can be traced to the decision by the Argentine and Brazilian governments to speed up economic integration on a bilateral basis through the Programme of Integration and Cooperation (PICAB). Paraguay and Uruguay joined in 1990, and a not yet full-fledged customs union was born in 1995. In 1996 the remaining South American members of LAIA began to associate themselves with MERCOSUR through FTAs.

Given the relative economic importance of its member countries and the radical nature of trade liberalization measures adopted over a short period of time (1991–94), MERCOSUR epitomizes the new breed of SSRTA from which valuable lessons can be drawn, complementary to those from ASEAN (see below).

The development of MERCOSUR is premised on a strong political will among the four members and their associates to persist in their internal processes of economic reform and sustain the macroeconomic and sectoral conditions that enable enterprises, regardless of ownership, to compete in domestic markets, and regional and extraregional markets, especially those with the greatest purchasing power and potential.

The Treaty of Asunción, signed in 1991, was initially received with a shade of scepticism by both local and international business communities. Many years of failed attempts at economic integration and economic take-off in Latin America and the Caribbean weighed on the minds of investors. MERCOSUR initially faced a problem of credibility. Only with the success of the Convertibility and Real Plans in Argentina and Brazil, respectively, did MERCOSUR begin to get the desired response from the business community.

The first thing that attracts private sector interest, particularly that of enterprises ready to risk capital and adopt best-practice technological and management standards, is MERCOSUR's 200 million plus consumers. With the development of a network of FTAs between MERCOSUR and third South American countries (Bolivia, Chile and the Andean countries), began with that signed with Chile in July 1996, enterprises within the network face a market of some 300 million consumers.

Businessmen and investors are not being offered a captive market, as in the past. The idea of indefinitely reserved markets for chronic infant industries is alien to MERCOSUR's philosophy. Once of the clearest signals of this is the bloc's relatively low external tariff (12 per cent on average) and its openness to negotiation and trade with the whole world. Exceptions to the tariff liberalization schedule and the elimination of NTBs (which are residual and confined to a few subsectors mostly on grounds of protecting macro-economic stability rather than enterprises) are scheduled to be eliminated for the most part before 2000. In addition, the radical processes of privatization and deregulation under way open up highly dynamic markets to both global players and investors in general, and call for major investments, especially in telecommunications, transport, energy, public services and infrastructure.

MERCOSUR has become a pole of attraction for efficient advanced industrial countries and developing country competitors, such as from the Republic of Korea and Malaysia, which invest and locate facilities with a view to operating in the integrated market. In the automobile industry, for instance, some US$18 billion are earmarked for investment by the key world players up to 2000, especially in Brazil and Argentina. A similar upward trend is observed in subsectors such as food, petrochemicals and chemicals.

Anyone who produces in Argentina, Brazil, Paraguay or Uruguay has WTO-compatible guaranteed preferential access as of 1 January 1995, when the intra-MERCOSUR tariff became zero for the majority of goods contained in the tariff nomenclature and most NTBs were phased out. Even those goods which still levy an intra- MERCOSUR tariff enjoy preferential treatment in respect of those from third countries as part of a transitional list. Brazil's transitional list (that is, that of the largest market) is very narrow.

A firm from any member country can potentially reach many more than 200 million consumers since other world markets have become relatively more open over the last few years. With at least two of them, NAFTA and the EU, MERCOSUR is to reach agreements which will make reciprocal trade and investment flows even freer by the first half of the next decade. In the case of the EU, MERCOSUR concluded a framework agreement on interregional cooperation in December 1995, which is a first step towards a more ambitious political and economic alliance. This will benefit those enterprises able to meet the necessary standards in terms of scale, originality, quality and price.

Admittedly, much remains to be done to bring MERCOSUR to completion. Just as in the EU, eliminating tariffs does not necessarily guarantee free reciprocal market access. Ensuring full unrestricted reciprocal market access will still take some time. Governments still have much to do to turn customs, whose past chief role was to block the movement of goods and services, into facilitators of such a movement. None the less, full reciprocal market opening is being perceived by the economic operators as firm and irreversible.

It will also take time to achieve a level playing field in every subsector. Policy legacies cast shades of unevenness, especially in services and government procurement. Neither are there clear rules on unfair competition. These constraints are being addressed by MERCOSUR organs.

Barring major macroeconomic disturbances, businessmen and investors perceive that MERCOSUR remains firmly on track towards a full-fledged customs union. The signals sent to the markets when the Treaty of Asunción was signed in March 1991 have been effectively pursued. A zero tariff for intra-MERCOSUR trade and a common external tariff were to be promptly attained. Today they are a reality, even though the customs union still needs a few more years before it becomes fully in force in all subsectors.

Many enterprises took such signals at face value early on and positioned themselves to take advantage of the enlarged market. They realized that with democratic stability and current economic reform policies, MERCOSUR's potential for economic growth, largely driven by the profound transformation taking place in Brazil since the enactment of the Real Plan, is huge. They are aware that economic transformation in the subregion will not be linear processes and that ups and downs are inevitable since the hurdles are not trivial. But there is a distinct sense of direction. The expectation is that Argentina and Brazil will join the ranks of the industrialized world early next century, pulling their regional partners along with them.

Some estimates predict that Brazil's foreign trade will triple by the beginning of the next decade. In economic and social infrastructure alone, investments are estimated at some US$150 billion for the next few years. The constitutional reforms of 1995–96 opened the way to a bold process of economic deregulation and privatization, which is already stimulating strong investment in energy, oil, telecommunications, transport and physical infrastructure – just as in Argentina (see Chapter 9 and Annex 9A).

A knock-on effect on the other partner and associated countries is reflected in the growth in reciprocal trade and the development of large multinational infrastructure projects which have now become politically and economically feasible and which will require major investment in the next few years. Major cross-border investment by firms based in Chile (the most successful case of economic reform in the subregion) adds to this positive sum game, as does the imminent association of Bolivia and, further ahead, other neighbouring countries.

Gaining a lasting presence in the Brazilian market, with its size and dynamism, is the biggest challenge faced by enterprises based in the other member countries. The constraints on further access to the Brazilian market lie with the supply rather than with the demand side. If its momentum is maintained, the Brazilian market can serve as powerful engine of structural change for MERCOSUR as a whole. But getting to know the Brazilian market and its internal logic better requires a good deal of effort. Many enterprises, especially SMIs without international experience, can aspire to reach MERCOSUR markets and beyond through alliances with Brazilian enterprises.[4]

There is thus growing awareness that, in line with government efforts to create and sustain an environment favourable to competition at the national and subregional levels, enterprises need to devote substantial effort to attain acceptable levels of international competitiveness. Organizing and learning to compete is thus among the greatest challenges faced by governments, businesses and, in fact, social actors at large in all member countries. The businessmen of the subregion have taken up the challenge. Since the signing of the Treaty of Asunción, there has been intense activity by business to learn about the implications of MERCOSUR and, more importantly, to act upon such knowledge.

Reciprocal business missions to identify business opportunities have multiplied, especially since the entry into force of the customs union, as have official missions by top officials not just of central governments but also at the state, provincial and local levels. Business missions composed of both industrialists and top government officials across regions, particularly between ASEAN and MERCOSUR, have ceased to be a rarity.[5] Examples of such meetings are given in Box 12.2.

Box 12.2 Business diplomacy and information networks

The number of important MERCOSUR business meetings involving foreign investors has multiplied, both abroad and in the region. Only in 1996, hundreds of businessmen and government officials attended MERCOSUR forums organized in Buenos Aires by the Davos World Economic Forum; the meeting on MERCOSUR organized in Brussels by IRELA and the Europe–Argentina Club, under the auspices of the European Commission; the Annual Symposium of IDEA held in Bariloche and the 3rd Southern Cone Marketing and Business Congress, held in Florianopolis. These meetings included presidents and ministers of the MERCOSUR countries.

(continued)

Box 12.2 continued

Other business promotion meetings, on the investors' forum model, are held periodically under multinational programmes especially aimed at promoting business cooperation, such as the Bolivar Programme under the auspices of the Inter-American Development Bank (which held its Second Latin American Enterprise Forum in Arequipa, Peru in December 1996), or by national governmental, mixed and private institutions which operate on a bilateral level and whose purpose is to promote the internationalization of SMEs in MERCOSUR and globally, such as the Brazilian Service to Support Micro and Small Enterprises (SEBRAE). In October 1996, SEBRAE, which runs bilateral programmes with other MERCOSUR countries, organized a new version, the third, of Mercotrade in Río de Janeiro, with the participation of 1350 enterprises from MERCOSUR and seven other countries. The estimated business resulting from the forum amounts to some US$215 million.

Courses and seminars, postgraduate and multinational programmes, such as the special programme developed by the Argentine Business University with the Lutheran University of Brazil and the University of the South of Santa Catarina, on business management in MERCOSUR, round tables and workshops, with integration and MERCOSUR as the main theme, have multiplied throughout MERCOSUR. There are now thousands of professional people and enterprise directors who have participated in a whole range of events aimed at explaining MERCOSUR and providing information on how to operate across borders and, above all, how to take advantage of the business opportunities lying ahead. The online information networks and the wealth of information on MERCOSUR and its opportunities in the general and specialized domestic and international press, as reflected in a survey published in *The Economist* magazine of 12 October 1996, have opened access to economic and political information which businessmen, especially in SMEs, and those in the interior of their respective countries, need to operate in the integrated economic area.

In turn, chambers of commerce and other business organizations are getting their act together to participate intensively in the MERCOSUR process, at both national level and in the region as a whole. Many sectoral and top business institutions provide services to their associates in relation to MERCOSUR. In 1991 the MERCOSUR Industrial Council was set up by the principal industrial organizations in the four countries, and this is now a significant forum for dealing with economic integration issues from the standpoint of the industrial sector, although it has not yet achieved the position of influence occupied by the chambers of commerce and industry in ASEAN. In other cases, investors of one member country in another have organized means of grass-roots institutionalization and mutual cooperation in order to defend their interests and provide each other with mutual support. The best-known example is the Brazil Group which operates in Argentina with a membership of 200 Brazilian enterprises operating in the country. There is also the Cordillera Group, composed of Chilean and Argentine enterprises. The process of setting up the Argentine Group by Argentine businessmen operating or planning to operate in Brazil has just begun. All this is in addition to the traditional role fulfilled by bilateral chambers of commerce under the corresponding bilateral channels.

In the case of both financial institutions and consultancy firms, they are already positioning themselves with the integrated market in sight. A recent example is the Itau Bank which is opening a major network of branches in Argentina. It should be pointed out that international experience of services that can be provided by business chambers to facilitate the internationalization of SMEs, and their participation in the integration process, is wide-ranging. One of the most interesting to look at is the Confederation of Chambers of Commerce and Industry of Asia and the Pacific.

These initiatives reflect the interest of enterprises of all sorts, irrespective of size and ownership, in participating actively in MERCOSUR's future development. They cut across the whole gamut of economic activities. There is also awareness that SMIs will pose the greatest requirements for technical, information and other forms of support needed to enable them to adjust and take advantage of the enlarged market as well as to join business alliances to enter it, along with world markets. The industrial networks developed in Europe, especially in Italy, and in East Asia, which pool technological, financial, management and distribution services are among the most suitable mechanisms to help SMIs, and a rich source of experience for MERCOSUR.

ASEAN

Ever since ASEAN was founded in 1967 by Indonesia, Malaysia, the Philippines, Singapore and Thailand, and later joined by Brunei and Viet Nam, the original member countries (except the Philippines) have enjoyed sustained real GDP growth rates of over 6 per cent per year and real per capita GDP growth rates of over 4 per cent per year. As of the late 1980s, ASEAN growth rates have overtaken those of first-generation newly industrializing economies to become the fastest in the world.

Domestic political stability and economic prosperity of the individual member nations has fuelled the success of the regional grouping. In the 1990s, after two decades of thriving growth, progress of intra-ASEAN linkages accelerated, driven by private sector entrepreneurship and private/public sector cooperation rather than by government-to-government policies.

Export processing zones, also called free trade zones (FTZs) or 'bonded' factory sites, played a key role in the development of export orientation in ASEAN – which took place along with a number of import substitution policies. A tradition of largely unrestricted FDI operations originating in such zones gradually pervaded most of the host economies. Emphasis on FDI and export orientation in the ASEAN countries did not take place at the expense of, but were instrumental in, promoting national industrialization as the key growth engine.

Cross-border trade between FTZs contributed importantly to the growth of intraregional trade and is at the root of ASEAN growth polygons (see below). Much of such trade is intra-industry and takes place between subsidiaries of MNCs.

The uniqueness of ASEAN lies in the fact that it is a private-investment-driven rather than a trade-driven grouping. Trade follows cross-border investment and technology transfer, rather than the other way round. Its genuine open regionalism is epitomized by the fact that the ASEAN countries' unilateral tariff and NTB reductions of the 1980s and early 1990s applied to all trading partners, not just to fellow ASEAN members.

ASEAN's free trade area (ASEAN FTA) was formed in 1992 with a 15-year schedule as of 1 January 1993. A common effective preferential tariff (CEPT) scheme for manufactured products with at least 40 per cent ASEAN-wide content was established. The original goal was to reduce tariffs to up to 20 per cent in five to eight years, and to up to 5 per cent by 1 January, 2008. NTBs were also to be phased out. The Fifth ASEAN Summit gave a further boost to the ASEAN FTA by agreeing to reach full implementation by 2003. Some member nations have unilaterally broadened the range of products with tariffs to be set at up to 5 per cent by 2000. The ASEAN Secretariat expects most intra-ASEAN traded items to be essentially liberalized by that year, that is, three years in advance of the WTO's deadline for developing countries. In addition, the implementation of the Green Lane Systems started on 1 January 1996 will expedite the clearance of CEPT products through all ASEAN borders.

ASEAN's 1995 Summit agreed to establish the ASEAN Investment Area (AIA). AIA is designed to promote FDI inflows by transforming ASEAN into a single investment region through simpler and more transparent and harmonized codes and procedures. The steps to be taken in this direction are a comprehensive survey of FDI in the area, an expert group meeting on the promotion of FDI in AIA, a round table on the formulation of a common strategic plan for the promotion of FDI in AIA and a training course for ASEAN policy makers in the FDI field.

ASEAN's private sector embraces a dynamic mix of local and foreign, Chinese and indigenous enterprises which interact cooperatively as well as competitively with each other and with SOEs. Flexible adaptive strategies, such as alliance and coalition building, consultation, negotiation, bargaining and compromise are key ingredients of such interaction.

Flexibility and pragmatism are key to ASEAN's strategy, by allowing individual countries to opt out of particular cooperation schemes as they choose, thus proceeding on a lowest common denominator path to attain group-wide consensus. This is aptly conveyed by the '$x + y = 6$' formula put forward by former Singapore Prime Minister Lee Kuan Yew. It means that a common ASEAN policy or position could be reached despite the fact that some of the six member countries may not agree to participate, so long as they do not object.

ASEAN has instituted various mechanisms to further production specialization at the subregional level. They include the ASEAN Industrial Projects (AIPs), Industrial Complementation (AIC) and Industrial Joint Venture (AIJV) schemes.

AIPs are large-scale, capital-intensive public/private sector projects in which all the member countries hold equity shares and whose output enjoys tariff preferences within the subregion. Examples include urea plants in Indonesia and Malaysia. Through the AIC scheme preferential tariffs are granted to specific manufactures traded among private firms within the subregion (see Figure 12.1). It has been applied to automotive parts and components under a brand-to-brand complementation scheme joined by

Malaysia, Thailand and the Philippines. Japanese auto companies and their local partners with plants in various ASEAN countries have benefited from this scheme in their parts and components exchanges. The AIJVs seek to promote relatively small-scale private sector projects by granting 90 per cent tariff preferences if formed by partners from two or more ASEAN countries (auto components and processed foods are examples). The AIJVs are guaranteed against expropriation and nationalisation. Foreign investors are allowed to hold up to 60 per cent of equity or more under certain conditions.

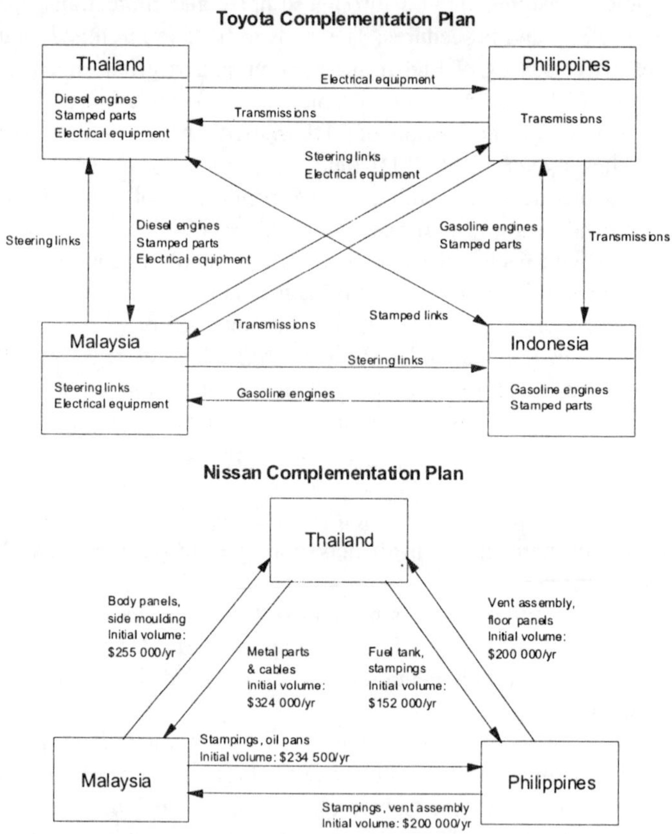

Source: Rushton (1990)

Figure 12.1 ASEAN automobile complementation scheme

The initiative of the ASEAN Chambers of Commerce and Industry (ASEAN CCI) has been key in the enactment of the AIC and AIJV programmes. ASEAN CCI comprises the national homologues in all ASEAN countries. Their membership consists mostly, but not exclusively, of local firms. The ASEAN CCI sponsors various working groups (on industrial cooperation; trade; food, agriculture and forestry; and transport and communications); Regional Industry and Commodity Clubs and National Industry and Commodity Clubs. It has also set up joint business councils with the private sector in ASEAN's major trading partners. The ASEAN CCI Secretariat is rotative and sponsors a research institute (see Figure 12.2).

The ASEAN CCI is actively involved in the formulation of cooperation programmes with private sector participation. Thus, for instance, the ASEAN Regional Industry Clubs have contributed to the development of the AIC scheme. The Industry Clubs, which span a broad cross-section of industry, perform as the regional counterpart of national industry associations involved in information gathering and sharing, issuing of policy proposals and policy dialogue with governments. Thus, for example, the ASEAN CCI and the ASEAN Automotive Federation worked with the ASEAN Committee on Industry, Minerals and Energy (COIME) to set up the AIC scheme for the automobile industry.

Although these formal ASEAN-wide schemes by no means exhaust the scope for intraregional private and private/public sector cooperation, the ASEAN CCI and its Regional Industry Clubs are effective means of facilitating cross-border business contacts and bringing business opportunities to fruition by sharing expertise and other resources. The ASEAN CCI has fully supported AFTA and advised governments on its implementation. It has also advocated the prompt admission of new members (Viet Nam, Cambodia, the Lao People's Democratic Republic and Myanmar), the promotion of growth polygons and links with other RTAs.

With noticeable national variations, the ASEAN countries as a whole tell a success story about fulfilling a great deal of the transition from a resource-based to an efficient industrial powerhouse within a short period of time. These countries have undergone a remarkable pace of structural transformation. This, however, can hardly be understood as a set of purely domestic phenomena (see below).

ASEAN's subregional growth areas (also called 'growth triangles' or 'polygons') are trans-border economic zones which comprise contiguous provinces or states of the member countries. They seek local development by promoting the intraregional flow of resources rather than just trade in goods

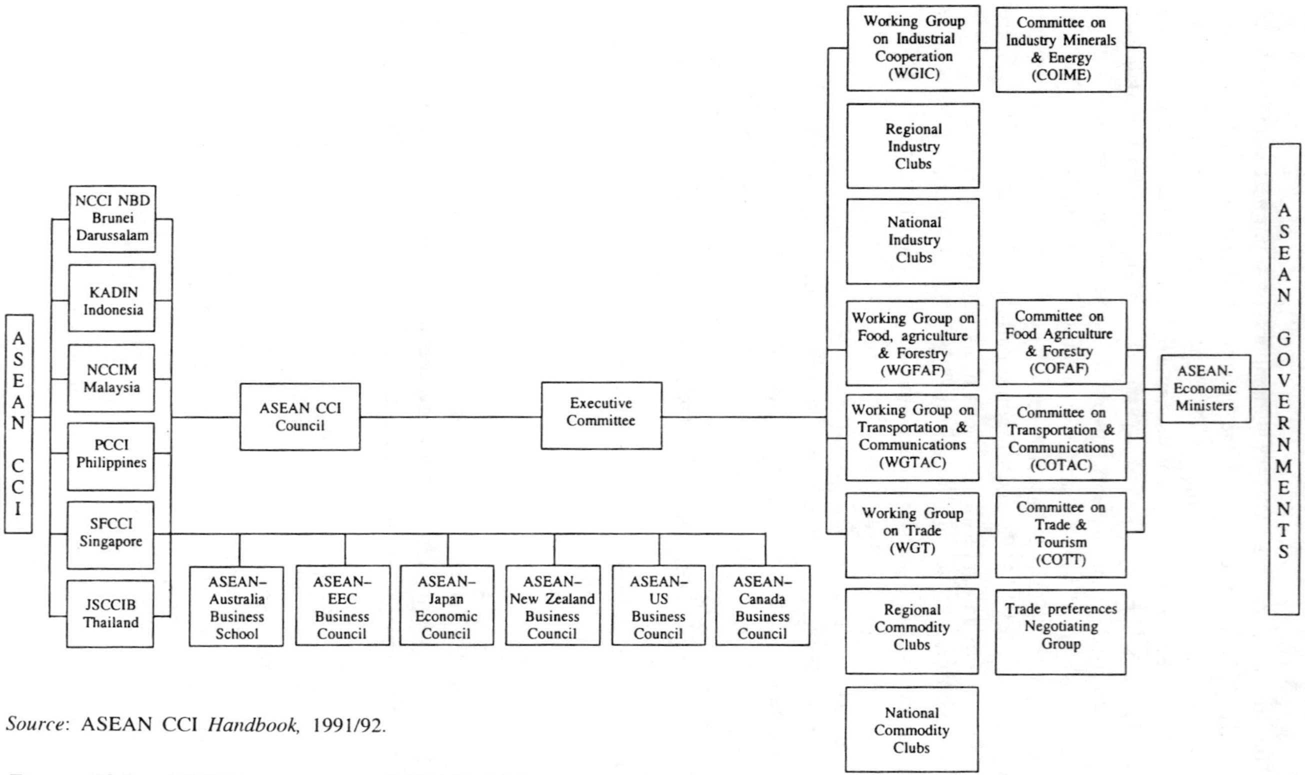

Source: ASEAN CCI *Handbook*, 1991/92.

Figure 12.2 ASEAN government/ASEAN CCI interactions

and services. They are not discriminatory towards the rest of the world. Governments play a facilitatory/catalytic role through joint infrastructure development projects, coordinating investment policies and sponsoring business missions to third countries. Private initiative does the rest. The key objective of these growth areas is the exploitation of actual or potential resource complementarities to foster growth and efficiency as well as competitiveness on a global scale. Private investors find in them the necessary framework conditions to embark upon projects and networks of projects anchored on matching resource endowments across borders, involving the movement of capital, labour, skills, technology and information. Because these projects take advantage of externalities that spill across national boundaries, the market alone fails to guide the seizing of the ensuing opportunities. What matters most in the growth areas is the expansion of resources and the growth of future output rather than static efficiency gains from using existing resources. This is attained by means of specialization and relocation of economic activity, leading to intra-industry trade, as a key to improving the efficiency in resource use and promote growth.

The first and most successful subregional area so far is the Indonesia–Malaysia–Singapore growth triangle (IMS GT), which comprises the whole of Singapore, the southern part of the Malaysian state of Johor, and the islands of the Riau Province of Indonesia (its coverage is now being extended to the Malaysian states of Malacca, Negri Sembilan and Pahang and Indonesia's Western Sumatra). IMS GT matches Johor's and Riau's cheaper land and labour with Singapore's technical and managerial skills, capital, technology and transportation and communications infrastructure to attract ASEAN and non-ASEAN investment to all three locations (see Tables 12.2 and 12.3).

The IMS GT contains Indonesia's Batam FTZ which was first developed in 1987 to compete with Singapore as an oil services trans-shipment port, export location and tourism centre, but it actually took off when it became integrated into the IMS GT two years later. The IMS GT contains, *inter alia*, a number of industrial parks, some high-tech facilities, an industrial training institute and technical and financial support services. Most of the economic activity in the triangle owes to the private sector and comprises manufacturing, processing, property development and tourism. Singapore has relocated both multinational and locally owned labour-intensive manufacturing operations into the triangle, particularly in Johor, in order to regain export competitiveness. With growing shortages of land and labour in Johor itself, relatively underdeveloped Riau became the next frontier within the triangle.

Table 12.2 Comparative advantages in the IMS GT

Business or activity	*Singapore*	*Johor/Riau*
Electronics	Major regional base for manufacturing; major international procurement office	Lower labour/land costs for labour and land-intensive assembly operations
Oil	Refining/petrochemical processing, trading, storage and distribution	Riau islands (e.g. Karimun Island) offers environmentally isolated space for oil storage
Maritime services	Full range of ship-building, repair and maintenance activities	Johor and Riau islands (e.g. Singkep) offer sites for shipbuilding/repair
Telecommunications and business services	World-class information technology infrastructure and wide range of business services; operational headquarters of many large MNCs	Many manufacturing, marketing, procurement and technical support activities by MNCs requiring coordination
Logistics and distribution	Excellent telecommunication/transportation facilities and logistics management services	Wide range of export manufactures requiring transportation and logistics management support R&D
R&D	Large pool of R&D scientists and engineers; R&D manpower training facilities and supporting infrastructure	MNC products requiring applied R&D and design for local market adaptations; MNC operations requiring process improvement R&D
Tourism	Excellent air travel gateway for tourists; emerging regional sea-cruise centre; cosmopolitan shopping centre; multicultural city	Abundant leisure resources such as beach resorts, golf courses, etc.; cultural diversity
Agribusiness	Food processing technology and biotechnology R&D capability	Abundant land resources for agriculture and animal husbandry

Source: Wong (1992).

Table 12.3 Johor (Malaysia): approved manufacturing projects, 1981–90

1981	1981	1982	1983	1984	1985	1986	1987	1988	1989	1990[a]	Total
Number of approvals (%)											
Johor	69.0	79.0	66.0	129.0	102.0	80.0	82.0	183.0	208.0	204.0	1 202.0
Malaysia	596.0	468.0	490.0	749.0	625.0	447.0	333.0	732.0	784.0	906.0	6 130.0
Johor share	11.6	16.9	13.5	17.2	16.3	17.9	24.6	25.0	26.4	22.5	19.6
Potential employment	6 028.0	5 436.0	7 337.0	12 920.0	7 450.0	8 910.0	12 829.0	27 815.0	36 226.0	28 413.0	153 364.0
Proposed paid-up capital (M$ million)[b]	157.1	152.3	118.7	161.5	292.7	184.7	265.0	728.0	1 004.6	841.7	3 906.3
Malaysian equity (M$ million)	81.6	100.2	86.5	90.5	242.2	82.6	65.3	170.4	193.4	182.8	1 295.5
Bumiputra	34.88	59.6	47.6	43.3	184.2	52.9	27.6	69.5	74.3	91.0	684.8
Non-Bumiputra	46.8	40.6	38.9	47.2	58.0	29.77	37.7	100.9	119.1	91.8	610.7
Foreign equity (M$ million)	75.5	52.1	32.2	71.0	50.5	102.1	199.7	557.6	811.2	658.9	2 610.8
Loans (M$ million)	260.3	238.9	184.1	295.8	534.8	255.2	438.0	1 101.4	1 697.9	1 248.3	6 254.7
Total proposed capital investment (M$ million)[c]	417.4	391.2	302.8	457.3	827.5	439.9	703.0	1 829.4	2 702.5	2 090.0	10 161.0

Notes: [a]January to December.
[b]Proposed paid-up capital = Malaysian equity + foreign equity.
[c]Total proposed capital = proposed paid-up capital + loan.

Source: Malaysian Industrial Development Authority.

Real-estate projects and tourism account for a good share of foreign investment in Batam (mostly from Singapore). Singapore–Johor and Singapore–Riau are the strongest sides of the triangle, while Johor–Riau side is the weakest.

The Brunei Darussalam–Indonesia–Malaysia–Philippines Growth Area (BIMP GA), also premised on the above-stated principles, seeks to accelerate economic growth in areas which are relatively disadvantaged *vis-á-vis* other regions of the countries involved. It is also being expanded to include seven additional provinces in Indonesia. Over the last two years 13 working groups have been established in BIMP GA to implement cooperative initiatives aimed at facilitating the movement of people and resources. BIMPGA is also setting up a growth fund (initial capitalization US$ 300 million) to finance infrastructure and commercial projects in the region. The Asian Development Bank has just completed a report which identifies some 150 policy, programme and project initiatives for public and private sector implementation in BIMP GA.

To sum up, ASEAN's subregional economic zones are a unique bottom–up and decentralized form of regional cooperation which evolved from the experience with EPZs, industrial and technology parks and other subnational zones. All of them contain industrial and technology parks and EPZs. It is worth noting that Article 4 of ASEAN's charter explicitly refers to subregional arrangements with non-member countries. Examples are the China–Singapore Suzhou Industrial Park established in the town of Suzhou in Jiangsu Province and the India–Singapore technology park in Bangalore, in both cases set up with important private sector involvement.

Domestic conditions have played a key role in the success story of the ASEAN countries. These began to pursue export-oriented strategies earlier than the MERCOSUR countries. At the same time, they exhibited a high degree of resource mobility and flexibility in resource allocation. Had these domestic conditions been absent, the story would be different.

Yet, beyond domestic factors lies the fact that the ASEAN countries belong to what might be called a 'strategic group' of countries, whose core members are Japan and the first-generation newly industrializing economies, China and Viet Nam. In conjunction, they are part of a highly informal and yet well-structured, cross-border regional economic integration process. This process has been aptly conceptualized (originally by K. Akamatsu) in the metaphor of the 'flying geese pattern'. It operates by means of highly interdependent 'billiard-ball-style' type shifts in trade and industry. ASEAN's private-enterprise- and investment-driven regional integration process can only be properly grasped as part and parcel of a broader pattern, featuring Japan as 'lead goose', first-generation newly industrializing economies in second line, the ASEAN-4 (Indonesia, Malaysia, the Philippines and Thailand) in third line, Viet Nam in fourth line, and India and Pakistan further behind. China's place in this sequence is not clear due to its leapfrogging in some areas, its muscle as a second-rank trade power and the size of its domestic market, all of which endow it with a dynamics of its own.

As prosperity and trade surpluses bring higher wages, labour shortages and stronger currencies, higher relative domestic production costs incite firms from the relatively most advanced countries to relocate labour-intensive manufactures in neighbouring countries. As these acquire manufacturing experience, they do not just become more export-competitive in consumer goods, but also start broadening and deepening their manufacturing base. As the pool of cheap labour becomes exhausted, and upward pressures on domestic wages ensue, they begin to lose competitive edge in simple, labour-intensive manufactures and start going up the skill- and technology-intensity ladder towards more sophisticated manufactures so that new countries replace them as most advantageous locations for producing labour-intensive, low-skill manufactures.

Relatively less developed countries gradually catch up with the more advanced ones according to shifting comparative advantages. Both the catching-up and the caught-up countries adjust flexibly in such a way that the whole region moves along a pattern of dynamic equilibrium growth. On these lines, first-generation newly industrializing economies shift towards more technology- and skill-intensive manufacturing exports while the ASEAN countries move from primary to labour-intensive products. In fact, the process is so rapid that the ASEAN countries are already overcoming the labour-intensive stage and giving increasing emphasis to more skill- and technology-intensive manufacturing. Private enterprises, particularly MNCs based in the more advanced countries, are the key agents of this comparative advantage recycling process. It goes without saying that the metaphor refers to 'stylized' facts, that is, it is not designed to provide a full account of all frictions or exceptions that occur along the way (see below).

This process can be illustrated by the case of the electronics subsector (see Table 12.4). Owing to the appreciation of the yen, production of higher-end electronic products, like computer peripherals, has lost its cost advantage in Japan and has thus shifted to the first generation newly industrializing economies. Production of standardized products such as large colour TV sets and air conditioners has shifted to the more advanced ASEAN countries, such as

Table 12.4 'Billiard-ball-style' shifts in ASEAN (electrical and electronics industry)

Major product	*What remains in Japan*	*What moves out of Japan*	*What moves out of Singapore*
Audio-visual products	Colour TV (digital, high-definition) Wide-screen TV S-VHS LD-player High-end hi-fi equipment	Conventional colour TV, including large-size conventional types VCR (standardized, hi-fi) Audio-visual products for export (high-priced, standardized)	Colour TV (small size) Audio-visual products (lower-priced)
Computer electronics	Display for computer (17/21-inch) Customized semiconductor	Display for computer (14/15-inch) Computer peripherals 16 MDRAM (mega-DRAM) 3.5 HDD (hard-disk drive) Semiconductor (integrated production)	Assembly of computers FDD (floppy disk drive)
Home electronics	Fully microcomputer-controlled automatic washing machine	Air conditioner (for export) Ceiling light	Twin-tub washing machine Compressor
Electronic devices	Superconductivity Capacitors (e.g. for TV)	Cathode-ray tube Electronic devices/parts, coil, transformer, filter, resonator, spindle-motor, etc.) Compressor for refrigerator	Battery Electrical parts Capacitor (standard type) Coil (standard type)
Telecommunication equipment	Facsimile (office use)	Cellular phone (standard type) Facsimile (standardized models)	

Source: Nomura Research Institute.

Malaysia. Finally, production of lower-end products, for example cassette recorders, has shifted from the NIEs and the more advanced ASEAN countries to Indonesia and China. While subsidiaries of MNCs located in ASEAN countries are mainly export-oriented, their counterparts in China are more geared towards the domestic market. Within ASEAN, lower-priced products are now being transferred from Singapore and Malaysia to Indonesia and the Philippines, while capacity for middle-priced products so far produced in Japan are being relocated in Singapore and Malaysia. These shifts largely occur across borders but within companies. Strategies differ between set manufacturers and parts and components manufacturers. Large set manufacturers place emphasis on the skill and technology levels as well as on access to local sources of parts and components. For these producers, particularly those relatively lower-priced, availability of cheap labour is crucial, along with regional market size. In the case of semiconductors, most assembly is outsourced, while fabrication remains in the most advanced countries (that is, in Japan and the Republic of Korea).

Integrated manufacturing of semiconductors has already started being outsourced to ASEAN, especially Malaysia, *in toto*. At the same time, ASEAN is substituting first-generation newly industrializing economies as suppliers of standardized, low-skill intensive electronic products, while the latter (and Japan *a fortiori*) focus on more technology-intensive lines such as liquid crystal displays and precision parts. Ten years after the major relocation of facilities by Japanese firms to ASEAN began, a significant local base of supporting industries has developed including plastic and packing materials and metal parts, which is not the case in other subsectors (see below). Sophisticated materials continue to be produced by Japanese subsidiaries in ASEAN.

As the regional market for parts and components develops and supplies from Japan and first-generation newly industrializing economies continue at a price disadvantage, the scope for expanding R&D activities, especially in Singapore and Malaysia, correspondingly broadens. The latter have a better supply of technical and engineering skills than their ASEAN partners. This explains their higher reliance on domestic parts and components suppliers (some 80–90 per cent of parts and components of standardized audio-visual products are locally produced in Malaysia and Singapore after relocation from Japan; most electronic parts and components required in Indonesia are imported from Malaysia and Singapore). In contrast, key elements such as laser pick-ups for CD players and special plastic materials are still imported from Japan. They amount to some 10 per cent of the total value for ASEAN-made electronic products. Yet, as FDI inflows from Japan and other advanced countries continue, there are increasing instances in which the above-described hierarchical pattern breaks down. For example, Sony produces cathode ray tubes in Singapore and assembles them in Malaysia, while Toshiba manufactures them in Thailand and assembles the colour TVs in Singapore.

As ever more FDI in Asia shifts from production for exports to third markets such as NAFTA and the EU to production for final consumption within Asia, FDI interdependence and division of labour among Asian countries is on the rise.

The north American share in Japanese manufacturing FDI went from two-thirds in 1988 to just over one-third in 1993. Over the same period, Asia's share went from just over one seventh to one third, that is, it has already become as important as that in North America. The share of intraregional FDI in Asia rose from about 36 per cent of total FDI in 1992 to almost 52 per cent in 1993. ASEAN countries have become the most important recipients of intra-Asian FDI, although they are being overtaken by China. This trend has been coupled with the above-mentioned substantial increase in intra-Asian FDI, particularly that from first-generation newly industrializing economies in ASEAN countries, which now has surpassed in value that of Japan itself (some two-thirds of intra-Asian FDI now comes from first-generation newly industrializing economies). Particularly in electronics and electrical machinery, increasing production costs triggered by higher wages, labour shortages and currency appreciation, have led Japan and the NIEs to locate new capacity in the ASEAN countries. And, along the way, the latter are also raising the local content ratio of parts and components production (see Table 12.5).

Successful technology transfers by Japanese electronic firms to ASEAN countries since the 1980s and the latter's readiness to create a conducive environment for inward FDI through sound macroeconomic management, liberalization of FDI codes and strong investment in infrastructure and technological upgrading has fuelled the working of the flying geese pattern. The rapid transformation of, and ensuing competitive threat posed by, the ASEAN countries has, in turn, prompted first-generation newly industrializing economies such as Taiwan Province and the Republic of Korea to speed up efforts to catch up with Japan in high technology areas while relying on the ASEAN countries as a production base for labour-intensive manufactures.

The subsequent process of cross-border outsourcing takes place largely within firms. These often simultaneously diversify across subsectors at home

Table 12.5 Local content ratios in ASEAN

Product	Place of production	Local content ratio (%)[a]
Mini/midi hi-fi stereo (for export)	Singapore/Malaysia	Over 90
VCR (standard model)	Malaysia (including Singapore)	Around 80
CD radio-cassette recorder	Malaysia (including Singapore)	Around 90
Radio-cassette recorder (standard model)	Malaysia	Almost 100
Radio-cassette recorder (standard model for export)	Indonesia	50
Mini hi-fi stereo	Indonesia	Around 40
Colour TV	Malaysia	50–60
	ASEAN	80–90
Air conditioner	Malaysia	Around 80
	ASEAN	Around 90
Electronic parts[b]	Singapore/Malaysia	50–60
	ASEAN	70–80

Notes: [a]This ratio is based on the sum of locally available parts and components in the region (in value terms).
[b]Computer peripherals, batteries, resistors, transformers, coils, motors.

Source: Surveys by the Nomura Research Institute.

and undertake outward FDI in the same sectors, which leads to a strong expansion of intra-firm trade. Underlying this trade, there is an intense cross-border movement of factors of production, including management and production know-how, skills, capital and technology. The specific mix of these resource transfers is determined by the rate of return that the firms expect to get upon relocating overseas.

Rapid long-term growth in Asia (averaging 7–8 per cent per year in the newly industrializing economies plus China), matched with much lower expansion in NAFTA and EU countries, is abating the dynamism of exports to these countries and replacing it by production aimed at the Asian markets themselves as a growth engine. This circumstance, coupled with FDI flows that are still largely influenced by trade restrictions rather than by resource endowment and costs, as is still the case in ASEAN automobiles and high-market consumer electronics in China, limits the scope of the flying geese paradigm.

The ASEAN countries still have a good way to go before joining the ranks of advanced industrial countries. In recent years, massive FDI inflows from Japan and first-generation newly industrializing economies have spurred structural change. One key reason for this is that such FDI has focused on manufacturing rather than on natural resources. Thailand's trade structure, today similar to that of Taiwan Province in the late 1960s, is already reaching the 'young NIE' stage and, before the 1997 crisis, was expected to become a 'mature NIE' before 2000. Malaysia and the Philippines, unlike oil-dependent Indonesia, were expected to reach the 'young NIE' stage by the turn of the century (see Figure 12.3).

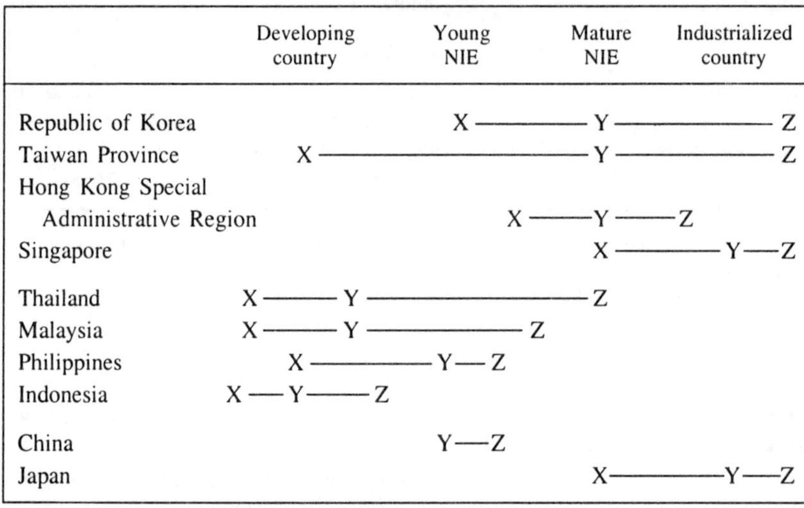

Note: X = 1965; Y = 1992; Z = 2000 (forecast).
Source: Nomura Research Institute

Figure 12.3 Asian countries' stylized stages of trade structure

Coordinating the cross-border flows of labour is a key issue in the context of Asian regional cooperation. Such flows have accelerated over recent years. The ASEAN countries are both sources and recipients of migrant labour (the Philippines is the only large net emigration country within the grouping).

WTO 2000: A REGIONAL AND SECTORAL COMPARATIVE PERSPECTIVE

The Challenge

The diverse approaches countries are taking in the countdown towards 1 January 2000, when the period of transition to comply with WTO TRIMs is due, offer insights into disparities in microeconomic policy. No clear consensus existed before 1997 as to what precisely is the meaning of such a transitional period. The disruptions provoked by the crisis have made things even more blurred.

From a sectoral perspective, two distinct approaches were apparent. While some countries were using the transition period as a time of progressive convergence towards achieving TRIMs standards, others saw it as a race against time offering a chance to employ policy instruments and practices that, as of 2000, or 2002 for LDCs, will be sanctioned as bad practice. The latter were doing so in order to place themselves in the best possible position in terms of technological learning and manufacturing competitiveness in selected activities they consider crucial, as well as in the expectation of being able to postpone the deadline for compliance by resorting to exception mechanisms.[6] This alternative became all the more likely with the crisis.

The recent escalation of cases before the WTO, coupled with their regional and sectoral biases, appears to relate to this diversity of approaches as well as to the shift towards a rule-based international trade system. Between 1 January 1995 and 18 September 1996, 54 disputes concerning 34 regulations were brought before the WTO, compared with 196 disputes during the 47 years of the GATT's existence. This 457 per cent increase in the monthly average is symptomatic of a heightened awareness of the need for reciprocal monitoring, as much as of a hectic accommodation to the new international economic order. Table 12.6 gives an idea of the geographical distribution of recent cases brought before the WTO by advanced industrial countries regarding developing countries' practices.

Of 25 disputes submitted to the WTO involving Asian developing countries, either as plaintiffs or as respondents, 6 relate to the automobile industry while the remaining 19 are spread throughout ten different subsectors. As one of the sectors most exposed to trade disputes, this industry probably best illustrates the diversity of approaches to the new international economic order.

Table 12.6 Cases brought before the WTO by the advanced industrial countries (1 January 1995 to 18 October 1996)

	Absolute no.	%
Asian developing countries	11	0.65
Other developing countries	6	0.35
Total	17	1.00

Source: Asian Development Bank (1997), p. 201.

Progress towards WTO 2000 must take into consideration China, whose influence permeates the whole of the Asia–Pacific region and beyond. China is unlikely to agree to comply, except partially, with WTO disciplines before 2010 at the earliest.[7] Because China is the world's fifth largest trading power and the recipient of 35 to 40 per cent of total FDI flows going to developing countries and economies in transition, this raises vital questions as to how level the playing field will be as of 1 January 2000.

ASEAN Policies for the Automobile Industry

Before the crisis, the world automobile industry was expected to reach a capacity to produce more than 210 000 vehicles per day by 2000 against 178 000 today. More than 40 per cent of excess capacity was expected to be located in Asia (Deloitte & Touche Consulting Group, 1997).

Within ASEAN, Thailand is the main assembler, accounting for some 40 per cent of supply, followed in descending order by Indonesia, Malaysia, the Philippines and Viet Nam (see Table 12.7).

Thailand takes advantage of its privileged position *vis-à-vis* its ASEAN partners in terms of its domestic market size, good infrastructure, accumulated experience and development of the auto parts industry.[8] With plans to become the Detroit of ASEAN, it pursues a more open policy than its partners. Almost all of the large world automobile enterprises and a good many of their respective suppliers – particularly those of Japanese origin – have already set up shop in Thailand or were planning to do so by early 1997.

The case of General Motors (GM) merits special mention. It negotiated a US$750 million investment in Rayong to produce 100 000 units annually as of 1999, 70 per cent of which were destined for export markets starting from

Table 12.7 ASEAN: country-wide distribution of current and projected automobile supply

Country	1995	2000 (projected)
Thailand	571 000	850 000
Indonesia	380 000	600 000
Malaysia	296 000	320 000
Philippines	129 000	275 000
Viet Nam	15 000	60 000
Total	1 391 000	2 105 000

Source: UNIDO.

the second year of operation. GM expected that some 30 of its component suppliers, particularly those of Opel in Germany, would follow it to Thailand or other neighbouring countries since intra-ASEAN trade is to be almost fully liberalized as of 2003. GM was granted a wide range of incentives, including those applied to investment in rural areas, duty-free machinery and equipment imports for two years and export tax exemptions for eight years followed by a 50 per cent reduction over the subsequent five years. It also obtained an income tax reduction for ten years, amounting to as much as 25 per cent of its investments in infrastructure and 200 per cent of its expenses for transportation, electricity and water. Import duties on some raw materials will also be reduced. Furthermore, the Thai government agreed to provide US$15 million to set up an education and training centre.

But the most salient and unusual feature of the deal negotiated between the Thai government and GM was the cancellation of local content rules (LCRs) for automobiles. Besides having traditionally been more open to FDI than its neighbours, starting in 1998 Thailand was to be the only ASEAN country preparing to fulfil its TRIMs commitments with the WTO in advance.[9]

By contrast, both Indonesia and Malaysia were pursuing their respective national car projects (dubbed 'Timor' and 'Saga', respectively). These include highly selective promotional regimes that comprise fiscal and tariff exemptions as well as subsidized financing, which keeps prices considerably below the competition. A key feature of these regimes is compulsive rules for gradually higher LCRs.

Malaysia, the more advanced of the two, proceeded with an unusual blend of state support and entrepreneurial drive, particularly in terms of technology mastery.[10] In 1996, Proton, the leading Malaysian automobile company, acquired an 80 per cent share of Lotus, United Kingdom in order to have access to design technology and, thus, reduce its dependence on Mitsubishi, which has an 8 per cent stake in Proton. Several Lotus engineers began working for Proton's R&D division to develop an integrated engine and gearbox system. In 1997 Proton was also negotiating the purchase of Royal Begemann, a Belgium gearbox producer, for US$126 million. Proton exports 18–20 per cent of its annual production to some 30 countries, including Australia, Chile, France, Indonesia, Singapore and the United Kingdom with margins close to zero. The company is considered by Prime Minister Mahathir Mohamad as one of the keys to his plan to turn Malaysia into an industrialized country by 2020.

Malaysia's budget for 1997 included incentives to limit imports of intermediate goods, parts and components by means of the gradual elimination or reduction of tariff and sales-tax exemptions. Faced with the forthcoming constraints associated with its WTO commitments, the Malaysian Government is pursuing an accelerated deepening of the industrial structure and fostering a greater use of domestic inputs, particularly intermediate and capital goods. Development of industrial clusters, with activities ranging from final products to manufacturing and service support activities, are aimed at strengthening intrasectoral linkages, increasing domestic value-added and reducing import dependence. Eighty-five per cent of the value of manufacturing exports is currently made up of imports. Capital goods imports, which still account for nearly half of the value of investment, must be accompanied by offset programmes, including the transfer of technology.[11]

Before its 1997 agreement with the IMF, the Indonesian government had reiterated its strong commitment to the development of an independent automobile industry. This meant preference for local ownership, development and use of domestic technology and enforcement of LCRs. Only the Timor project, carried out by a local enterprise associated to Kia, from the Republic of Korea, qualified for special treatment. The Timor car is a four-door, 1600 cc sedan whose domestic production was scheduled for 1998 after an initial year when all completely built-up units were to be imported tariff-free from the Republic of Korea for local sale. The cars were to be exempt from domestic sales and luxury product taxes so that they could be sold at half the price of the competition. The project also enjoyed subsidized financing and benefits from government procurement guidelines.

The EU, the United States and Japan accused Indonesia of violating the non-discrimination and most favoured nation principles as well as the TRIMs agreement, whereby its extant policy in the automobile sector should have been notified in 1995 and no new non-complying regulations introduced since then. Since an agreement amongst the parties was not reached in bilateral negotiations, the WTO instituted a panel to settle the controversy along procedural guidelines in force. By the time that the panel would have reached a decision, Indonesia expected to be beyond the point of no return in the execution of the project. However, the 1997 crisis proved to be far more expeditious in deterring the Indonesian government's plans than the WTO's dispute settlement mechanism.

A sharp disparity between generic and selective policies was apparent in ASEAN in general and Indonesia in particular. While being criticized by the largest trading powers for its policy in the automobile sector, Indonesia was also being commended by the World Bank as 'South-East Asia's most liberalized economy' since the government introduced its 1995/96 deregulation package. Yet this deregulation had not affected NTBs relating to LCRs, investment licences, government procurement and export restrictions on certain products. The average rate of effective protection for 269 categories of manufactured goods was estimated before the crisis at 52 per cent. This level was due to go down over time as a result of scheduled reductions in nominal tariffs to 0–5 per cent in 1998 and 20 per cent in 2000 according to different product categories.

For comparative purposes, Table 12.8 reports on LCR conditions in ASEAN countries and some other countries around 1996. It contains information on the respective rules to be complied with by the enterprises and on effective LCR levels achieved and programmed. This information permits to draw the following conclusions:

1. In all ASEAN countries, except Thailand, there was a prevalence of policies aimed at a progressive increase in LCRs over time — this also applies to China and India.
2. LCRs have little relation to the level of per capita MVA (see Figure 12.4). Such rules are not a reflection of existing industrial capabilities but, rather, of intended ones.[12]

Table 12.8 LCRs in ASEAN and other countries (automobile industry)[a]

Country	Automobiles (%)	Commercial vehicles (%)	Per capita MVA 1993 (in US$)
Indonesia	(up to) 65[b]	(up to) 30[b]	167
		40 (Bakrie pick-up in 3 years)	
		60	
Philippines	40	45	198
Malaysia	(up to) 60[c] Kijang ASTRA (60 per cent in 1998)	45	724 (1991)
	46 (Saga Proton)	70 (INOKOM pick-ups and light trucks in 3 years)	
	75 (City Honda)		
	58	17 (Toyota Land Cruiser Prado)	
		51 (Hicom/DRB/Isuzu trucks in 3 years)	
Thailand	54[d]	72 (Ford/Mazda pick-up)	607
	60 (City Honda)	80	
	70 (Toyota Soluna)		
	65 (GM Opel, 1999 in 10 years[e])		
Viet Nam	30		39
Taiwan Province	50[f]		3 202
India	80 (Fiat)		59
	70 (Peugeot 309)		
	90 (Maruti 800)		
China	80[g]		
	90 (Santana LX, 2.7%, 1985)		190
	80 (Santana 2000, 60%, 1995)		

	90	(Jetta)			
	65	(Audi)			
	85	(Citroen 1988)			
Russian Federation	65	(Kia in 5 years)	65	(Kia in 5 years)	628
Hungary	10	(GM engines)			716
Botswana	20	(Hyundai from 1998)			101
Argentina		The regime has been essentially liberalized[h]			1 498
Brazil	85	actual average, liberalization ongoing			596 (1991)
Mexico	36	(since 1985)			464
Turkey			50	(Kia pick-ups)	630
Italy	75	(Mitsubishi Pajero, 1999)			3 503
United States	75	(Toyota Camry)			4298
United Kingdom	90	(Nissan Primera)			2 954

Notes: [a]In all ASEAN countries, except Thailand, a progressive increase in local content was scheduled before the 1997 crisis. Thailand had already decided to abolish LCRs in 1998.

[b]Depending upon installed capacity.

[c]30 per cent for automobiles with over 2851 cc, 45 per cent for those with 1851 to 28 500 cc and 60 per cent for those with up to 1850 cc. The government of Malaysia has warned that it will exclude from the calculation of local content those parts and components with high import content subcomponents.

[d]In this case the local content is not measured according to the value of the parts but with a weighing system which assigns 'points' to each part of the vehicle so that they add up to 100.

[e]The actual local content is currently 5 per cent.

[f]To be eliminated when Taiwan Province joins the WTO. However, tariffs as well as NTRs in the automobile sector would continue for eight more years (see text). Currently, only automobiles from the United States and Europe can be imported. The tariff is 30 per cent for automobiles and 42 per cent for trucks.

[g]Since 1995 the automobile companies which installed capacity in China must ensure 40 per cent local content immediately, 60 per cent within the second year and 80 per cent within the third year.

[h]The share of domestic value-added in the value of production of the industrial sector fell from 51 per cent in 1984/85 to 35 per cent in 1994/95 (see text).

Source: UNIDO.

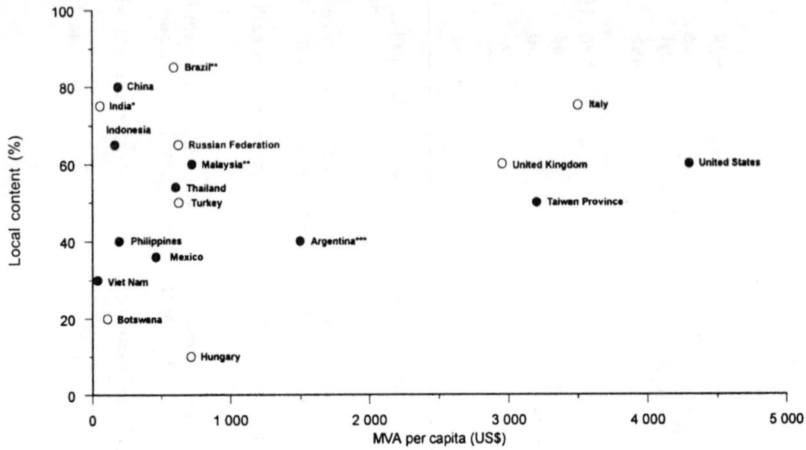

• Government regulation ○ Actual local content

Note: *1990; **1991; ***1992.

Figure 12.4 Automobile industry: local content versus MVA per capita (% and US$ in 1993, except where indicated otherwise)

LCRs and Industrial Strategy in ASEAN: Contrasts with MERCOSUR

LCRs are usually part of broader policies of indigenization or localization, import substitution, export expansion, mastery of technology, capability development and industrial deepening.[13] Hence such regulations are usually part of a entire panoply of complementary tariff and fiscal incentives, as well as special training, R&D, SMI and regional programmes. In addition, they are also used as bargaining chips *vis-à-vis* foreign investors and trade partners.

With Japan and the Republic of Korea as sources of inspiration, the ASEAN countries adopted policies aimed at promoting activities with increasing technological and skilled-labour content to face domestic upward pressures on unit labour costs and attaining AIC status within a couple of decades. In Thailand, for instance, medium- and high-technology-product exports exceeded those of labour-intensive products in 1993 for the first time, and have since then continued growing at a much higher rate than the latter. Thailand's current Industrial Master Plan resorts to the 'cluster approach' as a means of deepening the industrial structure and complete the process of transition towards becoming an industrialized economy. The absence of cluster development is perceived as a market failure which makes it necessary to resort to policy measures geared to increase the local content and induce upward development, including manufacturing and service support activities.

The ensuing increase of MVA as a proportion of the value of production in the ASEAN countries before 1997 appeared in marked contrast with the MERCOSUR countries, where the opposite trend was observed (including the anticipated dismantling of local-content-related measures). Thus, for instance, in Argentina the share of local MVA in the value of industrial production declined from 51 per cent in 1984/85 to 36 per cent in 1994/95. There was a similar, albeit more moderate, trend in Brazil. Allegedly, this is part of a more efficient linkage with the 'global network economy', whereby no nation can afford to keep very high levels of vertical integration. Yet the acid test is still to be passed by showing how such efficiency gains will help to lower levels of unemployment that have recently reached historical peaks and remain chronically high.

The contrast is also shown at the aggregate level by comparing the of imports and exports (see Chapter 6, Figure 6.2). Over the first half of the 1990s Argentina and Brazil applied relatively import-driven opening strategies compared to the more export-driven strategies of the ASEAN countries.[14]

The above highlights some of the contrasts to be found in the industrialization patterns of both regions before 1997. The view in ASEAN was that, having prioritized manufacturing-led export development, the time has come for a deepening of the industrial structure (calling for policies out of synchrony with the timing of introduction of the WTO disciplines). On the other hand, MERCOSUR countries pursued the reverse sequence over the 1990s, with a more modest outcome in terms of growth (although more attuned to WTO 2000). In fact, even before the 1997 crisis, voices were heard in ASEAN which warned against the premature introduction of LCRs, precisely in order not to restrict export development as a result of the limited competitiveness of domestic intermediate and capital goods attained so far. As will be seen, these voices reflected internal tensions which will reach a climax by the turn of the century.

The Race Against Time

Commitments that individual country governments have made with the WTO will eventually have to be reconciled with those they have made *qua* members of free trade and economic integration treaties. For instance, whilst the TRIMs come in to force in 2000, the ASEAN Free Trade Area (ASEAN FTA) will start in 2003, the ASEAN Investment Area (AIA) in 2010 and the trade and investment liberalization programme of the Asia–Pacific Economic Cooperation agreement (APEC) in 2020 for its developing members. Indications stemming from public debates and, more to the point, private sector investment decisions and related agreements with host governments in the ASEAN countries suggest that the ASEAN FTA, AIA and APEC schedules are being kept at least as close to the top of the agenda as the WTO's. The need to make these different schedules converge is not an idle question: do ASEAN FTA, AIA and APEC deadlines need to be accommodated to those of the WTO or the other way around?

Except for Thailand, which had decided to abolish LCRs in 1998, the governments of the other ASEAN countries were subject to various domestic pressures to alter their conformity to WTO 2000 before the 1997 crisis. Firms that were carrying out pluri-annual investment programmes to attain progressive higher percentages of local content, as mandated by regulations in force until the end of 1999, potentially faced considerable losses if their markets were opened to more efficient international competitors. Governments, in turn, would find it hard to ignore the social consequences of this type of situation.

Efforts can be expected, therefore, to exploit grey areas in the TRIMs agreement such as possible exceptions and differences of interpretation.[15]

From 2000, low-level tariffs are due to be the only best-practice substitute for LCRs and other NTBs. Hence the race against time is on to attain domestic manufacturing capabilities efficient enough to compete in world markets, with low margins of effective protection.

The Philippines private sector has requested its government to revise its commitment with the WTO to liberalize the automobile industry by 2000, on grounds that the auto part firms need more time to adjust to the new situation. The request calls for retention of LCRs as well as foreign exchange restrictions applied to domestic car production and assembly of completely knocked-down units. Another item in the petition is a postponement of the liberalization schedule until 2010, an idea which is gaining currency in other ASEAN countries.

Significantly, the Philippines Investment Council (IC) has adopted such proposals with the stated intention of helping the domestic automobile industry attain international competitiveness. Moreover, the IC supports an increase in mandatory local content from 40 per cent today to 50 per cent in 2000. Despite the fact that the way to harmonize such a measure with the tariff reform programme under way is still to be worked out, the IC regards it as a necessary step to develop the local auto parts industry.[16] IC is also considering levying a 7 per cent specific on completely knocked-down units, thus increasing the tariff applied to car parts and components from the current 3 per cent to 10 per cent. These proposals are contained in the document Philippine Automobile Vision 2020 which sets out the strategy for the sector.

In contrast with the sparsity of clear signals in respect of WTO TRIMs deadlines, the Philippines government has declared that, complementary to the ASEAN FTA and according to the AIA schedule, it favours liberalization of FDI incentives within South-East Asia by 2010. Under the ASEAN FTA, tariffs will go down to 0–5 per cent in 2003. In addition, ASEAN-CCI is currently studying the setting up of a regional LCR of 50 per cent on capital goods.

Outside ASEAN, Taiwan Province of China, although ready to abolish LCRs in its bid to enter the WTO, is negotiating compensatory measures aimed at lessening the impact of WTO 2000 and stretching it over time.

The government of Taiwan Province contends that were it to accept WTO disciplines *in toto*, the output of local automobiles firms would fall by 60 per cent and their market share to 30 per cent from the current 67 per cent. Auto parts production would fall by half, with only 35 per cent of the domestic auto parts producers surviving the abolition of the LCRs. It is estimated that only three or four of the 11 automobile assembly firms in operation would survive as such in a liberalized market, while the remainder would become sellers of imported brands. In its negotiations with the WTO, the Taiwan Province government is trying to safeguard the position of activities that it considers vital for the domestic economy, such as automobiles and consumer electronics, which would continue to be highly protected. Only those subsectors that have already gained a competitive edge, such as informatics and petrochemical products, will be substantially liberalized. The government has granted trade concessions in the shape of import quotas for automobiles to those countries that have agreed to support Taiwan Province's entry into the WTO under these conditions.

Thus, for instance, Taiwan Province has agreed to a grace period of eight years after its entry into the WTO with Japan, which includes a progressive lifting of the 20-year ban on imports of Japanese automobiles. A tariff-based quota system would be implemented by which no more than 7 700 small cars would be imported in 1997, with a 10 per cent average annual growth until 1999, when the increase would stop until entry into the WTO takes place. Once this happens, the annual quota will be automatically raised to 10 000 units to grow from then onwards at 20 per cent annually. The automobiles imported within the quota would be charged a 29 per cent tariff during the first year after entry. From then onwards, the tariff would decrease gradually over the grace period down to 22.5 per cent. Imports in excess of the quota would attract a 60 per cent duty. After the grace period, the QRs would be removed and all imported automobiles would be subject to a uniform 22.5 per cent tariff. The current local content of 50 per cent for locally assembled automobiles would be abolished immediately upon the Taiwan Province's entry into the WTO.

Taiwan Province is negotiating similar agreements with a number of other countries. To counteract the expected impact that removal of LCRs will have on auto parts firms, whose production may fall by up to 50 per cent, active programmes are under way to encourage gains in efficiency through process automation, improved product quality, better management, technology updating and strengthening of marketing networks. This is expected to help retain around 75 per cent of the domestic market.

Given their current policy orientations and stage in the technological learning curve, the MERCOSUR countries would meet fewer difficulties than those of ASEAN in complying with WTO 2000 (see Figure 12.5). It may be hard for most of the ASEAN countries, as well as several others of Asia, including China and India, to be able fully to adopt the WTO TRIMs disciplines by 1 January 2000. This is due to these countries' relatively late entry into such subsectors as automobiles and capital goods, regarded by them as vital tools of technological progress. This situation may invite resorting to exception mechanisms, based on the 'special difficulties' provision allowed for by the WTO. An alternative might be to make LCRs consistent with TRIMs through their application at the ASEAN level. A 50 per cent rule has been put forward for capital goods. On the other hand, none of the MERCOSUR countries has embarked on'national car' policies, as have Indonesia and Malaysia.

Both China and India have decided to develop their own, self-reliant automobile industry since they count on the market needed to attain scale economies. This poses a major challenge for the ASEAN countries. The most apt response would be to pursue intra-industry specialization at the regional

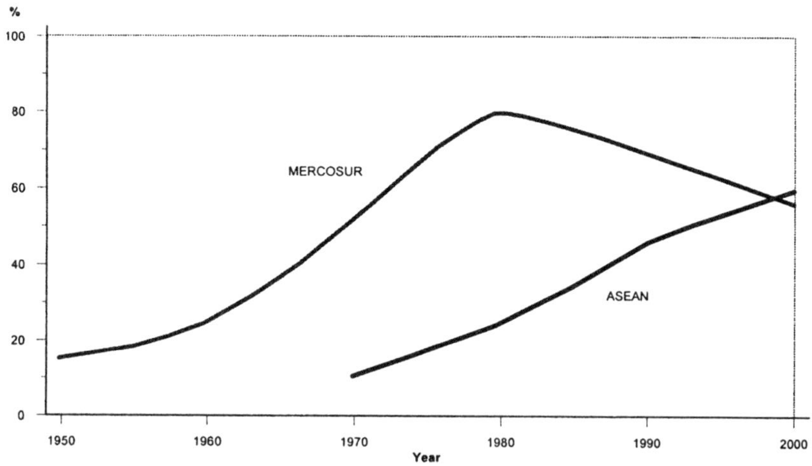

Figure 12.5 ASEAN and MERCOSUR: stylized evolution of local content in the automotive industry, 1950-2000

level. Yet, so far, Thailand is the only ASEAN country that has favoured a regional approach in the automobile sector.

ASEAN's AICO scheme may be used as a tool to encourage the increase of local content at the regional level with low intraregional tariffs. Because it will come into effect only in 2003, the scheme's impact is unlikely to be felt fully before 2005 or 2010. One of the difficulties with AICO is that each member country applies different exception regimes (for instance, regarding local content), so that harmonization raises non-trivial problems.[17]

Final Remarks

There is a lack of consensus in defining precisely the meaning of best practices, particularly in the microeconomic context. Policies in this sphere are guided, on one hand, by the institutional and historical legacy of each country and, on the other, by the nature of the policy goals pursued which, in turn, cannot be divorced from geopolitical considerations.

To varying degrees, for instance, ASEAN countries try to emulate the experiences of Japan first, and the Republic of Korea second, so as to join the convergence club in a couple of decades. Yet it is not precisely this type of emulation that drives the WTO disciplines, since the former entails priority for policies aimed at substantially modifying the initial resource endowment over time, rather than taking it as given in terms of defining the future.

Underlying these differences two alternative paradigms can be distinguished with respect to the meaning of convergence and the level playing field. In one, levelling the playing field means policy convergence today. In the other, it means convergence in levels of development tomorrow. And the debate continues.

NOTES

1. This chapter is based on Sercovich and Peña (1996) and Sercovich (1998).
2. See Krugman (1992).
3. The specificities concern, *inter alia,* varying propensities towards acting by consensus, different roles of MNCs and expatriated entrepreneurs (see below), and dissimilar stages of industrialization which have an impact on approaches to commitments towards the WTO.
4. The automobile and food subsectors illustrate the future of competition in MERCOSUR. In both, large international manufacturing and marketing enterprises mobilize hundreds of suppliers who are beginning to discover the need for and advantages of getting ready to operate in MERCOSUR. This entails a thorough reorganization and technological upgrading. Businessmen know that those who do not do it will not be able to survive. The case is similar in many other subsectors.
5. The multiplication of initiatives and forums aimed at furthering business contacts confirms the growing private-sector-driven nature of the MERCOSUR economic integration process.
6. The distinction is not that clear when the measures resorted to are part of policy packages agreed in the framework of economic integration treaties (see below).
7. The ambiguous position of Hong Kong Territory, a WTO member and now part of China, cannot be expected to simplify or shorten procedures.
8. Only about one third of the nearly 600 Thai auto parts firms would be internationally competitive. Many of them are Japanese enterprises, which relocated to avoid high wages and the appreciation of the yen.
9. GM took good advantage of intra-ASEAN rivalry to attract FDI, in this case between the Philippines and Thailand. President Ramos had negotiated personally with GM's CEO the most enticing incentive package ever offered by the Philippines, including a free site for five years, compensation for investments in infrastructure, a training school worth US$20 million and other benefits. The Philippines offer was useful to GM in its negotiations to have the Thai government lift LCRs 18 months ahead of schedule.
10. For an in-depth study of another interesting case of such a rare blend see Sercovich (1980).
11. The view of the government was stated by Mr Mahathir Mohamad, the Prime Minister, at the launching of the Seventh Plan, which runs until 2000: 'Some people believe that the way to diminish the balance of payments deficit is to reduce the rate of growth of the economy. The simple answer is that it is necessary to reduce imports and increase exports. The local content of exports is still low and must be raised ... The worst thing to do is to slow down growth by increasing interest rates ... The domestic industry ought to produce everything that goes into the fabrication of the components of the final product. This way, increases in exports will not result in similar increases in imports. There will still be imports, but these will consist of low value raw materials for the most part ... The Government will actively support R&D to increase the local content and enable domestic enterprises to manufacture goods bearing their own brands.'

12. In the case of most advanced industrial countries LCRs are superfluous, except when they agree on rules of origin with trade partners.
13. The sharp contrast between this type of strategy and the 'maquila'-type strategy is evident, for instance, with regard to the need to prioritize the development of a formal and well-financed and equipped education and training system able to turn out workers with the necessary skills. On the links between domestic learning, technical change and competitiveness see Sercovich (1988).
14. Later, these countries began to face problems partly associated with a deterioration in the terms of trade and partly due to some macroeconomic slippages. As far as the trade balance goes, ASEAN countries faced different prospects from those of the MERCOSUR countries (in particular if only the trade balance in manufactures is considered). The latter offset deficits in manufactured goods with surpluses in primary goods. On average, the relative endowment of natural resources versus skilled labour of the MERCOSUR countries is higher than that of the ASEAN countries. Their respective export profiles partly reflect this fact, although this has little to do with the contrast between import- versus export-driven strategies pointed out above. For further analysis on this see Wood (1997). For a comparison between ASEAN and MERCOSUR, see Sercovich and Peña (1996).
15. The key unknown refers, of course, to China, which is negotiating substantial exceptions and grace periods with the WTO. China had offered to abolish its NTBs in the automobile sector, which it regards as a 'pillar industry', after 15 years (later shortened to 12 years).
16. The private sector has also requested a raise in the mandatory (foreign exchange) offset margins from the current 50 per cent of total sales to 65 per cent in 2000, which would not be WTO-consistent either.
17. AICO is a common preferential regime which will allow qualified enterprises (those which operate in a member country and have at least 30 per cent local shareholding) to enjoy tariffs of 0–5 per cent immediately after its start-up in 2003. The enterprises will also be given non-tariff incentives and regional local content accreditation. AICO is an accelerated benefit of the ASEAN FTA and will replace the ASEAN Industrial Joint Venture (AIJV) and brand-to-brand complementation (BBC) schemes.

REFERENCES

Asian Development Bank (1997), *Asian Development Outlook 1997 and 1998,* New York: Oxford University Press.

Deloitte & Touche Consulting Group (1997), *The Automotive Industry: Strategies and Priorities in a Global Environment,* May.

Krugman, P. (1991), *Geography and Trade,* Cambridge, MA: MIT Press.

Rushton, K. (1990), 'Auto parts complementation in ASEAN', *Southeast Asia Business,* no. 23, Spring/Summer.

Sercovich, F. (1980), 'State-owned enterprises and dynamic comparative advantages in the world petrochemical industry', Harvard Institute for International Development, Harvard University.

Sercovich, F. (1988), *Domestic Learning, International Technology Flows and the World Market,* Geneva: ILO.

Sercovich, F. (1998), 'Best practices, policy convergence and the WTO trade-related investment measures', *ECLAC Review* **64,** April.

Sercovich, F. and F. Peña (1996), *Forging Partnerships for Global Competitiveness in ASEAN and MERCOSUR,* Vienna: UNIDO.

UNIDO, *Industrial Development Policy Report*, Vienna: UNIDO.

Wong, P.K. (1992), 'Economic cooperation in the southern growth triangle', University of Singapore.

Wood, A. (1997), 'Openness and wage inequality in developing countries: the Latin American challenge to East Asian conventional wisdom', *The World Bank Economic Review*, **11** (1).

World Trade Organization (1994), World Trade in 1994 and Prospects for 1995 and 1996.

ANNEX 12A. COMPARING ASEAN AND MERCOSUR

The population of ASEAN is about twice as large as that of MERCOSUR, while its wealth in terms of GDP is only three-quarters that of MERCOSUR. As a result, ASEAN's GDP per capita is less than half that of MERCOSUR (US$1273 against US$2805 in 1995). This snapshot, which leaves aside inter-country differences, may suggest that both groupings find themselves at two distinct stages of development. Yet, although there is grain of truth in it, this conclusion may be quite deceptive even if serious valuation problems are disregarded (wealth measured at domestic prices and converted at market exchange rates, when compared with corresponding values in international prices and purchasing power parities, is consistently understated for both groupings).

The share of ASEAN countries in world wealth increased by 2.5 times, while that of the MERCOSUR countries increased by 10 per cent between 1970 and 1995. Today they account for 1.9 and 2.5 per cent of world GDP respectively. The contrast is sharper in terms of manufacturing value-added (MVA). The share of ASEAN in world MVA grew over the same period 4.5 times, while that of MERCOSUR fell by 13 per cent. It must be pointed out, however, that during the 1990s the MERCOSUR countries have reversed their declining trend, although they did not reach the remarkable and steady growth rates exhibited by the ASEAN countries. Today the share of ASEAN and MERCOSUR in world MVA amounts to 2.5 and 2.3 per cent respectively.

Although, as noted, the contrast in economic performance has narrowed considerably over the first half of the 1990s, the pace of gross capital formation still remains about twice as rapid in ASEAN as in MERCOSUR (regional averages were 33.7 per cent against 17.6 per cent in 1993). This particular disparity has not diminished over time. The ratio of gross fixed capital formation to GDP is higher in the ASEAN country where this ratio is the lowest (the Philippines, 24 per cent in 1993) than in the MERCOSUR country where it is the highest (Paraguay, with 21 per cent in 1993).

The extent of exposure to international competition as measured by the ratio of trade to GDP still remains much higher in ASEAN: some seven times. Such a ratio is almost twice as high in the least open ASEAN countries (Indonesia and the Philippines) than in the most open MERCOSUR countries (Uruguay and Paraguay).

Over the first half of the 1990s both groupings exhibited very high rates of growth of labour productivity in manufacturing. In this case, the average annual rate has been substantially higher in the MERCOSUR (4.1 per cent) than in the ASEAN countries (3.2 per cent). Not even Singapore, which enjoyed the best productivity performance in ASEAN, managed to do better on this account than Argentina (5.6 and 6.1 per cent, respectively).

However, productivity growth in MERCOSUR has been attained at the expense of growth in employment (it remained stagnant in net terms between 1990 and 1995), while such has not been the case in ASEAN (it went up by 6 per cent per year over the same period). As in many other respects, here the Philippines also displays a behaviour similar to that in MERCOSUR. Singapore experienced a rather low average annual increase in manufacturing employment by ASEAN standards (1.8 per cent) but in this case there is a phenomenon of deliberate relocation of investment in labour-intensive manufactures, particularly in favour of other ASEAN countries and China, that has to be factored in.

The behaviour of unit labour costs has been more favourable for MERCOSUR than for ASEAN. Such costs declined by 1.3 per cent per annum in MERCOSUR and by 0.5 per cent per annum in ASEAN. Indeed, the net decline in MERCOSUR as a whole owes exclusively to a steep fall in Argentina (at an annual rate of 5.6 per cent). Similarly, Thailand's fall (1.7 per cent per annum) reversed an otherwise positive, if very moderate, rise in the other ASEAN countries.

Finally, the share of ASEAN in world trade has gone up 3.3 times since 1970, accounting today for some 6.3 per cent. The share of MERCOSUR in world trade has remained stable at around 1.5 per cent (despite some improvement during the early 1980s).

Name Index

Subject Index